Responsibility in
Mass Communication

Responsibility in Mass Communication

by Wilbur Schramm

HARPER & BROTHERS · PUBLISHERS · NEW YORK

P
90
S383

This volume has been prepared under the
direction of a study group authorized by the
Federal Council of Churches in 1949. In 1950
the Federal Council was merged into the
National Council of Churches. The Federal
Council has retained its corporate entity and
continues to hold the copyright. The National
Council of Churches points out that the volume
is not a statement or pronouncement of the
National Council. The author is solely responsible for its contents.

92859

Contents

Foreword

by CHARLES P. TAFT
*Chairman of the Department of the Church and Economic Life
and of Its Study Committee*

This volume forms part of a larger study of Christian Ethics and
Economic Life which was begun in 1949 by the Department of the
Church and Economic Life of the Federal Council of the Churches
of Christ in America. At the beginning of 1951 the Federal Council
was merged with other interdenominational agencies to form the
National Council of the Churches of Christ in the United States of
America, made up of thirty Protestant and Orthodox church bodies
within the United States.

In recent years religious leaders have recognized that the ethical
problems of economic life have become increasingly urgent. The
ethics of everyday decisions and practices in economic life, both
private and public, are matters of wide concern. We need to go behind
individual acts and group pressures for a deeper understanding of
the motives underlying what people do in their economic activities, of
how the system fits together, of how close our preconceived ideas are
to reality.

Change is dominant in our national life and perhaps nowhere so
much so as in its economic aspects. During the past half-century
our ways of life and work have undergone a vast alteration. The change
has been accomplished without violence and without great apparent
upset, but the tempo of its pace is revolutionary. Certainly if people
whose span of life was in the nineteenth century could see what we
see in everyday life, they would hardly accept any word but revolution for the process that has brought it about.

This accelerated change demands that all thoughtful people understand its effects upon ethics and human values. How shall we deal
with the dynamism in our economic life so as to preserve and extend
the dignity of the individual, respect for the rights of minorities,
sensitivity to the public welfare, and free discussion and peaceful
persuasion? We cannot rely upon business statistics to measure these
intangibles. Judgments of even the best qualified individuals about

actual or impending changes, affected as opinions are by individual temperament, vested interests, or political partisanship, are also inadequate if considered separately. The fullest use of all our resources for information and discussion is required for sound progress toward solution of our complex problems.

There is no vital threat to our inherited and cherished values either in the *status quo* or in change as such. We cannot separate ethics from practical economic concerns. What is needed is a better understanding both of economic facts and of those ethical convictions and values which have special significance in the meaning and direction they should give to economic activity.

In many parts of the world we find a fanatic cynicism or a false philosophy in opposition to the foundations upon which Western society is based. What earlier generations took for granted, such as the value and integrity of the individual, the character of government as a tool for service of the people, the capacity of human life for essential decency and justice—these are now challenged by conflicting assumptions also claimed to be moral or at least essential for an efficient society.

Here lies the real crisis of the second half of the present century. We must meet this challenge, in so far as it is evil, and clarify in relation to our own institutions the basic ethical affirmations which we support.

The Federal Council of Churches conducted for many years an educational program on the ethical issues involved in economic life. Many denominational bodies have likewise been active in this field. It has become clear, however, that we need a more careful and realistic investigation of economic life and its relation to spiritual and moral values in a Christian frame of reference. We need to make use of the capacities of social scientists and theologians, in close association with other persons drawn from many occupations.

Accordingly, a three-year study was begun in 1949 under a grant from the Rockefeller Foundation, and continued under a further grant from the same source in 1952. The Foundation has not sought to exercise any supervisory control over the study and does not assume responsibility for any of the findings. The results of the study so far are presented in nine volumes: *Goals of Economic Life, The Organizational Revolution, Social Responsibilities of the Businessman, American Income and Its Use, The American Economy—Attitudes and*

Opinions, Christian Values and Economic Life, Social Responsibility in Farm Leadership, Social Responsibilities of Organized Labor, and *Responsibility in Mass Communication.*

Among the other volumes planned is one which continues the social responsibilities theme with respect to the churches themselves and their agencies in so far as economic policies and practices are concerned. Another volume is being prepared by a group of faculty members at Wesleyan University on formulating public policy in a democratic society in relation to economic growth. The final volume planned will subject to further analysis and interpretation some of the major issues of the study as a whole in their bearing on the work of the churches in social education and action.

Gratitude is due to the several authors for their devotion and creativity in the writing of these books. In all the volumes of the series, the authors have been free to write as they wished and to accept or reject suggestions or criticisms; each book is the responsibility of the individual writer.

Others have made valuable contributions to the total study effort of which this volume is an important part. The Reverend Cameron P. Hall, executive director of the department, has given the project his unfailing and effective administrative support. Professor Howard R. Bowen, former economic consultant to the study, made an invaluable contribution in the formulation of the project and aided also in criticism of manuscripts. The Reverend A. Dudley Ward served as director of studies from the beginning until the fall of 1953. He carried out his responsibilities as organizer and coordinator with imagination and efficiency, and also gave help after he had left for other important work. Since September 1953 Dr. F. Ernest Johnson has been in charge of the studies. His long experience in research and education with the Federal Council, and in other connections, has made him exceptionally qualified for this service.

A study committee of the department, including both lay and clerical members and representing a variety of occupations, has reviewed the program of the study at various stages. Mr. Charles H. Seaver, editorial consultant and secretary of the study committee, has carefully edited the manuscripts and has been available consistently for counsel.

The National Council of Churches has taken no official position and assumes no responsibility regarding the content of any of the volumes. In no sense, therefore, can or should any statement in the series be regarded as an official declaration of the National Council of Churches or of any of its units.

Introduction

by REINHOLD NIEBUHR

No organ of the Christian Church should be in need of apologizing for sponsoring a study such as this one by Mr. Schramm on the problem of responsibility in mass communication. The Church can be creative only as it enters responsibly into all the ethical problems of our culture and our nation. Some of these problems involve technical details which must be taken into account by any person or organization that would speak with any degree of authority on moral problems.

The most dominant characteristic of modern culture is the mastery of technics by the culture and over the culture. Western democracy is conditioned on every hand by the technical efficiency of our civilization. This is true of America in a special way, for we have probably the most efficient technical enterprise and are so preoccupied with technics that our French critics define our culture as "technocratic."

Among the technical advances of our culture, nothing affects the spirit of man, the richness and variety of the culture, and the solidity of the democratic political order more than the advances in the field of commnunication. One of the many virtues of Mr. Schramm's study is his excellent historical survey of the development of technics in this field from the invention of printing through the power press, the invention of the telegraph, and then in rapid succession the development of motion pictures, radio, and television. All these technical advances in the field of communication have affected the spiritual texture of our society even more than the rapid means of locomotion and the ever-rising living standards, due to productive efficiency.

As Mr. Schramm points out, the latter two developments—radio and television—have established a direct contact between the event and the audience. These and previous developments have made communication all-pervasive in the life of the nation, and they have also made for bigness in the organs of communication. The range of these organs is wider than ever before, yet the organs are fewer. Mr. Schramm points out that it has become much more difficult to launch a journalistic enterprise and, while the number of newspaper readers has constantly increased, the number of newspapers has decreased. The problem of bigness in the field of communication is aggravated even more in the final technical triumph of mass communication, television, because there are only limited air frequencies upon which the words and images can run, so that television is naturally dominated by the big "chains."

All these developments raise moral problems, which may be divided into two categories. The first has to do with organizing the means of communication so that the freedom of the person and the vitality of the culture will be preserved even while the community as a whole is served with information and entertainment. The second embraces problems of personal responsibility and decision making, which remain no matter what system is adopted. Mr. Schramm's study is particularly rich in offering case studies of the personal moral decisions which the agents of communication face on every level of responsibility. These decisions may, in turn, be placed in two groups.

In the first group are decisions in the making of which integrity is required in order to withstand, for the sake of the public good, the pressure of antisocial parochial and private interests and powers. These case studies prove conclusively that there is no substitute for ordinary integrity in this, as in any, field of human relations. The temptations to dishonest coloring of the news and to withholding news are many.

We ought not to be concerned as members of the Christian Church that there is no distinctively Christian approach to the problem of integrity. A former British ambassador in Washington once declared: "I have served His Majesty's government in many cultures and climes, which were informed by many religions, but I noted that in all of them there was no difficulty in distinguishing an honest from a dishonest man." After the Second World War the late Bishop Wurms of Germany, active in the resistance movement against Hitler, objected to the questionnaires by which our occupation authorities tried to separate the sheep from the goats, the Nazis from the anti-Nazis. The Bishop admitted that objective tests were valid in the case of the heroic anti-Nazis and the hard core of Nazis. But for the general population who in a corrupted society were in various ways involved in corruption the Bishop declared, "You must know the people in order to know the dishonest from the honest ones."

As Christians we believe that love is the ultimate norm of conduct; but we must also know that in public affairs love must be transmuted into the sense of justice to be effective. And in the private decisions affecting justice, the case studies of Mr. Schramm prove conclusively that integrity is the servant of justice. We may, as religious people, speculate on how best to achieve the standards of integrity which are essential in the management of the communication system, and we might insist that the highest standards are possible only if there is a sense of being judged beyond all human judgments. But we dare not as Christian people advance our piety as proof of our virtue. We can assert that it is the root of virtue but we must humbly abide by the general criterion, "By their fruits ye shall know them," and acknowledge that a technical society requires in all fields, particularly in the field of communication, a high degree of integrity; Christians, rather than claim a monopoly of the virtue, should be assiduous in supplying men with the resources for achieving integrity in situations of temptation.

Mr. Schramm's case studies prove that there is another type of situation in which responsible decisions are dictated by wisdom in addition to honesty, because these decisions require the weighing of conflicting loyalties, values, and claims, such as the right of personal privacy against the right of the public to know; and the right of the accused to a fair trial against the right of the public to know details of a crime which, if publicized, might prejudice the verdict; or the concern for an innocent person implicated in another's wrong-doing against the felt obligation to tell the full story. Mr. Schramm's case studies of the problems which face the managers of the communication system will give both the general public and the schools of journalism much food for thought, and they will offer indubitable proof of the necessity of acknowledging the responsible freedom of the person in any system.

But individual integrity, while always necessary, cannot solve the problems of making a vast system of communication, with its big units of management and ownership, compatible both with freedom and with the order and welfare of the community. Some over-all philosophy of mass communication is required. Mr. Schramm distinguishes four theories. Two of them, designated as the authoritarian and the totalitarian, are ruled out by definition. They are incompatible with the standards of a free society. This leaves two theories, which Mr. Schramm denotes as the "libertarian" and the "social responsibility" theories. The libertarian theory is the analogue in the field of communication of the laissez-faire theory in economics. As propounded by John Milton and John Stuart Mill, it rests on trust in the "free market of ideas" and in the superior power of unimpeded truth to drive out error. In any case it does not trust any government agency to define truth and error.

This libertarian theory is in broad agreement with the presuppositions of a free society but, as Mr. Schramm points out, it presupposes a rather more optimistic view of human nature than the facts warrant. It assumes that men are sufficiently rational and interested to detect error when it is in competition with the truth. It also assumes that there is always a "free market" of ideas. But that market, as is true of all markets, is not so free as the eighteenth and nineteenth centuries assumed. For the forces that enter into the market are unequal. The producer certainly has more power than the consumer, except as consumer interest is organized.

For these reasons Mr. Schramm prefers what he calls the "social responsibility theory" of mass communication. The theory is only a slight variation of the libertarian theory. It disavows governmental control in the field of ideas as fully as does the latter. Thus it could not modify the theory of a free market in ideas, as modern mixed economies have modified the laissez-faire theory by government regulation of the economy. The theory therefore emphasizes that every freedom has a corresponding responsibility; and that if a free press is not adequately responsible for the preservation of the public's interest, and for telling the truth and giving a fair and balanced interpretation of the events of history, it will imperil the very foundations of a free society.

This is about where the Commission on Freedom of the Press came out in its study made in 1946-47 under the chairmanship of Robert Maynard Hutchins. The Commission, not willing to invoke state authority to police the communication system, proposed the organization of a voluntary agency which would watch the communication industry and would condemn flagrant violations of accepted norms and periodically single out for special mention high standards of excellence in the press. Mr. Schramm criticizes the press reactions to this proposal, which assumed that the Commission was proposing state intervention. This was not a harmless misunderstanding but was prompted by the press's resentment of any outside interference. Bearing this stillborn proposal of the Commission in mind, Mr. Schramm moves a little closer to the libertarian theory. He hopes that, while the theory of a self-righting market of ideas is too optimistic, the market can nevertheless be partially righted by a greater responsibility on the part of the communicator, and through a wholesome interest on the part of the "consumer" in the product. Such interest would be represented by various civic and other organizations, whose interest and criticism would correct abuses in the communication industries.

The difficulty with this solution is that unorganized consumers, like unorganized voters, have only the power of a final veto. If consumers organize they become a "pressure group" like the Legion of Decency, which may preserve certain standards appreciated by its own group but which may endanger the freedom of the whole community to have access to various types of art or entertainment. The parochialism of these groups can be corrected only through a multiplicity of groups with different viewpoints. Such groups would mirror the realities of a pluralistic society. But since their intervention would be more negative than positive they might reduce the mass entertainment industry to a new low of sentimentality and inanity. There is, in short, no easy way of forcing people to be responsible against their own inclination and beyond their capacity. The social responsibility theory is distinguished from the libertarian by its emphasis on the fact of responsibility itself and by its insistence that the producer of news and entertainment, and not the viewer alone, has responsibility for the product.

It is difficult to enforce responsible behavior upon the producer, though the theory is right in holding the producer morally responsible for the product of news and entertainment in the mass media. It is difficult to compel responsible behavior. On the one hand, while state regulation may be used moderately in the mixed economy which has displaced a laissez-faire economy, regulation is too dangerous in the realm of ideas. On the other hand, securing consumer pressure to police the media is even more difficult than in the case of the market for goods. Consumers in ordinary markets can simply refuse to buy inferior goods, but in the realm of entertainment the attractiveness of the shoddy is precisely the problem.

Mr. Schramm gives some interesting examples of the tendency to vulgarize art in making it acceptable to a mass audience. One of his examples is the motion picture adapted from the play "The Voice of the Turtle." The play's moral is commendable; but in presenting it, the immoral past of the two principals, who have found the joy of true love, is hinted at. This hint of immorality is deleted from the movie, and the play thus becomes inane and pointless. There are many such instances of a superficial morality contributing to shoddy art.

It would be wrong to accuse the mass media of downright vulgarization of the culture. Leslie Fiedler is probably right in defining the effect of the mass media upon the culture as a paradoxical one, in that they elevate "low brow" and debase "high brow" art to a consistent "middle brow" level. Certainly the mass media have broadened the popular appreciation of good music. Television drama, on the other hand, is not as good as good movies, and certainly not as good as good original drama. The debasement occurs through the cultivation by the mass media of material that will appeal to mass audiences and must try to reach a common denominator of taste. The audience of special competence and refined taste thus tends to be excluded from the mass media.

Mr. Schramm gives many excellent examples of individuals in the management of the media who act responsibly and resist pressure in order to improve the standards of entertainment or to prevent their debasement. But the question still remains whether something must be done to a "system" that tends to exclude specialized audiences who appreciate and support the finest kind of drama, music, and other art. If the system does not encourage discriminating judgment we cannot expect a few managers to sacrifice themselves for the sake of purity in art.

Of Mr. Schramm's four theories three are systems as well as theories, in the sense that it is possible to organize power and responsibility in terms of the theory. Even the libertarian theory becomes a system by its insistence that no communal authority of any kind shall be used to enforce standards, on the assumption that the market will accomplish this, just as it is supposed to regulate prices. It is only the "social responsibility theory" that cannot be embodied in a system. It must content itself with emphasis on the proposition that the producer has responsibilities commensurate with his freedom.

Mr. Schramm gives evidence, already alluded to, that the managers of the mass media are resentful of any supervision, even if it is not political. While the proposal of the Commission on Freedom of the Press for an unofficial review board can scarcely be dignified as a part of a new system, and while any system of regulation that deals with more than minimal standards, outlawing obscenity and libel, is questionable for the reasons which the libertarians advanced, one must nevertheless raise the question whether the danger of vulgarization of the culture of a technical civilization, through the influence of the mass media, is not so great that steps must be taken to modify the "system" which expresses the libertarian viewpoint. Any such modification must not strive for regulation, for obvious reasons. It must, rather, strive to eliminate two weaknesses in the present system. The one is the tendency of the mass media to vulgarize the culture by reducing every work of art to the level most acceptable to mass audiences. The other is the vulgarization of the entertainment through the obtrusiveness of the "commercials," i.e. advertising.

Mr. Schramm rightly regards advertising as a prerequisite of "free" or nonpolitical mass media. But if criticism of the text in an introduction may be allowed, I do not think he gives due consideration to the fact that advertising in radio and television is quite different from the older newspaper advertising for two reasons: 1) The advertising is more obtrusive, particularly in television, than in the press. It cannot be avoided by those who are not interested, as the newspaper reader can avoid it. Mr. Schramm commends the artists who have resisted pressure from the sponsors to become "pitchmen" for the product. But even if the artist has some concern for his dignity this does not eliminate the ever greater frequency and garishness of the commercials. 2) The advertisers in radio and television have a more intimate relation to particular items of news and entertainment than they have ever achieved in the press. Mr. Schramm presents evidence that in television they have less responsibility for the presentation of the feature than they had in the earlier stages in the development of that medium. Nevertheless we have no newspaper in which the editorial or the chief news item is brought to us by the courtesy of a well-known toothpaste.

While the press critics of TV and radio have made much of the obtrusiveness of the commercials, they are probably not as great a danger to the integrity of the culture as is the cultivation of the mass audience. Both dangers can be mitigated by a modification of the system, and only in this way, because we cannot expect managers and owners of the media to sacrifice themselves for the sake of lifting the level of the entertainment. Nothing radical is intended. The only modification that would not be dangerous is one that would not regulate but would set standards and make the cultivation of specialized audiences possible, through the organization of a quasi-governmental agency such as the British Broadcasting Company or the Canadian Broadcasting Company.

In the case of Britain it has already been proved that without competition even the high standard of entertainment offered by a public service corporation tends to become stodgy. Thus after long debate commercial television is allowed to compete with the BBC. In the case of Canada, the governmental agency has always been in competition with United States commercial broadcasts. But both ventures have proved that the extreme libertarian fear of "political" authority is groundless, because it is possible to organize a public service corporation which is not political, which is also not commercial, and which may have exactly the same degree of freedom from political control as a good board of regents of a state university has in our American experience.

Though the entertainment of these public service corporations tends to become stodgy and lacks the flair of our best commercial TV programs, nothing in commercial broadcasting has ever approached the mature culture of the "Third Program" talks over the BBC. This matter is important because we must confess that the mechanics of television have tended to reduce the quality of "good talk" on scientific and other subjects. Perhaps it is wrong to mention "scientific" talks in this connection because on scientific subjects television does a splendid job in making abstruse and complex subjects interesting. It has, however, reduced the quality of talks in the general field of the "humanities" by its natural insistence on graphic material. The use of graphic material in subjects other than scientific ones tends to lower the range and maturity of the discussion. On the other hand, television has contributed considerably to widening the public's interest in civic and political problems. No newspaper can equal the survey of foreign affairs conducted by CBS correspondents each year's end under the chairmanship of Edward R. Murrow.

The means of rapid communication, beginning with the telegraph and ending with television, have done much to give political stability and unity to the nations, particularly to a nation as large as ours. It may be questioned whether we could have achieved the continental unity of this nation, across the wide expanses of North America, if the country had not been founded just before, and expanded just after, the invention of the means of rapid locomotion and communication. This made it possible to govern the great nation from a single center and to give it a sense of national unity and integrity.

But the political gains from the pervasiveness of the means of communication, both in giving the nation a sense of unity and in making the electorate more competent to follow the ever more complex problems of domestic and foreign policy, must be balanced against the losses in the culture. For it can hardly be denied that the mass media, particularly since the advent of television, have supplied the national culture with an intensity of social cohesion which makes for uniformity and conformity. This conformity is not to be compared with the hard conformity of totalitarian states, in which fear of political power enforces obedience. Our danger is rather a soft conformity in which the community, rather than the state, becomes the arbiter of opinion, and in which nonconformity is made difficult by the weight of standardized opinions—not only in politics but in all manner of taste and standards of living. The community becomes the tyrant through the conception of itself projected by the images of the mass media. The fact that we have a productive culture which requires luxurious living standards for the absorption of its ever greater volume of products tempts the advertising agencies to use every pressure, to force these living standards on a reluctant market by every appeal to pride, envy, and the sense of social acceptance.

Thus the problem of conformism, standardization, and the subordination of the economy to the culture, resulting from the pervasiveness of the new means of communication, is really greater than the more obvious problem of preventing vulgarization of the culture. It may in fact present the Christian faith with the primary spiritual, rather than merely moral, problem. It presents the religious tradition with the challenge to maintain the validity of the Scriptural principles embodied in the injunction: "And be not conformed to this world but be ye transformed by the renewing of your mind," and in the warning: "For a man's life consisteth not in the abundance of things which he possesseth."

Both problems are derived not merely from the potency of the means of communication but from the combination of that potency with the efficiency of a technical civilization. We Americans resent the charge that we are "materialistic," when it is obvious that our critics, whether in France or in India, have failed to achieve the standards of civic justice which we have achieved both through our abundance and through the sense of the common good which the means of communication have inculcated. But we must admit that we are relatively too successful in all our technical achievements, and that we are therefore in danger of becoming slaves of the instruments of production and communication which have initially served us so well.

It is significant that these ultimate problems dealing with the vitality and creativity of our national culture, with our sense of values, and with the very meaning of human existence cannot be met in purely "ethical" terms, if we limit ethics to the sense of duty. In Christian thought, at least before the modern period, a great emphasis was placed upon "grace," rather than duty. This emphasis was derived from the Pauline thought that man is too weak to do his duty, if he is not helped by what later was defined as "enabling grace." Paul confessed, "The good that I would, I do not; but the evil which I would not, that I do." This confession confronts us with the dynamics rather than the norms of the good life. We know the norms quite well, though in the complexities of modern life there are some difficult choices to make when different norms conflict. But the more important problem is "how to perform that which is good," to use the Pauline phrase.

If we regard the rich material presented by Mr. Schramm concerning one important sector of a technical society, we will realize that the problem of grace appears as frequently as the problem of norms. It appears first in those instances which, in Calvin's phrase, manifest the necessity of "common grace." These are the instances in which the *esprit de corps* of an organization, the standards set by a tradition, and the mutual loyalty within a unit of responsibility, give power to the individual to do what is right. It is significant that though there are always occasions when the individual must consult his own conscience and when he may be finally forced to declare, "Here I stand, I can do no other, God help me," yet there are other occasions in which he has the resource of a tradition or an organization to help him to perform the right action.

But there is another aspect of grace, which is manifest particularly in the communication industry. This might be defined as a secularized version of grace, if we remember that grace always means freedom, including freedom above and beyond duty, and freedom above and beyond the ordinary. Thus scholarship is good if it obeys the standards of objectivity and honesty. But it may still be nothing but pedantry if the grace of imagination is not added. In the communication industry, in which news and entertainment are variously compounded, imagination is necessary in interpreting the news, and even more in projecting the various art forms. No degree of honesty can obviate the necessity of imagination in the managers of mass media if the vitality of our culture is to be preserved against the sheer weight of mechanics. Therefore the community will hail every artist and producer who has the imagination to make his medium a servant rather than the master of an old or a new art form. Here the Church must modestly realize and confess that it is not by moral censoriousness but by inspiring the imagination and by gratefully acknowledging the greatness of a creative imagination, wherever manifested, that it best serves the spiritual values in a technical culture.

We ought, as members of the Church, to confess that religious institutions have been rather remiss in projecting the best in their traditions through the mass media. Religious programs have been too largely either sentimental or irrelevant. The most popular religious program is a Catholic one, in which Bishop Sheen presents the truths of faith so that they are relevant to the interests of a mass audience. It could not be said that he manages to convey the majesty of that ancient religious tradition. When he affirms that the radio is like the Old Testament, and television like the New Testament in that it represents not only a voice but an Incarnation, one has the feeling that modern prejudices rather than ancient wisdom have been cleverly expressed.

We must all confess, whether we are members of churches or secular citizens interested in the common welfare, that every moral and spiritual agency has been lagging in adjusting its methods to the requirements, and in preserving its traditional treasures against the perils, of a technical society. The virtues and the vices of technics are always raised to the highest degree in the realm of communication because it is the realm where the spirit of man is nourished by knowledge, inspired by great art, and placed in closer contact with his fellows; but also the realm where human sensitivities may be corrupted, imagination debased, and the bond between men reduced to artificial and technical dimensions.

It is because this realm of technics is so important and because the traditional institutions of culture, including the Church, have been so remiss in exploiting the possibilities and reducing the moral and cultural perils of the ever more elaborate media of communication that one must welcome a study by a Christian layman, under Church auspices, which seeks to explain the intricacies of this world to the lay mind and to explore, for and with the practitioners of the arts of communication, the moral responsibilities of the new powers inherent in modern communication technics.

It is worth noting in conclusion that the Church in America is forced by the magnitude of existing problems, and by its close relation to the national culture, to be able and willing to sponsor such an enterprise. In its willingness and ability to do this it may be distinguished from the churches of Continental Europe, which at their best preserve the treasures of faith in less secularized form than the American churches, but at their worst, pursue theological and liturgical interests without regard to all the problems which have engulfed a technical society.

The Church in America is, at worst, in danger of becoming engulfed in the characteristic prejudices of a technical society and thus of losing its own peculiar prophetic genius. But at its best it is more closely related to the multitudes and in more organic relationship to society than any European, at least any Continental, Church. It has this close relationship paradoxically enough because the dominant churches of America grew out of a sectarian base, which disavowed all responsibility for the common welfare in the pursuit of religious purity. In the process of doing this they built integral religious communities which emphasized lay responsibility and activity, and which preserved the loyalties of the common man more successfully than the churches of Europe. Thus the original intention of creating a "separated" or exclusive religious community had the effect of creating multifarious religious communities that were much more nearly co-extensive with the total civil community than is the case in Europe. In this way was established the integral relation between the Church and the community which gives American religious life its unique color.

On the other hand, the Church has been challenged to consider the new complexities of a technical civilization in this nation because technics have become more consistently pervasive in the culture than in any other nation. We are thus forced by both duty and potential ability to direct our conscience to problems which have been regarded as outside the proper domain of the Church, but which cannot be outside of that domain if any human interest or perplexity is its proper concern. Therefore this excellent study is commended to the churches and particularly to the laity. It should give them a new sense of the urgent need for appraising, from the Christian viewpoint, the impact of mass communication on our culture.

It is to be hoped that this confrontation of the real facts and mechanics of responsibility in the mass media will give many laymen a new sense of the importance of these media and of the virtue of those practitioners who exercise their responsibilities with integrity and with wisdom. But however that may be, it will certainly throw light on common problems of all practitioners in the mass media by its careful analysis of the salient moral problems which they confront, and by its wealth of detailed case studies which give substance to the conclusions of the author.

Responsibility in
Mass Communication

To be above the beasts is to be *able* to make moral decisions and to act on them . . . to be below the angels is to be *obliged* to do so . . . the minimal requirements of morality are freedom and obligation.

—J. L. MOTHERSHEAD, *Ethics*

1

The Thesis

The thesis of this book is that the present is a time of important change in mass communication; that a time of change is a time for redefining standards and responsibilities; and that these new standards and responsibilities as they emerge are defining and delimiting a new philosophy of public communication for the United States.

The sense of new problems is everywhere around us. Within the last few years, codes of ethical conduct have been made in almost all the branches of mass communication. The industry has been looked at hard, from within and without. There has been an impressive amount of questioning and soul-searching by editors, publishers, broadcasters, and film-makers, and by associations and working groups made up of these men. There has been an increased governmental interest, indicated by Congressional committees, certain decisions of the Supreme Court, and the Federal Communications Commission—and in Great Britain by the Royal Commission. There has been also a considerable increase in public interest and concern regarding the social responsibility of the broadcasting industry, the film industry, and some branches of the printed media. This has been typified by printed and voiced criticism, by listeners' councils, by organizations to view and make recommendations on films, by the privately-supported Commission on Freedom of the Press, and by a series of well-publicized controversies, which in many cases took on the stature of debates.

In the first section, this book examines the directions and dimensions of the change which lies behind this new sense of problems. We shall try to describe and explain the coming of largeness and fewness to mass communication, the changing structure of the industry, and the supposed effect of the mass media on their audiences. The second part of the book traces the main currents of change in public philosophy of mass communication—the old authoritarianism; the coming of libertarianism; the growth of a new and aggressive authoritarianism in the Communist states, with built-in, factory-made ideological and ethical filters; and, on our side of the world, a groping out of 19th-century libertarianism into a new and ill-defined concept of mass communication which will better fit our times than what we have had, and which for want of a better name we have called social responsibility.

The import of the first two parts of the book, then, is that in this century we are being presented with a new and different mass communication system, to which society, including the directors of the system, must make an adjustment.

Consider what has happened. Nineteenth-century mass communication was almost wholly by means of print. The newspapers were numerous and comparatively small, so that every group of the population could be fairly sure of having its shade of opinion represented. When Hartford, Connecticut, for example, had thirteen thousand people it had 13 newspapers. Today, we have in the United States one daily paper for approximately every ninety thousand people. Only 6 per cent of our cities with a local daily newspaper have competing ownership. Bigness and fewness have come to mass communication.

Furthermore, our century has seen the growth of the great media which, later in this book, we shall call machine-interposed—that is, films, radio, television. Drawing partly on the tradition of the theater, partly on the circus and vaudeville, partly on folk art, they have brought into existence a new form of entertainment which we call popular art, meaning a form of art intended for very large numbers of people, the success of which is to be judged primarily by the amount of money it makes.

The inexorable trend of economics and applied science which has brought bigness, fewness, centralization, and popular art to mass communication has brought with it striking new problems. Popular art, for instance, has raised questions which were never very important in the relatively restricted arts of theater, circus, and vaudeville, or the relatively indigenous folk art. What influence, for example, can a widespread popular art be permitted to exert on public mores, values, and tastes? Furthermore, such art is controlled by a relatively few people who are at a relatively great distance from the audiences they serve. The main sources of influence through popular art on public taste and mores are a few centers—New York and Hollywood, principally—and a few great production units—less than a dozen studios, a few great publishing houses, four radio networks, three television networks, all gigantic in size. In each of these a few people must prepare identical products for vast numbers of people. The old indigenous quality of folk art, as well as the ability of circus, vaudeville, and theater to adjust readily to the interests of small audiences, has been lost. This is a new problem, requiring as it does decisions on a gigantic scale that will balance the tastes, needs, and interests of smaller groups within the great audience against the common-denominator wishes of the great audience itself; and requiring also a set of basic decisions on what may acceptably be done with a medium that comes into the home and reaches as many as 50 million people with a single production.

In some ways the changes in the information media have been even more dramatic than the development of the popular arts. For, with the coming of bigness and fewness, the separate, clashing voices are no longer raised so readily in a "free market place of ideas." No longer is it easy for the self-righting process described by Milton and Mill, the very cornerstone of libertarianism, to operate. A new responsibility has come to rest on our news and opinion media. Whereas formerly they were responsible only for voicing clearly and vigorously the views each represented, in full confidence that the public would be able to read contrary views and decide between them, now it is coming to be obligatory for these media actively to seek out and represent *all* significant points of view.

Centralization of the information media has tended to change the old relationship of media, government, and people. The small, numerous media, as we knew them in the eighteenth and nineteenth centuries, were representative of the people in their checking on government; in fact *were* the people. But the larger and more centralized media have to some extent withdrawn from the people and become a separate set of institutions, parallel and comparable with other power centers such as business and government. And this in turn raises two other sets of problems.

For one thing, there is the problem how these larger and **fewer** and more centralized institutions of communication shall maintain their representative quality. In the second place, there is the problem how these institutions shall behave in their dual capacity as great business organizations and great communication organizations. For each of the great media organizations is really two enterprises, not completely compatible with each other. At the same time and under the same management, they are carrying out much the same responsibilities as a school system and a department store. They must maintain a certain level of economic strength and solidarity before they can properly carry out their communication responsibilities, but nevertheless their business responsibilities must not be allowed to interfere with their informational responsibilities. As business organizations they would readily be subject to the same close legal accountability as other business. Zechariah Chafee correctly observes that mass media are the only powerful business enterprises in the country which are subject to very little legal accountability. Our Bill of Rights begins with an explicit direction that mass communication shall not be restricted in any way that would affect freedom to say and comment. The result of all this is a delicate balancing of responsibilities and requirements, indeed a balancing act of the first order.

So much for the first two sections of the book, which are past and prologue and attempt to set the stage for a more detailed consideration of standards and responsibilities. In the second part we shall examine some of the developing problems. Insofar as possible we shall try to look at them, not on a high abstract level, but rather as they appear to the media—in the context of practical decisions that have to be made day by day. Wherever possible, we shall try to illuminate these decisions by relating them to the currents of communication history and by trying to suggest where, in the midst of all the crosscurrents of conflicting responsibility and pressure, the new and somewhat shadowy border line between responsibility and irresponsibility seems to lie. We have gathered these problems into four large areas, which we shall identify as follows:

FREEDOM

Obviously, the basic responsibility of the mass media is to remain free. Their freedom must be defended against challenge from whatever source—whether from government, from opposing political philosophies, from business and class allegiances, from power and pressure groups, and from special-interest forces within the media themselves. What form does the threat of government control take in the mid-twentieth century? By many it is argued that the greatest threat to communication freedom is no longer the government, but rather forces from outside the government. For example, is communication "monopoly" a threat to freedom? What control over communications is exercised through financial support? To what extent do class or group allegiances, pressure-group activities, and favors threaten communication freedom? And how serious is the impact of expert manipulation of the media by public relations men and political leaders? These are all questions which must be faced up to in trying to assess responsibilities for maintaining a free communication system.

THE RIGHT TO KNOW

The mass media must be free in order to represent the public's right to know. But what are the limits on that right? For example, what happens when the right to know conflicts with other old and honored rights: the right of an individual to privacy, the right of an individual to fair trial, the right of government to withhold information when it feels the public interest requires it, or the media's right to serve their own interest in withholding information? These are questions of conflicting responsibilities, which cannot be answered simply by saying that the public's right to know is overriding, and the right of free press is bounded only by law. In all these cases the boundaries of responsible performance need to be adjudicated and redrawn.

TRUTH AND FAIRNESS

If the preceding area was concerned with a *quantitative* ethic—*how much*, under given conditions, it is the responsibility of the media to tell the public—this area represents the *qualitative* responsibilities of a free and responsible communication system. Essentially, this is the problem of presenting a true and balanced picture of the world. What standards of accuracy shall be required? What are the obligations regarding objectivity as opposed to interpretation? What does it mean in practice to say that the media should be fair to minority viewpoints, to opposing political viewpoints, and to targets of attack? What is a "balanced picture"? These obligations are clearly not the same as they were one hundred years ago, when there were more newspapers per community, and when an editor or publisher could afford to operate his own political prism, confident in the knowledge that other political prisms were filtering the light in their own way, and the public could take its choice.

POPULAR ART

As the two preceding areas concerned chiefly the informing side of the media, so this one concerns the entertainment aspect. It is the problem of redefining standards in view of the new and unprecedentedly large audiences that have come with mass circulation and the electronic media. Within this area fall such questions as these: Should the public be given "what it wants" or "what it needs"? What is a "bad" picture, in the Platonic sense in which that question is usually asked? What constitutes indecency? When do the media threaten the social mores; when is the content "dangerous"? What are the assumptions regarding the nature of man and the world, and of media effect on man, which underlie the media codes and media practice, and are these adequate assumptions? Finally, what constitutes an adequate program service—in view, that is, of differing tastes, minority interests, and the broadest concept of public good? These are not all new questions, but the mass media and the great audience require that they be asked again and reanswered in terms of the new conditions.

Part III, then, indicates the nature of the ethical problems which changes in the media have brought. In part IV, we face the question of whose responsibility it is to do something about it.

Our viewpoint is that the responsibility is shared by government, media, and public.

We could sum up by saying flippantly that the government's responsibility is to keep its hands off, the media's responsibility is to do for themselves what their critics want the government or some other policing body to do, and the public's responsibility is to be a responsive and critical audience. But this is too simple.

Therefore we shall have to ask, what are the limits on what government can and should do toward contributing to responsible communication? Of course, government should have as little as possible to do with the apparatus which exists to check on government, and indeed it may require a high order of responsibility for government to keep its hands off the communication system as much as it should.

But, within allowable limits, what can government do? For example, what aspects of performance should it look at when it assigns broadcast channels? When and how, if at all, should it supplement the offerings of the privately owned mass media? If there must be some governmental check on motion pictures and textbooks, what are the responsible limits of that activity?

Then we shall look at some of the things communicators themselves can be expected to contribute to responsible mass communication. In general, the efforts of communicators have taken one of two forms: the adoption of self-regulating codes of ethical conduct, and the gradual professionalization of the industry. The first of these is swift and dramatic, but we are not persuaded that it can do what most needs doing. In any case, we must ask just what codes can do, and what they cannot; and what the present codes have accomplished. But we have more hope for the slower method, the gradual growth of the industry in responsibility and professional spirit. Under this heading, we must look at what has been accomplished and what might be accomplished by the increasing amount of professional education in the field, the activities of professional and trade associations in mass communication, the beginnings of self-criticism in the media, and the effects of awards and prizes for excellent performance in mass communication.

Finally, to what extent can the great audience be expected to take full partnership in the task of keeping mass communication responsible? Is the mass communication audience doomed to relative passivity or inarticulateness, to be represented only by a few organized minority groups and articulate critics? Is the stereotype of a "mass" audience, with tastes as simple as a baby's or as malleable as jelly, essentially correct? Or is it possible that an articulate, critical audience may develop to provide the check on mass communication which everyone feels is needed, but which nobody feels should be provided by government? Hardly anything would make as much difference in mass communication as an alert audience expressing to communicators its opinions and needs. And if indeed there are strong feelings within the public as to what kind of performance is wanted from mass communication, through what machinery can and should those feelings be expressed?

These are the matters that concern us in the next several hundred pages.

PART I

The Growth of Mass Communication

Thou hast most traitorously corrupted the youth of the realm in erecting a grammar-school; and whereas, before, our forefathers had no other books but the score and the tally, thou hast caused printing to be used; and, contrary to the king, his crown, and dignity, thou hast built a paper mill.

—WILLIAM SHAKESPEARE, *Henry VI*, part II

2

Its Development

About the year 1450, in Mainz, Germany, there occurred one of those conjunctions of an idea, skills, and materials that historians later write about. In this case, the materials were the wine press used for centuries in Western Europe; cast metal type, invented 50 years earlier in Korea but rediscovered independently at Mainz; and paper and ink, both of which had been developed many centuries earlier in China and brought to Europe by way of the Near East. The skills were those of calligraphy and block printing, developed to a high level by Asians and by Europeans especially in the medieval monasteries. The new idea was to print from movable metal type, so that a piece of type might be used interchangeably in many jobs. The result was a machine for the rapid duplication of writing—the writing being standardized into type faces.

That was the beginning of modern communication. The story of those 500 years of development in communication is a story of man's changing relation to machines in the communication process. The difference between communication before and after 1450 was simply that man had finally made an efficient machine to duplicate interpersonal communication. Then, a long time after 1450, man made a machine which he could interpose in the communication process to see and listen for him. That was the second great step in the history of modern communication. A little later he developed the skills and techniques that make possible efficient communication between man and machines. And in our time he has unlocked the wonders of machine-to-machine communication, and we have automatic factories and devices that remember facts and make decisions. Those four steps are the ones that have made modern communication what it is.

But let us return to the events just after 1450. That first step into modern communication—how did man take it? What was the first thing he printed from movable metal type, there beside the River Main in Germany? Was it something like "What hath God wrought?"

which Samuel Morse sent over the first telegraph line? Was it a medieval version of "Now is the time for all good men. . . ."? Was it the printer's name, set in a stick of type to be marveled at? We do not know. The earliest dated piece of printing that remains is a papal indulgence, struck by Fust and Schoeffer, in 1454. The first book was apparently the 42-line Bible, which was done not later than 1456, and of which the printer is believed to have been Johann Gutenberg.

Thus at its very birth the new art was pressed into the service of the chief power center of the times: the Church. And if the printing press had been a different kind of machine, it could have been restricted—as certain other communication devices, like heraldry, or the semaphor, have been—to one master, or one class, or a certain kind of job, or a certain topic. But the peculiar characteristic of machine-duplicated communication was that it became involved everywhere with all the public affairs of man. How swiftly that converted wine press spread from the Rhineland around the world! Caxton was printing in England, Aldus in Italy, by 1494; Juan Pablos in Mexico City less than 50 years after Columbus first saw the new continent. Everywhere it went, the printing press involved itself in the matters that exalted or stimulated or troubled man. It served the parties in power, but it also served all the revolutions of the spirit and the body politic. It served the Church and also carried the great debate on the Reformation. It circulated the precious books of Aristotle, which had been chained to the library desks of the Middle Ages. It carried far and wide the extraordinary intellectual output of the Renaissance. It carried commercial news to the merchants of England and North Germany, and also revolutionary pamphlets—in fact so many of them that anonymous pamphlets are even today the symbol of revolution in many European countries. Without the press there might possibly have been an Enlightenment, but it is a matter of grave doubt whether there could ever have been a French or American revolution.

The press served all masters who would have it. In the great ground swell of democracy toward the end of the eighteenth century, the press led the people toward their new-found importance. And just at that time, shortly after 1800, man succeeded in making the first major modification in his remodeled wine press. He added a new source of power to it. This was the gift of the industrial revolution. Steam—later electricity—replaced man's muscles. It was the same old press, but it worked faster; the same product, but more of it. The exciting thing about the power press was that it came at just the time when it was needed to reach the masses of new voters. To those who couldn't read, it offered an easily seen incentive to learn to read, and thus it was closely involved with the growth of public education. Then smart merchandisers found out they could sell papers for a penny and still make a profit if they sold enough, and if they sold enough they could also sell advertising, and so we had "mass" communication—prices at a level the common man can pay, enormous circulations, advertising, large publishing organizations, the attractive concept of the new machine as the voice and servant of democracy, and the misleading and erroneous concept of a "mass audience."

Meanwhile, in the mid-century, the telegraph and the cable had speeded communication, and the camera and photo-engraving had added vividness to the printed word. But all this was still nothing fundamentally new. The Washington hand presses that rode west in the American covered wagons were essentially only a hardier version of the press that Gutenberg had at Mainz in 1450. The presses that printed the Gettysburg Address were essentially the same machines, run by steam. They were still a part of the great wave of communication that began to break at Mainz in 1450. And the accomplishment of that first wave, as we have said, rested entirely on its ability to make very swift duplicates of writing on paper.

The first fundamentally new development came three quarters of the way through the nineteenth century. As the first wave of modern communication can be dated back to Gutenberg in 1450, so the second can be dated, if not to Samuel Morse and the telegraph, at least to Alexander Graham Bell in 1876. He gave us the telephone. A few years later, Edison's phonograph and his movie camera and projector made it possible to store sounds and moving sights. DeForest's triode vacuum tube in 1907 opened the world of radio and television.

The difference between communication before and after 1876 was that man had finally begun to make efficient machines that could be interposed in the communication chain, and trusted to listen and see for him. In a sense, of course, the printing machine had been interposed in a communication chain, but it merely duplicated; it did not communicate directly. It made a product that could be read at leisure, the reader taking the initiative, setting his own pace, selecting from the copy as he wished. The second wave of modern communication made a profound change in that it shifted the initiative, partly at least, from receiver to sender. Once the receiver had made his basic choice, the sender was in charge. The machine, or the force behind it, controlled the pace, the repetitions, the emphasis, the timing.

The new machines were faster than the press. They brought tidings more quickly, answered an argument more swiftly. They had about them a sense of reality, a sense of immediacy, that print never had. They had an emotional quality that was hard to get into print. And yet we must admit that the second wave has not yet involved itself in social change as the first wave did. While print is five centuries old, we have had the telephone only three quarters of a century, and radio and television are newcomers within our time. These newer media came into being when Western countries were being urbanized. They came into being when the work week was being greatly shortened, and people began to have more leisure. They came into being at a time when America was on the verge of a striking change from what David Riesman[1] calls "inner-directedness" to "other-directedness"—from an individualistic work-success ethic and a future-time orientation, to a hedonistic present-centered ethic concerned greatly with group relationships and opinions. These new machines were exactly what people needed to keep them informed of the other people around them. They were sociable little machines. They brought personalities into one's living room, and transported one into countless other living rooms and chambers of state. More than print, this new machine-interposed communication extended man's environment and dominated his leisure. More than print, it offered opportunities to manipulators.

When one tries to add up the social impacts of machine-interposed communication, he concludes that as print had come to play a part in certain great revolutions of the mind and the state, so films and broadcasts came to play parts in a great change within our way of life. It is still too early to assay the exact part they have played in the change to "other-directedness," but it must have been significant. This, I think, we can say: that while print first commended itself to man for its ability to inform, films and broadcast commended themselves for their ability to entertain. And, whereas print began as the most private and the smallest of media and grew into mass communication, films and broadcasts were born into mass communication and never knew anything else. Even more than print, they demanded large communicating organizations to produce them.

These are the parts of modern communication with which we are going to be concerned in this book. But we should be telling less than the whole truth if we did not fill in the rest of the picture, the other two waves.

The third wave of modern communication was developing at the same time as the second, but came slowly and reached its crest only in the twentieth century. This was communication between men and machines. It developed slowly as man became more ingenious at making dials and gauges that would give him information, and instruments on which he could register his wishes. It now seems ordinary to us, but it would have seemed fantastic only a few decades ago, that a man would be able to fly an airplane when ground and horizon were completely invisible to him, simply by means of messages sent him by a panel of instruments designed to say how high he is, how fast he is going, where he is heading, whether his wings are level, and how fast his engine is turning. If that would have seemed fantastic in 1915, the idea of ships seeing the shoreline or planes seeing the ground quite clearly through clouds and fog would still have seemed fantastic in 1935. Yet in the 1940s we had a machine that operated through an electronic screen and conveyed exactly this kind of information, in the most minute and exacting detail, to humans. We call it radar.

The third wave in modern communication, then, developed slowly for a hundred years and came to a peak in the fourth decade of the twentieth century. The fourth wave has broken really only in the last ten years. It can pretty well be dated to a paper by Claude Shannon in the *Bell System Technical Journal* for 1948.[2] The article began modestly: "The recent development of various methods of modulation . . . has intensified the interest in a general theory of communication." That is exactly what Shannon set about providing. The effect of his paper, and the formulas in it, was to stimulate a great outpouring of developments in the area of communication between machines.

Let us not say arbitrarily that we are uninterested in any communication that seems not to involve humans, because this fourth wave has the most direct and important implications for humans. As machines in the early nineteenth century had come to do the work of man's muscles, so now these new machines were able to do some of his thinking for him. In our own time, therefore, we have had the excitement of watching a major scientific idea develop into use. The great computers, with their brain-like qualities, have all come into being in the last two decades. The concept of feedback of information, which made possible such relatively simple devices as the thermostat, has been so developed that it is now possible to put a machine in charge of other machines and to build a factory to run itself. It is mathematically possible even to build a machine to duplicate itself. Literally we have built machines able to take over many of the qualities thought previously to be man's unique preogative. Under the name of automation, this fourth wave of modern communication has already had great effects on American industry, and may have profound effects on man's concepts of himself and his place in the world.

Let us be clear that the reason we are limiting ourselves to the first two waves of modern communication is not that the third and fourth are any less exciting. Indeed, the most exciting communication developments ahead of us are undoubtedly in the area of machine-to-machine communication, and 25 years from now this may well be the largest branch of the communication industry. Nor are we limiting ourselves because the two later areas do not furnish ethical problems. On the contrary, we may expect automation and the "thinking" machines to provide ethical problems at least as severe as any of the other kinds. We are limiting ourselves precisely because the two newest kinds of communication are so new. Young as machine-duplicated and machine-interposed communication may be when measured against the whole history of man's communicating, they are still old when compared to man-machine and machine-to-machine communication. They are old enough to have acquired an ethic and to have been incorporated into philosophies.

For another reason too we are particularly concerned with the first two waves of modern communication. The great voice of print was caught up in the ground swell of democracy and the sharply breaking waves of revolution in the 17th and 18th centuries; and the impressive new technology of the media (the power press, photoengraving, stereotyping, sound and sight recording on film and transmission by airwaves) was caught up in the almost unbelievable growth curve of economics in the 19th and 20th centuries. As a result, the tiny hand press, the squeaking earphones, the flickering film, have in our time grown into vast business enterprises: daily newspapers, publishing houses, radio and television stations and networks, and film studios and theater chains. We call these developments mass communication because of their massive product and the enormous audiences they have come to serve.

At the beginning, print was used mostly to meet *specific* needs and *specific* interests. Thus the merchants needed business information, the Church needed certain religious documents in a form that could be more readily circulated, the government needed a way to duplicate certain products of legislation and executive authority. Gradually print began to have more general uses. The newspaper came into being. As Robert E. Park pointed out, the first newspapers were mostly devices for organizing gossip.[3] And yet they were more than that because their growth was intertwined with the growth of schools and cities and people's governments. It is no accident that Shakespeare talked about schools and printing, together, in the sentence with which we introduced this chapter, or that early newspapers in this country tended to appear where there were post offices and to grow as school population grew.

The social history of newspapers is the history of a battle for circulation. As communities grew larger, the newspapers began to take over some of the functions that were served in villages by face-to-face contact. Villages operate by the kind of public opinion that grows out of gossip and the understanding that grows out of familiarity. And so the newspaper tried to organize gossip and keep its readers familiar with what they could not themselves see or find out. To do this, it needed an audience that could read, which was gradually provided by public education. It needed a way to circulate speedily and cheaply, which was gradually provided by the clustering of people in large communities and by postal services. It needed a way to print fast and cheaply, which was provided at last by the power press. And it needed a way to become important to large numbers of readers, a way which was provided by the growth of political democracy.

In its first century the newspaper was essentially a newsletter. Political pamphlets circulated separately and often surreptitiously because the political content of the newspapers was controlled by authority. In the 18th century, these functions of print were married, and there was born the party paper. This was a journal of opinion which took over from the broadside and pamphlet the task of representing political discontent. It developed in time to be fired at the Bastille and at the Stamp Tax and to lead the great movement toward popular government and democracy.

Thus all the dams broke at once and loosed the torrent of communication. More people went to school. There they learned to read and became more deeply interested in their governments and in the world beyond the realm of their eyes and ears. The growth of popular governments required people to inform themselves and helped them to do so by providing schools and facilitating the distribution of newspapers. And newspapers, given cities full of people, many of whom now could read, and most of whom felt a need for political information in order to take part in government, helped break their dam by developing the power press. Thus the newspaper grew on the mighty yeasts both of the industrial revolution and the democratic political revolution.

The newspaper in this country and western Europe has evolved beyond the party press to a more general newspaper. As Park pointed out, when someone in the 19th century referred to "the power of the press" he was referring to the power of the editor and the editorial.[4] On the other hand, when someone today speaks of the power of the press, he is almost certainly talking about the power of the reporter and the news. In the 19th century, our influential papers were journals of opinion. At best, these papers were like Horace Greeley's New York *Tribune*, which Charles Francis Adams said "during those years was the greatest educational factor, economically and morally, this country has ever known."[5] At worst, they were journals in which news was regarded very much as it is regarded in present-day Communist papers: as merely an excuse for editorial comment.

In several ways the party papers were anachronistic. For one thing, there tended to be so many of them. Each such paper tended to gather a party, or a splinter of a party, behind it. The little town of 12,000 persons in which I grew up had at one time five newspapers, all representing different political viewpoints. The tendency of papers was, therefore, to proliferate, to divide their potential audiences in terms of ever more sharply defined differences of opinion. On the other hand, the tendency of the industrial revolution, in which the growing newspaper was involved, was toward consolidation. Greater profits were to be made by selling more units of a single kind. Furthermore, costs were swiftly rising, partly because of increasing mechanism requiring greater skill on the part of a staff, partly because more machines and more complicated machines had to be bought, partly because the public learned to demand more expensive services (for example, wire news, syndicated columnists, feature services, pictures, cartoons, and a good local news coverage). Many newspapers also came to have a revulsion against subservience to a political machine or party, and to note on the part of the people a decreasing appetite for the owners' ready-made, one-sided opinions and an increasing appetite for news.

For all these reasons, the party press was not a suitable mold for the future. More and more papers broke away from it and began to serve larger segments of the people with a product in which news was more important than opinion, and feature news often more important than hard news, and in which advertising grew rapidly with circulation and came to be an important determinant of the paper's success. Many American papers went through a period of "yellow" journalism, in which they subordinated other services to the production of sensation, fantasy, highly emotionalized news. They were trying to reach the people, as Walter Lippman said, "who find their own lives dull, and wish to live a more thrilling existence."[6] Under the competition of the machine-interposed media and the pressure of needs for other kinds of service, our press has come through its "yellow" age and now exists in a spectrum which extends from the *New York Times*, which tries to carry "All the news that's fit to print," to the most sensational tabloid and *Confidential* magazine. Some of the inheritance of the "yellow" period remains with us, however, in comic strips, in the high proportion of feature and human-interest stories, and in the playing-up of sensational news as a stimulus to circulation.

It is important to notice that the general pattern of the industrial revolution (toward larger and fewer manufacturing units) has been reflected in newspapers. Even while the national population has more than doubled, and while total circulation of daily newspapers has increased twelvefold in 75 years, the number of daily newspapers has significantly decreased. The number is still decreasing, through mergers, sales, and suspensions, and very few new dailies are being started. Thus we have fewer and larger newspapers.[7] Indeed, only 6 per cent of all the daily newspaper cities in this country now have competing dailies. The figures in the table below show what the trend is in relation to the national population. They are assembled from the N. W. Ayer *Guide to Periodical Literature*, the yearbooks of *Editor and Publisher*, and the United States Census reports. Here is the story:

	Number of Dailies	Total Circulation	U.S. Population
1888	1,442	4,543,713	61,000,400 (est.)
1900	2,120	9,330,930	75,994,575
1914	2,442	25,426,911	96,000,000 (est.)
1920	2,042	27,790,656	105,710,620
1930	1,942	39,589,172	122,775,046
1940	1,878	41,131,611	131,669,275
1950	1,772	53,829,072	150,697,361
1956	1,760	56,147,359	162,000,000 (est.)[a]

The trend with respect to competitive ownership of daily newspapers in the United States is indicated in the following table:

	Total Dailies	Total Daily Cities	Cities with Competing Dailies	Percentage of Cities with Non-competitive Ownership
1909-10	2,202	1,207	689	42.9
1920	2,042	1,295	552	57.4
1930	1,942	1,402	288	79.4
1940	1,878	1,426	181	87.3
1944-5	1,744	1,396	117	91.6
1953-4	1,785	1,448	87	94.0[a]

[a] This table is from an article by Ray B. Nixon, "Concentration and Absenteeism in Daily Newspaper Ownership," *Journalism Quarterly*, 22 (June 1945) 97-114, updated by the same author, "Trends in Daily Newspaper Ownership since 1945," *Journalism Quarterly*, v. 31 (Winter 1954) pp. 3-14.

This is a dramatic development indeed, and it makes for an obvious difference in the relation of a newspaper to its public. The whole essence of the party press was the ability of each opinion group to be represented by its own paper. This would be very hard to accomplish in the 94 per cent of our cities which do not have competing dailies. The kind of service that a paper in a single-ownership town sells therefore must be different from the kind of service a party paper sold. By its very nature it has to be big. It has to sell many copies, to sell large amounts of advertising to pay its bills, and to serve more people better. The process is obviously circular. In order that it may sell many copies it must serve many kinds of people representing many political viewpoints. Therefore, it cannot afford to represent one political viewpoint only, as could the party press. It finds that representing all significant viewpoints on controversial questions is usually profitable, whether or not otherwise desirable.

Even though its publisher may be anti-Roosevelt or -Truman or -Eisenhower, the paper cannot afford to carry only anti-Roosevelt or -Truman or -Eisenhower news. Even though it is big business by virtue of the costs of producing it (which we shall have occasion to discuss in greater detail in a later chapter), it cannot afford to be an apologist only for big business. This is a new kind of responsibility, one which the party press never had to think of, and to which the yellow press paid little attention. The effort of newspapers to analyze this new obligation has made for much of the preoccupation with ethical problems in the mass media during recent years, and indeed represents much of the reason for this book.

We have been talking about print. The machine-interposed media came along relatively late in the industrial revolution and therefore had relatively short histories of smallness and fewness. They were caught up in the tidal wave of growth almost as soon as they had a marketable product. Motion pictures were already in 1920 attracting weekly audiences equivalent nearly to one third of the people in this country. Radio, which had 30 stations and 60 thousand receivers in 1922, had 3400 stations and over 100 *million* receivers in 1956. Television reached barely 75,000 homes in 1947, but in 1956 went into three quarters of the homes of the country—about 36 million. The later these media came along, the more fantastically swift was their growth. The Columbia Broadcasting System has recently compiled a table showing the time it took certain industries to put their products into 34 million homes in the United States. There are the figures:

Telephone	80 years
Electric wiring	62 years
Automobile	49 years
Electric washing machine	47 years
Electric refrigerator	37 years
Radio	25 years
Television	10 years[a]

[a] From *Network Practices*, a handbook of testimony prepared by the Columbia Broadcasting System for hearing before the Senate Committee on Interstate and Foreign Commerce, June 1956. The CBS statisticians have cheated a little here, because, of course, there were not 34,000,000 homes in the United States when these earlier industries were founded. Nevertheless, the growth of the later industries has been significantly faster.

Another way to show the swift growth of mass communication in this country is to tabulate the estimated size of the advertising pool, a very large part of which, of course, goes to the support of the mass media. These are the best figures it is possible to assemble on one of the more dramatic growth curves of the industrial revolution:

Year	Estimated Total Advertising (in millions)
1880	200
1890	360
1900	542
1910	1,200
1920	2,935
1930	2,607
1940	2,087
1950	5,710
1955	8,500*

* These are *Printers' Ink* estimates.

This is what we mean by the growth of mass communication. Dramatic as they are, the figures are merely incidental to what has happened. For the truth is that we have, in the lifetime of many of us, been presented with a *new* system of public communication. The social bulk of these new enterprises is as different from that of the tiny printing enterprises of the 16th century as the 16th-century enterprises were different from the *Acta Diurna*, the wall newspaper used to record the decisions of the Roman Senate. But it is not necessary to go back as far as the 16th century to find a contrast with our present mass communications. One hundred years ago there was no radio, no television, no movies; newspapers were mostly party papers, and magazines and books were small industries indeed. Only 50 years ago there were no radio and no television; movies were represented by a few nickelodeons; newspapers were a combination of party papers and yellow press, and still growing in numbers. The dramatic coming of largeness and fewness to newspapers was still in the future, and so was the passing of the party press. Radio and television were still to be born, and the days of mass audiences for films were still to come. All these developments have come about in the last 50 years.

There is another way to symbolize what has happened. What would people have thought a century ago, if someone had predicted that it would be possible not too far in the future to buy for five cents a newspaper connected by leased wires and reporters to all the principal cities of the world, no more than minutes removed from a news event anywhere, and indeed only a few hours from news pictures wherever they are taken, and maps and charts wherever they are available? What would people have thought 50 years ago, if someone had told them that in the future most homes would contain a relatively inexpensive little box into which one could look and see and hear the Metropolitan Opera, the New York Music Hall stage, the Olympic games in Melbourne, the meetings of the United Nations, the fighting in a distant part of the world, and the candidates for national office?

There is yet another way. What would anybody have thought, if someone had predicted that these little boxes we have been talking about would be used, on the average, about four hours a day in every American home where they are available; that another box called a radio would be used, on the average, a little over two hours a day; and that the average American adult would spend, on the average, thirty minutes a day with his newspaper? On the basis of various data, it has to be concluded that most Americans now spend between three and six hours a day, on the average, with mass communication. This probably compares with not much more than an hour 50 years ago, and considerably less 100 years ago.[8]

These developments in communication have made a profound difference in the way we receive information, and in the kind and amount of information we receive. For communicators they have made a profound difference in the opportunities they offer and the responsibilities they enjoin. The implications of these developments will concern us throughout this book.

3

Its Structure

What can we say of the structure and function of mass communication that will help us comprehend its responsibilities?

Its Pervasiveness

In the first place, mass communications are extraordinarily *pervasive*.

Suppose we were describing our culture to a visitor from another planet. We should have to report a set of experiences which come to practically all of us throughout all except the first year or so of our lives. In imaginative language, we might call these the *teach-please* experiences (after Horace), or the *inform-entertain* experiences, because each of them is intended, in some proportion, to teach and please, inform and entertain. A newspaper is more on the informing side; radio, television, and films, more on the entertaining side. A magazine of large general circulation is usually a fairly even combination. Textbooks are mostly to inform; novels, mostly to entertain. And so on. But each of these teach-please experiences comes from mass communication. And we should be hard put to it to name any man-made products except food, clothing, and shelter which are more widely pervasive throughout our lives and our communities.

Much of our population depends on these teach-please products for a large part of all the information and entertainment they receive during life. Over 90 per cent of all the homes in the United States receive a daily newspaper, containing several hundred news and advertising items. Over 90 per cent of all our homes have radios which will play music, news, drama, or offer other information or entertainment, practically any hour of the day or night, although it is sometimes hard to get the particular music you want when you want it, or to get a newscast precisely when you need it. However, most of these radios will pick up from 6 to 50 stations, and in that group there is considerable choice at any hour. Over two thirds of all

26

American homes take magazines regularly. Perhaps one third of all Americans see motion pictures with some regularity, and perhaps one fourth of them read books with some regularity. The larger part of this movie-going and book-reading is by individuals below the age of 21, and we might speculate on the meaning of that fact. But these are impressive figures, nevertheless. When one can record that 56 million copies of daily newspapers are sold every day in this country, that approximately 100 million radio sets are in our homes, offices, and cars, that books and magazines can be bought even in the drug stores, and that movie houses are available almost everywhere in the country, then the word "pervasive" takes on new significance.

Furthermore, these teach-please products are becoming even *more* plentiful. Daily newspaper sales have been steadily increasing. The number of radios is steadily increasing. The number of television sets has increased at an almost exponential rate!

The very pervasiveness of mass communication is itself a fact of importance for anyone who is examining the responsibilities of the media. These enormous circulations act as a sounding board to magnify every act of the mass media. Furthermore, the fact that so many people depend on the media raises a bothersome problem, for these people are different in needs and tastes. One of the hardest questions mass communicators have to decide is whether to meet all the different needs of the different groups within their audience, in which case any program will serve only a minority of the audience—or to try to meet the broad common needs of the largest possible audience, in which case various individual and group needs may go unmet. Actually, for example, the art of program-making on radio or television, or the art of magazine-making, is necessarily a set of compromises, made in the most skillful way possible so as to meet as many needs and interests as possible and attract as broad an audience as possible to the magazine or the station. But the sense of these unmet needs, and of the responsibility for meeting them, is the reason behind educational broadcasting, "good music stations," and special-audience magazines and newspapers of all kinds which supplement the great circulations of the more general media.

The Industry that Produces It

What can we say about the importance of the industry that produces mass communications?

It isn't big, at least not by motors or utilities standards. Altogether, it represents about two per cent of all the business done in the United States each year. To get an idea of the relative size, we might remember that the total annual sales of all our book industry equal less than a week of the sales of General Motors.

More important: the mass communication industry is diffuse. That is, it has a great number of individual producing units. The automobile industry, which also turns out pervasive products is really only half a dozen companies (that is, companies turning out passenger cars as the finished product), and one of these does more than half the business. On the other hand, there are 1760 daily newspapers, over 8400 weekly newspapers, over 500 television stations, over 3400 radio stations, several hundred book publishers who produce each year over half a billion copies of 13,000 titles, somewhere around 50 substantial movie producers and over 18,000 movie theaters, and so many magazines of so many kinds that one never knows where to draw the line around the definition of a magazine and therefore whether to say there are 5000 or 7500 of them.[1]

This is important for us to notice, because it means that many branches of the communication industry have local responsibilities and special interests to meet. Newspapers are almost always local in their orientation; the editor is choosing news for his *local* clientele, the advertiser is advertising for his *local* market, the editor is giving editorial advice to his *local* readers. Magazines, though many of them strive to be national in their scope and audience, are still so numerous that many of them are set up to serve special needs and interests. That is, we have women's magazines, farm magazines, teen-agers' magazines, plumbers' magazines, etc. Radio and television are less local than newspapers, less special than many magazines, but stations still have a local personality and local responsibilities. And, as large newspapers have grown larger and fewer, at the same time small papers and bulletins—neighborhood papers, company journals, Chamber of Commerce bulletins, et cetera, local or private by intention—have proliferated, with the intention of serving local needs and interests.

But we must not lose sight of the strong centralizing tendency in the mass media. Although mass communication output has grown steadily larger in the last 40 years, production has tended to concentrate. As we have already pointed out, the number of daily newspapers has steadily decreased for 40 years. A dozen publishers sell a very large chunk of all magazine circulation. Six studios make a large proportion of all movies. A very large part of all broadcast programming comes from four national networks for radio, three for television; in each case two do the lion's share of the business. Few newspapers have Washington or foreign correspondents any more; their distant news is fed them by one or more of the three large wire news services; much of their feature and entertainment material comes to them through syndicates. Thus you can go from one end of the United States to the other today and read about the same news and entertainment, except for materials of purely local interest, in almost any town where you stop. You can hear the same radio, watch the same television, see the same movies, buy the same paper bound books.

It is harder to enter the communication industry than it used to be. It used to be possible to start a newspaper in New York City, one hundred years ago, with 15,000 dollars of capital. Now it would take 5 million dollars of risk capital to compete successfully with large dailies, and even then the chances of succeeding would be less than even. Marshall Field dropped a sum that must have been in the millions on *PM* and the Chicago *Sun* before accepting failure. Other media have gone through the same metamorphosis. *Life*, one of the few large magazines started in recent times, dropped somewhere near five million dollars before it began to make money. There was a time when to start a small paper anywhere one had merely to acquire a press and a few fonts of type; to start a broadcasting station anywhere one had only to put together a tiny transmitter from used parts; to start as a book publisher one merely needed capital of ten thousand dollars or less. Now it requires somewhere around half a million dollars to equip a television station, if one can get a station at all. Small newspapers are selling for up to a quarter of a million dollars. Publishers advise you to stay out of "big time" mass communication, unless you can bring very substantial capital. In other words, whereas it used to be easy for any person or group of persons with initiative and an idea or a viewpoint to get into mass communication, now it is much harder. There are high economic barriers in the way. The following table summarizes the situation.

MASS COMMUNICATION MEDIA IN THE UNITED STATES

Medium	Number of Units	Circulation and Audiences	Financial Support
Books	300 publishers of five or more titles annually. 30 publish 60% of books; 100 publish 85%.	13,000 titles 600 million copies per year.	By sales Estimated in neighborhood of .75 billion annually.
Daily newspapers	1,760 dailies*	56 million copies a day	70% from advertising; 30% from circulation. Total between 3 and 4 billion
Magazines	6,000 plus 6 large publishing houses	20 magazines have over one million circulation each.	Advertising and circulation in varying proportions. Total, estimated near one billion
Television	460 stations 3 large networks	36 million receiving sets	Advertising mostly; some from talent. 20 educational stations non-commercial, subsidized. Total over one billion.
Radio	2,896 AM stations 530 FM 4 large networks	Over 100 million receiving sets	Advertising and talent. 100 educational stations subsidized. Total, estimated near .7 billion.
Films	100-plus studios 6 very large ones 18,000 theaters	Weekly attendance estimated near 45 million	Attendance, plus small local advertising income. Estimated, one billion plus.

* There are also about 8478 weekly newspapers, circulating somewhere above 18 million weekly, supported by advertising and circulation, with total support somewhere near 200 million a year.

Each year, *Editor* and *Publisher*, the newspaper trade journal, publishes balance sheets for typical newspapers of different sizes, compiled from figures supplied anonymously by newspapers throughout the country. The average total of operating revenue for a news- *high* paper of 50,000 circulation, in the year 1955, was 2.7 million dollars![2] Paper and ink for that paper alone cost nearly 600,000 dollars, and it cost over half a million to run the composing room. Even these costs are small, however, beside the gargantuan economics of television. Here is what it required in the way of man-hours to produce one hour of network television (the program was "Climax" on CBS):[3]

	Personnel	Man-hours
Producer	1	60
Director	1	100
Program staff	5	216
Story editor and staff	10	98
Script	1	Varies greatly
Writers for script adaptation	3	240
Music scoring	5	36
Music record library	3	4
Cast	30	1,700
Total	59	2,454 plus

When you recall that many of these 59 persons are very highly paid, and that the time charges for network television are in the neighborhood of $1,000 a minute, you begin to realize what sums are involved in lighting up a television screen in an American home.

Costs like these have forced the communication industry to centralize. They could not otherwise meet the demands on them. Americans would not be satisfied any more with the kind of newspaper that used to be printed with a few fonts of type on a hand press, with no wire service and no syndicated features. Americans would not be satisfied with the kind of station KDKA was when it broadcast records from a garage in Pittsburgh in 1920. But nevertheless when mass communication becomes hard to enter, and when ownership and production tend to concentrate, these are significant developments worthy of concern in a democracy. These developments may not be bad; actually they may turn out for the good. The chances are we get better papers, better broadcasting, out of them. But they impose certain special responsibilities on mass communications to represent a variety of ideas fairly. This kind of responsibilty we shall have a great deal to say about in the pages to come.

Mass communications in this country support themselves. They are not run or subsidized by the government. Different branches of the industry support themselves in different ways: newspapers and magazines, by selling both advertising and circulation; radio and television, by selling advertising; books and motion pictures, by selling circulation. As we have said, the total support of mass communications is small compared to that of utilities or motors or other leviathans of American industry. But communication is still big business. To support mass communications in the United States last year cost somewhere over eight billion dollars.

The first responsibility of an American mass communication organization is to support itself, because only by so doing can it continue to live, and only by remaining economically strong can it be free of outside influences and able to handle facts and ideas as it believes it should. But this very fact suggests that there might be some conflicting responsibilities built up around the need for support. This would be especially true in the case of media which live wholly or in part by selling advertising space or time. Here one might with good reason expect some conflict of interest as between service to the advertiser and service to the public. And indeed a whole family of ethical and responsibility problems arises over this aspect of communication, as in later pages of this book we shall see.

THE FUNCTIONS OF MASS COMMUNICATION

What do mass communications do?

Think of society as a large group of communicating mechanisms, bound together by intricate and interconnected networks of communication, influence, and obligation. Some of these mechanisms will distinguish themselves from the others by having a relatively large communication output in proportion to their input. These may be the ministers, teachers, writers, artists, and political orators of the society. Some unkind *men* might say we are referring to the wives of the society. But in any civilized society there are certain communicating organisms whose output is vastly greater in proportion to their input than is that of any individual. These are the mass communications.

The mass communication organizations are in some respects like individual communicators. Like the individuals they fit into the endless communication chains which cross and crisscross society and help bind it together. Like the individual writers and artists and teachers, the mass communicators are connected to many receivers. Like the individuals, the mass communicators are complete communication units. That is, they receive and send messages, decode what they receive and encode what they wish to send, and interpret the flow of communication through them. Their performance may be measured in the same terms as the individual performance—that is, in terms of capacity, fidelity, reliability, accuracy, etc.

Furthermore, mass communicators have essentially the same functions as the individual communicators—insofar as these functions are public, rather than private. Face-to-face communications obviously make certain contributions to our everyday living which we would never delegate to mass communicators. A private communication such as, say, a proposal of marriage, is more appropriately performed by an individual communicator than through a mass medium. At the same time, it should be noted that much supposedly private communication—gossip, rumor, "intimate confessions," etc.—does get into the mass media, and in conspicuous places. And, in truth, most of the functions which man has ever given communication have been turned over in some degree to mass communication. This is especially true of the traditional public functions of communication, which are the same now as they were when the first tribes assembled on the beaches and in front of the caves.[4]

Thus, mass communication *helps us watch the horizon*, as the ancient messenger used to do. Instead of a running messenger or a distant drum, now we get news bulletins, or on-the-scene broadcasts, or advertisements of opportunities.

Mass communication *helps us correlate our response* to the challenges and opportunities which appear on the horizon, and *reach consensus* on social actions to be taken. We used to do this through tribal councils or town meetings. Now we turn to mass communications to read the rival arguments, see the rival candidates, and have the alternative courses of action explained to us.

Mass communication *helps us transmit the culture* of our society to new members of the society. We have always had teaching at mother's knee, and imitation of the father—and still have. For thousands of years we have had schools in some form or other. But mass communication enters into this assignment by supplying text-books, teaching films and programs, and a constant picturing of the roles and accepted mores of our society. I once asked a large group of immigrants, "How did you first learn what American life was like?" Some of them had received letters from relatives, but their chief source was our picture magazines. "How did you get your first English lessons?" I asked them. "From your movies," they said.

Mass communication *helps entertain us.* The ballad singer, the dancer, and the traveling theater (even the pitch man) of older times have now gone on television, radio, and films. The story-tellers are chiefly in print.

Finally, mass communication *helps sell goods for us* and thus keeps our economic system healthy. We used to listen for the town crier's advertisements, the word-of-mouth tidings of bargains to be had, the bells of the traveling store-wagon. Now we read the ads in the papers or the magazines, see the ads on television, or hear them on radio.

We have been talking about similarities between the individual and the mass communicators. Now let us mention some dissimilar-ities. Whereas the individual's decoding, interpretation, and encoding are carried on in the central nervous system, the central nervous system of mass communication is an organization of individual com-municators who themselves make up a highly intricate communica-tion network. When one analyzes the complexity of the assignments and the interrelationships that exist within a communication organi-zation, it seems a minor miracle that a daily newspaper ever gets out, or a television show ever gets on the air.

A NEWSPAPER'S DAY

To an outsider a newspaper office looks casual and fairly relaxed, except sometimes just before deadlines. The complexity is hidden in well established patterns and good management. Yet if we were to describe in any detail the communication that takes place, let us say, inside a newspaper office during a single work day, and the complicated nature of decision-making that lies behind such an outwardly simple act as publishing 24 pages of newsprint, we should find ourselves talking on an almost unbelievable level of intricacy.[5] This is what, in a mass communication organization, takes the place of the human nervous system.

You may get a sense of this complexity if we describe, even without all details, what happens in a newspaper during the process of publication. The day begins with a sort of accordion movement, in and out. The teletypes begin to clack and clang with news from all parts of the world. The phones jingle as people phone in items or classified advertisements. Meanwhile the reporters and photographers are getting their assignments and are making their first 'phone calls of the day preparatory to covering their special stories and their beats. The advertising salesmen are preparing to go out to call on merchants. The printers are at work setting up the copy that is ready —the features that come in from the syndicate, the late news from the previous day. The ads are already set in type. The editors are marking the early copy, so as to keep up a steady flow to the composing room. They are studying the competitive papers, the wire news budget, the previous day's paper, and all the other news forecasts they can get, so as to give assignments and predict the flow of news that day. The editorial writer or writers are deciding what topics should be included that day, after which they will be looking up information and perhaps talking it over with some of the reporters or editors, or with the publisher. The publisher, all this time, is less caught up than the others with daily decisions. His problems tend to be of longer range: Should we buy a new press? What about a campaign for better schools? Who should replace the managing editor who is getting near retirement age? Can we afford to give the typographical union the increase of 25 cents an hour it wants? You see that different problems are being met at different levels of the hierarchy, but at some point all the decisions must mesh and produce a newspaper.

Now the reporters are coming back with their notebooks full of details to write. Some of the hot stories are being phoned in by "leg men," and written in newspaper style by "rewrite men." The reporters and rewrite men are sitting in front of their typewriters, making the countless little decisions that go into forming a story: What is the most important idea, to be featured? What should we tell the public in the first paragraph (it may not read the second!)? What facts about the story are worth reporting, and which ones should be discarded? When there is an apparent conflict in fact, where does truth lie, or what conflicting views must be presented?

The advertising salesmen are coming back. Display advertising is usually dummied the day before publication. Orders are being noted, and space assigned. Ads are being written and designed and sent to the clients for approval. Two clients want the space on the sports page next to the big game; one of them has to be disappointed. A client has submitted an ad which may be contrary to good business practice; that issue has to be decided.

Material is now flowing to the copy desk from the teletypes, from the reporters, from the photographers' darkrooms. Some of the stories are being rewritten. All are being copyread and marked for the printer. The pictures are being cropped and marked for size. Facts are being checked as well as possible. The compositors are ringing for more copy, and the copy boy is sent down with a handful of the tawny newsprint reporters and editors write on.

By this time a fundamental decision has been made: how many pages should the paper "go" today, and how big will the news "hole" be? The amount of advertising will determine this, because it takes a certain amount of advertising to pay for a certain number of pages. Roughly, half to two thirds of the space will go into advertising, and about two thirds of the paper's income will come from advertising.

When this is decided, then the editors will have more to go on. The paper is beginning to take shape. The early pages are already made up. Now the editors will know which stories will have to be shortened or discarded, and what size headlines they will need. The question how to make up the front page now comes up. This is the newspaper's showcase. It is the editors' pride. Here they will put the most exciting merchandise they have to offer. What story will they give the banner headline? What stories will they put in the prize spots above the fold? They will want a feature or two to put under three-column heads toward the bottom of the front page; which should those be?

Now the ads are all set in type, made up, and proofread. The sports and society news have been "put to bed" in their metal frames. The last of the news copy is flowing through the copy desk, down to the compositors. The pressmen have come to work and are wiping off the big rollers in preparation for printing. About this time, last-minute problems begin to occur: a big story breaks on the news wire; a fire starts in the business district. The editors have to decide how to remake the front page, whether to try to cover the story with a bulletin or at length, or wait until tomorrow.

Now the tempo eases off upstairs, speeds up in the press room. The reporters are tapping out copy for tomorrow; the ad men are getting together their copy for the next day; the city editor is making up his assignments and filling up his future book; the sports editor is making arrangements to have all tonight's games covered; and the society editor has gone to report a society tea. Downstairs, the last corrections are being put in the type forms, the mats are being made, and the metal half-cylinders are being cast for the press. And now the press starts to roll, slowly while the pressmen examine the first copies, then at top speed. The papers come swiftly through the folder and pile up where the counters and wrappers can get at them. For the last 30 minutes there has been subdued but increasing activity in the circulation department. Now the trucks are ready and many of the carrier boys are gathered with their bicycles and canvas bags, waiting to fold their papers. The first loads of papers come down to the "out" room; the first carrier boy counts out his 78 papers and starts folding; the first truck is loaded and on its way to the news stands, hotels, drug stores, and suburbs. And so the flow of the newspaper to the community begins.

A Television Station

Now let us look at what is happening in a television station.[6]

The station's day revolves around a detailed schedule of programs and announcements, compiled in the front office and distributed to all the other departments of the station. The program director, the producers and announcers, the newsman, the advertising manager and salesmen, the engineers and camera men, all have this schedule, and it is probably the first thing they look at when they come to work. For, just as the newspaper is built around available space, so is broadcasting built around meticulous timing and ruled by a clock.

The engineers are likely to be the first employees at the station in the morning. Some of these are in the main station building beside the studios. Others are some distance away, in the transmitter building which sits on high ground or in an open space beside the steel tower. They come in early to warm up the tubes, and to put the station's signal pattern on the air so as to check the signal and help service men tune up new sets. And soon after them come two camera men and a producer or director, who look at the schedule and begin to arrange their equipment.

The announcer who has the first shift is likely to be next in the studio. He looks at the schedule and picks up his copy. He has the routine announcements which put the station on the air, and also a number of commercials, written by the continuity department and timed to fill exactly 30 seconds or one minute, or whatever the commercial time allows. He reads these over, to spot hard words and check some of the timing. He slicks down his hair, straightens what advertising men call a "sincere" tie, and goes into the studio to sit down at a little desk with his copy in front of him.

The announcer, the producer, the camera men, the engineers, all watch the clock. Nobody, not even a bored office worker, watches the clock more closely than do broadcasters. The secondhand starts climbing toward the top of the dial. The producer holds up a warning hand. The engineers wait with hands on switches and dials, to turn on the sound and the first camera. The hand reaches 12. The producer points. Then, like a well-coached team, the group all step into action. The engineers turn their switches, moving hands swiftly to other duties. The announcer smiles at the camera and bids the audience good morning. A slide with the station's name and channel number goes in front of the camera. Then the announcer says, "Our national anthem!" The engineers switch on a record, and a film of a rippling flag goes into the film camera. That done, the announcer reads a brief commercial, looking the camera sincerely in the eye. Then the engineers switch to the network for the morning show, and the announcer can come out of the studio for a cigarette.

As in the case of a newspaper, much of the material that goes to the audience is being prepared away from the local plant. In the case of a newspaper, it is coming from the many arms of the wire news service. In the case of the broadcaster, it is coming from the network. The middle morning, most of the afternoon, and the best viewing hours of the evening, are usually furnished by the network. They come, usually from New York or Hollywood, over long lines or by microwave from tower to tower. They come into the studios, are fitted into the pattern of local commercial announcements, then are sent by wire or microwave to the transmitter, whence they go out into the air again toward the waiting antennas of receivers.

While the network starts the program day, other departments of the local station are springing into action. The advertising men are checking their accounts, making telephone calls and visits, preparing commercial copy. The news teletype is clacking, and the announcer who has the first local newscast of the day is sorting the news items that come out of the machine on yellow paper, checking the morning papers, putting together whatever the schedule allows him. He times it carefully, discards or adds a few sentences to space it out evenly, reads it several times to become as familiar as possible with it. Ideally, he should memorize it, so that he could always look the camera in the eye, but that is asking too much; so he merely tries to become familiar enough with it to be able to look up frequently. If he has time, he tries to prepare some "visuals" to go with the newscast— some maps, or film footage, to illustrate the day's news. He works swiftly toward his deadline, with frequent glances at the clock.

In the continuity department, a girl is looking blankly at a typewriter trying to compose an announcement assigned her by the advertising department. She gets an idea and begins to pound away.

There is a controlled but steadily rising tension in the second studio where the late morning local show is being rehearsed. A director is there, with three engineers, two camera men, a female announcer, some miscellaneous studio crewmen, and half a dozen local performers. The director is trying to explain to the amateurs how they must keep "on camera." They must use restrained gestures and movements, not the sweeping ones of the stage. They must look at the camera, not at scripts. He rehearses them painstakingly, looking up often at the clock or at his wrist watch to check the timing. Rehearsals for television are much longer and more careful than for radio. They take more people, and the new performers take more coaching. The camera men, too, must carefully plan the angles and distances they will use. To an outsider it is amazing how many people it takes to put on a television program, and wondrous how they keep out of each other's way. This little rehearsal group gradually works up toward what the producer considers to be a satisfactory level of performance; then he lets them go out into the hall for a soft drink or a cup of coffee before the show.

In the front office, the station manager is working with the program

director and the advertising manager on some changes in the master
schedule. The manager's phone rings. He speaks into it soothingly.
Somebody is angry over a violent bit of action in a children's program.
While he talks, the program director and the advertising manager
watch the morning musical from the network, which is on the
station manager's television set. The manager has no sooner finished
his call than his phone rings again. A local politician wants equal
time to answer what he says is a political attack on him by the mayor
in a television talk the preceding evening. The manager tells the
program director to schedule the politician for 15 minutes at the
same time as the mayor's talk had been. The three go back to their
conference. They are talking about an idea for selling a filmed show
to a local advertiser. The program director wants to add another
announcer to his staff. The advertising manager says some of his
clients are complaining that their commercials are not getting
favorable times. The manager's phone rings again.

Now it is time for the local show. The network program comes
to an end. The engineers smoothly switch from the microwave to
the local cameras. The announcer goes into his commercial. In the
larger studio a tense little group is poised. Their faces have been made
up to photograph clearly. The producer smiles encouragingly at
them. The camera men move around to get a little better angle. In
the darkness of the control room, the engineers are watching the
television screens connected with the several cameras. The producer
is talking to the camera men through wires to their earphones, telling
them to move closer or come back or take another angle.

The commercial ends. The clock hand climbs to the top. The
producer points to the female announcer. She smiles prettily and
introduces the program. And the whole team plunges into its
amazingly intricate pattern—the performers playing to the cameras,
watching the producer's signals out of the corners of their eyes; the
camera men circling, moving in, moving out, changing lenses and
focus, in response to the voice in their earphones; the engineers with
their skillful hands on dials and switches, their eyes on the monitors
in front of them and on the producer; the announcer coming
smoothly in and out as the script requires; the studio crew handling
the lights and sets; the producer keeping his control like the conductor of a symphony over the whole team, and his eye on the
script and the clock.

The minute hand is nearing 15, and the engineers look at the master schedule to see what will be required of them next. Already a male announcer is in the small studio with two commercials in front of him, waiting for the clock. One engineer checks the microwave monitor to see that the signal will be all right when it is time to bring the network back. In the continuity room, the writer is pounding copy which sings, she hopes. The advertising manager goes out to try to sell the new program idea to the hoped-for client.

And so the day goes on, and the programs go to the transmitter and out from the tower to the tuned-in sets.

THE MOVIES

The media are interestingly alike and unlike in their act of production. One of the differences one first notices between newspapers and television, on the one hand, and film-making,[7] on the other, is that a very large part of the newspaper and the broadcast programs comes from outside the local production unit. As intricate and well coordinated as are the team performances and the city newspaper and the local television station, yet they would be far less effective without the wire service and the network. In other words, these two media have powerful production units working for them in faraway points: the wire service with its correspondents and its exchanges in every part of the world, the network with its two great centers of skill and talent in New York and Hollywood, and with its ability to exchange among stations any station-produced programs which are deserving of exchange. Motion-picture studios have no such exterior source of production. They exist to produce films, which are in turn to be distributed to the public by theaters.

However, two very important parts of motion-picture production are outside the studios. These are—in the case of most studios—ownership, and in the case of all studios, stories. Whereas the studios make their own pictures in Hollywood or on location, most of them are financially accountable to a head office in New York. This means that financial decisions are ultimately made elsewhere and referred up from the level of the producer. So far as stories are concerned, Hollywood is constantly in the market for the best stories it can get, especially for stories which have already been a success as novels, magazine pieces, or theatricals, and have therefore been advertised to the public.

A film studio is likely to cover a number of acres of valuable Southern California real estate, and the closed studios and offices are likely to be a fairly small part of the plant. Much of the studio is "lot"—simply an outside space to take advantage of the California sunshine. The lot is covered with sets, which may be anything from a replica of ancient Rome to an artificial ocean in which floats an artificial Santa Maria, or to a replica of the beach at Iwo Jima. The shells of buildings, discarded automobiles, chariots used in an ancient epic of some kind, these and many other sets and props are spaced around the lot. Inside the main buildings of the studio are, of course, beautifully equipped sound stages, enormous costume collections, dressing rooms, cafeterias, swank offices for the top men, lesser but still very substantial offices for the writers and the technicians. There are cutting rooms, projection rooms, film storage rooms. It is a huge layout.

The film day begins early for actors and directors. They report at least by 8 o'clock to take advantage of as much sunlight as possible. On any day, at least one, often four or five, films are likely to be in progress on the lot. Another one or two may be "on location"—for example, on the desert, or in a city, or in Europe. In an ordinary year, the studio we are imagining is likely to make 40 films. Of these, perhaps 10 will be "A" films, the big productions costing over a million dollars each. Inasmuch as shooting time of an "A" film is likely to be two months or more, and of "B" film anywhere from three weeks to two months, there is always a considerable amount of activity on the lot, and in the offices, studios, and cutting rooms.

There is another characteristic that sets film-making apart from newspaper or television-making. Films are not made consecutively. Newspaper stories and television programs (except those that are filmed) are fashioned smoothly and directly from beginning to end, but movies are shot by scenes. These scenes are not necessarily made in the order in which they will appear on the screen. In fact, they almost never are. They are shot in whatever order is most convenient or economical. Then they are put together, with suitable additions or deletions, in the cutting room. Literally, a movie is made in the cutting room. The typical film goes into the cutting room with several times as much footage as the final product will have.

But what is happening in the studio on a typical day? Three or four films are being shot on the lot. One is a drawing room comedy, one a "horse opera" with cowboys and Indians, one a war story with armies and guns, et cetera. Let's look at the horse opera. This is using the same set where dozens of other westerns have been made: two intersecting streets, with a row of false building fronts and a few buildings finished in—the bar, for example. Here is a team in action, even more numerous and more complex than we saw in the television studio. The captain of the team is a producer. He is responsible for the picture—responsible to top management, that is, for making a picture that will make money. He has set up, in consultation with the director, a shooting schedule, a cast, a prop and set list. He, or one of his assistants, has arranged for the extras, who will ride or walk or lounge through the scenes without any specially written part in the show.

But the executive who is really in charge of the shooting is the director. He is the man who has to see that the story gets told, that the script gets transferred to celluloid. He sits in his folding chair on the lot, saying a word here and there to his assistants, telling the actors by gestures what he wants, sometimes stopping the action to explain a scene or give an actor more directions. He has now gone through a scene four times without photographing a foot. The camera man, the sound technicians, the extras, the horses, are all waiting. The three principals—hero, villain, and girl—are simply meeting on the street. The girl and the villain are walking down the street, and the hero confronts them in a way that indicates he suspects "monkey business." The extras and the rest of the cast are there because everyone thought the scene would take only a few minutes, and then they could take part in one of the big crowd scenes. But already the director has spent an hour and a half on it. Tempers are getting a little frayed. People are getting impatient. The producer is mentally counting up the lost time he is paying for. The director patiently explains what he wants out of the scene that he isn't getting. The cast listens carefully. They are professionals; they are used to taking direction. "All right, now, let's go through it once more, then we'll shoot," says the director, and the girl and villain start sauntering for the fifth time down the street with its fake fronts.

That kind of thing is happening on the lot. What is going on inside?

In individual offices, the writers are scowling at their typewriters.

Some of these writers have become famous for their books or their plays. That was before they came to Hollywood. Few Hollywood writers ever become famous. They are employees. Their job is to do what the producers and directors tell them to do. More often than anything else, their job is to "lick" a story. That means they are to take a story which has been successful in some other medium, and make it fit the demands of the screen and the requirements of the Motion Picture Code. Most of them, especially those used to writing books, plays, and stories, find it frustrating business.

But the writers are working on manuscripts which have been bought, often for very large sums, by top management, and they are producing scripts which will go up again to the front office to be approved or rejected, returned with directions for changes, or assigned to some other writer. Most of these larger decisions are made in the front offices by the executive producers. It is these men essentially, always in consultation with New York, who decide how many and what pictures will be made each year, about how much can be budgeted for each, who will act in them, who will produce them, who will direct them, and finally whether and in what form they will be released.

On any given day, therefore, while the directors are directing, the producers producing, the actors acting, and the writers writing, a series of highly important decisions is likely to be in progress in the front offices. Shall we buy the prize-winning novel by that new author, and if so shall we get him to try to do a script for us? The author's or publisher's agent wants $100,000 for movie rights; maybe we can talk him down to $75,000. The writer will have to get $1,000 a week, and he probably won't be able to turn out a decent movie script, but it will be good publicity. And whom shall we get for the leads? We have stars A and B on contract for another picture this year, but they would be better in our new musicale. Perhaps we can borrow C from another studio. Or why not give D a chance when she is through with that horse opera? Sometimes a western star can step up to A pictures. And then, if we buy it, who's the best director we have for it?

These are the kinds of decisions the top producers make. These and others. For example, the western picture is overrunning its budget; can we cut it back to size, or shall we fire the producer and give it to someone else? The Code office is objecting to the love scenes in our new Parisian picture. It will cost us $100 thousand to reshoot the footage they don't like. Shall we go along with them, or shall we release it anyway and take a chance on getting around the Legion of Decency and the state censors? And the New York office is disturbed because the American "epic" we produced is falling below the expected gross. They are saying nasty things about our artistic director E, and about this kind of film in general. They say, make more musicales and westerns; those always pay back. An actors' agency is on the phone; they have a new beauty contest winner they want us to look at. A writers' agency has a story. Our best music director has an offer from a rival studio. And one of our leading actresses is supposed to be getting into a marital row, and the question is whether the publicity will help or hurt us. These too are problems of the kind going through the front offices at the studio, problems hidden behind the huge incomes, the tremendous estates, and the dark glasses.

So the work of the studio goes on: the production team struggling with a script on the lot, the writers struggling with scripts in their offices, the managerial group struggling with problems basic to all the others, and in the dark rooms the cutters, the directors, the producers working over film footage, scissoring it, pasting it, watching it over and over again, putting together a film from scenes. That night perhaps there will be a sneak preview at some nearby theater, and the audience will be asked what it thinks. Some weeks later, if management and ownership all approve, the film will go out in metal cans to the first-run theaters.

A Complex Process

That is the way mass communication comes into being. A correspondingly complex internal network goes into the production of radio, magazines, and books. Each of these is in its way different, and yet they are all basically similar. One way in which they are similar is the common pattern of decision-making which goes through them all, and which we can indicate in a little table:

This may make it sound simpler than it is. There are hierarchies within these hierarchies. For example, a newspaper printing shop will have its own division of responsibilities among superintendent, foremen, compositors, make-up men, proofreaders and pressmen, although the general responsibility of the whole group will be to get

Who Has	*Newspapers*	*Magazines*	*Books*	*Radio, TV*	*Films*
General responsibility	Publisher	Publisher	Top executives	Top executives	Top executives
Operating responsibility for financial support	Advertising and circulation executives	Advertising and circulation executives	Sales executives	Sales executives	Distribution executives
Operating responsibility for content	Editors	Editors	Editors	Producers, directors	Producers, directors
Working responsibility for content and performance	Reporters, writers, artists	Authors, artists, staff-writers	Authors	Writers, composers, actors, broadcasters	Writers, composers, actors
Working responsibility for technical production	Printers and circulation workers	Printers and circulation workers	Printers and circulation workers	Engineers, and sound men, etc.	Camera men, sound men, etc.

the copy in type and on paper. Similarly, the working responsibility for content is sometimes inside, sometimes outside the communication organization. Some magazines are staff-written, some written by outside authors. Some textbooks are written by authors in colleges or schools; other textbooks, and parts of many textbooks, are written in the publishing house. Some decisions can be made locally, some far away. The local broadcasting station is responsible for what it puts on the air, but by signing a contract and granting option time to a network it mostly gives up the right to decide what goes into its transmitter during certain hours of the day. The editorial policy of the newspaper may be determined by an owner who never steps inside the news room. Many decisions on motion pictures are made across the continent, in New York, where the chief owners have their offices, and where the last word is spoken on what films go out to the theaters. The amount of local control thus varies between media and even within media (for example, a chain newspaper vs. a locally owned newspaper), but in general the same pattern of responsibility runs through all the media, and when we come in a later chapter to talk about the ethical problems that present themselves to the different media we shall find that there is a fairly common pattern of decision-making.

What kind of structure have we, then, in mass communication? In each case we have a tremendously intricate production network interposed in the communication process to do a highly important task for society. In each case, the top management of this network is responsible for both the financial and the teach-please sides of the business, and for all basic policy, although many lesser policy decisions are distributed along the hierarchy. In each case, this network feeds a machine—a printing press, a broadcasting microphone and/or camera chain and a transmitter, or a film camera chain and film printer—which steps up the output enormously over any level we have ever reached by interpersonal communication, enabling this network to reach a vast number of individuals at the same time with the same message. But, for the very reason that so many are reached in mass communication, the feedback from audience to communicator is weak. In interpersonal communication—in talking with our friends, for example—we can watch the face of the person we are talking to, or listen for his quick answers, and thus tell in a fraction of a second whether our message is being received, whether it is being understood, whether it is being accepted. But we cannot watch the faces of our mass communication audiences, and we get precious little mail and phone calls from them in proportion to the size of our audiences; therefore we spend a great deal on audience research, which is seldom wholly satisfactory as feedback, but usually the best we have. The fact of this weak feedback from an audience on whose approval mass communication has to depend, and for serving whom mass communication has certain special obligations, makes it all the more essential for a communication industry in a time of change to review its social responsibilities.

4

Its Social Effects

At this point it is necessary to turn aside briefly and ask: how much effect does mass communication have, anyway?

This sounds like a ridiculous question. It is *assumed* that mass communication has an effect on human beings. If not, why are we writing this book?

Furthermore, all of us have seen the effects of communication, in a small way at least. We have given an order and seen it obeyed. We have, when young, asked a girl for a kiss and observed the effects of that communication (sometimes our cheeks have smarted from the effects). We have noticed that even nonverbal communications like traffic lights can affect our actions, and that certain communications, verbal or nonverbal, can stimulate our adrenal glands and cause us to feel wrath. It is contrary to all our experience to doubt the ability of communication to have an effect.

And in truth, there is little doubt of the effect of face-to-face interpersonal communication. But it is necessary to record that there are real differences of opinion concerning the effects of *mass* communication.

For example, here is Senator John F. Kennedy of Massachusetts, writing in *The New York Times Magazine:*

Today the challenge of political courage looms larger than ever before. For our everyday life is becoming so saturated with the tremendous power of mass communication that any unpopular or unorthodox course arouses a storm of protest.[1]

Here is A. C. Spectorsky, writing in *The Exurbanites:*

Here walks a man whose political opinions are shaped by what he reads on the editorial pages of *Life.* There goes a woman who sneers at such-and-such a movie because she subscribes to *The New Yorker.* Yonder totters an ancient whose tic is ascribable to the fact that he cannot shake from his mind's ear the words, 'Don't be half safe,' sung to the tune of 'The Volga Boatmen.' That teen-ager insists on scuttling her naturally fresh appearance in dutiful response to some offhand remarks in *Madamoiselle*. The pinched expression on this man's face is habitual since his wife has been on the wonder diet touted by a woman's magazine. . . . On every hand the results are tangible, often depressing, and frequently comic.[2]

On the other hand, here is a contrary view from Professor Richard T. LaPiere, writing in his book, A *Theory of Social Control:*

In the opening chapter of this work it was pointed out that a current version of the *Gesellschaft* concept of society revolves around the idea that the mass media—the newspaper, magazine, radio, motion picture, and television—determine in significant measure the conduct of modern peoples. Crucial to this idea is the assumption that modern society, in categorical contrast to premodern forms of social life, is an aggregate of semi-autonomous individuals, each responding independently of all the others to communications that come to him via the mass media. The fundamental error of this assumption and hence of the ideas derived from it should now be quite evident.

The recent and continuing stress on the powers, for good or evil, of the press, radio, motion pictures, television, etc., is a consequence of the newness of these means of communication rather than their actual impact on human affairs. . . . The conduct of men cannot be determined by anything analogous to mass production means.[3]

In general, the scholars have tended to be bearish, the laymen and the educators bullish, concerning the probable effects of mass communication. The laymen have observed, or think they have, what mass communication can do. The scholars have been more aware of the complexity of social causation, and have for the most part been unable to relate mass communication directly to any very abrupt or striking attitude change.

The situation obviously calls for arbitration. If the effects of mass communication are as doubtful as LaPiere indicates, this book can be shorter; indeed, it can end with this chapter, and thus save a considerable amount of time and work for both of us. On the other hand, if it is as powerful as Spectorsky and Kennedy suggest, then we must ask whether we have raised up like Frankenstein a monster that might destroy its creators. Where does the truth lie?

Not all scholars or observers of mass communication take such firm positions on one side or the other of the controversy as those quoted. Readers who seek a more balanced treatment might well start with an essay by Paul F. Lazarsfeld and Robert K. Merton, entitled "Mass Communication, Popular Taste and Organized Social Action."[4] This is a keen and perceptive piece in which the authors cut the ground out from under the critics who feel that "the power of radio can be compared only with the power of the atom bomb," but still try to isolate and analyze certain effects which are attributable to mass communication: the power of conferring status, for instance; the power of enforcing social norms by giving publicity to deviation from them; the power of helping to maintain the *status quo* by drugging its listeners into passive reception rather than action. This last is what the authors call the "narcotizing dysfunction" of mass communication. Lazarsfeld and Merton also perform a useful service by calling attention to the fact that mass communication is likely to have more effect under some conditions than under others. For example, it can probably accomplish more when it has a *monopoly*. That is why dictators try to keep contrary communication away from their audiences. It is also why Kate Smith was so effective in her war bond sales, according to Merton[5]—because no one rose to challenge the appealing radio image of her that had been built up. Mass communication can accomplish more by *canalizing* an existing drive. Cigarette advertising, for example, can pay for itself by directing an *existing* habit of smoking cigarettes *toward a particular brand*. Likewise, mass communication can be effective in *supplementing* face-to-face contacts. The Lazarsfeld-Merton article is useful at this point in our discussion and is recommended as an antidote to statements of the kind we quoted earlier.

Let us see what kind of sense we can make of this varied set of judgments concerning the effects of communication.

First of all, let us distinguish between what we have called the *services*, and what we have called the *effects*, of mass communication.

There is no real doubt that mass communication contributes to the functioning of our social order by taking over much of the responsibility which precivilized societies handled by word-of-mouth communication. These we mentioned in the previous chapter: the *watchman* function of reporting dangers and opportunities on the horizon; the *council* function of presenting alternative arguments and alternative candidates, and thus helping us to reach consensus and decisions on important social questions; the *teacher* function of passing the funded culture of the society on to the new members of the society; the *entertainer* function of making us laugh and marvel and relax; the *business* function of speeding and extending our commerce. The evidence is clear for all to see regarding these services. In each of these respects, mass communication provides information and other communicable materials which enter into our interpersonal relationships and contribute to the efficient functioning of our large social groups.

Over a long term the mass media thus drip into us. They give us a constant series of reports from parts of our environment we have never seen, and thus contribute to our picture of environment. They give us a concept of status in the society around us simply by making us more familiar with some names, faces, and voices than with others. A few years ago a radio newscaster, who was distinguished chiefly by being given a favorable hour on a powerful station, came within a few votes of being elected governor of a populous Middle Western state. Later he was put into an important national office. These results unquestionably could be traced to the status which rubbed off on him from his radio time and position. Likewise, by familiarizing us with some art rather than other art, the mass media doubtless contribute to the forming of our taste for art. By connecting some forms of conduct with status figures, they may contribute to our preferred conduct. In other words, over a long period they help fill in the ground for the figure of our decision-making.

So much for the long-term service effects. Concerning the immediate effects, the picture is less clear. In the laboratory we have in a number of instances succeeded in causing individuals to change their opinions by exposing them to mass communication. In field studies, on the other hand, where individuals were exposed to mass communication but no effort was made to communicate with them face-to-face or to change their group relationships, we have seen no comparable effects. There have been only a few cases when mass behavior could be clearly attributed to mass communication. The most famous of these was the Orson Welles broadcast, in 1938, of a fictional invasion from Mars. In the Welles case, you will remember, a panic was created among less critical members of the audience, and thousands of people left their homes and sought refuge from the Martians.[6] But, as we said, cases like this have been few. Election studies, for example, have indicated that the media apparently have little direct and immediate effect in changing voting decisions—

rather, people tend to select from the media what will reinforce their existing predispositions. At the same time, think how difficult it would be to run a candidate for any except a neighborhood office if that candidate had not been "built up" in the mass media. And recall what happens when a great mass-media personality like Mr. Eisenhower finds himself in resonance with a great public motivation and uses the media to announce that he will go to Korea to try to end the war. How many votes for ending the war were thereby canalized into votes for Eisenhower?

Mass communication can canalize existing attitudes and thus affect human attitudes and behavior. This is what advertising most often does. Identifying existing needs and desires, it rouses these, and then points out ways in which they may be satisfied. Do you want to smoke? Try Buckies. Do you wonder whether you may be "only half safe" from body odors? Try Smelless. Do you want to buy a car? Look at the Elephantine Eight. Do you want to buy a house? Here is one for sale. Here we have some impressive results indeed. Most of us can remember the time when women had to sneak their smokes in cloakrooms or behind drapes, at the very time when they were tired of inhibiting their wish to smoke in public, and were looking for an excuse to cast aside the old social taboo on women's smoking. The tobacco companies played this game skillfully. You can probably recall some of the ads from that period. They showed distinguished female opera singers and other prestige figures gaily smoking in public. They furnished such slogans as "Reach for a Lucky instead of a sweet," by means of which women could rationalize doing what they wanted to do anyway. We do not have the field research by which to prove that these ads themselves released the pent-up drives that determined women's behavior, but to observers it seemed obvious. And this same canalizing power of advertisements applies also to other media content and other behavior. For example, a boy who is full of unexpressed hostility and feelings of rejection may pick up a crime technique from a crime program, whereas a well-adjusted boy will merely use the same program to get rid of some of his aggressions without harming anyone. There is no real doubt that mass communication can have effects like these.

Mass communication never acts *by itself* on an individual. Whatever effect mass communication has, it will have jointly with other determining forces, of which the most important are two: the individual's personality resources and his group relationships. By personality resources I mean the stored knowledge we have available for use; the values and attitudes we have built up to govern the *direction* (favorable or unfavorable) of our responses to almost everything with which we have had experience; and the motivations we have at any given time for doing a certain kind of thing. These are usually called our cognitive states, our dispositional states, and our motivational states. Together with our group relationships they pretty much determine what we do with any mass communication we receive.

By group relationships, I mean the groups of persons we work with, play with, and live with, the standards and customs and opinions we share with them, and how much we value the privilege of belonging to the groups and are therefore willing to defend the group standards, customs, and opinions. Man lives in groups. These groups may be as small as a family or as large as a whole society. But much that he does he learns to do from group association and does because of some group reason. For years, one of the greatest villains in keeping us from understanding more clearly the social effects of mass communication was our ancient concept of a "mass" audience—that is, an audience of separated individuals, receiving mass communication like a hypodermic under their individual skins, and reacting individually to it. We know, now, that this is not the case. At the end of the communication chain is an individual who has certain important and often overlapping group memberships. Among these are family, coworkers, play groups, religious and political groups, etc. Most opinions are discussed and some generated in these groups. Opinions are more stable if they are shared in the groups. Indeed, an individual member will tend to bring his own opinion into line with the norm of any group he values, and he will defend the group norm elsewhere. He will tend to ask and respect the opinion of leaders in these groups. Sometimes these leaders change according to the subject under discussion. For example, in the family, father may take the lead on politics, mother on food and manners, son on football and "bop."

Man is far from a *tabula rasa*, or clean slate, for mass communication to write on. By the time a voter sees a Presidential candidate on television he has had at least 21 years of experience with human beings. He has learned what to expect from political oratory. He may have enough knowledge to challenge a wild statement if the candidate makes it. He has built up a sense of values which lead him to react positively or negatively to much of what the candidate will say. He may or may not be motivated in the direction the candidate wants him to go. And the voter will have a strong sense of group belongingness by that time. Perhaps he will have built up a loyalty to a political party. Certainly he will have a sense of how the people he admires think about this election, and how the people in his "set" or his union or his luncheon club evaluate the candidate. In other words, before he ever sits down to the television set, he is prepared to react in a pre-set way to whatever comes out of it.

Take the boy who learned the crime technique from the broadcast (and doubtless later put it into use). Most lads of this kind feel rejected by society. For belongingness they have turned to a peer group which admires violence. The boy was probably getting ready to impress this group by his knowledge of how to commit a crime. He was looking (unconsciously, of course) for some way to satisfy his aggression drive.[7] The boy who did *not* pick up the crime technique did not need to look for extralegal ways to satisfy his aggressions. He was probably well adjusted in a group that did not value violence as the first boy's group did. Thus, if we had known enough about these two boys we could have predicted in advance, from their personality resources and their group relationships, how they would probably be affected by a crime program. And in the same way, every member of the mass communication audience will bring with him his own set of personality resources and his own set of group relationships, and mass communication can affect him only in combination with these.

In things that matter, the individual and his social organization are generally inclined to resist change. On any subject where his attitudes are long and firmly established, where they have an emotional content, where they relate to things he deeply values, the individual is highly resistant to change, whether it is suggested by mass communication or any other source. Indeed, he will often reject or ignore messages that challege his firm attitudinal structure, or will distort them so that they seem to agree with him. This is what happened in the famous case of the Mr. Biggott cartoons,[8] a series of satires on prejudice which were published by an organization dedicated to the eradication of race prejudice. When the cartoons seemed to be having no effect, field research revealed that they were *being taken seriously and literally* by prejudiced individuals. The satire was being completely missed because it conflicted with strong predispositions.

Likewise, any individual is reluctant to go against the norms of groups in which he values membership. Kurt Lewin tried to persuade housewives, in wartime, that they should serve various unpopular cuts of meat, in order to conserve the supply.[9] He tried this by lecture method, and failed abjectly. He tried by group discussion, and had notable success. The reason he succeeded was that, through discussion, the individuals were able to modify the group norm and thus gain some reinforcement for the idea of serving the previously unvalued foods.

Therefore, mass communication faces a powerful built-in resistance whenever it tries to effect a change in its audiences. This doesn't mean that mass communication has nothing to do with building up the personality resources and group standards by which the individual resists change. Quite the contrary. The individual learns a great many of the facts he knows from mass media. His concept of the status different individuals hold in society is largely determined by mass media. Many of his tastes have been developed by exposure to popular art and fine art through the mass media. And the mass media have had something to do with the group standards he supports. One of the things we have recently come to understand about mass communication is that it feeds facts and ideas to groups. Actually, it seems to feed the group leaders more than the followers, for research indicates that the leaders are keenly alert to mass communication, particularly in their area of leadership. Mass communication thus provides ammunition and information for the leader. It helps provide a common background of knowledge for all the members. When a message comes to one member or more, it often bounces around the group. It is discussed with the influentials, squared with the group norms. One of the most spectacular ways in which mass communication serves groups is by punishing deviates from the group norms. For example, an athlete takes a bribe, a politician refuses to support his party's candidate, a prisoner of war declines to come home, a public figure has bad table manners, an interracial marriage takes place, a husband is unfaithful: in all these cases the mass media have the power to make the deviation widely known and punish it more severely than might be done by legal and administrative means.

The import of what we have been saying is that, with due allowance for different viewpoints and language, LaPiere, Kennedy, and Spectorsky may all be right. As LaPiere says, most social control is effected by groups. As Spectorsky says, mass communication can have striking effects on taste and fashion, and it fills in much of our environment for us. As Kennedy says, mass communication may exert a terrific pressure in political life by giving publicity to politicians' deviations from group norms.

Mass communication does not often work "like an atom bomb" (perhaps the reaction to the Orson Welles broadcast was as close as it has ever come to that). It does not work like a hypodermic, moving swiftly through biologic channels to bring about the predicted result. It does not often succeed by itself in making abrupt and notable changes in attitudes. Rather it works in a long, slow rhythm, and in combination with the audience's individual predispositions and group norms. In this way, it does have an effect, although not quite so striking and explosive as some laymen attribute to it.

If you want a metaphor for its way of working which will be better than the "atom bomb" or the "hypodermic" metaphor, say it works like a creek. It feeds the ground it touches, following the lines of existing contours but preparing the way for change over a long period of time. Sometimes it finds a spot where the ground is soft and ready, and there it cuts a new channel. Sometimes it carries floating material (an unpleasant symbol for a status figure!) which helps to change the appearance of the banks of the stream. Occasionally, under most favorable conditions and in time of flood, it washes away a piece of ground and gives the channel a new look. This, like all other metaphors, has its inadequacies, but it is better than the other ones.

PART II

The Philosophy of Mass Communication

And though all the windes of doctrine were let loose to play upon the earth, so Truth be in the field, we do injuriously be licensing and prohibiting to misdoubt her strength. Let her and Falsehood grapple; who ever knew Truth put to the wors, in a free and open encounter?

—John Milton

5

The Four Concepts of Mass Communication

Since Johann Gutenberg printed his first book from movable metal type, western man has held only four major concepts or theories of what mass communication should be and do. It might be more accurate to say that there have been only *two* major concepts. Certainly there have been only two lines of development.

Modern communication was born into an authoritarian society and developed an authoritarian theory around itself. Ever since that time, authoritarianism has been the most widespread and influential philosophy of mass communication, and is still to be found, although sometimes disguised, controlling the communication systems of many countries of the modern world. In our time, authoritarianism has taken a spectacular new turn: the authoritarian Soviet Communist concept of mass communication. Because this is such a radical development from the older authoritarianism, we are going to treat it by itself rather than as a part of the parent theory.

Another concept of mass communication came into practice during the social and political revolutions of the seventeenth and eighteenth centuries. As these revolutions opposed authoritarian political systems, so this new concept was an alternative to authoritarian control of communication. We have called it the libertarian concept. This has given central direction to our own communication system, and is paid at least lip service in most of the non-Communist countries of the world today. In our country, Great Britain, and a few others, however, libertarianism has taken a new trend which is as different from its parent theory as Soviet Communist theory was different from the older authoritarianism. For want of a better name we call this emergent new libertarianism the theory of social responsibility. It is the concept of mass communication which is developing around us today, and which we are helping to shape by deciding what kind of responsible behavior we expect from our communicators.

This, then, is what you might call the intellectual history of mass communication: two lines of development, authoritarian and libertarian; and within each of these an older and a newer form, although all four concepts are still in use and may be observed side by side in different parts of the world.[1]

AUTHORITARIANISM

A social system like communication always reflects the social and political structures within which it operates. In trying to understand why mass communication develops as it does in different societies, then, we begin by looking at the societies. And we start with a look at certain basic assumptions which any society holds—assumptions concerning the nature of man, the nature of society and the state, the relation of man to the state, the nature of knowledge and truth and moral conduct.

Modern communication was born in 1450 into an authoritarian society. The essential characteristic of an authoritarian society is that the state ranks higher than the individual in the scale of social values. Only through subordinating himself to the state can the individual achieve his goals and develop his attributes as a civilized man. As an individual, he can do only a little; as a member of an organized community, his potential is enormously increased. This means not only that the state ranks the individual, but also that the state has a certain amount of caretaker function and the individual has a degree of dependent status.

Furthermore, individuals within the authoritarian state differ greatly in status. Authoritarian philosophers like Hegel ridicule the democratic belief that "all should participate in the business of the state."[2] In the authoritarian state there is a sharp distinction between leaders and followers. Only a few are cast in the role of leadership. Sometimes they are believed to be in their high positions because of divine selection, as, for example, were the Renaissance monarchs who claimed to rule by divine right. Sometimes they are leaders because of what is believed to be their superior intellect, wisdom, or experience. In any case, always in an authoritarian state a man or a few men are in position to lead and be obeyed. These are rulers or advisers to rulers, and they stand at the locus of power.

What is the source of truth in an authoritarian society? It may be an accredited divine revelation, the wisdom of the race, or simply the superior ability of a leader or group to perceive dangers and opportunities. It may be, on the other hand, after a floundering reaction from disappointment with previously accepted truth, and emergent new promise—as sometimes happens when a country in desperation turns to a dictator. But whatever the source of truth it has two characteristics. It is restricted; not every man has access to it. And it becomes the standard nevertheless for all members of the society. As Siebert says, it "acquires an absolutist aura which makes change undesirable, and stability or continuity a virtue in itself."[3] One of the functions of the authoritarian state, therefore, is to preserve unity of thought and action among its members, and to maintain continuity of leadership. To this end the authoritarian state employs such tools of persuasion and coercion as it commands.

Three powerful strands entered into the Renaissance authoritarianism which first played host to modern communication. One of these was the doctrine of divine right by which such monarchs as the Tudors and Stuarts claimed to rule, and which set apart a bevy of hereditary nobles from the rest of the population. The hereditary leaders, of course, protected their status in politics and war.

A second was the authoritarian tradition of the Roman Church, which had grown powerful in the Middle Ages. The Church considered itself the repository of divine revelation. Its responsibility, as shepherd of mankind, was to protect this revelation from being contaminated and to protect its sheep from impure doctrine. Where its authority reached it permitted debate, but not on basic assumptions, and not outside the qualified members of its own order. The Church enforced its dictates where it could by the use of imprimaturs, book proscriptions, and even excommunications. In many countries, for some centuries, it could command and usually receive the co-operation of the state in such control of opinion and expression.

A third strand was the long history of authoritarian political philosophy, stretching back to Plato. For all his idealism, Plato had argued that, once authority in a state is equally divided, degeneration sets in. Just as a man must govern his own baser instincts and appetites by intellectual control, so must the rulers of the state keep the material interests and selfish passions of the masses from dominating society. Plato's own theoretical "Republic" was governed by philosopher-kings. Plato's own master, Socrates, while vehemently arguing his freedom to deviate from the laws of Athens, just as readily admitted that the authorities were entitled to enforce those laws no matter how wrong. We sometimes forget how strict Plato was in the realm of art and thought. As MacIver writes, "Plato wanted to 'co-ordinate' the life of the citizens under a strict cultural code that banned all modes of art and even of opinion not in accord with his own gospel. Very politely, in the *Republic*, he would 'send to another city' all offenders against the rigid rules prescribed for the artist and the philosopher and the poet. With equal politeness, in the *Laws*, he would require poets first to submit their works to the magistrates, who should decide whether they were good for the spiritual health of the citizens."[4]

This tradition of authoritarian political philosophy was carried up to the early centuries of printing, though in quite different ways, by many other philosophers: Machiavelli, for example, who advocated that all else must be subordinated to the security of the state, and that nonmoral actions by the political leaders, as well as strict control of discussion and of dissemination of information are justified to that end; Thomas Hobbes, the naturalistic philosopher, whose theories of the state and its relation to the individual did much to justify the authoritarian policies of 17th-century governments; George Hegel, who has variously been called the father of both modern fascism and modern communism, and who gave to authoritarian philosophy its final idealistic touch by saying that the state is the "ethical spirit . . . Will . . . Mind . . . the state, being an end in itself, is provided with the maximum of rights over against the individual citizens, whose highest duty is to be members of the state."[5]

This was the tradition into which machine-duplicated communication was born. At first the tiny infant voice of printing was no threat to government, and there was no need to do anything about it. Before many decades, however, it became apparent that a new great voice was being heard in the land. This voice could be dangerous or helpful, according to who controlled it. The governments began making use of the regulative authority they possessed.

One of the first things they did was to control access to the new medium. By issuing patents or licenses to printers and publishers, they assumed the power of determining who could enter the business. Since each licensee had a monopoly, or at least a grant of great privilege, he was all the more likely to publish what the ruler wished.

But even this was not entirely satisfactory to the rulers. They instituted censorship, which required that all manuscripts or proof had to be examined and passed by a representative of government before being printed. Censorship, however, fell of its own weight, late in the 17th century. It was too cumbersome, too laborious. The coming of newspapers made too much to read. Clever journalists could get around it too easily. Even the censors disliked the job.

So censorship was largely replaced by the threat of punishment *after* printing—such as prosecution for treason (writing intended as a part of a plot to overthrow the government) or sedition (which is to treason as the flea-bite to the snakebite). And some governments went in for publishing their own papers, paying or bribing writers (Walpole's government was notorious for this), or subsidizing existing printers; but for the most part the media in this stage of authoritarianism were permitted to be privately owned.

The concept of pubic communication which developed in these first 250 years of printing was exactly what would be expected in an authoritarian setting. Printing was simply another tool to promote unity and continuity within the state. It was to carry wisdom and truth as wisdom and truth were identified by the rulers. Access to the medium was to be restricted to those individuals who would operate for "the good of the state" as judged by the rulers. The public at large were considered incapable of understanding political problems, and communication was therefore forbidden to "disturb the masses" or interest them in something they could not "understand." The media were not expected to criticise the rulers or political leaders, and above all they were not permitted to attempt to unseat the authorities. Discussion of political systems in broad principles was permitted (as is not the case with Communists); and it was all right to question the political machinery, but not the manipulators of that machinery.

The basis for communication ethics in such a system is easy to perceive. Negatively stated, there should be no publishing which, in the opinion of the authorities, would not be good for the state and (consequently) for its citizens. More positively, all publishing should contribute to the greatness of the beneficent state, which would as a consequence enable man to grow to his fullest usefulness and happiness within the state. But the important thing is that there is always an authority to serve as umpire. One need not decide himself. There is always revelation (if one can know it), the wisdom of the race or the past (if one can perceive it); or the guidance of the leader (the easiest to perceive and the commonest of all the guide-posts).

Communication authoritarianism waned notably by the second half of the 18th century. By that time a line of liberal thinkers had thrown stones at the theory, and in several western countries a succession of democratic revolutions had knocked holes in the practice. The tide seemed to have turned away from authoritarianism. The new concept of public communication was that it should serve the individuals, not the state; that it should not offer unity, but rather diversity; that it should contribute to change as well as to continuity; and that it had every right to criticize the government in power. We shall have more to say about this later.

But let us not end this brief account of the older authoritarianism without pointing out that it did not die in 1750 or 1800. In many parts of the world it continues today, even though it may be disguised in democratic verbiage and in protestation of press freedom. Wherever a government operates in an authoritarian fashion, there you may expect to find some authoritarian controls over public communication. For example, the International Press Institute, which has its headquarters in Zurich, made an attempt in 1953 to assess the amount of press control and freedom throughout the world.[6] Altogether 248 editors in 48 countries answered the Institute's detailed questionnaire. On the basis of their replies, the Institute felt able to say: "Freedom of information is being especially threatened today." The report named specifically the following types of authoritarianism:

1. Countries where press control is complete—e.g., the Soviet Union and its satellites, also China, Yugoslavia, Portugal, Spain.

2. Countries where political criticism by the press is formally possible, but where censorship operates—e.g., Colombia, Egypt, Syria.

3. Countries where special laws or other discriminatory legislation expose editors to arrest and persecution—e.g., Union of South Africa, Persia, Pakistan, India, Iraq, Lebanon.

4. Countries where unofficial methods discourage press opposition—e.g., Turkey, Argentina, Indonesia.

These facts were for the year 1953. In some of the countries the situation may have changed by now. But the fact remains that authoritarianism has for more years in more countries been the dominant philosophy behind public communication than has any other pattern of thought.

LIBERTARIANISM

All through the 16th and 17th centuries a new theory of mass communication struggled to be born, drawing its prenatal strength from the great revolutions of the popular mind and the body politic which characterized western Europe in that period.

It was a time of great change, you will remember, succeeding apparent or relative changelessness. First there were the startling developments in geography and science, which challenged the traditional knowledge and seemed to vindicate the power of human reason as against inherited and revealed knowledge. There was the Reformation which challenged the authority of the Church of Rome, and resulted in a pattern of discussion and argument at variance with authoritarian patterns. There was the swift new growth of the middle class and of capitalism, challenging the old idea of fixed status, and ushering in a world of social mobility to replace one relatively fixed and permanent. There were political revolutions, like the one in England against the Stuarts, challenging the right to arbitrary rule.

But most importantly, the new theory put its roots down into the kind of intellectual change represented by the Enlightenment of the 17th and 18th centuries. This was one of the greatest revolutionary intellectual movements of all time. As Cassirer said, the basic idea of the Enlightenment was "the conviction that human understanding is capable of its own power and, without recourse to supernatural assistance, of comprehending the system of the world, and that this new way of understanding the world will lead to a new way of mastering it. Enlightenment sought to gain universal recognition for this principle in the natural and intellectual sciences, in physics and ethics, in the philosophies of religion, history, law, and politics."[7] In other words, what was happening was that man who had already proved the world was round, who had looked at the planets through telescopes, who had discovered the circulation of the blood, and who had challenged the Church of Rome in argument, was now feeling his muscles and throwing down the gauntlet to all the old custodians of power and wisdom. He was declaring independence of all outside restrictions on his freedom to use his understanding for the solution of religious, political, and social problems.

In a sense, the intellectual revolution was chiefly a secular revolution, not only because it challenged the authority of the One Church, but also because it tended to transfer the rewards for good conduct nearer to the arena of worldly gains. It is hard for us now to realize the change in business and economics which was under way in the hundred years between the middle of the seventeenth and the middle of the eighteenth centuries. Heilbronner reminds us that in 1644 one Robert Keane of Boston was nearly excommunicated—not fined or imprisoned, *excommunicated*—for the crime of charging too much interest on a shilling loan, and the minister of Boston seized this opportunity to point out certain behavior which was unacceptable and well-nigh unforgivable.[8] This included:

> That a man might sell as dear as he can, and buy as
> cheap as he can.
> If a man lose by casualty of sea, etc., in some of his
> commodities, he may raise the price of the rest.
> That he may sell as he bought, though he paid too dear.

"To seek riches for riches' sake," cried the minister, "is to fall into the sin of avarice." Yet, only a little over 100 years later, business was booming in America and England very much as it is now, and Adam Smith was preaching the laws of classical economics, including the commandment that government shall never (well, hardly ever) interfere with the market. Leave the market alone, he said, and it will regulate itself. Thus to Adam Smith, as to Jefferson, the best government is the one that governs least. In the eighteenth century, the central ethic was already coming to be the work-success ethic, in which man found his own level by the skill and hard work with which he seized opportunties in the free market.

To an even greater degree the intellectual revolution was a secular one for the reason that it succeeded in transferring the focus of interest from theology to science; that is, from theological controversy to scientific inquiry. Here again the rewards in the secular arena were great and enticing, both economically and intellectually. And the pattern that emerged from the scientific inquiry was rather well in phase with the new economics and politics. For here were Newton's idea of a universe which ran by itself like a time-machine and Lamarck's and Darwin's ideas of evolution in which the fittest survived in a free contest very much like Adam Smith's free market. If it were possible now to graph the focus of attention of men from the beginning of printing through the beginning of power printing—that is, from 1450 to a little after 1800—the result would certainly be a sharply rising line of secular interest, and a sharply falling line of sacred interest. And if we could guess where the lines crossed, we should probably place that point somewhere in the seventeenth century.

We are not implying that this change was all to the good. Indeed, a few paragraphs by Arnold Toynbee are worth pondering at this point.[9] He says:

The enlightened and well-intentioned authors of our seventeenth-century Western spiritual revolution did not succeed in achieving their two aims. They succeeded in establishing in the West a spirit of tolerance which lasted from the close of the seventeenth century until after the opening of the twentieth; and they accomplished this, as they had planned, by diverting Western Man's attention from theological controversy to scientific inquiry.

But this "transvaluation of values," which our seventeenth-century predecessors began, has gone, between their day and ours, to lengths which they would have deplored. The banishment of Christian fanaticism from Western souls has been followed by the eclipse of Christianity, while science and technology, after diverting Western Man's interest from theological controversy, have gone on to divert it from religion itself. Technology, instead of religion, is what our Western Civilization has come to stand for by our time, some three hundred years after the seventeenth century beginnings of our revolutionary Western "transvaluation of values." In making this diagnosis today, a non-Western observer of our twentieth century Western Civilization would be right. Yet we ourselves are speaking the truth when we declare that for us Western Civilization stands for not technology, but for the sacredness of the individual human personality.

We twentieth-century Westerners hold personal freedom just as sacred as our predecessors did: but here is the paradox in our present position. In becoming devotees of science and technology we have not ceased to be devotees of freedom. But, in relinquishing our hold on Christianity, we have deprived our belief in freedom of its religious foundations.

What has happened, therefore, is that the intellectual revolution, which formed the basis of the libertarian concept of mass communication, has run somewhat off the track on which it was started by the philosophers of the Enlightenment. And I think we shall see, later in this book, that the extent to which it has run off the track corres-

ponds pretty closely with the extent to which we are today dissatisfied with the working of the theory of libertarian communication.

But let us return to some of those philosophers who have contributed doctrine and fighting phrases to what we call the libertarian
theory of communication. Descartes was one of the first, and his
great influence derived from his emphasis on reason as a road to
truth. In England perhaps the most influential was John Locke. As
we read back over him today, we can see how pivotal he was in the
intellectual changes that we are considering. He argued, you will
remember, that the center of power is the will of the people. The
people delegate their authority to government and can at any time
withdraw it. The people—each individual among them—has certain
natural rights which cannot justifiably be abridged. In a rational act
man has surrendered some of his personal rights to the state, but only
in order that his natural rights may better be maintained and defended. The state, Locke argued, must be centered on the will and
well-being of the people. It must maintain religious tolerance and
freedom of individual enterprise. Many of Locke's phrases, as you can
see, found their way into the American Declaration of Independence
and the French Declaration of the Rights of Man.

John Milton's *Areopagitica*, a century before Locke, was one of
the earliest of the great anti-authoritarian documents of this period.
This is an eloquent argument for freedom of the press from governmental restriction. It was based on the premise that men have reason
and wisdom to distinguish between right and wrong, good and bad.
But they can exercise this ability to its full power only when they
have a free choice. Given a "free and open encounter," Milton said,
truth will demonstrate itself. Rational argument is a kind of "self-
righting" process, by means of which the sound and true will survive.
Therefore, government must not interfere with the argument. There
must be no artificial restrictions on the free market place of ideas.[10]
The relationship of the "free market place of ideas" to Smith's later
self-running, self-controlling economic market and to Darwin's "sur-
vival of the fittest" in a kind of social market, will be clear.

Milton's argument had little effect in his own time, but in the
eighteenth century it was revived and expanded by men like Thomas
Paine, John Erskine, and Thomas Jefferson. Erskine, for example,
defended Paine in a memorable court trial when Paine was accused
of grievous error in publishing *The Rights of Man*. In the course of

that defense Erskine stated a position which was instantly caught up by the defenders of the new theory of communication.[11]

The proposition which I mean to maintain as the basis of liberty of the press, and without which it is an empty sound, is this: that every man, not intending to mislead, but seeking to enlighten others with what his own reason and conscience, however erroneously, have dictated to him as truth, may address himself to the universal reason of the whole nation, either upon subjects of government in general, or upon that of our own particular country.

Notice carefully that phrase, *not intending to mislead*. Erskine would doubtless have said that a man who communicates in bad faith forfeits the moral right to defense of his freedom to communicate, even though the *legal* right may have to extend farther than the moral one.

Jefferson carried the point of view still farther. He contended that, just as the function of government was to establish and maintain a framework within which an individual can develop his own capabilities and pursue his own ends, so the chief function of the press is to inform the individual and to stand guard against deviation by government from its basic assignment. A constant victim of press vituperation during his own political career, Jefferson nevertheless maintained that a government which could not stand up under criticism deserved to fall. His general view of the press was stated in these words:

No experiment can be more interesting than what we are now trying, and which we trust will end in establishing the fact, that man may be governed by reason and truth. Our first object should therefore be, to leave open to him all the avenues of truth. The most effectual hitherto found, is the freedom of the press. It is therefore the first shut up by those who fear the investigation of their actions. The firmness with which the people have withstood the late abuses of the press, the discernment they have manifested between truth and falsehood, show that they may safely be trusted to hear everything true and false, and to form a correct judgment between them. I hold it, therefore, to be certain, that to open the doors of truth, and so fortify the habit of testing everything by reason, are the most effectual manacles we can rivet on the hands of our successors to prevent their manacling the people with their own consent.[12]

Here are most of the elements of the new theory—the reliance on reason to discriminate between truth and error; the need of a free market place of ideas in order that reason may work; and the function of the press as a check on government.

In the 19th century, John Stuart Mill defined the market place a bit more clearly. "If all mankind minus one," he wrote in a famous essay, *On Liberty*, "were of one opinion, and only one person were of the contrary opinion, mankind would be no more justified in silencing that one person, than he, if he had the power, would be justified in silencing mankind." Why? He answered that question with four propositions: First, if we silence an opinion, for all we know we may be silencing truth. Second, even a wrong opinion may contain the grain of truth that helps us find the whole truth. Third, even if the commonly held opinion is the whole truth, that opinion will not be held on rational grounds until it has been tested and defended. Fourth, unless a commonly held opinion is challenged from time to time, it loses its vitality and its effect.[13]

This was the philosophical tradition out of which the new theory of mass communication grew. It was foreshadowed in the sixteenth century, envisioned in the seventeenth, fought for in the eighteenth, and finally brought into widespread use in the nineteenth, when power was added to the printing press and machine-duplicated communication could be brought to a large part of the public. By that time the authoritarian system of communication was vanquished at least on the surface. Most countries had adopted at least the language of the new libertarianism, although many of the practices of authoritarianism still remained below the surface, and indeed still remain today.

To see what a revolutionary change this is from the authoritarian theory, let us ask of libertarian theory the same questions we asked of authoritarianism. The nature of man? According to authoritarianism, you will remember, he is a dependent animal, able to reach his highest level only under the guidance and care of the state. According to libertarian theory, he is an independent rational animal, able to choose between right and wrong, good and bad. In authoritarian theory, as you will remember, the state out-ranks man on the scale of values. In libertarian theory, on the other hand, the state exists only to provide a proper milieu in which man can develop his potentialities and enjoy the maximum of happiness. The state exists only because it has been given that assignment; if it fails in that task, it can be abolished or radically changed. As Siebert has remarked, the libertarian theory of knowledge and truth somewhat resembles early Christian theology, as opposed to the authoritarianism of the medieval church.[14] The power to reason was conceived in the 17th, 18th, and 19th centuries to be God-given, just as the knowledge of good and evil was God-given. Truth was therefore discernible by thinking men. Although that truth might be different from truth as previously perceived (as the Reformation contended), although the path to truth might lie through " a morass of argument and dispute" (as practice indicated), still as Emerson said, "The sun shines today also!" To every man is given this present power of discerning truth. Not the select few. Not the ruler alone. But potentially *every* man.

The task of society, then, is to provide a free market place of ideas, so that men may exercise this God-given gift of reason and choice. That is the essence of libertarian theory. The less control by government, the better. In place of more formal controls, libertarianism chose to trust the self-righting process of truth. That implies, of course, a truly free market place. Everyone must have access to the channels of communication. No viewpoints or opinions must be silenced, unless they are truly dangerous to the welfare of the whole group, and even that is hard to prove. Ideas must have an equal chance—and this has always been one of the hardest conditions for libertarianism to meet, because voices in the market place are not equal. Some viewpoints have a big paper, a big name behind them; others do not. Nevertheless, the goal is attractive, and the whole theory with its refreshing idealism and its complimentary view of man, is an extremely appealing one.

What kind of mass communication did libertarianism result in?

In theory, at least, it would be private enterprise, privately owned media competing in an open market. In theory, anyone with sufficient capital could start a paper or a magazine or a publishing house, and the capital demands should not be so severe that many viewpoints would be squeezed out of having their media spokesmen. The profit should be determined by the ability of the medium to satisfy customers. Thus the success of a communication enterprise, and hence its right to continue, would be measured by the final judges of its social usefulness—the public.

And it is true that in the United States and Great Britain, cradles of libertarianism, the printed media did develop very much as predicted. Notably in the 18th and early 19th centuries there were many small, privately owned papers, standing for every shade and variation of political viewpoint. For a long time in America and Britain, and even up to the present time in certain countries, the press was a "party press," representing and often supported by political groups. It was easy to enter publishing, and so practically every party found a voice. Unfortunately the party press was a severe strain on the vaunted ability of man's reason to discriminate between truth and falsehood, because its news was just as slanted as its editorial opinion.

After the middle of the 19th century, however, a change began to take place in the press. Its support began to come in larger measure from advertising rather than political subsidy. The cost of entering became greater. The attitude of some editors and reporters began to be that of observers, rather than participants in the politics of the day. It became a matter of pride, especially among American newsmen, to distinguish sharply between news and comment. A theory of what was called "objective news" began to be heard and followed. According to this theory, news should present only the raw facts of the day's events. News objectivity has become a favorite subject of argument in the last two or three decades, its opponents contending that it neglects to tell the whole truth or fill in the background for a news event. Many libertarian countries never adopted the idea of objective news at all. But it is perfectly true that the idea of news objectivity arose both from the new demands of wire services and from an honest desire to keep from contaminating the "free market place," and its development was one of the great accomplishments of western journalism.

When motion pictures came in they posed a special problem. Movies came in, strangely enough, under authoritarian, rather than libertarian, theory, though they became popular not long after 1900. This was because of their close relation to the theater. No one bothered to make a stirring plea for freedom of the theater, as Milton, Erskine, Paine, and Jefferson did for freedom of the press. The theater had been licensed and censored for centuries. Films, with their vast audiences and apparent potential for good or evil, naturally fell under the same kind of restrictions. But libertarian countries like the United States and Britain have become increasingly uneasy under this practice. Exactly how can film licensing and censorship be squared with libertarian theory? Exactly what differentiates films from newspapers and magazines, so far as censorship goes? The film also purveys opinions. It also has a news reel. It also watches the horizon, assists us in arriving at consensus, and transmits our culture to the new members of our society. Why, then, should it not function in a free market place just as does the newspaper? The problem is a thorny one, which has only partly been solved by adoption of a "voluntary" code on the part of the producers, and by ameliorating decisions on the part of the courts.

Broadcasting also poses a problem. There are not enough channels for everyone who wants to broadcast. In order to avoid chaos on the air, and thus look after the public's interest, someone must distribute the channels. The obvious choice to represent the public in performing this task is the government. But on what basis will the channels be parceled out? The government must to this extent interfere in the free market place of ideas. The best standard we in the United States have developed is that of "public interest, convenience, and necessity"[15] a vague yardstick at best, and putting altogether more responsibility in the government's hands than Milton or Erskine or Jefferson might have approved. Actually, the American system of broadcasting, which is privately owned, comes closer to the principles of libertarianism than most other broadcasting systems throughout the world. In most countries, broadcasting is a government monopoly.

Thus survivals of authoritarian theory still exist, so far as films and broadcasting are concerned, even in the countries where libertarianism is strongest. And even in the case of the press, the libertarian theory was by no means adopted everywhere.

Many of the underdeveloped areas of the world have found it impossible to transplant the western ideas of a free press and support the resulting papers by private enterprise. In other countries, sometimes enthusiastic approval, sometimes lip service, was given the idea, but authoritarianism was too deeply grounded in the political system to be replaced. Dictators have in general found libertarianism too inefficient for their manipulative purposes. As a result the mass communication systems of Nazi Germany, Fascist Italy, and Communist Russia were built on authoritarian theory.

Even in democratic countries certain developments have in the twentieth century caused thoughtful people to question whether libertarianism is the ultimate in press theory. For one thing, to enter the mass communication industry is no longer easy; only a man with enormous capital can do it in any substantial way. That places a new responsibility on the mass communication media: to make a *restricted* market place truly a *free* market place of ideas and facts.

Furthermore, many of the fundamental philosophical bases of libertarianism have recently been challenged. As Carl Becker said:[16]

What confuses our purposes and defeats our hopes is that the simple concepts upon which the Age of Enlightenment relied with assurance have lost for us their universal and infallible quality. Natural Law turns out to be no more than a convenient and temporary hypothesis. Imprescriptible rights have such validity only as prescriptive law confers upon them. Liberty, once identified with emancipation of the individual from governmental restraint, is now seen to be inseparable from the complex pattern of social regulation. Even the sharp, definitive lines of reason and truth are blurred. Reason, we suspect, is a function of the animal organism, and truth no more than the perception of discordant experience pragmatically adjusted for a particular purpose and for the time being.

Even without adopting this pragmatic viewpoint, it is still possible to question some of the fundamental libertarian tenets. And increasingly that has been happening: men have been asking whether libertarianism is really the last stop on communication's road toward the ultimate wedding of freedom and responsibility.

But before taking up the two communication theories which in our own time and on different sides of the world have tended to supplant libertarianism, let us ask what are some of the implications of libertarian theory for communication ethics. And we have to answer, I think, that the chief implication is in regard to truth and the individual. With libertarianism, the well-spring of truth lies in reason, and with the individual's *own* reason. Therefore, it is assumed, he does not go to authority or custom for primary guidance as to moral conduct, but rather searches his own heart and mind.

Furthermore, it becomes a major matter of ethics for communicators to communicate the truth as they see it. Whether this is done by objective or subjective reporting will vary as between countries, even as between papers, but in either case it is of the greatest importance to extract and unveil. Especially it is important to reveal truth about government. And finally, the stimulating of controversy about politics, or attacks upon existing government, is in no way unethical, according to libertarianism, because of the God-given ability to reason and discriminate, and the right to know what one's government is doing so that the government's master, the public, can decide whether to change it.

The ethical responsibility of the publisher under libertarian theory might therefore be expressed by John Locke's phrase, "enlightened self-interest." The degree of "enlightenment" varies greatly with different individuals. At one extreme might be a Pulitzer, who wrote that "nothing less than the highest ideals, the most scrupulous anxiety to do right, the most accurate knowledge of the problems it has to meet, and a sincere sense of social responsibility will save journalism. . . ."[17] At the other extreme might be put the statement attributed to William Peter Hamilton, of the *Wall Street Journal*: "A newspaper is a private enterprise owing nothing whatever to the public, which grants it no franchise. It is therefore affected with no public interest. It is emphatically the property of the owner, who is selling a manufactured product at his own risk. . . ."[18] The second of these quotations is obviously an *abortion* of the theory. The first is a *development* of the theory, away from the abortions and toward some of the needs which have appeared in our own time, and which we shall be considering in this book.

SOVIET COMMUNIST THEORY

In our own century both of the older concepts of mass communication have gone through a kind of cell division, so that now, as we have suggested, we actually have not two, but four, patterns existing side by side. The old authoritarianism survives stubbornly in countries like Spain and Portugal, to give two examples only. Libertarianism exists little changed in countries like France. In Great Britain and the United States, men are groping their way toward a new offshoot of libertarianism which, for want of a better term, we have called the theory of social responsibility. The Soviet Union and its allied and satellite countries practice a new version of communication authoritarianism, which we shall call Soviet Communist theory. This last is the concept to which we are going to devote the next few pages.

Soviet Communist communication theory is a kind of phenomenon in that, as an attendant on a spectacular change in governments, it burst suddenly upon the world, after the October revolution of 1917, rather than developing at the snail's pace with which the other communication concepts have come into being. Furthermore, hardly any other theory can be traced so directly and positively, as can the Communist theory, back to its source. The basic source of communism, of course, was Karl Marx. Like most great conceptualizers, Marx was a synthesizer rather than an originator. He was a child of his time. He had men around him like Engels who contributed to the development of the theory. But the place to start in trying to understand the Soviet Communist theory of communication is with Karl Marx, the German exile working in England a hundred years ago on a book which would have its greatest impact on Russia.[19]

Soviet theory is Marxist, but not Marx. Indeed there is good reason to think that Marx (who, it is reported, once said, in disgust, "I am not a Marxist") might be startled to see what has happened to his theory in the Soviet Union. Nevertheless, it is clear that Marx contributed a general frame of mind and three sets of ideas on which the Soviet leaders built their new kind of authoritarianism.

The frame of mind was authoritarian, but with a difference. Marx felt he was constructing a *general* theory of history. He felt confidently that he could explain great areas of human behavior on the basis of a small set of economic facts. Thus, Marxism is a neater, tighter system than democracy. Democracy insists on the right of men to disagree—with each other, with religions, with their governments. Marx and his followers, on the other hand, as I have said elsewhere,[20] placed an almost mystical value on "Unity"— unity of the working class, unity of the Party, unity of choice among alternatives. "How could one of your elections possibly be free if the wrong side won?" a Russian once asked me; and in that one question is illustrated much of the difference between their position and ours. As we are apt to think that people *should* hold different ideas and values, and therefore to encourage the arts of compromise and majority rule, so the Soviet theoreticians are apt to think that men should *not* hold different viewpoints, that compromise is a sign of weakness, that there is one *right* position to be found in Marxian interpretation, to be defended, propagated, and enforced. To us, what Muller calls the "famed Russian unity" seems reactionary and tyrannical.[21] To the Russians, our lack of agreement, our permissiveness toward argument, compromise, and criticism, seem anarchy or chaos. This is the general frame of mind which the Soviet leaders inherited from their ideological fathers.

Within this framework, Marx put together the three sets of ideas which we have mentioned. The first of these was his dialectic of social change. It must be remembered that Marx was a child of change. He grew up in a period of great change—scientific, industrial, and social. He gloried in change, rather than in changelessness. Indeed, as Brinton says, he tried "to find in change itself the riddle of change."[22]

He found the answer he sought chiefly in Hegel. This was the famous *dialectic*—the concept that two opposing forces (*thesis and antithesis*) resolve their difference in a *synthesis*. The synthesis in turn becomes a thesis, which is opposed by a new antithesis, and so on. Marx used the dialectic to interpret history as a succession of class struggles. In particular he predicted that the next great struggle would pit the working class (antithesis) against the bourgeois (thesis), with the result being victory for the workers and formation of a new classless society (synthesis).

But in adapting this pattern from Hegel, Marx turned Hegel's doctrine upside down. Hegel was an idealist. For Hegel, it was "the idea," the life process of the human brain, that made the dialectic work. Marx said that for Hegel dialectics "is standing on its head. It must be turned right side up again, if you would discover the rational kernel within the mystical shell."[23] Marx argued that the material conditions of life—man's way of making his living and the kind of living he makes—determine man's ideas. In other words, material determinism, and chiefly economic determinism, is the central factor of the life of man, according to Marxian theory.

Reflecting on this pattern, Marx concluded that productive forces would always change faster than producers' relations, thus throwing society out of balance. As he analyzed the situation, capitalism contained the seeds of its own destruction. It would always have depressions and economic crises. The rich would grow richer and fewer; the poor, poorer, more numerous, and more desperate. The last stage of capitalism would be imperialism, which would breed wars and more misery. Finally the working class, unable longer to contain their misery and frustration, would rise, liquidate the surviving capitalists, and take over the means of production on the base of which to build a new classless society. And, inasmuch as all society is economically determined, Marx said, the political system, the arts, religion, philosophy, and all other components of culture would change with the economic system.

The goal of the social dialectic, as we have said, was thus seen to be a classless society. But it is also seen as a *stateless* society. Looking at the formidable Soviet bureaucracy and military establishments, we sometimes forget this. But Marx insisted that the state is merely a device for one class to exercise control over another. With a classless society, therefore, the state is by definition obsolete. And Engels said: "The first act in which the state really comes forward as the representative of society as a whole—the seizure of the means of production in the name of society—is, at the same time, its last independent act as a state."[24] From that moment on, the state must "automatically wither away."

This is the inheritance from Marx: on the one hand, the extraordinarily optimistic view of man as being ultimately able to live without government; on the other, a view of man as moved like a pawn by economic forces. And the dynamics of the situation require that man shall be organized into "a machine to change society," as Stephen Spender put it, so that society in turn can remake man.

But when the Soviet leaders had a chance to apply the theory, after 1917, they found it rather incomplete. Marx had never explained how the Golden Age was to be run. Industries were to be nationalized, of course; private holdings were to be expropriated. But what else? How was the Party, once it had seized power, to turn Soviet man into the "near-Godlike" creature, able to live without government, which Marx and Engels had envisioned?

It was somewhat more of a job than had been anticipated. The Party was never more than a small percentage of the Russian people, and therefore it had a constant problem of maintaining its own power and security. The Russian economy was primitive. There was no chance to let the state wither away; indeed, it had to be expanded manyfold. For a while, it was convenient to ignore this; then Stalin explained that as long as the Soviet Union was ringed around by enemies it must maintain a strong central government and military establishment. Furthermore, Marx had said next to nothing about mass communication. But in an amazingly short time, by trial and error, and under the force of need, the Soviet leaders evolved their theory.

Before analyzing the theory, let us make clear why we are going at such length into general theory, as opposed to communication theory. In the Soviet system, there is not a theory of the state and a theory of communication; there is only one theory. Soviet mass communication developed as an *integral* part of the Soviet state. Nothing could be farther from Soviet thinking than our concept of the press as a Fourth Estate to watch and report on and criticize the government. Soviet mass communication is an *instrument* of the government. All the media are conceived of instrumentally. They are tools to do the work of the state. Private ownership of the media was therefore no more thinkable than private ownership of heavy industry, which also was a tool to do the work of the state. Furthermore, inasmuch as the problems of the state are pressing and serious, the mass media should be turned to pressing and serious problems. Recreation is generally an unworthy use of such tools. As Lenin said, the press should be "collective propagandist, collective agitator . . . , collective organizer."[25] Keep in mind this integral and instrumental concept of the media as we examine the doctrine which lies behind their use.

The Soviet leaders believed, of course, that power is resident in people, latent in social institutions, and generated in social action. But it can only be realized when it is joined with the ownership of natural resources and the means of production, and when it is organized and directed. The media must therefore be owned and used by the state. But how must they be directed? The Soviets believed that only the Party has the power and vision (and the Marxist theory) to lead and organize the masses. Therefore, the direction of the media must also ultimately lie with the Party (and it is true that media policy and control both now head up in organs of the Party).

How is truth derived for expression in the mass media? In the early years of Soviet power, it was assumed that truth was arrived at through collective deliberation of the party. Each Party member was supposed to have full freedom of discussion until a Party Congress reached a decision. As early as the tenth Congress in 1921, however, Lenin expressed grave doubt about the efficiency of this system. During the 1920s, control passed rapidly from broad discussion and Party Congresses to a small group of top Party leaders. The appropriate behavior of a Party member today, says Margaret

Mead, "is to know the principles of Marxism-Leninism and to apply them as directed by the Line, not to think about them."[26]

Truth, for the Soviet communicator, therefore, is of two kinds. The basic unchangeable truth is the Marxist doctrine, as interpreted by his top Party leaders. Thus the Soviet editor is committed to a concept of material determinism and class struggle, and on an issue like this there can be no compromise. As Lenin said flatly, "the teachings of Marx are immovable because they are true." But there is another level of truth, having to do with actions of the state and things happening to the state, on which considerable latitude of interpretation is permitted. Permitted, that is, not to the editor, but to the top Party members. In essence, the Soviet policy is to do whatever will contribute to the basic Marxist goals as we have stated them. This leads sometimes to the most radical and surprising changes in "line." Editors were caught red-cheeked and flat-footed when Stalin signed his treaty with Hitler. Many of them were equally embarrassed recently when top Moscow leadership turned against the cult of Stalin. Yet these policies were regarded by top leadership as justified at the time. Thus the communicator is compelled to listen constantly and carefully for new Olympian rumblings from Moscow. And he is often required to be nimble and agile indeed in order to keep up with the vibrating line.

In the preceding chapters we have talked about the relation of man to the state in the various systems. Let us here say merely that the Soviet state, as it now exists, is a dictatorship in which the power pyramid rises very sharply from the proletariat to a few select Party leaders. It is a caretaker state in which Soviet man, for the most part, is regarded as not yet ready to participate to any great degree except as a worker—an engine to improve society. As Mill would improve society by first improving man, so the Soviets would improve man by first improving society. There is a long, long gap between the Marxian concept of man as able to live in a people's state without government, and the present Soviet Communist concept of man as an instrument for improving society, an instrument to be played on by all the devices of mass media and organized coercion, an instrument to be shaped and directed by a Promethean few in the Party.

Let us now sum up some of the things we have been implying about mass communication under the Soviet Communist system.

In the first place, mass communications are used instrumentally— that is, as instruments of the state and the Party. They are not privately owned, or privately intended. They are owned by the state, controlled and directed by agencies of the Party, and closely integrated with other instruments of state power. They are used as instruments of unity within the state—that is, to tell Soviet citizens what to think about a given event and what to do. Actually, a very large part of the Soviet press is intended for the direction and information of the Party. Outside the Soviet state, they are used exactly as Soviet diplomacy, economic policy, and military power are used —to advance the cause of the Soviet state and the Marxist concept of social change.

They are a *planned* press, as compared to our rather spontaneous mass communication system which grew up to meet needs as seen by entrepreneurs, advocates, and consumers. The Soviet newspapers, magazines, and broadcasting are assigned like soldiers to the task of the state's and the Party's communication with a given area, or group, or industry. They have no responsibility for originating public opinion or pushing the state into a policy decision. A "personal paper" like the *Chicago Tribune* under Colonel McCormick, an independent critical journal like *The New York Times*, a radio network with opposing opinions from its commentaors like ABC, are not within the Soviet concept. Even a *newspaper*, as we know it, is un-Soviet; timeliness of news is a rather unimportant quality in the Soviet system; rather the important thing is to select and interpret the news in such a way as to advance the cause of the Soviet state. Which is simply to say again that the Soviet communication media are intended to be efficient pipelines, efficient instruments of the controlling hierarchy. And they are held to this assignment by a strictly enforced responsibility.

It may be helpful at this point to say a few words about the Soviet concept of freedom and responsibility, which is obviously different from ours. To us, the Soviet media seem "kept" and "servile." To the Soviets, our media seem "irresponsible" and "disorderly." To them, our media seem to be full of "twaddle." To us, their media seem not to be directed to the needs and wants of the people. And yet both of us talk about freedom of the press, often almost in the same words.

In order to understand the Soviet concepts of freedom and responsibility, let us remember that from the Marxist point of view complete freedom is impossible. Anything else said by Soviet apologists is for the sake of argumentation and diversion. As Lenin wrote, "to live in a society and be free from this society is impossible."[27] But from the Soviet point of view, what is worth while in "free" communication is what the Party conceives to be the truth. In other words, the Party and the state have access to a body of authoritative doctrine which they believe to be the absolute and basic truth. Freedom to communicate *this* truth is what is valued.

The state, or more accurately the Party, being custodian of this truth, it is incomprehensible to the Soviet spokesman that our media should seek freedom *from* the state; the Soviet media are expected rather to seek freedom *within* the allegedly beneficial state which protects them in doing what the state says is "good for them." Therefore it is obvious that in the Soviet state no freedom *against the state* can be tolerated. As Vyshinsky said, "there is and can be no place for freedom of speech, press, and so on for the foes of socialism."[28] Likewise there can be no freedom for communication from outside which might contaminate the Soviet citizens' ideas. As Muller says, the Soviet leaders feel they must protect their citizens "from powerful, irresponsible men who want to promote their own selfish interests at the expense of others, and who in the democracies largely own the 'free' press." That is why they raise an Iron Curtain. On the other hand, the Soviets feel that by owning the facilities of mass communication they eliminate concealed class controls with which they charge our press.

Finally, let us record that freedom and responsibility are inseparably linked in Soviet theory. The *results* of communication are always in the Soviet eye. Communication media are *instruments*. The Soviet theorists value the instrumental result, as we value the *abstract right* to speak freely. That is why we permit no consideration except the most serious matters of national security or human rights to limit us in the exercise of press freedom, and that is why the Soviet spokesmen call ours an irresponsible press. First of all, the Soviet press is expected —indeed, compelled—to be responsible for possible results of what it says. First of all, the Anglo-American press is expected—indeed, enjoined—to speak freely. And therefore we have merely a new version of the old contrast between authoritarian and libertarian systems, although the Soviet spokesmen, with different and skillfully chosen vocabularies, also talk about a free and responsible press.

The differences between Soviet authoritarianism and the non-Marxist authoritarianism will now be clear.[29] Typically, of course, the media under the old authoritarianism were and are privately owned, except in some countries in the case of broadcasting. These media were and are controlled by patents, licensing, guilds, government pressure, and censorship. Soviet media, as we have seen, are controlled by ownership, by Party personnel in key positions, by directives, review, criticism, and censorship. But the essential point is that in the older authoritarian systems the media have typically been part of the business system, and to that extent, less exclusively an instrument of the government. They have been in bondage to the state, but the Soviet media are *in* and *of* the state.

It is important that the Soviet system has removed the profit motive from publishing, and thus caused the rewards to lie not in the by-products of prosperity, but in the by-products of orthodoxy and skill in propaganda. It is noteworthy also that the Soviet system has succeeded in defining the function of mass communication positively (that is, *requiring* the press to do certain things) whereas the older authoritarianism defined it negatively (the press is *not permitted* to do certain things). The Soviet communications were built as a part of change and to accomplish a specified change; the older authoritarian media have been used mostly to maintain the *status quo*. Finally, it is obvious that the Soviet media are integrated, planned, used in a way that the older authoritarian media almost never were. The older ones were merely *controlled* media; the Soviet ones, as we have said, are planned media, serving the goals of the state in the same way as the steel plants or the infantry do.

Yet the ethical implications of the Soviet Communist communication theory are much like those of the older authoritarianism. There is always an outside check on what is right. In the case of the Soviet system, it is no longer the revealed Will of God, or the wisdom of the philosopher-king, or the will of the sovereign who was supposed to rule by Divine Right. Rather it is a body of doctrine through which all human events can be passed as through a prism, being separated thereby into certain common constituents. And this doctrine is subject to interpretation by a small group of specially informed leaders. Seldom are individual or human rights made the basis of ethical or responsible acts in Soviet statements of their theory. Rather, they speak of collective rights—"the classless society," "the people's state," etc. There is this constant emphasis, on the good of the state and society, the welfare of the proletariat, behind their ethic. For, as we have said before, according to the Soviet mechanics, the improvement of society must precede the improvement of man, and the good of man is necessarily dependent on the material welfare of the society in which he lives. The key word in the last sentence is *material*, for in Soviet theory ethical practice is referable always to its material and its social results, as opposed to its spiritual or human results.

This is the communication theory which is ranged opposite us in the world today, in control of mass media which serve almost a billion people.

Social Responsibility Theory

Those were the alternatives we had to choose from before the pattern of social responsibility theory emerged. That is, we could choose among the old authoritarianism, the new-model authoritarianism with Communist trimmings, and the libertarianism with which we were growing increasingly dissatisfied.

Why were we becoming dissatisfied with libertarianism? We have already suggested most of the reasons: the press growing big and concentrated, hard to enter, and farther removed from the people, so that the self-righting process was less likely to have a chance to work. Minority opinions were less likely to be heard, and there came to be less and less assurance that idea would clash against idea in a free market place. Furthermore, there was a great change in the ideological climate in the late 19th and early 20th centuries. We are only now beginning to assess the full dimensions of this change. But it is clear that the shadow of the Enlightenment, which was the basis of libertarian communication theory, falls less heavily on the modern world.

Recall that earlier climate of thought: Newton's perpetual motion machine, the universe, running according to immutable laws which rational man can search out and understand; John Locke's philosophy of inherent natural rights and rational man; Adam Smith's classical economics with its emphasis on the minimum of government restraint and its faith that "as men worked for their own self-interest they would inevitably work for the common good"; and John Milton's idealistic concept of a self-righting process by which truth, exposed to human view in an open market, would inevitably emerge from the free encounter of ideas.

What has happened to those ideas in the twentieth century? Newton's static and timeless concept has been challenged by discoveries about evolution, statistical mechanics, and relativity. John Locke's philosophy has been challenged by modern psychology, which sharply limits the rational capability of man, and by modern philosophy, which is inclined to doubt the existence of any right without a corresponding obligation. Classical *laissez-faire* economics is no longer widely accepted without reservation. We have come to hope, rather, that by interfering to some extent with the free operation of the market we may be able to avoid the disastrous troughs of the business cycle; and studies of "robber barons," with the muck-raking which came at the turn of the century, have led us to doubt that *laissez-faire* and "self-interest" are always equated with the common good. In short, our view of man and our view of society are altogether less optimistic and idealistic than they were in the Enlightenment. And, whereas in the Enlightenment one of the greatest needs of society seemed to be to free the press from the state so that it could operate as a check on government and as a vehicle by which rational man might discern truth out of a free clash of ideas, now the tendency is not to extend the press's freedom but rather to examine its performance and perhaps to lay some requirements on it which would be quite foreign to the spirit of the Enlightenment out of which libertarianism grew.

Mass communication has been subjected to an increasing wave of criticism. Actually, the first American book extensively attacking the press was published in 1859, but the chief wave of criticism followed the publication of a series of articles by Will Irwin in *Collier's* in 1911.[30] Irwin argued that the influence of the newspaper had shifted from the editorials to the news columns, that the commercial nature of the paper was responsible for many of its shortcomings, and that the press had become big business, entry into which was increasingly difficult for the newcomer. Upton Sinclair's savage *Brass Check* followed in 1919. George Seldes bitterly attacked the press in *Freedom of the Press*, 1935, and in a newsletter *In Fact*, published in the '40s. During the '30s, newspaper publishers shared the attacks made against businessmen generally, for example in such books as *America's House of Lords*, by Harold Ickes, and Ferdinand Lundberg's *Imperial Hearst*. This criticism has varied in degree of responsibility, but increasingly it has come to have a serious and thoughtful tone. The general themes of the critcism have been summed up as follows by Theodore B. Peterson:[31]

1. The press has wielded its enormous power for its own ends. The owners have propagated their own opinions, especially in matters of politics and economics, at the expense of opposing views.

2. The press has been subservient to big business and at times has let advertisers control editorial policies and editorial content.

3. The press has resisted social change.

4. The press has often paid more attention to the superficial and sensational in its coverage of current happenings, and its entertainment has often been lacking in substance.

5. The press has endangered public morals.

6. The press has invaded the privacy of individuals without just cause.

7. The press is controlled by one socio-economic class, loosely the "business class," and access to the industry is difficult for the newcomer; therefore, the free and open market of ideas is endangered.

In these statements Peterson is using "press" to mean all mass communication. It is obvious that some refer chiefly to media other than the newspaper.

Along with this criticism, there have been also positive developments of importance. For example, journalism schools have been created (the first one 50 years ago), and they have helped to provide more professionally-minded employees for the media. This is in itself a significant step away from the days when a newspaper was operated by an itinerant printer as a free channel for anyone who would support it. The adoption of codes by practically all the media is another notable step. We shall discuss these codes at a later point in this book. Suffice it to say here that of all these codes only the newspaper code, adopted by the American Society of Newspaper Editors in 1923, seems to follow rather closely along the lines of libertarian thinking.

Furthermore, during the last half century the media have taken steps toward responsible action and responsible thinking that would have astonished the American mass communicator of a century ago. As Charles Beard said, freedom of the press a hundred years ago meant "the right to be just or unjust, partisan or nonpartisan, true or false, in news columns and editorial columns."[32] Frank Luther Mott has called the early nineteenth century, which we are inclined to think of as the high point of press freedom and libertarianism in this country, "the Dark Age of Partisan Journalism."[33] But almost exactly a half-century ago, Joseph Pulitzer, who was then one of the most prosperous as well as the most influential of newspaper publishers, wrote the statement we have already quoted "nothing less than . . . a sincere sense of moral responsibility will save journalism from a subservience to business interests, seeking selfish ends, antagonistic to public welfare."[34]

Nearly fifty years later, the stockholders of the small *Park Ridge Echo* at Alexandria, Minnesota, met to adopt a declaration of aims for the paper, which read in part: "To begin with we must realize that a truly great newspaper must be greater than any one of, or the combined consciences of its editors, in that, when it speaks, its words are of someone far wiser, far more reasonable, far more fair, far more compassionate, far more understanding, and far more honest than those men, crippled by human weaknesses and failings, whose task it is to write those words."[35]

These are samples of a quite remarkable series of statements, which are oddly at variance with the statements of earlier libertarian editors and owners. But let it not be thought that American mass communication has limited itself to *talk* of responsibility. The responsibility of being the only paper in a city has led a number of leading American newspapers—for example, the Cowles papers in Minneapolis and Des Moines, the Louisville *Courier Journal*—consciously to apportion their output so as to represent, as far as possible, both sides of a controversial question fully and fairly. Such a network as CBS has set a very high standard for its news coverage, and for the separation of news from comment, and all networks have been most scrupulous about giving an individual or an organization free and equal time to answer a broadcast attack. The codes we have been mentioning have been *voluntarily* adopted. Most of the media have gone to great lengths to help the public *understand* questions of public policy. All these are impressive examples of a concept of communication public service far different from the belligerently libertarian statement we quoted in an earlier chapter: "A newspaper is a private enterprise owing nothing whatever to the public. . . . affected with no public interest."[36]

It is therefore clear that a new concept of mass communication is emerging. We have called it the "social responsibility" theory for want of a better name, but it is distinguished from its parent libertarianism chiefly by a greater sense of responsibility on the part of the media. Theodore Peterson, who has written on this topic, has tried to state this new theory, and has come out with this description:

> Freedom carries concomitant obligations; and the press, which enjoys a privileged position under the Constitution, is obliged to be responsible to society for carrying out certain essential functions of mass communication in contemporary society. To the extent that the press recognizes its responsibilities and makes them the basis of its operational policies, the libertarian system will satisfy the needs of society. To the extent that the press does not assume its responsibilities, some other agency must see that the essential functions of mass communications are carried out.[37]

This new theory has unfortunately been associated in the public mind, and especially in the mind of mass communicators, with two Commissions which were appointed in the late '40s and early '50s to examine the performance of the press. One of these was the Commission on Freedom of the Press, established in this country by private philanthropy and chaired by Robert Maynard Hutchins. The other was the Royal Commission on the Press, established by royal decree in Great Britain. Press reaction to the former of these, especially, was bitter, and the report when it appeared was given the silent treatment. Yet the Commission really had little to say which could not have been echoed and, indeed, was not said in advance by leaders of mass communication.

This new theory of mass communication we are talking about is not something which has grown out of the deliberations of a few scholars on a commission. It is something to which the media and the whole culture have contributed, and it is a change so obvious that no objective scholar could look at the communication system of a hundred years ago and the system today, and say that they were operating under the same concept of communication. The aspect of the Commission's work which so irritated the press was not the positive doctrine enunciated in regard to the responsibilities of mass communication, but rather the fact that outsiders were criticising the always sensitive press, and, above all, the fact that the Commission dared to wave a big stick at the press. "It becomes an imperative question," said the Commission, "whether the performance of the press can any longer be left to the unregulated initiative of the few who manage it." And again, "Those who direct the machinery of the press have engaged from time to time in practices which the society condemns and which, if continued, it will inevitably undertake to regulate or control." *Regulation* has always been a red flag word to the press!

But the responsibilities of the press, as stated by the Commission, would arouse very little disagreement among communicators: to provide "a truthful, comprehensive, and intelligent account of the day's events in a context which gives them meaning"; to serve as "a forum for the exchange of comment and criticism"; to give "a representative picture of the constituent groups in society" (in other words, minorities as well as majorities); to help in "the presentation and clarification of the goals and values of the society"; and to provide "full access to the day's intelligence." As we say, no mass communicators in this country are likely to object to having those responsibilities assigned them. They objected to a group of "outsiders" saying that they were not in all cases meeting these responsibilities, and suggesting that they should be required (possibly by government) to live up to them.

Therefore, it is well at this point to try to forget the verbal battles and the strained relationships between press and commissions, and to try to consider instead the characteristics of the new concept of mass communication which we see all around us.

Essentially, the new theory is a turning away from rationalism, from a self-centered and *laissez-faire* ethic. For example, what of *truth* in terms of social responsibility theory? As the Commission says, the media are expected to provide "a truthful, comprehensive, and intelligent account of the day's events in a context which gives them meaning."[38] Under libertarian theory this requirement could hardly have been so posed. Under libertarianism, the media were expected to reflect the world as their owners saw it. They were permitted to distort, to lie, to vilify, all with the confidence that when all the distortions, the lies, the vilifications were put together, then rational man could discern truth amongst the falsehoods. But the requirement under the new theory is clearly different. Even in later states of libertarianism, the requirement was different, for papers separated news from comment, and then developed the concept of "objective" news reporting. Objective reporting meant simply that the reporter would present the facts without comment or explanation. This was obviously intended to aid the self-righting process: by seeing the facts raw and unadorned, man could more easily distinguish truth. But the viewpoint of the new theory is that objectivity is not enough. "It is no longer enough to report the *fact* truthfully," said the Commission; "it is now necessary to report the *truth about the fact*."[39] This is a new and severe responsibility to be placed on the mass communicator, incomparably more difficult than the task of "objectivity." For now the media are enjoined to try to present the whole, the balanced truth. As Elmer Davis says:

> The good newspaper, the good news broadcaster, must walk a tightrope between two great gulfs—on one side the false objectivity that takes everything at face value and lets the public be imposed upon by the charlatan with the most brazen front; on the other, the 'interpretive' reporting which fails to draw the line between objective and subjective, between a reasonably well-established fact and what the reporter or editor wishes were fact. To say that is easy; to do it is hard.[40]

In libertarian theory, full responsibility for deriving the truth was placed upon the public. In this emergent theory, the media become full partners with the public in this responsibility. Another aspect of the search for truth in which the media have a new responsibility is the presentation of comment and criticism. In libertarian theory, the press was expected to present the one set of opinions for which it stood. In these days of one-paper towns, and a shrinking number of owners, many newspapers have come to accept the greater responsibility of presenting all sides of a controversy fairly and equitably. "We are common carriers," said Norman Isaacs, managing editor of the *Louisville Times*. "The freedom of the press was given for that purpose—and for that purpose alone. Freedom of the press cannot mean the license to keep people from knowing."[41] Edward Lindsay of the Lindsay-Schaub newspapers writes that newspapers have a new "responsibility to minorities in the publication of complete and objective news accounts. They have a responsibility at the business level. Newspaper publishers are denied the luxury of refusing to deal with those whom they dislike or of using their control of a medium of communication to punish those who patronize a competitor."[42] And the television code, it will be remembered, advocates that stations should "give fair representation to opposing sides of issues which materially affect the life or welfare of a substantial segment of the public." Thus a broader responsibility in regard to the searching out and presentation of truth is assigned the mass media under the new theory. The assumptions behind it are obviously (a) that man is not so adept at deriving truth as had been believed, and (b) that libertarian practice, in this age of few and big media, no longer provides a truly free market place of ideas.

We have now for some time been suggesting the view of man which appears to underlie the new theory. Let us turn our attention more directly to it. Under the older, libertarian theory, as Peterson sums it up:

Man was regarded as primarily a moral and rational being who was inclined to hunt for truth and to be guided by it. Every man by nature wished to aid the quest for truth, and every man could serve its cause, for even the most seemingly preposterous idea was worth expression. Only if all men spoke freely what was on their minds, the ridiculous as well as the sublime, could they hope to discover truth. Given freedom to speak and to publish, men would express themselves. They would do so temperately and without capriciousness. There was no need to remind publishers of their public responsibilities; they would assume them without exhortation because of the moral sense which gave them their dignity. Nor need one worry about the occasional publisher who, because of human frailty, lied or distorted. Other publishers would find it profitable to expose him. His lies and distortions would be recognized, for the public would put his utterances to the powerful test of reason.[43]

The proponents of the newer theory say, on the other hand, that the libertarian theory simply hasn't worked out that way. The communicator has not always shown a high moral sense. Man has not always behaved like a rational and discriminating being. Rather he has behaved like a lethargic being, seldom showing those innate natural qualities with which the Enlightenment credited him. Capable of using his reason, he is loath to do so, says Peterson. "Consequently he is easy prey for demagogues, advertising pitchmen, and others who would manipulate him for their selfish ends. Because of his mental sloth, man has fallen into a state of unthinking conformity, to which his inertia binds him. His mental faculties have become stultified and are in danger of atrophy. If man is to remain free, he must live by reason instead of passively accepting what he sees, hears, and feels. Therefore, the more alert elements of the community must goad him into the exercise of his reason. Without much goading, man is not likely to be moved to seek truth. The languor which keeps him from using his gift of reason extends to all public discussion. Man's aim is not to find truth but to satisfy his immediate needs and desires."[44]

Furthermore, the trend of the theory of social responsibility is to place a lower evaluation on man's morality than did the libertarian theory. Milton's concept was that man cannot be regarded as truly moral unless he has been tempted, and that he is therefore better off learning of evil through the mass media than at first hand. The general view under that theory was that man is the heir of certain absolute principles of ethical behavior through which, by the exercise of reason, he could distinguish right from wrong. But to judge from the motion picture, radio, television, and comic book codes, man is quite a different creature. He is easily susceptible to temptation; he is easily degraded morally; he is like a child in the face of the immorality which is supposed to appear in the media. Therefore, it is the responsibility of the media to protect him from temptation beyond his ability to resist.

The kindest thing to say about this view of man is that it is more realistic than the libertarian view. It is clear that man is no longer considered the shining creature, standing only a little lower than the angels, repository of natural rights and the exerciser of reason, which the Enlightenment made him out to be.

As to government, on the other hand, the newer concept is rather more favorable than the older ones. The libertarian view of government was derived from centuries of experiences with authoritarian rule; the social responsibility view grows out of experience with democratic rule. It is not entirely surprising, therefore, that some exponents of the new theory—notably the Commission on Freedom of the Press —are inclined to a more permissive attitude toward government's part in mass communication.

For the libertarians, the best government was the least government. In social responsibility theory, on the other hand, the government is expected to take an active part in promoting freedom. Indeed, the government is the only force strong enough to make sure that freedom can operate effectively. Therefore, when necessary the government should share with the citizens and the media the responsibility for media performance. Says W. E. Hocking, "government remains the residuary legatee of responsibility for an adequate press performance."[45] If a self-regulated press and a self-righting process in society do not obtain for citizens the communication services they need, says the Hutchins Commission, then government should step in. Of course, here is where the Commission on Freedom of the Press parts company with most of the spokesmen for the media themselves. For the Commission follows Hocking in believing that the government may justifiably legislate to correct abuses of the mass media, or it may enter the field of mass communication to supplement existing media. The media spokesmen, for the most part, vehemently deny to government much of that right. Government's right and responsibility stop with such housekeeping chores as giving out broadcast channels, say the media men, and even in so doing it should give no attention to the content of the channels.

Freedom, as defined by the new theory, is thus clearly freedom *for*, as opposed merely to freedom *from*. The freedom the libertarians sought was freedom from the encroachments and requirements of government, and other external restraining agencies. The freedom which appears to be the goal of this new and emergent theory is freedom for the kind of communication which fulfills society's needs. Libertarian freedom was a negative freedom; social-responsibility freedom is a positive freedom. Under libertarian theory, it was sufficient to remove the restraints and restrictions on man, and let his reason and his natural endowments work. But the man of today, who possesses negative freedom but no access to the press to express his views, has a rather empty freedom. The press that has freedom from outside restraint, but insufficient access to news or to channels, likewise has an empty freedom. According to Hocking, the press of today must have freedom "to have the use of one's powers of action (1) without restraint or control from outside, and (2) with whatever means or equipment the action requires."[46] Even the press itself has been retreating from its libertarian concept of negative liberty because of its concern for freedom of information. A system of negative freedom obviously provides no way of prying information from unwilling government officials. Therefore, the press has worked for open meetings, open records, face-to-face meetings with government executives—all of which fit under the concept of freedom *for* meeting society's needs, rather than any concept of freedom *from* outside restraint.

This is the theory of social responsibility as it seems to be emerging. Its goal? Obviously, the smoother functioning of society and the greater happiness of man. But beyond that the Commission on Freedom of the Press suggests a goal which contrasts interestingly with the goals of the other theories we have been describing. The purpose of the authoritarian press was obviously to maintain the power and position of the ruling forces. The main purpose of the newer authoritarianism, the Soviet Communist theory, is to maintain and advance the Soviet socialist system. The main purpose of libertarian theory was to represent the citizens in checking on government. The main purpose of the new theory, says the Commission, is to maintain free expression so as to raise social conflict "from the plane of violence to the plane of discussion."[47] Thus the shadow of the nuclear weapon falls across our thinking in this time.

What are the ethical implications of this theory? Let us treat that question only briefly here, because much of the remainder of this book will be concerned with the kinds of ethical problems that arise in this changing time of mass communication. But it is evident that under this new theory, as distinct from libertarianism, there can be no rights without corresponding duties. If man uses his right to free expression "to inflame hatred, to vilify, to lie, to contaminate the springs of truth," as Peterson puts it,[48] obviously he forfeits the right, and may be restricted from such use of it. He has the right to be in error, but not to be deliberately or irresponsibly in error. He has the right to express himself, but a corresponding duty to his conscience and to society. "The notion of rights, costless, unconditional, conferred by the Creator at birth, was a marvelous fighting principle against arbitrary governments and had its historical work to do," said the Commission. "But in the context of an achieved political freedom the need of limitation becomes evident."[49] And it is clear that the test of responsibility, under the new theory, has swung around from individual toward social responsibility, from rationalism toward a social conscience and a religious ethic. The communicator must satisfy his conscience, but he must also satisfy his perceived duty to society. As libertarian theory chose to emphasize the "enlightened self-interest" of Locke, so the theory of social responsibility tends to emphasize John Stuart Mill's "greatest good of the greatest number." In other words, the concept of freedom of the press as a purely personal right is a dying survivor of the eighteenth and nineteenth centuries. Its place is being taken by a new concept of the relation of freedom and responsibility.

These, then, are the four concepts of mass communication which are with us, in varying stages of rise and fall, in the world today, and which are the bases for communication ethics and responsibilities as seen and as practiced. (1) The older authoritarianism still exists in many countries of the world, although often dressed up in libertarian language. (2) "Libertarianism," as we have defined that theory, still persists in some parts of the world. (3) Behind the Iron Curtain a new, aggressive, positive authoritarianism has come into being to advance the cause of Soviet socialism. (4) In the western world, however, notably in Great Britain and the United States, a new concept is rising out of libertarianism—still tentative, still rather rootless, retaining many of the doctrines and goals of libertarianism, but turning away from individualism toward social responsibility, from rationalism toward a social and religious ethic.

The new concept is still emerging, still not quite clear, but clearly a creature of our own time, and likely to be with us for the rest of the century.

FOUR CONCEPTS OF MASS COMMUNICATION

	Authoritarian	Libertarian	Soviet Communist	Social Responsibility
Developed	Applied to modern communication in 16th- and 17th-century England; widely used and still practiced	In England, in U.S. and many other countries.	In Soviet Union beginning 1917; later, in satellites and China	In U.S. in the 20th century; also Great Britain, Canada, and some other countries
Based on	Long history of authoritarian philosophy	Philosophy of rationalism and natural rights	Marxist - Leninist - Stalinist thought	Changes in media, new thinking by communicators, commissions, and philosophers
Chief purpose	To advance purposes of government in power; to service the state	To inform, entertain, sell but; chiefly to discover truth and check on government	To advance the Soviet socialist system, and maintain dictatorship of Party	To inform, entertain, sell; but chiefly to raise conflict to plane of discussion
Media can be used by	Anyone who gets royal patent or similar government permission	Anyone with economic means to do so	Loyal and orthodox Party members	Everyone who has something to say
Media are controlled	By government patents, guilds, or censorship	By "self-righting process of truth" in "free market place of ideas," and by courts	Ownership, surveillance, government action	Community opinion, consumer action, professional ethics

Media are forbidden	To criticize political machinery, or officials in power	To defame, to be obscene or indecent, or to commit wartime sedition	To criticize Party objectives or depart from "line"	To invade private rights or vital social interests in a serious way
Ownership	Private or public	Chiefly private	Public	Private, except as supplemented by government
Essential difference from others	Instrument for effecting government policy, though not necessarily government-owned	Instrument for checking on government and meeting other needs of society	State-owned and closely controlled media existing solely as arm of state	Media must assume obligation of social responsibility; and if they do not, someone must see that they do

(Adapted from Siebert, Peterson, and Schramm, *Four Theories of the Press*.)

PART III

Ethics in Mass Communication

Liberty means responsibility. That is why most men dread it.

—George Bernard Shaw

6

Freedom

We have spent so much time on the four concepts of mass communication because when a man or a nation is in the market for a new model, it is good to be able to see the alternatives. In this case none of the old alternatives is satisfactory: neither the old tough, efficient authoritarianism under which mass communication grew up, nor the new efficient repellant authoritarianism which the Communist states have developed since 1917, nor the old permissive optimistic libertarianism under which our communication system has been operating for nearly two centuries. This is a new age. The new age requires a new 20th-century model.

But, when we abandon these three other systems, we abandon also road maps and directions. The old and the new authoritarianisms are imposed from the top and therefore relatively easy to codify. Libertarianism was built on the philosophy of the Enlightenment and on the thinking of New and Old World statesmen and communicators, and was grounded in a long period of practice. But the emergent system—social responsibility or whatever we call it—is new and uncharted, and not clearly based in doctrine unless one considers that the American and the British Commissions have stated the doctrine, which it would embarrass a number of mass communicators on each side of the Atlantic to admit. Therefore, we are on our own. We have to find our own way.

It is easy to say in a general way what this emergent concept demands of the mass media. Essentially it demands a combination of responsibility and freedom. More specifically, it demands that the media be accurate and full in their reports on environment; that they express adequately and fairly the conflicting views on public questions; that they entertain us with decency and taste, and give us an adequately balanced service; and that they keep themselves free from pressures, restrictions, or allegiances that might detract from the fairness, balance, and reality of their content. But these are big and fuzzy words. Our problem is to get down to cases and try to say what

these words are coming to mean in the emerging concept of communication responsibility. So doing, we must necessarily descend from
the fairly high level of abstraction where we have been operating for
the last several chapters, to the practical level of everyday decisions
in the media.

In the last hundred years ethical considerations and problems of
responsibility must have intruded in larger proportion into the
thousands of decisions which have to be made every day in an American communication organization. How large the proportion is, what
percentage of a communicator's working decisions involve conscious
ethical content, it is impossible to say. But the proportion must be
higher than it was a century ago. One hundred years ago, as we
have tried to suggest, the principle of *caveat emptor* applied in mass
communication almost as in business. One hundred years ago—long
before 94 per cent of our daily newspaper towns became single-ownership towns—an editor or publisher might operate his paper as one
particular political prism, through which to filter the light of his
environment. So doing, he could be confident that other editors, other
publishers, were applying other prisms, presenting counterbalancing
facts and ideas, and inviting the "self-righting" process to work. One
hundred years ago, the machine-interposed media had not yet introduced the problems of mass entertainment. One hundred years ago
the process of professionalizing the mass media had barely started
(and, as we have said, it is by no means completed today). The last
hundred years have therefore brought new responsibilities, a more
demanding public, and a growing sense of professionalism mirrored
by codes, professional training, and organizations like the American
Society of Newspaper Editors. The problems of responsibility have
clearly become more central and urgent than before.

An attempt has been made, as part of the preparation for writing
this book, to explore this new territory as realistically as possible, by
finding out what kinds of decisions now have to be made by the mass
media involving conscious ethical considerations. This has been done
by asking a number of mass communicators on all levels of the
hierarchy to remember the kinds of communication problems they
have faced in the few days preceding, and to recall and tell of the
decisions they have had to make which they have clearly perceived as
involving ethical questions or defining their responsibility. In order
to expand and get behind these cases, a number of these men have

been asked also to talk in more general terms about their understanding of communication responsibilities. Also the literature has been searched for relevant statements and discussions.

The result has certainly *not* been to assemble *all* the ethical problems which confront mass communication, or even all the *kinds* of such problems. Undoubtedly an overbalance of the cases has been collected from the press, simply because the press is older than broadcasting or films and has a longer tradition of experience with such problems, and also because the author knows more about the press.

We have organized the material in four categories: the problem of freedom and control; the problem of defining the right to know; the problem of truth and fairness; and the problem of popular art.

In the following chapters we take up these areas in order, illustrating them by examples of the kinds of day-to-day problems which communicators face, and endeavoring to point out some of the borderlines and limits which are beginning to be observable on the dubious terrain.

The basic responsibility of mass communication, in our system, is to remain free.

This is no less true now than in libertarian days. Justice William O. Douglas, of the United States Supreme Court, put in an eloquent way what most Americans feel today:

Man's right to knowledge and the free use thereof is the very essence of the American political creed.

We have staked our security, our ability to survive, on freedom of the mind and the conscience. So spoke Jefferson, Hamilton, and Madison.

So say the great majority of us today.

That conception of freedom is the most novel principle the world has known. It leaves political and religious discourse unlimited and unrestrained. It leaves the mind free to pursue every problem to the horizon, even though the pursuit may rile a neighbor or stir his ugly prejudices. . . .

The Founding Fathers believed that the antidote to advocacy was counter-advocacy. They believed that if a subversive idea was presented from a platform or a soap box, the remedy was not to jail the speaker, but to expose the fallacy or evil in his cause, to submit his ideas to pitiless analysis, to explode his thesis in rebuttal.

The concept of our Bill of Rights is the concept of a politically mature people. It is the concept which makes the American way of life the ideal for every people. For its essence is tolerance for all shades of opinion, persecution for none. Under our way of life a man should never go to jail for what he thinks or espouses. He can be punished only for his acts, never for his thoughts, or beliefs or creed.

It is important, I think, to adhere to our first principles. We must adhere to them if we are to have the capacity to cope with the tremendous problems of this age.[1]

"Man's right to knowledge and the free use thereof" is or should be, therefore, the central concern of a responsible mass communication system today as yesterday. We cannot *assume* freedom today merely because in the 18th century we succeeded in freeing the press from government and writing a guarantee of that freedom into the First Amendment. As a matter of fact, the threat may be greater today than it has been for some time. And not only from big government, but also from political and social pressure groups within our society, from business relationships, from interlocking ownerships and other forces within the industry itself, and always from the competitive upsurge of peoples who hold to one of the authoritarianisms, old or new. It is a matter of more than arithmetical importance that today there are more people in the world who lack free communication than those who have it. Many of those who do not have it (the Communists for example) still talk of their communication systems as free. As John B. Wolfe said at the Minnesota symposium on science and freedom, "man can *seem* to be free in any society, no matter how authoritarian, as long as he accepts the postulates of the society, but can only *be* free in a society that is willing to allow its basic postulates to be questioned."[2]

Our political philosophy requires us to keep the basic postulates of our society open to question. Yet we are opposed in the world today by states which are fanatically sure of the rightness of *their* postulates, and in our own society we have influential groups who fear this aggressive competition and are therefore opposed to any such questioning or free argument concerning *our* concepts. All these are severe challenges to "man's right to knowledge and the free use thereof." And the essential meaning of the situation in which we find ourselves is that mass communication, having found how to free itself in the 18th century, must now find how to keep itself free in the 20th.

What is the kind of freedom we are trying to keep? When you look carefully at it, it breaks down into three parts:

Freedom to know—the right to get the information we need in order to organize our lives and take an intelligent part in governing.

Freedom to tell—the right to transmit information freely and to take a public stand on an issue and argue for it.

Freedom to find out—the right of access by communicating media to sources of information which needs to be told and known.

The first of these is a social right, belonging to all people. The second is the one we most commonly are talking about when we mention "freedom of the press." It too is the right of all people, but it is institutionalized in mass communication. The third right also belongs to all people, but is delegated to the chief finders in our society, the mass media. They are the ones who speak up when this right is infringed upon by closed meetings or withheld documents. Indeed, this third right is now probably the basis of more complaints from the media than either of the others. Without this third right, of course, they can hardly live up to their responsibilities under the first.

We consider it the fundamental responsibility of mass communication today ceaselessly to defend these three kinds of freedom. To defend them not only against government, but also against threats from any other quarter—from outside the country, from power groups inside the country but outside the government, and even from restricting influences within the media themselves. To defend them not only with protests and publicity, but also by taking the initiative in actions that will maintain and spread the bounds of freedom. For example, mass communication must keep itself economically strong so that it may remain impervious to threats, bribes, and subsidies, no matter what their origin, for these would control in some measure what the media say or do not say. Furthermore, mass communication must try to discharge its other duties so responsibly that there is as little incentive as possible for government or society to want to control or change its service.

As we see it, the best defense for freedom today, on the part of our mass media, is responsibility. This difficult and troublesome balance between freedom and responsibility is undoubtedly the major problem in mass communication today, and will be the concern of much of the remainder of this book. In the next pages we are going to examine some of the contemporary threats to communication freedom and talk in each case about the responsibility of the media.

THE PROBLEM OF GOVERNMENT REGULATION

Let us begin with the old bogeyman, government. What form does the threat of government control take today?

Zechariah Chafee, who knows as much as anyone about mass communication's relations with government, points out that mass communication includes the only large, wealthy, and powerful business enterprises in this country which are subject to very little legal accountability. "In the last hundred years," he says,

little news sheets issued by obscure printers have turned into enormous plants, in each of which a handful of men can inform and influence millions of citizens. Other business enterprises which have grown from small beginnings to great power during the same period, like Standard Oil Company, the New York Stock Exchange, chain stores and chain banks, have eventually aroused public alarm and been put under substantial government control to restrain public abuses. They can no longer run loose. Yet it is the first principle of our Bill of Rights that the government must let all the powerful enterprises in the press run loose.[3]

Mr. Chafee goes on to say that he firmly believes this is as it should be. We agree. We want to keep government regulation of mass communication at a minimum. We want the communication media to help us keep it that way. This they can do (a) by resisting encroachment of government on their freedom, (b) by accepting the responsibility of doing for themselves many of the things the law does for other enterprises. As Mr. Chafee says, it is a heavy moral responsibility "to prevent abuses of power and to make sure that the [press] increasingly performs the services which the American people need."

The Printed Media

Newspapers and magazines are in a relatively privileged position among the media in the United States so far as government control is concerned. They won this freedom in the eighteenth century and have firmly held on to it ever since. Print, like all the media, is subject to laws of libel, obscenity, copyright, et cetera, but these are not unpleasantly restrictive. The Post Office Department has sometimes held over the printed media the threat of withdrawal of second-class mailing privileges, and occasionally has actually removed the copies of a magazine (for example, *Esquire*) from the mails and withdrawn second-class privileges.[4] This kind of censorship is a dubious activity of the Post Office, and was properly protested and ruled unconstitutional at the time of the *Esquire* events. Certain state and municipal governments have tried to censor books and magazines, and the publishers have fought these governments bitterly, and usually won. A few states have moved to acquire a kind of oblique control over textbooks by making such requirements as affidavits of noncommunism for every author in a text—even for the authors quoted in an anthology. But on the whole these activities have not caused a great deal of trouble.

Most of the heat has been generated by two specific kinds of regulation. One of these is evil and pernicious and to be avoided at all costs. This is the political tax. It was only about a century ago that the last restrictive tax on newspapers was removed in England, and, as Gerald points out, the growth of the popular British press trailed that of the American Press by 60 years because of a stamp tax on advertising. In this country in 1934, a corrupt political machine in Louisiana tried to tax newspapers of that state into silence. The machine would have succeeded except for intervention of the United States Supreme Court. Gerald notes correctly that this intervention was made possible only by a remarkable "judge-made overturn in Constitutional theory by means of which the federal government moved to protect the press against state governments."[5]

There is another kind of encroachment which is directed at the commercial practices of the printed media. There have been several well-publicized instances of this government activity in the last twenty years. For example, there was the successful suit brought under antitrust laws against the alleged monopolistic advertising practices of the Kansas City *Star*. There have been cases in which the government sought to make the newspapers pay newsboys a minimum hourly wage, which the papers resisted, arguing that the newsboys were "merchants": that is, they really bought and sold their papers. This was not one of the arguments that showed the press in its most lovable light. But the best publicized of all was the Associated Press case.[6] This was a case brought against the AP under anti-trust laws, seeking to compel the agency to sell its wire service to all buyers. Formerly the agency, which is cooperatively owned, had protected its members by refusing to sell to their competitors. This was brought to a head in

Chicago where the new Chicago *Sun*, competing in the morning field
with the Chicago *Tribune*, was unable to obtain AP service. The case
came to be called by some people the *Sun* case, and by some punsters
the "Sun suit." The fact that the *Sun* supported Roosevelt against the
Roosevelt-hating *Tribune* added emotional overtones to the suit which
it might not otherwise have had. But let Robert Lasch tell the story:

> Almost to a man, the publishers of America interpreted the filing of
> this action as a foul assault upon the First Amendment, and with frighten-
> ing unanimity exerted all their power to impress upon the public that
> point of view.
>
> "We see in this, not the end perhaps, but surely the greatest peril,
> to a free press in America," said the Detroit *News*. From the citadel of
> its monopoly position in a city of 600,000, the Kansas City *Star* cried:
> "This is the sort of thing that belongs in the totalitarian states, not
> in a free democracy." "In the event of a government victory," said the
> New York *Daily News*, "the press services of the United States will be
> under the thumb of the White House."
>
> These were not extremist positions. They represented a fair sample of
> the opinion handed down by the press, sitting as a supreme court, long
> before the government brought its case to trial and won the first round
> in the United States District Court of New York. The Associated Press
> proudly published a volume of the collected editorial judgments for the
> instruction of the country.[7]
>
> The country rode out the storm with equanimity. Dimly or otherwise,
> the people perceived that the newspapers, once again, had proved unable
> to separate their commercial privileges from their civil rights.

In retrospect the press outcry about the AP case now sounds a
little silly. The government won the case, and the *Sun* got AP
service. The White House did *not* get its thumb on the wire services.
No newspaper was suppressed. No newspaper was restrained or
censored in what it wanted to say. The question was a commercial
one: whether a news service could be withheld from some papers for
competitive reasons.

The dangerous element in this case is that the newspapers put
themselves in the position of crying "wolf" when the wolf was no
more than a rabbit. It doesn't help public understanding of freedom
of the press or public respect for the First Amendment to have them
associated with problems of newsboys' pay or restrictive membership
in a news agency. I am not saying that the newspapers were not right

in fighting these issues—merely that there is considerable doubt whether they should have fought them on grounds of press freedom. The newspaper, like all mass communication, is at once a business and an informative public service. As Chafee says, it is something like combining in one organization a college and a very large private business enterprise, the one devoted to educating the public, the other to making money for a few owners. This combination is admittedly awkward, and yet constitutes one of the great strengths of a communication system free from government. We must maintain it, we must do everything possible within the law to keep our papers strong enough to stand independently of the government and report on it; and yet we must expect a rather unusual kind of responsibility from the owners of these papers. For they are like college presidents, as well as like business tycoons. Their responsibility in one capacity should temper their behavior in the other. And, at the least, they should try to think clearly and separate their freedom as free enterprise from their rather special kind of freedom under the First Amendment.

This is an excellent example of what we called the "difficult and troublesome balance" which our media are forced to maintain between freedom and responsibility. The media are enjoined to stay economically strong in order to remain free and independent. They feel that their economic position is threatened by some action of the government taken against them not as public service organizations but as business organizations, aimed ostensibly at bringing them into line with other business organizations. In the circumstances both government and media have a clear responsibility to think clearly and proceed slowly.

The government must ask itself whether the action it is taking is likely in any way to limit the freedom and independence of the media as communicating organizations. The media must decide whether the government action is indeed something to be opposed with the arguments of business or the arguments of communication. For "press freedom" is a precious commodity, not to be lightly drawn into a business argument. When the Postmaster General refused second-class mail privileges to *Esquire*, then the media could properly claim that an essential freedom was being abridged. When the same argument was raised in relation to the wages of newsboys, the cause was no longer so clear.

The essential point to keep in mind is that the mass media must always fight any government challenge to free expression of ideas. Not only the printed media. And not only in regard to editorial comment. In *Burstyn vs. Wilson*,[8] a case that involved the censorship of an Italian film called "The Miracle," the Supreme Court clearly extended the protection of the First Amendment to motion pictures as well as to print. In *Winters vs. New York*,[9] a case that involved the right to publish magazines consisting mostly of accounts of crime and violence, the court went still further and extended the protection of a free press to entertainment materials. Said Mr. Justice Reed in the majority opinion:

We do not accede to appellee's suggestion that the constitutional protection for a free press applies only to the exposition of ideas. The line between the informing and the entertaining is too elusive for the protection of the basic right. Everyone is familiar with instances of propaganda through fiction. What is one man's amusement, teaches another's doctrine.[10]

Walter Lippmann, in *The Public Philosophy*, distinguishes in an interesting way between the different amounts of government intervention that the media may expect by virtue of their different natures.[11] In our public philosophy, he says, freedom of speech is conceived as "the means to a confrontation of opinion—as in a Socratic dialogue, in a schoolmen's disputation, in the critiques of scientists and savants, in a court of law, in a representative assembly, in an open forum." Even in the canonization of a saint, he points out, the Church listens patiently to a "devil's advocate." This confrontation or debate is the basis of our provisions for freedom of speech. When genuine debate is lacking, then freedom of speech does not work as it is meant to. It follows, then, he says, that the degree of toleration that will be permitted in the media will be in proportion to the efficiency with which ideas can be challenged and rebutted.

In the Senate of the United States, for example, a Senator can promptly be challenged by another Senator and brought to an accounting. Here among the Senators themselves the conditions are most nearly ideal for the toleration of all opinions. At the other extreme there is the secret circulation of anonymous allegations. Here there is no means of challenging the author; and, without any violation of the principles of freedom, he may properly be dealt with by detectives, by policemen, and by the criminal courts. Between such extremes there are many problems of toleration which depend essentially upon how effective is the confrontation in debate. Where it is efficient, as in the standard newspaper press taken as a whole, freedom is largely unrestricted by law. Where confrontation is difficult, as in broadcasting, there is also an acceptance of the principle that some legal regulation is necessary—for example, in order to insure fair play for political parties. When confrontation is impossible, as in the moving picture, or in the so-called comic books, there will be censorship.[12]

This is undoubtedly true, and keenly observed. Yet it does not answer the question as fully as we need it answered, for we must further ask, *what* legal regulation? censorship of *what*? Take the motion pictures for example. What kind of censorship is permissible, and what kind is an undesirable encroachment on freedom?

Films

The First Amendment is clearly a concern of the motion-picture industry, and indeed that industry has strong Supreme Court backing for resisting censorship on all grounds except obscenity. In the "Miracle" case, the court ruled that a film might not be legally censored on the grounds of being "sacrilegious." Later, the court ruled that "LaRonde" might not be censored on the grounds of immorality. The Court also reversed Ohio's ban of the film "M" on the grounds of "tending to promote crime" and Texas' ban of the film "Pinky" on the grounds of inciting racial tension. It seems that only censorship for obscenity, as defined by the courts, will be tolerated by the Supreme Court under the First Amendment.

Perhaps the most interesting aspect of the motion pictures' relations with government has been the comparatively submissive attitude of the studios. How much of this is due to the constant harassment of pressure groups, how much to the threat of government intervention, how much to the personalities of the leaders of the film industry and the fact that much of the ownership is absentee, is hard to say. We do have Darryl Zanuck's statement in *Treasury for the Free World*:

Let me be blunt. The fear of political reprisal and persecution has been a millstone about the neck of the industry for many years. It has prevented free expression on the screen and retarded its development. The loss has not been merely our own. It has been the nation's and the world's. Few of us insiders can forget that shortly before Pearl Harbor the entire motion picture industry was called on the carpet in Washington by a Senate committee dominated by isolationists and asked to render an account of its activities. We were pilloried with the accusation that we were allegedly making anti-Nazi films which might be offensive to Germany.[13]

The case Mr. Zanuck was talking about was the investigation that followed Senate Resolution 152, August 1, 1941, introduced by Senators Nye and Clark, who vigorously opposed the entrance of this country into the war and were fearful that the film industry was making war propaganda. The investigation was never concluded and never got anywhere, unless it succeeded, as Mr. Zanuck implies, in frightening the film makers.

Another case where the government laid a hard hand on the industry was the anti-trust legislation, originally instituted in 1938, which resulted in divorcing the makers of films from exhibitors.

Less spectacular but of somewhat greater moment to film content is the series of state censorship actions. Most of these are on the grounds of indecency, but some are definitely on political grounds. For example, a film was banned in Ohio in 1937 because "the picture encourages social and racial equality, thereby stirring up racial hatred . . . all the above doctrines are contrary to the accepted codes of American life." A documentary film dealing with the Spanish Civil War was banned by the Pennsylvania Censor Board with the suggestion that the film would be acceptable if the words "Fascist," "Nazi," "Italian," "Rome," "German," "Berlin," etc., were deleted.[14] This decision was fought in the courts, and reversed. In fact, as Ruth Inglis says in commenting on this case, examples of this sort are rare, and the producer or exhibitor who fights a case of this kind in court is almost sure to win. The difficult cases are those which involve censorship on the basis of indecency or unfairness to some group or other. And the film industry has been somewhat less aggressive in fighting these cases than the printed media have been.

Almost all the observers who have studied the motion pictures as a public service have concluded that we need less, rather than more, government regulation. Miss Inglis, for example, in the book she wrote for the Commission on Freedom of the Press, decided that "the friends of freedom should fight governmental infringements of freedom whenever they occur."[15] On the other hand, we should ask of the film industry two manifestations of responsibility in return for the maximum of freedom. In the first place, the industry should itself resist encroachments on its freedom to make the best films it knows how to make, whether these encroachments come from governments or pressure groups. In the second place, like the press with its long-won freedom, the film industry should be scrupulously responsible with all the freedom it can win. And each of these behaviors will contribute to the other.

Broadcasting

The real heart of the problem of regulation lies in the broadcasting industry. This industry has most of the kinds of encroachment which the other media experience, and in addition one very important kind of its own. For example, its programs are frequently under attack for their "indecency" or their "political content." It has been and continues to be the object of anti-trust actions; an example of this was the divorcement of NBC's Blue and Red networks. It is the subject of keen and continuing interest on the part of Congress, which is aware of the political potential of radio and television, and has directed its comments from time to time, and sometimes its investigations, toward such topics as alleged Communists in the industry, monopoly in the industry, violence in programs, and political prejudice in news coverage. As this is written, the networks are being investigated by a Senate sub-committee on suggestion of monopoly, and we must say more of this later. But the point we want to make is that all these circumstances are the more threatening because the industry is under the continuing regulation of the Federal Communications Commission.

This is something which does not happen to either the printed or the film media. A similar pattern in the printed media, for example, would require newspapers to obtain a federal license before starting into business, and renew it—giving proof of good public service—every three years. Such a requirement would be intolerable to newspapers, and would be bitterly and properly resisted on the grounds that it is contrary to our concept of free communication and probably in violation of the First Amendment.

With broadcasting, the problem arises because there aren't enough channels for all the broadcasters who want them. More correctly stated, there aren't enough *desirable* channels. Somebody has to decide who gets what channel. As we found in the early 1920s it isn't feasible to let broadcasters choose their own, because they tend to cluster around the same channels, and the more the air fills up the more it is impossible for listeners to get anything except a cacophony of squeals and distorted programs. Furthermore, many agencies other than entertainment broadcasters have an interest in channels. The military, for example, the police, the transcontinental telephone and teletype, short-wave communication from and between automobiles and trains, the forest service, the rural electric service, and many others. Therefore a public policeman must be set up to lay out boundaries and police the fences. This is the job that was given the Federal Communications Commission.

Now, when the commercial broadcasters have to go to the FCC for their licenses, it creates a peculiar problem for a country which has been grounded in libertarian communication theory. For the user of a channel (1) is using a channel which others would like, (2) has made or is prepared to make a substantial investment in equipment to be used on that channel, (3) undertakes to perform a service with that equipment and that investment which, by all the patterns of libertarian theory, should be free from government licensing and review, (4) and yet somehow must be selected from among others who would like to use the same channel, and logically should be called to task, occasionally, to make sure he is using it well.

The nub of the problem is how the FCC should select the licensee when there is competition for a channel. Especially in television, this is often a very spirited competition. Great potential profits ride on the decision, many thousands of dollars in legal fees are put into preparing for the hearings, and tempers are raw. The FCC, represented by an examiner, must sit in judgment. The Communications Act has given him a rather broad yardstick by which to judge an applicant. This is the standard of "public interest, convenience, and necessity." The meaning of those three words has filled countless thousands of pages of hearings and debates.

How define the public interest, convenience, and necessity? For purposes of selecting licensees, the FCC has defined it by standards which the chief law digest, Pike and Fischer, lists under 25 headings:

1. fair, efficient, and equitable distribution of facilities
2. interference
3. financial qualifications
4. misrepresentation of facts to Commission

5. difficulties with other government agencies, involvement in civil or criminal litigation

6. violation of Communications Act or FCC rules

7. delegation of control over programs

8. technical service

9. facilities subject to assignment

10. local ownership

11. integration of ownership and management

12. participation in civic activities

13. diversification of background of persons controlling

14. broadcast experience

15. new station vs. expansion of existing service

16. sense of public service responsibility

17. conflicting interests

18. programming

19. operating plans

20. legal qualifications

21. diversification of control of communications media—newspaper affiliation

22. diversification—multiple ownership of radio facilities

23. effect on economic interest of existing station

24. "need"

25. miscellaneous factors

Studying applications for licenses the FCC will usually find a number of "differences" between applicants in terms of those 25 tests. It will tend to prefer an applicant with more broadcast experience, or with better financial backing, or representing local rather than absentee ownership, or representing more diversification of ownership (that is, one that tends to bring new blood into the communication business), et cetera. On the basis of these comparisons, it decides which applicant is better able to serve the "public interest, convenience, and necessity."

To discuss each of these standards would take us on a long side trip, and require us to delve into questions of law rather than questions of responsibility. But there is one standard which we cannot ignore, because it bears directly on the question of freedom. This, of course, is number 18—programming.

The idea of submitting the programs of a mass communication organization to government inspection is repugnant. In actual practice, the Commission has not taken a very hard look at programs. Yet the threat remains. A few years ago the Commission scared the broadcasters white by publishing a little "Blue Book" entitled "Public Service Responsibilities of Broadcast Licensees."[16] This talked about responsibilities for high-quality programming. It was promptly made the subject of bitter objection which invariably returned to the topic of communication freedom.

It is clear that some standards must be considered so that station applicants may be compared. It is just as obvious that the essential standard is programs, for all the other standards are secondary and contributory to the question of what kind of programs the station will carry. Well, how far do the people of the United States want the Commission to go into programming? I think we have to answer that we (and probably the people as a whole) don't know exactly. We are willing to have the Commission consider whether a station keeps the programming promises it makes when it applies for a license; to enforce its regulation on giving equal time for answer to an attack on the air; and to compare the programming promises of two applicants in broad terms. For example, if one applicant promises only popular records and wire news, and the other promises a network service, educational and cultural programs, wire news and local news coverage, et cetera, then we should certainly expect the Commission to concede an advantage to the second applicant. But, on the other hand, we don't want the Commission to pass judgment on what a station says about the government (if anything the station says is actionable in the courts, then let the case be tried there—but not in the FCC). We don't want the Commission to put itself in position to pass judgment on a specific news commentator, or a certain news broadcast, or a particular variety program.

Somewhere between these two kinds of action lies the borderline beyond which we are not satisfied that the Commission can safely go. [The nearer the Commission gets to questions involving *specific* programs or performers, the more dangerous the ground it is treading, the more likely it is to be encroaching on essential freedom. It is up to the government to keep behind that danger line, up to the public to help hold the line, up to the media to fight every invasion of the border and so to conduct their programming as to take away as much as possible of the temptation to invade and encroach.]

Court action is a less frightening prospect to broadcasters today than is Commission action, and Commission action is in turn less frightening than Congressional action. "If the threat of Congressional action hung over us in radio times, it hangs 100 times as heavy now that we are in television," a network head told me. This is because the political potency of the broadcast medium makes it a constant concern of officials who owe their positions to politics, and because of the broad investigative powers of Congress and the constant possibility of restrictive legislation.

For example, as this is written the Senate Committee hearings on network monopoly are under way in Washington. These illustrate not only the shadow of government intervention but also some of the rather dangerous assumptions that sometimes hang over these hearings. The hearing itself is directed at CBS and NBC, the two dominant television networks. They are the ostensible targets, but the real villain is the old problem of too few channels. Many important markets can have no more than two channels. Therefore, there is no room for a third network. The two dominant networks have affiliated with them a large proportion of the preferable outlets, most of the national advertising income, and most of the outstanding television talent. Therefore in a sense they are bordering on "monopoly." In fact, the third network, ABC, has been able to do better in competition with the two big fellows than anybody thought it could—thanks, as Jack Gould says, to Walt Disney and British movies. But the fourth network, Dumont, has found the situation pretty hopeless.

The thought behind the hearings, and behind the Bricker report which launched the hearings, is that if the two big networks could be limited in their affiliations or their coverage, it would be possible for other networks to operate, for local stations to do a larger share of the programming, and in general for control of the industry to be more diversified. It is not necessary for us to take a stand on this question, but it is desirable to say something about an implicit assumption which seems to underlie this hearing, and which also appeared to underlie the Blue Book and certain other expressions of the FCC.

This assumption is that concentration in the broadcast industry is necessarily undesirable; that the country is full of local stations anxious to present high-quality programs of public and local interest; but that the networks and multiple ownership are throttling the better impulses of these local stations, and forcing them to take inferior programs of a highly commercial nature.

That is a rather exciting picture—3,000 live broadcasting stations, programming to local needs and tastes just as newspapers try to cover the local scene and cater to local interests. But is it a realistic expectation? It was difficult in radio; in television, it is well-nigh impossible. High-quality local programming in television costs so much in skill and money that stations can't do much of it. They must depend on networks, because only through networks can they get the concentration of talent and program support which they need to present the kind of programs their audiences have come to demand. Furthermore, it is simply not true that the impulse to better programs comes from the local stations, rather than the networks. Both radio and television networks consistently offer a better average of programs than most of their affiliates will take. The figures on distribution of sustaining programs show this. Especially is it true in television, where local stations do not like to take sustainers; they want programs with income; in fact, it is the general consensus of opinion that the stations are more commercially-minded than the networks. Certainly, it is the networks rather than the stations which have been responsible for most of the important public service innovations of recent years—the documentaries, the 90-minute plays, the forums and discussions, the political conventions on the air, et cetera.

We are not trying to defend the networks or attack the Senate's investigation, but merely to point out that this government intervention, like many others, is on dangerous ground. For what is the alternative (as long as there are no more channels than at present) to having a few powerful networks in television? The only very clear alternative is a dominance of advertisers and advertising agencies. If stations are not organized in networks, they must be organized to be served by advertisers. For how otherwise will they get the expensive national programs they and their audiences want? And as between network service and advertiser service, there is little question which would provide the greater proportion of public service.

The Commission on Freedom of the Press had something to say about freedom in the broadcasting industry, with which we can bring this discussion to a close. The Commission recommended that broadcasting should be brought under the protection of the First Amendment just as the printed media have been. This idea seems sound, and is buttressed by Supreme Court decisions in cases like *Burstyn vs. Wilson*[17] and *Winters vs. New York*.[18] The ideal, of course, would be to have broadcasting as free as the press, but yet it can never be quite so free because of its very nature, as we have pointed out: because channels must be allocated, and some police power must be exercised, and because debate and refutation are not so automatic as in the Senate of the United States or in the newspaper press. Therefore, what we must work for is to make broadcasting as free as the press *within the limits* that are imposed on it by its nature. But nothing in its nature permits the government, through regulatory commissions, to have anything to do with specific programming. As the Commission said, we must keep broadcasting "free for the development of its own conception of service and achievement. It must be free for making its contribution to the maintenance and development of a free society."[19]

And so we return to the central theme: true freedom requires both liberty and responsibility. In the libertarian days we were preoccupied with keeping mass communication free (for whatever it wanted to do). In these new and somewhat different days we are inclined to see interdependence between freedom and responsibility. We are inclined to keep the media free so that they may be responsible, and to expect them to be responsible so that they may be free. In fact, we are now inclined to say that only by being responsible can the newer machine-interposed media win the kind of freedom that the printed media have won.

THE PROBLEM OF MONOPOLY

Monopoly is inimical to freedom of communication, because it puts difficulties in the way of the free flow of ideas into the market place. As a matter of fact, the shadow of monopoly, allied with bigness, has done as much as anything to bring about the rethinking of communication responsibility which we call the emerging social responsibility concept.

Concentration in mass communication is an economic fact we shall have to live with. The trend is strong, and there is no more likelihood of reversing it than there is of reversing the trend toward concentration in the making of automobiles, or in the ownership of grocery stores, or in the providing of light and power.

It is tempting to look back to the day when there was a newspaper for every thousand people. It is tempting to look back at some of the dreams the pioneers in broadcasting had for that art: that each station would be a program center reflecting local needs and problems, making most of its own programs from local talent, powerfully helping the newspapers to maintain the free flow of ideas and opinions into the market place. But there is no indication that we are going to move toward that kind of pattern.

As far as anyone can now see, the economic trend that has brought about this concentration is irreversible, except perhaps by a national economic catastrophe. Concentration has come about because it fits better into the national economic system. For one thing, capabilities for serving large numbers of persons have immensely increased: fast presses, quick transportation, wire news connections to all the world, powerful broadcasting stations, cheap receiving sets, efficient means of duplicating films, and the growth everywhere of motion picture theaters. While these capabilities have grown, the cost of labor and equipment has also increased immensely, so that to provide a service to a small audience would be prohibitively expensive, and all the economics of the situation are in favor of large audiences.

Furthermore, the tastes of the audiences have changed. They now demand wire news, syndicated features, and an efficient organization of local reporters and editors. Broadcasting audiences have learned to want big names, expert entertainment, the best in music, the kind of entertainment that would cost them thousands of dollars a year if they had to pay for it in theaters, night clubs, and concert halls. Motion picture audiences, too, would be unsatisfied with less than the expert film making and big-name actors they have become used to. They are even becoming used to wide screen and other special filming and projecting devices that represent additional investments for producers and exhibitors.

There is no sign whatsoever that *more* daily newspapers are going to be founded, or at least that any great number are going to be founded and survive. There have been some notable attempts in that direction in recent years—for example, *PM* and the Chicago *Sun*— but little success. All the economic currents are against it. There is no sign that more broadcasting networks could live if they were founded. As a matter of fact, the American Broadcasting Company television network was foundering only a few years ago, until it received a transfusion of motion-picture money.

The federal government has won three major engagements in the courts, within the last two decades, in an attempt to stop the trend toward concentration. It has succeeded in forcing the National Broadcasting Company to sell one of the two networks it owned (thus initiating the American Broadcasting Company as a separate organization); it has forced the Associated Press to sell its services to newspapers which were in competition with member papers (for example, permitting the Chicago *Sun* to buy AP service even though it was competing in the same morning market with the Chicago *Tribune* which had long been a member of the AP); and it has forced the motion picture studios to divorce themselves from control of strings of theaters. There have also been such lesser actions in the courts as the case against the Kansas City *Star*, forcing it to adjust certain practices which were said to be monopolistic—among others, its practice of requiring advertisers to buy advertising *both* on its radio station and in its newspaper in order to use one of them. We have already mentioned the Congressional investigation of television networks, one of a number of investigations of media practice, not many of which have had significant results in changing patterns. Undoubtedly the government had a responsibility to bring these actions and investigate these allegedly monopolistic procedures, just as it was the responsibility of the media to bring out an adequate defense of their practice. But in general it seems that the pattern is now pretty well set, and unlikely to be changed fundamentally through the courts or in Congress.

Therefore, the problem is to live with it. And here I should like to make two comments.

In the first place, it should be said to newspaper publishers especially and to other media heads less specifically, that they have lost as well as gained by the coming of bigness, fewness, and great prosperity to the mass media. For while they are in sounder financial position, and whereas they are able to furnish a much better service to their audiences, still they have lost a certain closeness to their constituency which was one of the greatest strengths of the libertarian press. In the days when many cities had a paper for every thousand people, the press in effect *was* the people. It was very close to them. When the press observed and criticized the government, it was therefore really speaking in the voice of the people, and the people thought of it as their own. The larger and fewer the papers have grown, the more they have withdrawn from the people. They do not speak so clearly in the people's voice. Indeed, the press has come to be thought of by the people, not as their own, but as another power center like the government or big business. And therefore the people do not so readily leap to its defense. They are more ready to criticize it and hear it criticized and to let the government act to control it. This is a penalty of bigness and fewness.

But, on the other hand, there is nothing to prove that the concentrated media offer any poorer service to the people than did the diffuse media. Indeed, most of the evidence is on the other side. Certainly, the coming of networks immensely improved radio and television, and the proliferation of networks would not likely improve it further. The roads to improvement are better in other directions. Similarly, where good newspapers exist, there is good reason to think that single ownership does at least as well for a community as multiple ownership. "Newspapers that don't have local newspaper competition are better able to resist the constant pressure to oversensationalize the news," says John Cowles, publisher of the Minneapolis *Star* and *Tribune* " . . . to resist the pressure for immediacy which makes for incomplete, shoddy, and premature reporting. . . . They usually are less inhibited about correcting their errors. . . . They can present the news in better perspective." Mr. Cowles' own Minneapolis and Des Moines papers are examples of how well single ownership can work.

The truth seems to be that there is nothing in concentration to keep the mass media from serving their publics at least as well as they could serve in competitive situations. In fact, there are factors in concentration that would tend to help them serve better—the economic strength to resist pressures, for example, and the absence of competitive time pressures to militate against balanced reporting. But with concentration comes a new and challenging responsibility. For, as we shall indicate later in these pages, the media must now take *special* steps to keep the free market place of ideas in operation. They must seek out and present fairly the opposing sides of a public question. They must be scrupulously fair in reflecting reality. Rather than relaxing under the absence of competition, they must be ever more intent on keeping their standards of service high.

There is little doubt that the standards of responsibility for concentrated media are higher than for diffuse and widely competitive media. There is also no question that, given responsible performance, the possibilities of public service are greater. Therefore, in a system of media concentration, the public can buy better service at the price of more careful vigilance. The media in return for greater rewards are asked to pay greater responsibility.

The Problem of Class Allegiances

Concentration in the media has made for concentration in wealth and property. Mass communication is big business. It is run by big business men. And this circumstance has led to much speculation by critics outside the industry, and much soul-searching by professionals inside the industry, as to whether a mass communication system that has become big business can fairly serve all other economic groups in society. In other words is the class allegiance of mass communications itself a threat to their freedom?

This concern has been most evident in the information branches of mass communication. Of these, William Allen White wrote these hard words:

Too often the publisher of an American newspaper has made his money in some other calling than journalism. He is a rich man seeking power and prestige. He has the country club complex. The business manager of this absentee owner is afflicted with the country club point of view. Soon the managing editor's wife nags him into it. And they all get the unconscious arrogance of conscious wealth. Therefore it is hard to get a modern American newspaper to go the distance necessary to print all the news about many topics. . . .[20]

In similar vein, Robert Lasch, another newspaper man, wrote as follows in *Altantic Monthly*:

In real life industrialists and department store managers do not pound on the publisher's desk and demand favorable treatment. They do not have to. An owner who lunches weekly with the president of the local power company will always grasp the sanctity of private ownership in this field more readily than the public-ownership ideas of a few crackpots. With the best of will, he may tell himself that his mind is open. Yet, as a businessman whose concerns are intimately bound up with those of other businessmen, he has a vested interest in maintaining the *status quo*.[21]

And so also Virginius Dabney, Richmond editor:

Today newspapers are Big Business, and they are run in that tradition. The publisher, who often knows little about the editorial side of the operation, usually is one of the leading business men in his community, and his editorial page, under normal circumstances, strongly reflects that point of view. Sometimes he gives his editor a free hand but far oftener he does not.[22]

Note well that we have been quoting neither social scientists nor professional critics nor the Commission on Freedom of the Press. These quotations are all from well-known and respected working newspapermen.

A well-known American editor told us this story:

Case 1. A machine tool company in our town was about to be taken over by a financial manipulator. Our financial reporter had the news, and wanted to present it. He took the story to our publisher. But it happened that the president of the company was one of the directors of our paper. He said, don't publish it. The publisher went along with him. Now it looks as though the company will be lost.

This is, of course, one of the most pernicious kinds of class control —the interlocking of other businesses with mass communication. This director was acting not as a responsible mass communication head but rather as a representative of his other business, and apparently short-sightedly at that.

The problem is not by any means limited to newspapers or even to the printed media. Magazines, some of them, are even bigger business than newspapers. Radio and television operations are very large business units, and their guiding personnel are among the business leaders in their communities. Motion pictures have long been characterized by extraordinarily large incomes on the part of top executives and star performers, and recently by a great deal of absentee ownership. So the possibility of class bias extends through all the media, and through entertainment as well as informational material. In the case of the former, our concern should be that popular art may not reflect adequately both the wishes and the needs of society generally. In the latter case, our concern is that the information media may not fairly reflect reality.

The owner of a mass communication organization is entitled to order whatever policy he wants, so long as it is legal. He might have trouble if he were to decree a policy that would drive away his audiences, but that too is his privilege, as long as he can afford it. As Royce Brier wrote in the San Francisco *Chronicle*:

Publishers and editors set editorial policy and establish viewpoint on news. If it is biased, hysterical, devious, or timorous, they are bound by that. If it is objective, calm, honest, and courageous, they are bound by that. Reporters and correspondents write news. If the boss wants it slanted, they slant it, or look for work elsewhere. If the boss wants it straight, they write it straight, or quit. Copy-desk men and sub-editors determine how the news shall be presented—where in the paper, what the heads shall say, what may be omitted. If that's the way the bosses want it, that's the way they get it.[23]

So likewise the publisher of a magazine, the head of a network or a station, the head or the owners of a studio, have final say as to what goes out and who comes in and what view of reality the operation takes. This is illustrated dramatically in what sometimes happens to mass communication with the coming or going of one man. Thus, the death of an owner of the Chicago *Daily News* has changed the entire character of that paper. The coming of E. P. Hoyt to be publisher of the Denver *Post* signaled a great change in that paper. In a similar way the later Chicago *Tribune* grew in the shadow of Colonel McCormick, NBC in the shadow of General Sarnoff, CBS in the shadow of William Paley, et cetera. And the smaller the city or the communication unit, the more likely it is to reflect the policy and intent of one man or a few men. Thus, as Zechariah Chafee says, in smaller cities "the quality of the facts and ideas conveyed to the particular community from its single newspaper depends on one man or a handful of men."

This "man or handful of men" do not necessarily exert any direct and obvious control. Occasionally they do. For example, here is a case reported by Michael Bradshaw in the *Atlantic Monthly*:

Case 2. On my first newspaper . . . I was city editor when we had trouble with the mayor's wife. She was a temperamental women; and once when the automobile she was driving collided with another car, she drove away in a huff without stopping to give her name as required by law. But someone got her number, reported it to the police, and we printed the story in our morning paper.

. . . The afternoon newspaper owned by the same company published an entirely different version of the same trivial accident, omitting the fact that the mayor's wife had driven off without stopping. After our morning staff reported for work, who should walk into the city room and go into a huddle with the police reporter but the publisher. Naturally we listened as he tried to explain the story to the reporter who had covered it. He wanted a little correction run the next morning, saying that the mayor's wife hadn't driven off. "But how can I say she didn't when she did?" the reporter asked as innocently as you please. To give the publisher due credit, he did, on that occasion, have the grace to blush and walk back into his counting office.[24]

More often, however, the policy control is indirect and often by inference. "Newspapermen are quick to get the idea of what the boss wants," says A. J. Liebling, "but those who get it first have usually had similar ideas right along. The publisher chooses some staff members as his instruments and ignores others (or, if they are obstreperous, gets rid of them)."[25] Some stories or pieces of editing are rewarded, others are not. Employees whose position agrees with the desired one are most likely to be put into responsible positions. For example, the remarkable policy control of the Chicago *Tribune* under McCormick was not attained by a series of directives, or by editorial rewriting, but rather by this indirect method—rewarding some behavior and not other behavior, providing an example in highly rewarded employees, and judiciously selecting newsmen for key reporting assignments in Washington and elsewhere. In the case of films, as several film men have reported, a popularly successful product may be rewarded, an unsuccessful one not. The pressure is on top management to repeat the success. This pressure is passed on down, and the tendency is always to repeat the formula, to do the sure thing.

We have not meant to talk as though owner control of policy is a dangerous thing. Dangerous or not, it is inevitable. Policy control goes with ownership, whether the owner is private or public. In a state-owned system, the government sets policy. I prefer private ownership. And, in a privately owned system, the fact that policy is controlled by a man who has a large income, and lunches with other big businessmen, may be a good or a bad thing, depending on the man. For example, in a certain network, the employees will tell you that the "conscience" of the network is its chief owner and its president, that these two men are responsible for many of the most liberal and courageous undertakings of the network, and that they have led rather than resisted the efforts of their staff to reflect reality fairly and meet the tastes and needs of all classes. Similarly, behind many of the most liberal magazines and newspapers of this country are men who prove that a publisher can be both liberal and "well-heeled."

What are we afraid of, then? Not that the owner or publisher or president, who happens to be a big business man, will decide between stories or actors or reporters or candidates or programs, which is his manifest right. Not that, but rather that these decisions will be made without his consciousness of a possible bias entering into them. In other words, we want our media to be as free from class bias as possible, and as a step toward that we are asking for an awareness of the possibility of *unconscious* class bias.

Every man tends to be more aware of other men's bias than of his own. In the days of many newspapers, bias on the part of media heads was less dangerous, because a reader could pick and choose among shades of political belief until he found the one nearest his own. Now, when we have few newspapers, an unconscious bias on the part of a medium's head is more dangerous. We can't expect the top media men to eradicate their bias; that would be superhuman. We can't expect to free them of allegiances and pressures. But we can expect them to perform responsibly to the extent of being aware of their class connections and allegiances, and to be on the lookout for any resulting bias that might filter down into the media operation. We can expect them, that is, to be aware of the possibilities and therefore a bit more careful in looking at their own decisions, particularly as to fair comment, objective news coverage, or an adequate entertainment service. That is all we can ask of them, and it is a great deal to ask.

CONTROL THROUGH SUPPORT

From the owners and top executives of the media, then, we ask responsible control. But how about control through support? Is that a threat to communication freedom?

Here we are talking mostly about advertising. The control which audiences exert by buying or not buying, viewing or not viewing, attending or not attending, is in general a wholesome thing, and quite properly paid attention to in managing the media. But advertising has been a favorite ogre of mass communication critics for years. Charges have been made that advertisers "really run the media"; that they "get the news slanted"; that they "control the editorial policy"; that they occupy exorbitant amounts of space or time and thus crowd out information and entertainment. It must be admitted that such charges have been more often made than proved, but in any case we have to ask just what kind of responsibility we expect of the media in their relationships with advertising.

First let us recall that advertising stands in different relationships to different media. The advertising support of motion pictures is so small as to be negligible, and the advertising is local and therefore has no relation to the making of entertainment films. Advertising support of the printed media is considerable (often two thirds or more of the total income of newspapers and magazines), but is quite separate from the news, editorial, and feature columns. That is, an advertiser buys space for his message but has nothing to say about the content of the material which the editor puts next to it. He may be able to specify that his ad appear, for example, on the sports page where it will have athletic stories near it and therefore supposedly be seen by the same persons who read sports news, but he does not have, or should not have, any control over what is said in those sports columns. The thing that chiefly worries critics, in the case of the printed media, is that the influence of the advertiser may cross over from the advertising to the editorial and news columns.

Advertising stands in a much different relationship to the broadcast media. For here, advertising support is total support. And, in radio and television, an advertiser does not merely buy a segment of time: he also "buys" a program, or a segment of time adjacent to a particular program. There are two principal kinds of broadcast advertising. One is the "spot" advertisement, which means that an advertiser buys a minute or half minute of free time between programs or, in some cases, within programs. In this case, the advertiser has nothing to say about program content, but he can specify, if time is available, what program he will be next to.

The other kind of broadcast advertising is the sponsoring arrangement, whereby an advertiser pays the cost of preparing a program and the time costs of putting it on the air. In this case, of course, he has the right of life and death over the program. He may produce the program himself, or more likely his advertising agency will produce it for him, or he can support a program the network produces. If the network produces the program, he can still say yes or no. The network also can say yes or no. It can refuse to carry the program. Or through its network acceptance office (a kind of benign censorship) or a station's local readers, it may ask for a change in detail. Thus what goes on the air, if it has advertising support, is the result of an agreement between the advertiser and the broadcaster. There is no fence, as in the printed media, between the advertiser and the information and editorial content. The advertiser must approve.

The advertiser's influence was probably greatest in the heyday of radio, when a very large percentage of all sponsored programs were prepared by advertising agencies for their clients, and the networks were chiefly in the position of furnishing time and channels. Of course, the networks and stations still had the right of refusal. But in this period the hand of the advertiser was most clearly visible in programs. This was the period, also, of the insistent and repetitive commercials, typified by those which George Washington Hill put into American Tobacco programs.

With the coming of television, the center of gravity for control has again moved back to the broadcasters. Now the advertising agencies produce relatively few of the large network programs; they are made either by the networks themselves or by a program-packaging house for the networks. No small amount of the country's film-making talent and facilities has been syphoned into these packaging houses. Some of them specialize in programs, others in commercials. And the result is that on the whole television commercials have drawn much less objection than did radio commercials at the height of radio, and that the broadcaster is more often in the position of selling a program than of merely selling time for a program. In other words, as television has developed, the relationship of advertiser to broadcast media has moved somewhat closer to the relationship of advertiser to printed media.

Now what principles of responsibility should govern that relationship of advertiser to media?

First, I think, we want to be sure that the information and opinion in the media are free of advertising control—except, of course, the advertising information, which also should conform to acceptable standards of accuracy and reliability.

Secondly, no matter who produces the programs or suggests the talent or authors, we want our media to be free of any advertising control that would militate against a well-balanced program service.

Thirdly, we want our media to be free from any advertising control that would keep them from fully exercising their responsibility to present a program service of high quality.

Finally, we expect the amount of advertising in our media to be in some equitable proportion to the amount of information and entertainment.

These are broad and high-sounding principles. Let's see how they apply in practice.

The most typical case involving possible advertising control is the threat of withdrawal of advertising.

Case 3. (Recorded by a reporter on a daily newspaper). The advertising manager came to me today and asked me for heaven's sake to give G a break. He said G was sore as the devil, and ready to pull out his advertising. Said we were not being fair to him in reporting a lawsuit against him. The ad manager said, couldn't we ever run a story favorable to one of our big advertisers? The city editor said to me, "call 'em as you see 'em."

Case 4. On penalty of canceling all theater advertising, theater owners in a small town demanded that the editor treat them more "fairly." Specifically: (a) Cease to publish news of other towns' closing theaters on Sunday; (b) Cease to publish letters to the editor complaining of the quality of pictures currently being shown; (c) Support candidates for city offices who are opposed to increasing the cost of theater licenses. The advertising involved is a considerable amount in the paper's weekly income. The editor compromised.

Case 5. A certain newspaper supported editorially the right of labor to organize in the plant of an advertiser who was engaged in a bitter fight with unions over that question. Advertising was withdrawn. The paper is said to have lost $200,000.

In any case like these, the only responsible course of action a newspaper or magazine editor or broadcaster can take is, after checking carefully the accuracy of his information and the fairness of his handling, to carry the information he feels his audience needs in order to make up their minds on the topic in question. His primary obligation is to his public. And there his real strength lies. For if he has an interested and faithful public, then it will always be profitable to advertise in his medium, and ultimately the advertiser who withdraws will have to come back. Most of the great newspapers and magazines of the country have histories of advertisers who have withdrawn and had to return. And, although in the meantime the paper has lost the income from these advertisements, still it has demonstrated its independence and its usefulness, and over all has probably made money by attracting other advertisers and larger orders.

A financial reporter for a large metropolitan newspaper reports this instance of how one paper handled this kind of problem:

Case 6. A large corporation withheld for 24 hours the announcement of a dividend increase on its common stock, enabling some company officials to profit substantially on the resulting market fluctuation. An enterprising reporter discovered the story. It was big news, but the company was a big advertiser. The reporter wrote the story but submitted it to his boss, the newspaper's financial editor. The managing editor was consulted. All three were in agreement. The story ran as the reporter had written it. In addition, the newspaper ran an editorial criticizing the company's "reprehensible behavior."

A high corporation official called the reporter into his office, claiming the story was unfair. The reporter said the executive protested strongly and threatened to pull out advertising. "I told him," the reporter said, "what an interesting story the threat would make for next day's paper. The advertising stayed."

Another case occurred recently involving a possible violation of release date. The part of the problem related to the release date need not concern us here, but the rest of it is germane.

Case 7. The *Wall Street Journal* obtained details of new General Motors models some time before the information was due to be released to the public. When the *Journal* published this information, GM cancelled $11,000 worth of advertising. The *Journal* stood by its guns.

As we said, we must beg the question here whether the *Journal* obtained its information legitimately and was or was not violating privacy or property rights in publishing it. We are not informed as to that. It is a matter which the *Journal* would have had to decide as responsibly as it could. But having once decided that the information is legitimately publishable, then the paper expressed its position about as responsibly as it could: its obligation is to its readers. It cannot fulfill that obligation and permit any news source, even an important advertiser, to censor the news. In fact, it would not be useful even to these censoring sources if it were to permit outside control over its news.

The editor of the *Journal* wrote:

Would they wish us to print only the banking news approved by bankers, only the steel news approved by steel officials, only the real estate news approved by real estate agents? If our readers thought that every story were censored by the industry or the company which it is covering they would not long have confidence in it. Nor would the situation be any better if we ourselves undertook to censor the news by our ideas of what is 'good for business.' If we reported only 'good' news, readers would not find the paper of value even in their own field.[26]

It is no accident that these cases happen to be cited from newspapers, rather than other media. Newspapers, because of their localness, tend to have a more intimate and direct contact with their local advertisers than a magazine has with its national advertisers. Nevertheless, a magazine has some problems of its own along this line. And broadcasters, of course, have them in legion. Here is a sample of the kind of problem that comes to broadcasters:

Case 8. Edward R. Murrow's "See It Now" program twice lost its sponsor because the sponsor, a large industrial concern, said it did not wish to be connected with the controversy the program generated.

Case 9. Drew Pearson lost his sponsor because the sponsoring company said that it did not want to be involved in the public mind with the kind of attacks that were being made on Pearson.

Case 10. Again and again, sponsors have insisted, through their advertising agencies, that the star of the show read some of the commercials. That is, they feel that the message will have more impact if it comes in the voice of Jack Benny or Ed Sullivan or the news commentator or someone else who has already won the confidence of the audience. Comedians and dramatic stars sometimes resist this additional assignment, but usually do it. Some newscasters do, and some do not. On one network, there is a standing rule that no newscaster shall read a commercial in connection with his own program.

Just as any advertiser has a right to buy space or not to buy space in a newspaper or magazine, so an advertiser has implicit and explicit right to decide to sponsor or not to sponsor a given program. That is not in question. An advertiser should put his money where it will do him, *over all*, the most good. The danger is rather that the advertiser's freedom of choice might force the broadcaster into making program changes that would give away some of his own freedom to serve the public. For example, it takes courage to continue a program that is controversial. It takes a real sense of responsibility to continue a program that is both controversial and unsponsored. And ultimately a program like that will probably have to go off the air, because network television cannot afford many expensive unsponsored programs.

Should the broadcaster avoid controversial programs? If so, he is not fulfilling his responsibility to explore public problems. Should he try to make his programs such as to deliver the largest possible audience to the potential advertiser? If so, the air will be full of giveaways, variety shows, sentiment and violence, and there will be no programming for the smaller, special-interest segments of the audience.

It is more than a coincidence that the advertisers who put the most money into broadcasting—for example, the soap and cigarette manufacturers—are concerned with a general, rather than a specific audience. They want to reach as *many* people as possible, *any* people, because a very large proportion of any audience will be in the market for soap and cigarettes. This means that advertisers of this sort are not much interested in supporting Omnibus, or the New York Philharmonic, or See It Now, or Invitation to Learning, because programs of this kind by their very nature and quality restrict their audiences. The biggest money in broadcast advertising is therefore for "common denominator" programs, for serving the broadest interests of the public, rather than the more specialized interests or the interests of groups within the public.

This is what makes the position of the broadcaster so hard. For, unlike the publisher, he has no second source of support, though he has a demanding audience. Therefore, he must constantly be serving two masters, the public and the advertiser, trying to sell for one, inform and entertain the other. And he must do as much as possible for the audience within the limits of what the advertiser will support. It is in every respect a more difficult problem of responsibility than the editor faces.

So far as Case 10 is concerned, this is the kind of problem in which the broadcaster must decide how free he should be from control over content. Actually, most local newscasters do read the commercial. Many network newscasters do not. There is a good argument in favor of introducing a new voice to read the commercial. For the news should be as objective as possible. Even the tone of the voice should reflect this care and objectivity. The commercial, on the other hand, is a sales message. Its purpose is to persuade and manipulate. Is it a good idea to mix the two? Should not the separation of news from selling be maintained on the air as in print, as a symbol of objectivity? Certainly a great many broadcasters think so.

Here is another example of the way in which the broadcaster must decide the amount of control over content he will permit:

Case 11. A certain comedian lampooned the commercials of another advertiser on the same network in a very funny manner. The advertiser protested. After considerable argument, the comedian dropped this kind of material from his program.

This is altogether a less important case than would be an advertiser's attempt to control what news items go out on a newscast. Even so, however, it presents one of the many situations in which a broadcaster has to sit down and think out his conflicting responsibilities. How important is this material to the comedian? To what extent does it come under the heading of free comment? To what extent will dropping it make the program less interesting to the public? In general, it must be admitted, the advertiser usually has his way over this kind of protest. But still, in many cases a broadcaster has been able to make an advertiser see that he stands to gain, rather than lose, from a good laugh at his expense, especially if he is confident enough to join in the laugh—that only the insecure person is afraid to have a joke told about him, and in any case that this is *free* advertising which keeps his name before the public.

One of the responsibility problems in this area is what we might call "subsidized" news. For example:

Case 12. (Michael Bradshaw, in the *Atlantic*): My second newspaper happened to be Josephus Daniels' *News and Observer*, which is deservedly called "the Old Reliable" because it prints the news without fear or favor. I had been on its state desk only a few nights—having moved up from a paper which didn't like a strike story cluttered up with unnecessary facts—when a man called up from a nearby town to say that he had a real news story which his home-town paper wouldn't print, and that if we would print it he would buy a thousand copies of our paper. Being new on the job, I asked the city editor about it. "If it's news," he said, "we'll run it because it's news. If it isn't, we won't." While I was there, that's how the *News and Observer* was run.[27]

Whereas a newspaper cannot afford to let its news be subsidized, a broadcaster is in the position of needing to have his news subsidized. And this puts the problem directly: how much control should an advertiser be permitted over the news program he sponsors?

The most desirable answer would be that he should have no control over it. Ideally, the broadcaster should sell time on either side of the news, as the newspaper sells space on either side of it. But, unless some other financial base is arrived at, the broadcaster is not likely to feel he can afford this. If the news is to be sponsored, then the problem of control almost inevitably enters. This is not likely to be direct control; the sponsor is not likely to try to censor the day's news, or give a directive to the newscaster as to what subjects he should omit, what positions he shall take. Rather, it is likely to be indirect. The newscaster is aware of his sponsor's interest and positions; consciously or unconsciously he may avoid going against them. And even though the newscaster and the broadcast executive together may keep this at a minimum, still the advertiser has the ultimate veto in deciding what newscaster to sponsor. There is a considerable history of liberal newscasters and commentators being dropped by conservative sponsors.

Ideally, of course, newscasters and commentators should not be sponsored. That would put the responsibility for reliable news squarely on the broadcaster, where it belongs, and would do away with a great deal of potential suspicion. If news has to be sponsored, then it would be better if only straight newscasts rather than news commentaries were sponsored. And, if both have to be sponsored, then it is simply up to the newscaster and the broadcaster to do the most responsible job possible.

Here is a problem of advertising control in reverse: It is reported by the publicity manager for a large milling company.

Case. 13. My boss says I'm the last guy who should write about ethics. But when a letter of mine to an editor of a metropolitan daily comes back with a note, "I think it would be wonderful if you were to advertise in our paper, then we could use your fine publicity to an extent," then I think I am in a position to ask, "Ethics?"
. . . Needless to say, we did not advertise.[28]

Let's hopefully say that this report is unrepresentative. For it is a shocking thing, in view of 150 years of libertarianism, that a newspaper should in effect be willing to sell a part of its news columns— and not only be willing, but offer such a sale!

Let us return to the problem of advertising in broadcasting, and talk about the effect of the present arrangement on unsponsored or less popular programs. For example:

Case 14. A television network recently dropped an unsponsored educational program and a sponsored educational program with a comparatively small audience, both for the same reason: that advertisers were unwilling to buy the time next to these programs. The advertisers (or their agencies) felt that an unpopular program decreases the audience for programs on either side of it.

Thus, even though a network can absorb a certain amount of unsponsored time, still it runs into this additional fact that any small-audience programming, no matter how high in quality, will make it harder to sell the time on either side of the small audience. This is one reason why so many public service programs are heard at odd hours, if they are heard at all.

The real problem is how dependent the broadcaster is on this additional support. The stronger the broadcaster financially, the better he can afford to put sustaining (unsponsored) programs on the air, or to program for special audiences. In the case of a network, this problem of dependence is multiplied by the interrelation among the stations. Typically, the network headquarters has trouble distributing its sustaining programs because the local stations don't like to take them; they prefer to sell the time. And in television, where program costs are high and rates are considerable, the problem is compounded.

Another kind of ethical problem in relation to advertising was suggested recently by Dean John Drewry of the University of Georgia. He asked:

Case 15. Should the local paper accept advertising from competing firms in nearby cities? Is it fair to local merchants?

Before answering these questions, the small town publisher must also ask himself this: Do I not also have an obligation to the individual reader—to the consumer as well as to the seller? If he can learn through an advertisement in my paper of lower prices in an Atlanta or Savannah store, is it not a social obligation of mine to open my pages to such an outside advertiser?[29]

Dean Drewry is quite right in pointing out the nature of the problem which is the conflicting obligation of the newspaper to its readers and to the business community of which it is a part. Furthermore, it has a certain obligation to give any qualified advertiser access to its pages. Most newspapers feel it is not irresponsible in this situation to take competing advertising. But Dean Drewry suggests a way out. He recalls that an Atlanta department store advertised in small Georgia papers with a map showing only two points— Atlanta and the town in which the advertisement was published. The copy read: "Try to get it first in your home-town stores. If they don't have it, it is only (number of miles) to (Name of Atlanta firm)."

Here is another example of media obligation not directly to any advertiser, but rather to the whole business community (which is also the advertising community). This is an example from Bradshaw:

Case 16. After the war had brought a horde of new workers to an industrial city in Ohio, our paper planned a series of stories showing how overcrowded housing conditions had created a serious health problem. We had a string of pictures of houses in which twenty, thirty, or forty persons lived, and we actually published one or two of them before a delegation from the real-estate board called on us. The most outspoken delegate said frankly that, if we published any more of the pictures, he thought the real-estate board ought to boycott our advertising columns; the others talked mostly about what a reflection they were on our beautiful city. And, for one reason or the other, we cut our exposure of deplorable conditions very, very short.[30]

These cases show how very difficult is the position of a medium which provides necessarily both a business and a public service. The case is a perfect example of the conflict. The publisher faced a chain of arguments like this: I am a part of the business community. What is good for this community as a whole is good for me. Therefore I owe some obligation, for self-interest as well as for public obligation, not to do anything which might be against the best interests of the business community as a whole. Furthermore, these men are my friends. I don't want to hurt them. I don't want them to see me in the position of dirtying my own nest.

On the other hand, he is faced with this kind of argument: I am the eyes and ears, and sometimes the voice, of the people of this town. They count on me to tell them the truth, without fear or favor. They don't want me to censor the news in line with what I think will be good for them, or what the businessmen think will be good for *them*. They want the whole story. They want me to be honest with them.

You saw how the paper in Case 16 decided the question. I can't believe that the decision was wise or responsible. For one thing, it was clearly placing the interest of a group within the community above the interest of the general public. It was a near-sighted, rather than a far-sighted view. It made for happier realtors. But did it, over the space of years, make for a better community? Did it lay the groundwork for future distinguished service by the paper? Just the opposite. For having once given up its responsibility to the public in favor of its responsibility to its fellow business men, the paper will find it ever harder to make a contrary decision in the future. I would guess that the editor and publisher would have slept easier if they had decided the other way.

We could go on citing cases of this difficult but necessary relationship between the communicator and the advertiser, but let us stop here with one final observation.

The stronger a medium is—whether a newspaper, a magazine, or a broadcasting network or station—the less difficult this problem is for it. It can afford to be independent and weigh its other responsibilities against its obligation to its advertisers.

The Royal Commission on the Press came to the following conclusions about advertising influence on the press:

So far as is consistent with its general character, a newspaper which is not very strong financially will therefore probably avoid taking a line detrimental to advertisers' interests, unless by so doing it can increase its interest to the public. If people are not interested in attacks on brewers or patent medicines, the paper will not make them: if they are, it will.

A newspaper which is strong financially or able to command a market which advertisers are anxious to reach is under no necessity to have regard to the interest of advertisers where those interests conflict with its own policy. If it does have regard to those interests it is in comparatively trivial matters.[31]

What the Commission found to be true in Great Britain is also true here. And it points to the real strength of the mass media in this difficult relationship. The real source of strength is the public. If the media are doing a good job with the public, they can afford to keep on doing it according to their lights. The advertisers will have to come to them. The public will support them. They can take a temporary financial setback in confidence that the future is sound. They can afford to be their own bosses.

CONTROL THROUGH FAVORS

The kinds of decisions we have been talking about are made chiefly by top management. There is another kind of responsibility problem which is faced by the lower echelons. This is the problem of favors and gifts becoming so influential as to threaten the freedom of mind and choice which we want our mass communications to have.

Favors and gifts range all the way from part-time employment to bottles of liquor at Christmas. Let us look at a few examples:

Case 17. In 1949, the St. Louis *Post-Dispatch* and the Chicago *Daily News* revealed that 51 Illinois newspapermen were on the state payroll, *sub rosa*. Some seemed to be doing work, some did not. The implication generally was that these men were being rewarded for political services.

Case 18. In 1954, the Providence *Journal-Bulletin* exposed a situation in and around Boston, involving 36 newspapermen, 10 of whom were receiving payment on the side from the State Government, the others from various horse and greyhound racing tracks. Some of these men had received over $12,000 in three years; some were on a steady payroll at $90 a week, over and above their newspaper salaries.

The action of the press itself in these cases was not all it might have been. In the Illinois case, it was some time before the news agencies circulated the story and before it was widely reprinted. Then, however, there were expressions of indignation from newspapers generally. The employees of chain newspapers and some of the lesser Illinois newspaper men were fired, but many of the newspapermen in question were publishers or owners; they defended themselves somewhat lamely, and kept on publishing. In the Boston case, the chief phenomenon was the way the story fell like a wet washrag in

the newspapers of the country. There was little publicity and surprisingly little editorial comment.

Yet this is a shocking thing. Our whole concept of mass communication rests on the assumption that the media can be trusted to be
our eyes and ears in places where we cannot go, and especially to
check on government and on public enterprises generally. In Illinois
and Massachusetts the public was really being asked to believe that
a newsman could write objectively and fairly, and criticize where
necessary, a government that was paying him under the table.

The trade weekly, *Editor and Publisher*, was worried about it.
Why have the newspapers done no more to clean house, *E. & P.*
asked:

> Why? Is it because editors figure the practice of outside payments is
> so prevalent in the newspaper business that it is no longer news? Is it
> because they don't want to "stir up the animals" in their own backyards?
> Certainly the Illinois and Boston exposés create suspicion that similar
> situations exist to varying degrees in other metropolitan centers. . . .
> Periodic exposés of the Illinois and Massachusetts variety do not do the
> newspaper business any good. They leave readers with the impression
> that the same thing might exist locally. Only the newspapers themselves
> can find out if that is true, take steps to correct it, and let readers know
> what has been done in their interest.[32]

The magazine suggests a way to get rid of the practice:

> We suggest that every editor and publisher declare a period of amnesty
> for their employees for 30 days during which they be requested to reveal
> voluntarily and confidentially any outside employment. There would be
> no punishment or retaliation for past indiscretions. And if management
> found that such work in no way conflicted with the reporter's duties or
> the interests of the paper it might be continued by agreement.[33]

The Associated Press, which dismissed an employee in Boston
because he had received some money from one of the tracks, was
even sterner in its stated policy. "We deem it wholly untenable for
any staff member to receive anything of value from any news source,
irrespective of its character or purpose and also irrespective of whether
the individual is actually in a position to benefit or disadvantage the
news source," said Frank J. Starzel, general manager of the news
agency.[34]

"Anything of value" is a stricter requirement than most media hold to. Christmas presents are commonly given and accepted. Free tickets are commonly given and accepted, both when the reporter is covering an event and when he is not. Free transportation is often given and accepted. But let us here note down some cases that show what kinds of problems the practice brings.

Case 19. A famous heavy-weight champion said that in his early days he paid 5 per cent of his purses to reporters to help publicize him. It was apparently a common and accepted practice.

Do you like the idea of reading a sports page where the writers are being paid by some of the athletes they write about?

A daily newspaper sports editor says this:

Case 20. I've been worrying about how much I should accept from the athletic department of the university? Free tickets to the games? Extra tickets? Entertainment? Travel? Gifts at Christmas time? Where do you draw the line? When do you build up such an obligation that you aren't any longer free to criticize?

Another example of this kind:

Case 21. The Cincinnati *Enquirer* forbade its employees to use complimentary tickets for the circus, except for the reporter and cameraman assigned to cover the opening performance. The *Enquirer* said that the tickets were taking the place of advertising.

This was reported by a city editor in a small town:

Case 22. Our paper accepted free season tickets to the movie theaters for ten of the editorial and advertising staffs. But by tacit agreement we were supposed to publish a pre-written story about the new films when the program changed. And when one of the reporters wanted to start a column of movie criticism, the advertising manager said that was contrary to the agreement with the theaters.

This came from a city reporter:

Case 23. We commonly exchange "courtesies" with the law enforcement officials. For instance, we neglect to notice that half a dozen bottles of whiskey are *not* destroyed after a raid, and the police on a beat neglect to notice a reporter's car parked too long in front of a fire hydrant.

The truth is, as the AP general manager said, that "anything of value" passing between newsmen and their sources is potentially dangerous and limiting. The writer may never think of it that way. He may feel that he can be completely objective about the news source. And yet, can he? Will a fifth of whiskey at Christmas time, from a friendly news source, influence you the next time you write about him? Will a free ticket to the motion picture theaters limit your freedom in writing about those theaters?

Here are two cases in which the "favors" were of considerable size:

Case 24. (From a metropolitan newspaper). A young reporter covering the financial beat received, for Christmas, a sealed envelope from an investment banking firm. Inside was a $100 bill.

"Just a remembrance at Christmas," a company official told him. There were no visible strings.

Knowing that he would continue to cover the financial beat, the reporter decided he could not accept the gift and still provide objective coverage of the company.

He mailed the bill back to the firm in a registered letter which explained his position.

Case 25. In the 1930s this reporter had a chance to make money out of his beat. A stockbroker offered to place his name on a "preferred list" of persons entitled to buy a new stock issue at the issue price. This meant the reporter could sell the shares for a profit at the higher market price after the issue was put on sale. The broker offered him $500 worth of the stock at issue price. The reporter knew other newsmen were participating in preferred lists. Even publishers were subscribing to new issues in this manner, and probably in much greater amounts. He decided that taking this opportunity for a fast profit would not influence his reporting the news of that stock or any news from the brokerage house that offered him a place on the preferred list. And he made a "modest" profit.

These cases both raise the same problem: is there any chance that this favor is limiting the freedom of the newsman to report and comment? The reporter in Case 24 thought it would; the reporter in Case 25, that it would not.

One of the commonest and most elaborate kinds of favors is the "press party." Merchants and manufacturers give them. University athletic departments give them. Publishers give them. Promoters and political parties give them. The ingredients aren't always the same, but usually they include drinks, food, and entertainment. Robert U. Brown, editor of *Editor and Publisher*, described a few of the more elaborate ones:

Schenley Distributors, Inc., [threw a] party for the first American importation of Canadian Schenley OFS, Original Fine Canadian. It seems that the first shipment was due in New York aboard the SS President Monroe. So a special car on a New Haven Railroad train was arranged to take the press representatives from New York to Boston, limousines in Boston, limousines to the waterfront, and an overnight trip on the Monroe to New York. The letter of invitation said: "I know you will thoroughly enjoy it, for we are prepared with sumptuous cuisine and delightful entertainment." An *E. & P.* staffer noted: "And with a boatload of whiskey, it sounds like the perfect lost weekend."

Chrysler entertained 500 newsmen who traveled to Detroit to view its "Theater in the Round" which included dancers, models, three bars, a 12-piece band, food—and the new cars.

Later 200 newsmen came to Detroit from all over the country, some by chartered plane provided by the host, to see the new Buick. A special train took them to Flint. After an elaborate luncheon, the "show" was put on in the Civic Auditorium—"Dynarama"—a stage show musical with a cast of 50 and a 30-piece orchestra. Of course the show theme had something to do with Buick—followed by the cars and the sales pitch. Oldsmobile put on "an Arabian Nights Fantasy" in Lansing with "26 Broadway and Hollywood actors." Chevrolet entertained at the G.M. proving grounds where the cars were shown, then back to Detroit for a big dinner with entertainment. Etc.[35]

Mr. Brown concludes that most of this is a waste of the newsmen's time and the advertiser's money. Certainly newsmen have a legitimate interest in the new cars, and they have to eat on the day they see them. But the very elaborateness of the program raises suspicion. Obviously every effort is being made to get the news written favorably about this new product. Is a newsman limiting his freedom when he accepts this food, drink, transportation, and entertainment?

I think the writing on the wall is clear: that the way ahead has little place for such favors. Bribes in the form of outside employment are now discredited. Elaborate gifts are looked on with suspicion. The more careful information media are inclined to turn down free tickets, food, and transportation except for working reporters and photographers, and some papers and magazines even insist on paying the way of the reporters they send to cover a story. Questions are being raised even about the press party.

I expect it will more and more come to be that the representative of an information medium will recognize the uniqueness of his position—that he is not in the same position as a businessman; that his freedom to write and comment must be bought at the price of acting like a professional man and maintaining the most scrupulous relationship with his news sources. And it may be hoped that news media sometime in the future will pay their reporters and photographers enough so that it will no longer be such a temptation to cadge free food and drinks, or take other favors or gifts.

Control Through Pressure Groups

These threats to freedom are perceived differently by different observers. The average mass communicator is most afraid of government regulation. The average social science critic has most to say about control by advertisers. The average layman is inclined to be most concerned over the influence of pressure groups.

And it is true that if one could in some way measure the area and intensity of outside pressures on the mass media—if there were some kind of foot-pound unit to apply—then probably the pressure groups would get top rating. For their pressure is continuing and broad, and is applied from top to bottom of the media structure.

There is nothing wrong with the idea of pressure groups. Indeed it is only through organization that the public can effectively represent its position to large communication organizations. The problem of responsibility which pressure groups bring to the mass media is one of weighing and balancing the complaints and suggestions from these groups. Responsible behavior does not consist in automatically rejecting and resisting the representations of these groups. It consists rather in considering the wishes of each group in relation to the needs of the public as a whole.

The editor of a strong Iowa newspaper described to Dr. Charles E. Swanson the chief pressures on him and his staff. Among them he listed:

1. Liberalism vs. conservatism. ("The strongest pressure that operates on our staff is one of liberalism vs. conservatism. Some of our staff members go to the clubs and they get this sort of pressure . . .")

2. Labor unions. ("We're careful about the unions because their feelings are hurt so easily. I was a _____ union member for seven years. I lean to management's side because their arguments are better. But I'm conscious of that. So we lean over backwards to be careful about the union side.")

3. Organizations. ("All the organizations want more publicity for whatever cause they're supporting.")

4. Religion. ("We get some [pressure] from the Protestants when we run news about the Catholics.")

5. Politics. ("We don't pay much attention to that. As long as the Democrats and Republicans squawk about us, we're all right.")

6. Advertisers. ("We've made about a half dozen 'mistakes' in news about a major advertiser in the last year, and he thinks we're against him. For example, the OPA fined him on some technical violation of the law. We ran the story. He thought it should have been left out. We couldn't do that. So he thought it should have been played down —a smaller head.")[36]

How do pressure groups actually operate to influence a newspaper or magazine? By every available channel. By sending committees or executive secretaries to call on the publisher or top editors. By telephone calls or letters—sometimes official, sometimes in organized but informal campaigns—of protest or compliment. By the relatively subtle method of personal influence and friendly contact at clubs or other social or business occasions. By favors, parties, entertainment. By threats. By making well-organized arguments available to editorial writers or reporters.

One rather frightening example of this last technique was cited by A. Gayle Waldrop in *Nieman Reports*.[37] He recalled "an extraordinary exhibit" of what appeared to be "an identical editorial appearing in 59 newspapers, without identification of its source. Its source," he went on to explain, "was the *Industrial News Review,* a clip sheet of E. Hofer and Sons of Portland, Oreg." The sheet is "distributed in the interests of private power companies and similar interests and financed by them." There is nothing wrong about clip sheets. They are often highly useful to an editor, and are used by many pressure groups from the government of the United States down to local industry. But this example of a large number of newspapers surrendering their editorial columns to a pressure group, without identifying the source of the comments, is hardly an example of responsible editing. If it is universally regarded as unfair and irresponsible not to inform the reader of the source of a news story, then what can be said of the practice of hiding from the public the source of an editorial?

On the whole, newspapers and magazines are somewhat less susceptible to pressure groups than are broadcasting and films. The motion picture industry, the Commission on Freedom of the Press concluded, "offers the most elaborate picture of accommodation to the pressure of the audience [meaning pressure groups]." This accommodation, said the Commission, "may not have gone quite so far as the present Code executive says it would have to go to satisfy all protestors: it has not limited the villain of the screen to 'a native-born, white, American citizen, without a job and without any political, social, religious, or fraternal affiliations of any kind.' But pressure groups, because they have or are thought to have influence on attendance, have shaped the motion picture to their desires."[38]

The motion picture is particularly vulnerable to such pressure because it is so open to the public gaze. Its total product is represented not by tens of thousands of news stories and editorials, nor by tens of thousands of programs, but rather by 300-400 major products a year, all of which are shown in all major cities. It is national, rather than local, and its point of origin is almost exclusively Hollywood—therefore it is easy to attack at the source. Furthermore, unlike the printed media, it has only one source of support.

Therefore the chief weapon of the pressure groups against the film industry is the threat, implicit or explicit, of boycott. Undoubtedly the strongest pressure on American entertainment films comes from the Roman Catholic church; especially from the Legion of Decency, which publishes a rating of all films in terms of their moral acceptability. There is some disagreement as to the effectiveness of this rating. Its A rating (A I means morally unobjectionable for general patronage, A II morally unobjectionable for adults) is regarded as advantageous audience-wise to a film. But a B rating from the Legion (meaning morally objectionable, in part, for all) is regarded by most of the industry as not serious. A C rating, however, meaning "condemned," frightens the industry. This rating threatens an organized boycott among Catholics, and also possibly additional pressure: for example, pressure from Catholic groups to pass restrictive legislation, or to sharpen the teeth of state or municipal censorship. Less than 3 per cent of all films reviewed in an ordinary year are given C ratings, but the possibility of such a rating hangs over the industry and leads it to be extremely careful of items that might offend the Catholics.

Again, let us be clear that the activities of a religious pressure group are not necessarily dangerous to freedom. There is a clear distinction to be drawn between the activities of a religious organization which are aimed at controlling the organization's own members and those

which are aimed at determining what the community outside the
organization may do. The first case is merely exercising church counsel
and discipline and is unobjectionable. The second may be interference
with free speech and press. In practical terms, there can be no objection to an effort of a religious organization to keep its own members from seeing a film, but when that organization tries to keep the
theater owner from showing the film or when it pickets the theater
in an effort to keep other people out, then that may well be a questionable pressure group activity.

There is no intention of implying that the Catholic organizations
are the only well-organized pressure groups affecting the making of
Hollywood films. Says Hortense Powdermaker:

> Complaints pile into the MPAA office from individuals and organiza-
> tions. The Women's Christian Temperance Union complained bitterly
> . . . over the number of Oscars going to pictures or actors portraying
> alcoholics. . . . The State Department, interested in carrying out a Good
> Neighbor policy with Mexico, asked that 152 feet of a film be reshot
> because it had shown some mass scenes with a number of Mexican
> children barefooted. . . . The burlesque of a United States senator . . .
> was protested. . . . Negro organizations protest stereotyping. Jews protest
> the making of *Oliver Twist*. Protestants complain that Catholic por-
> trayals are more favored than Protestant ones. . . . Parent-Teachers'
> organizations protest violence. . . . Members of various occupational
> groups, doctors, judges, lawyers, policemen and many others, remon-
> strate against the way they are portrayed. . . .[39]

If the complaints from members of religious, professional, racial and
national groups were all heeded, Miss Powdermaker concluded, it
would be impossible to make any picture with a villain in it!

This pressure on the film industry is heavy and continuous, operating through protests, formal or informal, to the Motion Picture Association (the code) office, or to a state or local censorship board or
through such rating guides as the bulletin of the National Legion
of Decency, and always with the threat of boycott or of legal restriction on censorship in the background.

An illustration of the way in which private pressure groups inter-
lock with governmental pressures on films is this case of "The Miracle," as told by Edwin S. Newman in *The Freedom Reader*:

> *Case* 26. The case of "The Miracle," an Italian motion picture film
> with English subtitles, had a double significance for the problem of

censorship in America. First, there is the legally significant development that through its opinion in this case, the Supreme Court extended the protection of the First Amendment to motion pictures. Prior to its decision in "The Miracle," a 1915 ruling was in force that motion pictures are entertainment and, as such, not entitled to the guarantees of freedom of expression. Second, the controversy itself was initiated and nourished by the attempt of private persons and agencies, representing a segment of opinion among Roman Catholics, to bar the showing of the film on the grounds that it was "blasphemous" and "sacrilegious." . . .

"The Miracle" was licensed by the State of New York and was offered at the Paris Theater in New York City, along with two other features, together titled, "The Ways of Love." A private organization within the Roman Catholic faith, the Legion of Decency, attacked the film as objectionable and urged movie-goers not to patronize it. To effect this end, picket lines were set up by Catholic War Veterans outside the Paris Theater; counter-pickets were stationed by other organizations which protested the attempt at boycott and censorship. At this point, the New York City Commissioner of Licenses declared the film "officially and personally blasphemous" and ordered it withdrawn at the risk of suspension of the theater's license to operate. The New York Supreme Court (lower court) held that the license commissioner had exceeded his authority, and, within one week of the closing, the film was again on the boards at the Paris. His Eminence Francis Cardinal Spellman, Archbishop of New York, soon thereafter condemned the picture from his pulpit and urged " all right-thinking citizens" to unite to tighten censorship laws. This set off a controversy among laymen and clergymen active in their various faiths and denominations. Even among Catholics there was not unanimity of opinion on the objectionable character of "The Miracle."

In view of the controversy, the chairman of the New York Board of Regents appointed a committee of three Board members to review the propriety of the licenses originally granted by the Motion Picture Division. After viewing the picture, the committee declared it to be "sacrilegious," and after hearing extended to the licensees, cancelled the licenses. The New York Appellate Division and the Court of Appeals (highest court) affirmed this action, and the matter was then brought to the U. S. Supreme Court.[40]

The Court ruled, as we have mentioned, that censorship of motion pictures on the grounds of being "sacrilegious" is unconstitutional. Similar verdicts, as we have indicated, have been given whenever a film has been censored for being "immoral" or "tending to promote crime" or "inciting race tension," whenever such cases have been carried to the Supreme Court by the producers or distributors.

Much the same kind of pressure operates on the broadcast industry, which has its network headquarters in New York and therefore is relatively easy to get at. Pressure groups working on the networks always have two threats implicit in their pockets: that they can exert influence on the advertisers who are the sources of broadcasting's support, and that they can exert influence on the Congress to pass stricter laws regulating broadcasting and on the FCC to exercise more rigorously its regulatory powers. Of these, the stronger threat has to do with the government. Broadcasting lives only by virtue of channels assigned it by the government. The fear of the broadcaster is, therefore, that pressure groups dissatisfied with broadcasts will influence legislation in an unfavorable direction. So far as advertisers are concerned, the fear is that dissatisfied pressure groups will lead them to withdraw their sponsorship of a program. Advertisers naturally want the largest possible audiences. They want pleased audiences, not audiences who will turn some of their disaffection for the program toward the product being advertised. Therefore, they are skittish about anything that looks like broad or organized objection, and the networks are skittish about the prospect of the advertisers becoming skittish.

That makes it sound simple. It isn't simple. These pressures and forces are subtle and many-sided. To a person observing them from outside they seem somewhat like microchemistry: that is, the network must assay a very small sample of what may be a very large force. Broadcasting's feedback from its audience is so slight that it has to make very important judgments on the basis of a comparatively few letters or telephone calls. "Twenty-five letters will often set a network on its ear," a prominent broadcaster told me. "One telephone call will do it, if it comes from a sufficiently important source. One editorial in the Hearst Press can be very bothersome." The networks' sensitivity to such symptoms depends on where the letters and the calls come from, and the subject matter they deal with. Some subject matters are far more delicate than others. Religion is one. Loyalty is another. General morality is a third.

How these combinations work may be illustrated by what happened in the following case.

Case 27. A well known entertainment personality made the remark on a pre-Christmas program, "let's have one Christmas program on which no one sings 'Silent Night.'" This seems like a relatively innocuous remark, and was made in the spirit of levity, yet for one reason or another it blew up a storm. For one thing it was obliquely related to religion. Certain religious groups picked it up and complained. The issue was attractive to sentimentalists, who complained that the network was attacking fundamental American values. To make things worse, the man who made it had been the subject of certain rumors (of a kind which start very easily in the entertainment industries) dealing with his membership in or association with Communist-front groups. Therefore, some high-placed and articulate persons linked the seeming irreligion to a political bias and cried "Commie!"

An advertising agency is said to have picked up the complaints, and put on its own pressure about a "Commie, atheist" performer. There was talk of letters to members of Congress and to the FCC. Therefore, although only about 200 letters had been received, the network found itself with a real crisis. Even then, it might have been possible to solve the problem by a good-humored apology on the next week's program. But by that time the performer had his own back up. The network had to issue a formal apology and take the performer temporarily off the air.

One way that political pressures operate on the media is illustrated by what happened to *Time* magazine in 1952. In November of 1951 *Time* ran a cover story about Senator Joseph McCarthy which was not entirely complimentary. A few months later, eleven national advertisers received a letter from the Senator reading in part:

Time's advertisers make it possible for the Luce chain to send into millions of American homes . . . dishonest, twisted news. . . . Many of those advertisers are militantly anti-Communist and intensely American. When I know they are not aware of the facts and because of that are unknowingly helping to pollute and poison the waterholes of information, I have a duty to bring that to their attention.[41]

Another, and particularly insidious, way of bringing political pressure is illustrated by what happened in Wisconsin in connection with the "Joe Must Go" campaign. It will be recalled that LeRoy Gore, editor of the weekly Sauk City *Prairie Star*, expressed his opposition to Senator McCarthy with a "Joe Must Go" club. He lost his battle and was forced to sell his paper. Then the leader of the opposition "Door for Gore" club undertook to put newspapers in their place. He warned the new editors of the paper: "If they keep their noses clean, they'll be all right. Expressing political opinions in newspapers in small communities just isn't the thing to do. Newspapers in places around Sauk City get along well by staying out of politics."[42]

Any student of communication history will recognize this for what it is: a straight throwback to authoritarian control of the media. It implies that the power group will determine what political ideas, if any, may be expressed in the media. This is what the whole libertarian revolution fought against. Fortunately, the Wisconsin Press Association recognized the threat and reacted. "We don't believe we would be doing our duty," they said, "if we were to slink down the back alleys, afraid to open our mouths to express an opinion on any subject that might be in the least bit controversial." And *Editor and Publisher* said, "It is an outright negation of the basic American principle of free exchange of ideas."[43]

It must not be supposed that all this pressure is on political grounds or from political sources. Philip Graham tells how the Washington *Post* reported the arrest of 20 ministers in Washington for failing to file marriage licenses. "The response was really incredible," he said. "Five of them canceled their church advertising. We said, 'Look, isn't that what you speak against when the distilling companies do that?' Five more said, 'We always thought we didn't mention the newspapers and you didn't mention the churches.' "[44]

The most common weapon of the pressure group is to threaten the financial support of a medium. Here are a few examples:

Case 28. Forever Amber was given a C rating by the Legion of Decency, meaning that it was "condemned." Cardinal Spellman declared in a letter to all pastors in his diocese, a letter which was read at masses: "I advise that Catholics may not see this production with a safe conscience." Cardinal Dougherty, in Philadelphia, gave an ultimatum to the Fox Theater to withdraw the film within 48 hours or be faced with a boycott on that theater and all other theaters in his diocese henceforth playing a film from the same studio. The studio cut and revised the film in consultation with the Legion, then made a public apology. The picture's rating was changed to B.

Case 29. (Reported by the editor of a small-town daily). The biggest department store in my town made noises as though it would withhold its advertising if I continued my campaign for an educational television station at the State university. The Taxpayers Association, to which this store belongs, is against the station as a waste of state funds. I know that *The New York Times* and the Chicago *Tribune* and so forth have let advertising accounts go on principle, and the advertisers have had to come back after a few months. They could afford it, but I'm not sure we could stand the loss of $200 a week. And, after all, it doesn't matter much to me personally whether the University gets its station. I've just been supporting it on principle. Maybe it's a question of do we live, or do we stand on principle?

Case 30. Ray Tucker wrote a column about the struggle among airlines for international routes, in which he discussed Pan American's lobbying activities. The day before the column was to be printed, Pan American's public relations manager sent the following telegram to all papers subscribing to the syndicated service which distributes Tucker's columns: "Pan American understands that you may be planning to publish a column by Ray Tucker containing numerous scurrilous references to Pan American. We feel it our duty to tell you that we believe a number of these statements to be libelous. You may also wish to take into consideration the columnist's obvious bias against the airline that has earned for the United States first place in world air transport." Many papers did not use the column.

As we have said, there is nothing basically wrong with the idea that pressure groups may convey their ideas and recommendations to mass media. The media, on their part, have every reason to consider these protests and suggestions most seriously. The only element of responsibility involved here is that the particular wishes and recommendations of the pressure groups should be considered in relation to the general public good. It is not always possible to please all groups equally. What pleases one group may very well be inimical to the interests of many other groups. Therefore, the media must be prepared to resist where it is desirable to do so.

The curve of willingness to resist runs upward from the film industry through broadcasting to the printed media. The motion pictures are least willing to resist a pressure group. Indeed, there is surprisingly little resistance. Insofar as possible, Hollywood tries to please everyone. It seldom fights back. And this in spite of the fact that in many cases a little trouble with censorship may help the box office, so long as the trouble does not go as far as a full-dress boycott. Hollywood's submissive attitude toward pressure groups contrasts with the militant posture taken by book publishers, dealing with the same material. For instance, take the case of *Forever Amber*. Book publishers fought through the courts and won their battle to present that story as written, whereas Hollywood at first made militant sounds but soon capitulated to the opposition.

The broadcasters are inclined to raise stiffer backs against pressure groups than are the film men, but the really firm opposition is found

in the printed media. These media are older, they have a stronger
libertarian tradition, and they deal in larger proportion with information as opposed to entertainment. Freedom of information is perhaps
easier to defend on ideological grounds. In any case there is in the
printed media a fine history of responsible conduct with relation to
pressure groups. One of the best examples of this we can give is the
reaction of the New York *Times* to what it considered "harassment"
by the Eastland Committee of the Senate. The *Times'* editorial tells
the story so well that we are going to reprint it in full:

The Voice of a Free Press: In executive hearings held recently in this
city, in public hearings held last summer in Washington, and now again
in public hearings held in Washington, a Senate subcommittee headed
by Senator James O. Eastland of Mississippi has been looking for
evidence of what it considers to be subversive infiltration of the press.
A number of employes of this newspaper have been called to appear as
witnesses before the subcommittee.

We do not question the right or the propriety of any investigation of
the press by any agency of Congress. The press is not sacrosanct. It is
as properly subject to Congressional inquiry as any other institution in
American life. It is the inescapable responsibility of Congress, however,
to make certain that any such inquiry be conducted in good faith and
not motivated by ulterior purpose.

A few employes of this newspaper who have appeared before the Eastland subcommittee have pleaded the Fifth Amendment. A few others
have testified to membership in the Communist party over periods
terminating at various dates in the past. So far as we are aware, no present
member of the Communist party has been found among the more than
four thousand employes on our rolls.

The policy of this newspaper with regard to the employment of
Communist party members has been stated many times, and may be
stated here again. We would not knowingly employ a Communist party
member in the news or editorial departments of this paper, because we
would not trust his ability to report the news objectively or to comment
on it honestly, and the discovery of present Communist party membership
on the part of such an employe would lead to his immediate dismissal.

In the case of those employes who have testified to some Communist
association in the past, or who have pleaded the Fifth Amendment for
reasons of their own, it will be our policy to judge each case on its own
merits, in the light of each individual's responsibilities in our organization
and of the degree to which his relations with this newspaper entitle
him to possess our confidence.

We may say this, however. We do not believe in the doctrine of irredeemable sin. We think it possible to atone through good performance for past error, and we have tried to supply the security and the favorable working conditions which should exist in a democracy and which should encourage men who were once misled to reconsider and to reshape their political thinking.

We have judged these men, and we shall continue to judge them, by the quality of their work and by our confidence in their ability to perform that work satisfactorily. It is our own business to decide whom we shall employ and not employ. We do not propose to hand over that function to the Eastland subcommittee.

Nor do we propose to permit the Eastland subcommittee, or any other agency outside this office, to determine in any way the policies of this newspaper. It seems to us quite obvious that the Eastland investigation has been aimed with particular emphasis at The New York *Times*. This is evident from several facts: from the heavy concentration of subpoenas served on employes of this newspaper, from the nature of the examination conducted at earlier hearings by the subcommittee's counsel, Mr. Sourwine, and from that counsel's effort, at those hearings, to demonstrate some connection between a witness' one-time association with the Communist party and the character of the news published in this paper.

It seems to us to be a further obvious conclusion that The *Times* has been singled out for this attack precisely because of the vigor of its opposition to many of the things for which Mr. Eastland, his colleague Mr. Jenner, and the subcommittee's counsel stand—that is, because we have condemned segregation in the Southern Schools; because we have challenged the high-handed and abusive methods employed by various Congressional committees; because we have denounced McCarthyism and all its works; because we have attacked the narrow and bigoted restrictions of the McCarran Immigration Act; because we have criticized a "security system" which conceals the accuser from his victim; because we have insisted that the true spirit of American democracy demands a scrupulous respect for the rights of even the lowliest individual and a high standard of fair play.

If this is the tactic of any member of the Eastland subcommittee, and if further evidence reveals that the real purpose of the present inquiry is to demonstrate that a free newspaper's policies can be swayed by Congressional pressure, then we say to Mr. Eastland and his counsel that they are wasting their time. This newspaper will continue to determine its own policies. It will continue to condemn discrimination, whether in the South or in the North. It will continue to defend civil liberties. It will continue to challenge the unbridled power of governmental authority. It will continue to enlist goodwill against prejudice and confidence against fear.

We cannot speak unequivocally for the long future. But we can have faith. And our faith is strong that long after Senator Eastland and his present subcommittee are forgotten, long after segregation has lost its final battle in the South, long after all that was known as McCarthyism is a dim, unwelcome memory, long after the last Congressional committee has learned that it cannot tamper successfully with a free press, The New York *Times* will still be speaking for the men who make it, and only for the men who make it, and speaking, without fear or favor, the truth as it sees it.[45]

CONTROL BY MANIPULATION

"We cannot say, 212 years after Jefferson was born, that our country is unalterably devoted to the principles of full information and free discussion which he made the basis of his life commitment," wrote J. Edward Gerald in a lecture on "Freedom in Mass Communication." He continued:

Men everywhere take more pains to interpret facts selfishly than they do to promote unrestricted communication. Sales talk is the bane of our political and business life. A newspaper which undertakes to report a national election, for example, finds less concern with standards of fairness than with demands for evangelism or partisanship.

Political parties and other special interest groups do not seem to want honest, ruggedly independent newspapers, but newspapers which will help them win elections, influence legislation, or pull the wool over the eyes of the people. The public never sees the parade of persons through newspaper offices in search of special advantage for themselves or their associates, and journalists have become so accustomed to the experience that, like bad weather or a nasty head cold, they take it in their stride.[46]

As Professor Gerald suggests, this is the disillusioning experience which every idealistic newcomer to the news media must expect: a very large proportion of the people who bring him news are not trying to help him, they are trying to use him. They are consciously trying to use the media for a manipulative purpose.

This is legal. It sometimes can be—often is—defended as an assistance to the newsgatherer. Thus the news bureau of the large governmental or industrial organization explains that it is in business to help the reporter get the information he needs. But there are two aspects of this manipulative practice which are especially threatening to the free flow of news, and these we must mention here.

Recently there was published a novel by J. G. Schneider, *The Golden Kazoo*.[47] This is a light-hearted fantasy on a future Presidential campaign in the United States. The campaign, it develops, is being fought out between advertising agencies. The candidates themselves are mere shadows. The political parties are not very important. The agencies, with their great manipulative skill and their command of the media, are the real actors.

There is just enough truth in *The Golden Kazoo* to send a cold chill down the backs of its more serious readers. For when one turns from this piece of imaginative fiction to a sober, solid book of scholarship, *Professional Public Relations and Political Power*, by Stanley Kelley, Jr., of the Brookings Institution, one finds documentation for much of the fiction. This book is a study of the part public relations has played in recent political campaigns. Kelley describes the activities of Campaigns, Inc. (Whitaker and Baxter) of California, in support of various candidates and of such causes as the American Medical Association's campaign against government health insurance; of Jon M. Jonkel, of Chicago, in the Butler campaign against Senator Tydings in Maryland; and of the various agencies which contributed the professional public relations skill to the 1952 Presidential campaign. Clearly, professional public relations is playing a more and more dominant part in contemporary politics:

At the national level [says Kelley] both major parties have had publicity specialists since Michelson and West took up their respective duties. The present public relations departments of the Republican National Committee and the Republican Congressional Campaign Committee are, in effect, commercial public relations agencies performing political functions. While themselves offering propaganda services, they have encouraged each of their party's candidates to retain his own counsellor, and many of the administrative assistants of congressional office-holders are in reality public relations men. The Democratic National Committee likewise now advises Democratic candidates to retain professional advertising and publicity experts.[48]

Increasingly, of late years, election campaigns have come to be stage-managed as carefully as theater or television. An important political appearance before the television camera is planned as painstakingly as a top network show, and a press conference or news release is designed as minutely as a battle plan. Public relations men help select the issues, and in some cases even help pick the candidates. A candidate is in a bad way without professional public relations counsel; at an early stage in the 1956 campaign much sympathy was expressed because one of the parties, somewhat low in funds, was said to be having a hard time finding an agency to take its business.

Well, what is wrong with all that? Hasn't a party, or a candidate, or an industry the right to present a case to the public in the best possible form?

Of course he has and it has that right. Our theory of communication freedom implies a free market place of ideas, in which all points of view have a fair chance to be heard, and opponents can confront one another in free and fair debate. What worries observers like Kelley is that this new kind of campaigning makes it more difficult, if not impossible, for the free market place of ideas to function.

To enter into this kind of campaigning, a candidate or the promoter of a cause must have two prerequisites: skill and money. If he has the money, he can buy much of the skill he needs from Whitaker and Baxter, or one of the other public relations agencies. But what does it mean to our concept of communication freedom to have political discussion increasingly monopolized by a restricted skill group? And what does it mean to our concept of political democracy to have such a high price tag put on political success? Presidential campaigns now are costing around 100 million dollars. Approximately eight million dollars is believed to have been spent in the last California election by the opponents and proponents of a single one of the two dozen or so state constitutional changes listed on the ballot. Whitaker and Baxter represented one side in this particular contest. And it has been pointed out that whereas Richard Nixon, during the 1952 campaign, could defend his financial record to 18 million people for only $75,000, which is about two fifths of a cent per person, still he could not have done so if he had not had $75,000 behind him.

Kelley quotes a decision of the U. S. Supreme Court regarding the advertising expenditures of the big three tobacco manufacturers. Says the court:

The record is full of evidence of the close relationship between their large expenditures for national advertising of cigarettes and resulting volume of sales. . . . Such advertising is not here criticized as a business expense. Such advertising may benefit indirectly the entire industry, including competitors of the advertisers. Such tremendous advertising, however, is also a widely published warning that these companies possess and know how to use a powerful offensive and defensive weapon against new competition. New competition dare not enter such a field, unless it be well supported by comparable national advertising.[49]

It is hard to see, Kelley says, why the Court's reasoning does not apply equally to competition in the merchandising of ideas.[50] This is the question which thoughtful observers of the media are now asking: Is this professional manipulation restricting the free market place? Are the entrance fees in money and skill keeping out many of the participants who should be heard from?

Furthermore, the whole spirit of this kind of manipulation is opposed to the idea of free debate. The intent of the public relations specialist, in fact what he is paid for, is not to get his client an even chance to be heard, but rather to get him a differential advantage in the use of the media. The techniques he uses are not those of the town meeting; they are the techniques of propaganda. If he can get his client a wider hearing than the opponent, why should he waste time on debating a question? To set up the kind of dialectic which Walter Lippmann proposes as the ideal of public communication,[51] or the kind of debate which the founders of our government envisaged as the process of political decision, would be to let the initiative and control of matters go out of the expert's hands. That would never do! The way in which these expert manipulators have entered into recent campaigns is, to say the least, eye-opening. When Jonkel took over the Butler campaign in Maryland, he found a little-known candidate with no special issues, facing a candidate who was well and favorably known. Jonkel made the campaign into a "merchandising of doubt", directing hatred and suspicion and prejudice toward Tydings. In fact, as you read the record of that campaign, it seems not so much to be Butler vs. Tydings as Jonkel vs. Tydings.[52] And so in many other campaigns: the experts choose the issues, tell the candidates what to do, control the image of the candidate which gets to the people. This is very far from the spirit of the free market place as we have understood it.

Edward L. Bernays, who has been the most articulate spokesman for public relations, speaks of this function of the public relations process as "the engineering of consent." He says: "The voice of the people expresses the mind of the people, and that mind is made up for it by group leaders in whom it believes and by those persons who understand the manipulation of opinion. . . . The sincere and gifted politician is able, by the instrument of propaganda, to mold and form the will of the people."[53] This is very far from the spirit of Milton and Mill. One wonders whether, if the sincere and gifted politician can do so, an *insincere* politician cannot do the same, provided he is gifted with "persons who understand the manipulation of opinion," and with enough money to pay them. In fact, as one well-known broadcaster said recently after watching a drippy political performance on the air, "If the American people don't learn to spot a phony on television, God help them!"

Now what does all this mean to the mass communicator? He can't reverse the trend toward public relations counsels and propaganda techniques in campaigns aimed at domestic public opinion, but he can at least be aware that here is one of the great forces which may impinge on the free market place. He can be more than a common carrier to transport whatever the expert manipulators give him. He has an obligation of his own to see that all pertinent sides of a question get an airing. He has the same obligation that earlier editors had, to seek out truth wherever it is hidden, to unmask falsehood, half-truths, double dealing, and chicanery. The first act of a dictator is usually to seize the mass media. Some people have been afraid that it might now be theoretically possible to "seize" the media by skill and ability to pay, and accomplish something of the same thing which dictators accomplish by force. However fantastic this may seem, the media are the first line of defense against any moves of that kind. They are the outposts. A well-propagandized public looks to them for warning and guidance.

We have been talking about the more spectacular manifestations of public relations in the media. A much simpler and more pervasive kind of public relations activity is visible every day and in every copy of every newspaper. This is the placing of a skilled public relations man or men between an important news source and the news-gatherers. Hardly a government bureau or department head now but handles its news through a press officer or the equivalent. Hardly a business or industry of any size handles its news except through this kind of expert representation. The editors of *Fortune* estimate that nearly half the contents of the nation's better newspapers now comes from publicity releases.[54]

There is nothing against having handouts carefully prepared to present the affairs of an organization in the best light. There is nothing against having a press or public relations officer to prevent public relations mistakes. There is nothing against having a press or public relations officer to protect some of the time of a busy executive, because otherwise the communication system might break down under the sheer overload of communication imposed on the top man. Moreover, newsgatherers usually admit frankly that they could hardly do their job today without the help of press officers, because the job of news coverage has become so enormous and so complex. Indeed, the press officer or the news bureau often performs the service of a middle man or translator, putting the news in terms the reporter and his audience can understand, and answering the questions the reporter asks in order to clarify his own understanding of the item. This is especially important when the news is highly technical, whether scientific, economic, or political. And many a reporter would waste valuable time without the guidance of a press officer in covering a large organization, because the press officer does not always prevent him from seeing an executive: more often, the press officer helps him find the *right* executive.

But, on the other hand, there is always a potential element of danger when the give-and-take between news source and newsgatherer is replaced by a relationship between an expert news manipulator and an expert reporter. What is the responsibility of the media in this situation? To be aware of what is going on. To recognize manipulation for what it is, to make allowance for it in reporting, to be a bit more suspicious than they might ordinarily be, to try unceasingly to get access to news sources which must be seen face to face in order to be reported adequately, and always to try to report the news behind the façade.

The responsible newsman must be skeptical of any manipulation of the news channels, major or minor, apparently benign or apparently malignant, political or economic or social or military. He will question it, and if he has real doubts he will pass them on to his readers.

THE BEST DEFENSE IS A GOOD OFFENSE

Looking back over the preceding pages, I am somewhat worried lest the responsibility of mass communication in regard to freedom be interpreted as a purely defensive one. Nothing is farther from my intention. The communicator must, of course, fight every government incursion into the content of his medium. He must be wary of pressure groups, influences, and favors. He must be alert to manipulation. He must make every effort to defend the free flow of his channel. But, as in competitive athletics, his best defense will be a good offense. The best way he can protect his freedom is to use it responsibly.

Defense of communication freedom is basically, therefore, a positive rather than a negative strategy. It is not chiefly a series of protests and court cases, a sort of border action against encroachments. It is basically a strong policy of using freedom in the spirit of our political system. That is to say, the use of freedom to feed and nurture the free market place of ideas. The use of freedom to bring about the kind of public debate from which truth is expected to emerge in a democracy. The use of freedom to meet the communication needs of all segments of one's audience. But we might talk endlessly about this without saying any more than the American Library Association and the American Book Publishing Council put into their eloquent May 1953 statement on "The Freedom to Read." which will make a good conclusion for this chapter.

"We affirm these propositions," the manifesto says:

1. *It is in the public interest for publishers and librarians to make available the widest diversity of views and expressions, including those which are unorthodox or unpopular with the majority.*

Creative thought is by definition new, and what is new is different. The bearer of every new thought is a rebel until his idea is refined and tested. Totalitarian systems attempt to maintain themselves in power by the ruthless suppression of any concept which challenges the established orthodoxy. The power of a democratic system to adapt to change is vastly strengthened by the freedom of its citizens to choose widely from among conflicting opinions offered freely to them. To stifle every nonconformist idea at birth would mark the end of the democratic process. Furthermore, only through the constant activity of weighing and selecting can the democratic mind attain the strength demanded by times like these. We need to know not only what we believe but why we believe it.

2. *Publishers and librarians do not need to endorse every idea or presentation contained in the books they make available. It would conflict with the public interest for them to establish their own political,*

moral, or aesthetic views as the sole standard for determining what books should be published or circulated.

Publishers and librarians serve the educational process by helping to make available knowledge and ideas required for the growth of the mind and the increase of learning. They do not foster education by imposing as mentors the patterns of their own thought. The people should have the freedom to read and consider a broader range of ideas than those that may be held by any single librarian or publisher or government or church. It is wrong that what one man can read should be confined to what another thinks proper.

3. *It is contrary to the public interest for publishers or librarians to determine the acceptability of a book solely on the basis of the history or political affiliations of the author.*

A book should be judged as a book. No art or literature can flourish if it is to be measured by the political views or private lives of its creators. No society of free men can flourish which draws up lists of writers to whom it will not listen, whatever they may have to say.

4. *The present laws dealing with obscenity should be vigorously enforced. Beyond that, there is no place in our society for extra-legal efforts to coerce the taste of others, to confine adults to the reading matter deemed suitable for adolescents, or to inhibit the efforts of writers to achieve artistic expression.*

To some, much of modern literature is shocking. But is not much of life itself shocking? We cut off literature at the source if we prevent serious artists from dealing with the stuff of life. Parents and teachers have a responsibility to prepare the young to meet the diversity of experiences in life to which they will be exposed, as they have a responsibility to help them learn to think critically for themselves. These are affirmative responsibilities, not to be discharged simply by preventing them from reading works for which they are not yet prepared. In these matters taste differs, and taste cannot be legislated; nor can machinery be devised which will suit the demands of one group without limiting the freedom of others. We deplore the catering to the immature, the retarded, or the maladjusted taste. But those concerned with freedom have the responsibility of seeing to it that each individual book or publication, whatever its contents, price, or method of distribution, is dealt with in accordance with due process of law.

5. *It is not in the public interest to force a reader to accept with any book the prejudgment of a label characterizing the book or author as subversive or dangerous.*

The idea of labeling presupposes the existence of individuals or groups with wisdom to determine by authority what is good or bad for the citizen. It presupposes that each individual must be directed in making up his mind about the ideas he examines. But Americans do not need others to do their thinking for them.

6. *It is the responsibility of publishers and librarians, as guardians of the people's freedom to read, to contest encroachments upon that freedom by individuals or groups seeking to impose their own standards or tastes upon the community at large.*

It is inevitable in the give and take of the democratic process that the political, the moral, or the aesthetic concepts of an individual or group will occasionally collide with those of another individual or group. In a free society each individual is free to determine for himself what he wishes to read, and each group is free to determine what it will recommend to its freely associated members. But no group has the right to take the law into its own hands, and impose its own concept of politics or morality upon other members of a democratic society. Freedom is no freedom if it is accorded only to the accepted and the inoffensive.

7. *It is the responsibility of publishers and librarians to give full meaning to the freedom to read by providing books that enrich the quality of thought and expression. By the exercise of this affirmative responsibility, bookmen can demonstrate that the answer to a bad book is a good one, the answer to a bad idea is a good one.*

The freedom to read is of little consequence when expended on the trivial; it is frustrated when the reader cannot obtain matter fit for his purpose. What is needed is not only the absence of restraint, but the positive provision of opportunity for the people to read the best that has been thought and said. Books are the major channel by which the intellectual inheritance is handed down, and the principal means of its testing and growth. The defense of their freedom and integrity, and the enlargement of their service to society, requires of all bookmen the utmost of their facilities and deserves of all citizens the fullest of their support.

. . . We do not state these propositions in the comfortable belief that what people read is unimportant. We believe rather that what people read is deeply important; that ideas can be dangerous; but that the suppression of ideas is fatal to a democratic society. Freedom itself is a dangerous way of life, but it is ours.[55]

7

The Right to Know

Let us sum up: The fundamental responsibility of the mass media is to remain free in order to represent the public's right to know. This principle is old and honored, and by and large the media know what is expected of them in defense of free communication.

But on the positive side of what mass communication should do to represent the right to know, there are still great areas of uncertainty. One historian has said that the mass media have spent two centuries fighting to be free, and only a few decades trying to be responsible. The so-called "new age of responsibility" we have been talking about has been characterized by thoughtful questionings on the part of the media concerning the boundaries of the right to know, the meaning in actual practice of truth and fairness, and what the public is entitled to in the way of popular art. In all such situations as these, as one editor put it, the media are still moving through virgin forests, proceeding cautiously, and blazing their trails.

Take the area, for example, in which the right to know conflicts with the individual's right to privacy, or his right to a fair trial, or the government's interpretation of what it should withhold in the public interest, or the media's own interest. These are not questions that can be settled by saying simply that the public is best served by the full facts. They present problems that must be solved carefully and prayerfully, attempting always to balance the conflict of interests and needs. The next three chapters all deal with areas in which a responsible communication system, assuming freedom, is trying to develop standards for the performance expected of it under the right to know. These patterns are emerging slowly. A good place to start to look at them is in the spot where the right to know overlaps the equally old and honored right of privacy.

The Right to Know vs. the Right of Privacy

The right of an individual to his own private life, his own thoughts, his own beliefs, has long been highly valued in Western culture, and has had increasing attention in U.S. law since a memorable article, by Warren and Brandeis, was published in 1890.[1] The battle for privacy is unabating. As this is written, for example, a group of California citizens are embattled, in their city council, because sun decks being built on a new apartment house will enable the apartment dwellers to look into the back yards of their neighbors! Peeping and prying by the media on ordinary citizens are no more condoned than peeping by neighbors from sun decks. But there is an area of uncertainty over the responsibility of the media particularly in regard to the privacy of public officials, of persons who are prominently in the news, and of persons caught in the backwash of the news. Let us look at several examples of each of those:

Public Officials

In general, a public officeholder or candidate for public office puts his career up for public scrutiny. The kind of political philosophy he expresses, his honesty or dishonesty, his skill or lack of skill with human relations, even his morality, are all questions of legitimate public interest, because they help the public decide whether he is a fit person to entrust with official responsibility. But the key question which helps to determine publishability of a particular fact or item is: does it reflect on the individual's ability to do the job he holds or is seeking? If so, it is the reporter's responsibility to the public to publish it. If not, it is the reporter's responsibility not to invade the individual's privacy by publishing it, unless, of course, there is some other good reason.

To illustrate how this line is coming to be drawn, let us note two instances reported to us:

Case 31. It came to the attention of a newspaper that the mother of a candidate for public office had been involved in a rather messy lawsuit in a neighboring state. This would doubtless be "interesting" to many readers of the paper, inasmuch as the election was getting hot. Question: whether to publish it?

Case 32. It came to the attention of a newspaper that a candidate for public office had been tried for manslaughter some years previously. The man was acquitted. Many voters doubtless remembered the case. Question: whether to publish this fact with the rest of the candidate's record?

The first case is relatively easy. It is hard to believe that a lawsuit participated in by a candidate's mother some years previously in a neighboring state would really affect the candidate's ability to discharge the duties of a public office. To spread these facts on the public record would be no more than indulging in malicious gossip, and the newspaper so decided.

The second case is a little harder. If the candidate had been *convicted* of manslaughter, that would probably be a fact of importance to the voters. But he was *acquitted*. Therefore, his record stands clear of the charge, and the newspaper should do nothing to retry the case in print. But this particular newspaper hung up on another aspect of the question. Some people in the town would remember the case. Others would doubtless hear that the candidate had been "involved in manslaughter," without further details. Would it, therefore, be more merciful to the candidate to respect his privacy by ignoring the old case altogether, or by stating the fact that he had been *acquitted of manslaughter*, and thus respond to the public's right to know the facts. The newspaper which faced this problem searched its conscience long and hard on this case, and finally decided to quiet the rumors by printing the truth matter-of-factly.

In general, a public figure in a public place is also fair game for photographers and reporters. But there are exceptions, as the following case illustrates:

Case 33. A news photographer brought in amusing candid shots of a candidate eating at a public picnic. The candidate was obviously enjoying himself, obviously relaxed and unaware of photographers. The table manners he was exhibiting would cause him great embarrassment and might affect his political fortunes. Incidentally, the paper opposed this particular candidate. The photographer argued that the candidate is in public life, and the picnic was a public place; therefore, what the candidate does there is public property. He says the public has a right to know how one of its candidates acts. Question: would publishing the pictures unduly invade the candidate's right of privacy?

We presented this case to a number of newspaper editors. They split almost evenly on the question of whether to publish the pictures, but their comments revealed some important reservations. For example:

We would publish it. A candidate for public office, especially when he displays himself at a large gathering, is exposed to the view of a large percentage of the electorate. There is no reason why the rest of the public shouldn't see him. However, if the "relaxed pose" is sought because the paper is opposing him for office, the picture then becomes as slanted as a news story would be were the reporter to write just the facts the paper wants published.

In other words, this editor is introducing the test of truth and fairness. The candidate probably gives up his right to privacy by appearing at the picnic, but the newspaper is still responsible for seeing that an unslanted picture gets to its readers. They have a right to know, but especially in the noncompetitive news world of most newspaper towns, the newspaper has a new responsibility for seeing that its readers have a chance to get a true and balanced picture. As another editor said: "Pictures should not do something we refuse to do in print: hold someone up to ridicule needlessly. We would be particularly careful in our treatment of a political figure we opposed on the editorial page."

Another kind of problem involving privacy vs. the right to know sometimes comes up because of the *way* a story is obtained. Thus:

Case 34. A reporter got a story by having a drink in a bar with a newly elected public official. The reporter hid the fact that he represented a newspaper, and the official opened up and talked quite freely about his plans for the office—a matter which he had so far refused to discuss with the press. When the reporter revealed his identity at the end, the official was restrained with difficulty from attacking the reporter physically. The reporter admitted that he might have used dubious professional ethics, but argued that any such story which the official was willing to tell to a chance acquaintance in a bar should hardly be kept out of the public press. Question: whether to print?

The official in this case was indeed most indiscreet, and by his very indiscretion robbed himself of much of his right to privacy. Yet it cannot be denied that the story was obtained under false pretenses —by methods more acceptable to spies than to professional newsmen. It is not quite sufficient to say that the official talked freely to an unknown person; anyone is more likely to think twice before making a statement which he knows is destined for the public press, and to grant him that chance to "think twice" is only doing unto others what any newsman would like done unto him. Therefore, the situation is clouded. When we presented it to editors, we got answers which ran the gamut. For example, here was one extreme: "Print it. Public official should have discussed his plans freely with press. His plans are public matters. Any means of learning them is ethical, for it is to public benefit."

This is libertarianism speaking, out of three centuries of battling for access to news about government. Yet the logic in this reply is specious, for it implies that the end ("public benefit") makes any means ethical. Another editor gave this answer:

We would not print the sneaked story as such. We wouldn't think very highly of the loose-tongued official in question, but we grant him the right to know the identity of his audience. I would handle it this way: I would build interview questions around the material the official disclosed, then send the reporter back to conduct the interview. I doubt if the official would refuse to discuss the matter this time, knowing that "no comment" answers would leave him in a peculiar position.

There is little doubt that newspapers and other newsgathering organizations are moving toward this latter position.

Prominent Figures in the News

Public officials, as we have said, have become newsworthy of their own volition. That is, they have deliberately put themselves before the public eye, so that the public could decide on their qualifications and judge their performance. But their is another group of newsworthy figures who have come into the public eye in quite a different way. These persons have *done* something newsworthy. They have invented something, or created something, or flown the Atlantic, or run a mile faster than anyone else, or some similar striking performance. There is no doubt, of course, that the *performance* should be covered fully by all the news media. The problem comes in deciding how far the public's right to know *extends* into the private life of the performer.

Here the mass communication media have a somewhat ambivalent responsibility. On the one hand they represent—in this country—the boundless curiosity of the American people. Americans like people; they are interested in how they live, what they do, even how they think; and mass communication has helped to extend this natural gregariousness and curiosity outside the neighborhod by making many distant parts of the country seem almost like next door. Hollywood, for example, is "next door" to many Americans. Some Broadway columnists and writers have succeeded in making New York seem like next door. Many sports fans feel very close to the great figures and centers of athletics; I give you, for example, the phenomenal extent of Notre Dame's "synthetic alumni." Now the news media are responsible as representatives of this extended curiosity, which they themselves have helped create. But they are also responsible for the protection of an individual's right to privacy. This results in an uncertain borderline. When are the media merely being Paul Pry, and when are they acting responsibly?

Let us admit that a majority of such public figures welcome a certain degree of prying into their public lives. Publicity is helpful to them. Favorable mention, of course, is to be preferred, but even unfavorable publicity is usually to be preferred to no publicity at all. Many a public-relations-wise person has said, "Attack me if you will, but in any case mention my name." For example, actors and actresses thrive on publicity and are usually not too unwilling to have their love entanglements, their tiffs, their home lives described in detail for their fans. Professional athletes, too, usually consider that publicity will help their "box office," and hence their salaries. But the difficulty comes in the case of a newsworthy figure who sincerely wants to avoid the public eye.

For example, Mr. William Faulkner, one of our few Nobel Prize winners in literature, stated his position this way in *Harper's* magazine:

> My belief [has been] that only a writer's works were in the public domain, to be discussed and investigated and written about, the writer having put them there by submitting them for publication and accepting money for them; and therefore he not only would but must accept whatever the public wished to say or do about them from praise to burning. But that, until the writer committed a crime or ran for public office, his private life was his own; and not only had he the right to defend his privacy, but the public had the duty to do so since one man's liberty must stop at exactly the point where the next one's begins.[2]

Mr. Faulkner was objecting to a two-part profile of him published, against his wish, by a national magazine. His position is clear: he argues that the public's right to know extends only so far as the individual puts himself into the public eye.

It can be guessed that Mr. Faulkner's publishers may not have agreed with him on the two-part profile, which very likely interested prospective readers and boosted sales. The need of economic support for literary and artistic activities clouds this issue. The responsibility for protecting the privacy of such an artist as Mr. Faulkner rests jointly on the entrepreneur, the public, and the mass media. Undoubtedly the mass media will grow up toward the day when they will be willing to discuss only Mr. Faulkner's books and not Mr. Faulkner—if he wants it that way. But they will be helped toward that position if they are put under less pressure from the salesmen who want publicity for their authors, and from the public which is willing to buy peephole materials rather than other kinds.

However, there are a number of cases of this kind which are much easier than the one we have been talking about. For example, here are two cases in which media practice has been roundly condemned by responsible media men in many places and positions:

Case 35. A photographer for a tabloid crowded the Lindbergh automobile to the curb—at the time when the Lindbergh kidnapping story was at its height—in order to get a picture of little Jon Lindbergh. The family had steadfastly refused to let any picture of the child be taken for news purposes. The photographer said that the child was "news," and he therefore had the right to get the picture by "ingenuity." The child's caretaker was badly frightened, thinking that another kidnapping might be taking place. The incident is said to have played a large part in the Lindberghs' decision to leave this country, as they did for several years.

Case 36. A notorious incident involving the right of privacy took place at one of Toscanini's concerts. Photographs had been forbidden, and news photographers were not admitted. One reason for this was that Toscanini's eyes were extremely sensitive to light. A photographer paid his way into the concert and took a flash-bulb picture of Toscanini while he was bowing at the end of the selection. The conductor was temporarily blinded and groped his way off stage. The photographer defended his act by arguing that the concert was news, and the public wanted to see it.

In each of these cases, there was a clear reason why the right to privacy would take precedence over the public's right to know. Certainly the face of the Lindberghs' surviving child was "news," but hardly sufficient reason to further torture a family which had already gone through the experience of having a child kidnapped and murdered. Christian mercy and gentleness would not have condoned the act of forcing the car to the curb. In the second case, it is worth pointing out that ordinarily a concert picture of this kind would have been permitted. The record does not say why a single posed picture was not arranged, with the conductor having eyes closed. Apparently in this instance, it was not permitted out of deference to a venerable and beloved old man's dislike of photographers. But isn't the dignity of the press above that kind of trick?

Let us ask, why did the photographer go to such lengths? To protect the people against a dangerous act of government? To reveal a great opportunity or a great threat? No, the suspicion is that he was doing a "stunt"—showing that he could beat the restriction. This is not a very high motive to justify what he did.

An editor reported this instance:

Case 37. Like other papers, we sent reporters and photographers to cover the honeymoon of Mr. and Mrs. X, whose marriage had been exciting news. The honeymooners tried hard to give the press the slip, and were naturally quite irritated at being followed. It seemed to me that famous people have to get used to little privacy, but the idea of following them on their honeymoon bothered me a little.

Here again, the media are under the same kinds of pressure as we have been talking about—the entrepreneurs who want publicity for their stars, and the public which has an avid appetite for the vicarious kind of sex experience one gets in such stories. Yet there is clearly a limit on the right of the public to know such things, when the individuals concerned do not want them known. Good taste and the Golden Rule suggest a standard to follow in these cases. Some of the coverage of honeymoons has been nauseating. There was at least one famous example when a press motor boat cruised most of the night around the yacht in which two well-known people were spending their marriage night. This is hardly worthy of a great and dignified press. On the other hand, some honeymoon coverage is clearly within bounds. For example, when Grace Kelley, an internationally known film star, and Prince Rainier, the head of a sovereign principality, went on their honeymoon, it was only proper that the Prince's subjects and Miss Kelley's fans should be told where they were going, and that the Monacans might be permitted to see some pictures of their new and lovely princess taken during the course of the honeymoon trip. This does not mean that Monaco and the United States need know the color of the sheets on the nuptial couch or the actions of the happy couple at breakfast the next morning.

There is another kind of problem involving privacy which is illustrated by this report:

Case 38. We had a story about a hunchback, and the question came up whether to mention in the story that he *was* a hunchback. Clearly that was a part of his description, as much as describing a girl as a blonde, or a man as tall or muscular. To mention that would have given a much more colorful picture of what took place. We finally decided not to mention it because it was not essential in the story.

To my way of thinking the decision was made like a responsible paper.

The press has traditionally been depicted as "cold," "brassy," "impersonal," "hard-boiled." That squares poorly with the experience of anyone who knows responsible newsmen. They are careful with evidence, searching in their questions, but they are also considerate, kind, and fair, and one reason why they get *better* stories is that people trust them.

At the other end of the news spectrum, however, is a group of publications that deal in sensation, "private lives," "revelations," and, in general, life seen through a keyhole. The motto suggested for this group is "all the dirt that's fit to dig." They would hardly be worth time to discuss here, were it not that they pride themselves on serving public's right to know. Invariably, when attacked on grounds of bad taste or indecency, they point to their healthy circulations as evidence that the public wants the kind of information they have to sell.

Confidential Magazine is one of the currently most successful members of this group. On a television program last fall, *Confidential*'s publisher and editor faced two newsmen: John Crosby, columnist of the *New York Herald Tribune*, and Max Lerner, editorial writer of the *New York Post*. Here is how Terence O'Flaherty, the radio and television columnist, recorded the program:[3]

John Crosby led off: "As a responsible journalist, I'm shocked by this magazine and all others like it. They're inaccurate, badly writttten, and employ the coward's tactics of smear by inuendo. . . ."

Publisher Harrison swelled like a frog: "There are four million people who buy it—and that's justification for it!"—an argument he was to repeat several times in the evening.

Columnist Lerner: "If the FBI didn't crack down on the sale of narcotics, there would be millions more taking them."

Crosby: "What function—beyond making money—do you serve?" (Big audience applause.)

Harrison: "These are all truths. The only way to smear a man is by a lie. When a man steps into the limelight he forfeits all privacy. . . ."

Lerner: "You mean that because a person is a celebrity there is no place into which you have no right to pry? I mean with all this disgusting detective work—at what point do you stop?"

Breen (with a mocking laugh): "When we run out of film. . . ."

Lerner: "I repeat—at what point do you stop? Are you going to do it to the Senators? Would you do it to Mr. Stevenson. . . ."

Harrison: "We already had one on him."

Lerner: "What about the President—would you stop at the Presidency? What about General Eisenhower?"

Breen: "We investigated him and could find nothing there within our realm. . . ."

Lerner: "Well, suppose you *did*—would not the President be outside your scope?"

Breen: "No, he would not."

Lerner: "I would like to return to the discussion of 'invasion of privacy.' You claim you are telling the story behind the story. I maintain you are telling the *irrelevant* story."

Harrison: "The fan of a public figure has the right to know everything about him. Take George Washington. What do people remember most about him? He cut down the cherry tree! I suppose you'd consider that irrelevant."

Lerner: "No, Mr. Harrison, not irrelevant. The object of the episode concerned Washington's integrity. You would have told about chopping the cherry tree only—and not the moral it involved."

Breen: "The newspapers do the same thing every day. . . ."

Lerner: "There is no similarity whatsoever. When a person has taken an overdose of sleeping pills or is accused of murder, this is a legitimate point for newspapers to move in with stories—not before."

Crosby: "There is a sense of taste in every newspaper office in America —a sense of decency that is missing in your magazine."

Harrison: "Well, it has a circulation of four million. Someone must like us."

Breen: "Actually we're performing a public service. I'd like to read this letter here we received from an old lady. She says, 'I'm an old lady past 80 and I want to subscribe to your magazine. I read the Bible every day. The Bible showed all about how people lived in ancient times, and *Confidential* does the same thing today. . . .'" (Audience laughter and boos.)

Lerner: "Comparison with the Bible! This is the ultimate. . . ."

Let us draw the curtain here on this painful scene. There is little more to say about the kind of responsibility *Confidential* illustrates. But the significant fact in this interview is the repeated mention of four million circulation. This is indeed an impressive figure. Only a tiny handful of magazines in all the world are bought by more people. *The Atlantic, Harper's,* the *Saturday Review,* the *Reporter,* and most religious magazines are bought by less than one tenth as many people as *Confidential.* It is clear that large numbers of people want to know what *Confidential* can tell them about prominent people.

And this leads us to point out that responsibility for handling news of these people does not rest solely on the newsmen. It is a shared responsibility. Notably it is shared with the public. Are the four million purchasers of *Confidential* free from responsibility for its existence?

Mr. Lerner mentioned the narcotics trade. There are three possible ways to decrease this undesirable business: salesmen of narcotics can become fewer or less active; government can more successfully inter- dict the sale and transportation of the drugs; or fewer people can decide to buy them. We have the same three avenues for lessening the trade in keyhole journalism, except that the government can't come into the picture unless the material can be proved obscene or criminally libelous or otherwise actionable legally. (As this is written, some public officials in California are investigating *Confidential's* per- formance to see whether it is legally actionable.) For the most part, we concentrate most of our effort on the working press, and urge them to "higher standards." About the buying public we do very little, and yet here is the key to the whole problem. For if the business were not enormously profitable, there would be no *Confidential.* Is it realistic to expect the public to do anything about its own communication behavior? Is it too much to hope that public taste might rise to the point where publishing a magazine of this sort would no longer be greatly profitable? If that is, indeed, too much to hope, then I am afraid that (a) we are putting a very heavy burden on the ethics of publishers and editors, and (b) we are inviting government to inter- vene.

Figures in the Backwash of the News

There is another group of individuals whose privacy comes under the challenge of the newsgatherers. These are the persons who come into the stream of the news not of their volition, or because of something they have done, but because of their relationship to some other newsworthy figure. A few examples will illustrate the nature of the problem.

MacDougall and others have mentioned this one:

Case 39. The son of a Senator came to New York intoxicated and was arrested. The Senator, his father, was a rabid prohibitionist. Some newspapers played up the story, using the angle of the father's views vs. the son's conduct.

There is no doubt in this case that the story is news, and the name of the father, and his position on prohibition, are part of the news. The question is merely how much should be made of the ironic contrast between the father's views and the son's conduct. Many a father has had an erring son or daughter. Many a school teacher has had a child expelled from school or flunked out. Many a minister has had a child who has committed a moral crime. Many a merchant has had a child who stole.

In none of these cases has the child's action necessarily discredited the father, and yet each one has caused bitter grief and disappointment to the father concerned. In each case, the friends of the father have rallied around to try to soften the blow. Only the enemies, and the jealous, have gloated. The suspicion is aroused that a newspaper which played up strongly the contrast between father's views and son's conduct was in the position of gloating over the failure of the father's ideas. In other words, the paper's own attitude toward prohibition or toward the father may have had more to do with how the story was played than did the story's news value.

Another kind of situation is illustrated by the following:

Case 40. A photographer took, and his newspaper published, a picture of a grieving widow at the funeral of her husband. Friends of hers later told him it was a low-down trick: that she obviously wouldn't want that grieving mask preserved in public.

It is worth pointing out that grief is no disgrace, and that the face of a widow grieving at the funeral of her husband is not ordinarily something that should embarrass her in later years. The question is simply how far does the right to know extend when it represents the morbid curiosity of the public, and how far can the newsgatherers conscientiously intrude into the privacies of people in order to represent that interest? Certain pictures of funerals—for example, the funeral procession of a President, a President himself entering the church for a funeral of a distinguished man, pall-bearers carrying the casket of a distinguished man—pictures like that are clearly within the public domain. They are parts of history. But it is worth asking whether a responsible press should not consider itself justified in failing to represent some of the lesser curiosities of its readers, and in leaving individuals alone without benefit of flashbulbs in moments of grief and intimacy when privacy is most valued.

Case 41. A reporter posed as a coroner's assistant to question relatives of a man who died under mysterious circumstances. He got the story, the details of which definitely suggested foul play. He defended his action by saying that all other sources of news were closed to him on this particular case, inasmuch as it was under investigation, and the public was entitled to know the truth. The relatives were angry, and accused the paper of bad faith.

There are two noteworthy elements in this case. One of them is the fact that officials apparently would give out no news on the case. This is doubtless sometimes justified by the nature of the case, but often does more harm than good. Actually, reporters, when not faced with a blanket of secrecy, have turned up material which has helped solve many important crimes. The reporter in this case, therefore, may have had some justification for impatience. But was he justified in posing as a coroner's assistant? We presented this problem to a number of editors and publishers, and they voted two to one that it was a wrong action. Examples of their comments:

The foul play in the case is in doubt. However, the foul play by the reporter is clear. One wrong does not justify another wrong and the paper had better look to its own reputation. The story can probably be smoked out in other ways that are legitimate. Got a Grand Jury in the county, maybe?

I wouldn't be very happy with the reporter who impersonated an officer. We're strictly against that sort of thing.

It's bad practice to pose as an official. If I had such information, however, I would use it this way: I'd take it to the district attorney and let him carry the ball from there.

The conclusion is that, except under the rarest of circumstances, a responsible reporter is not justified in posing as anything but a reporter if he is collecting facts for publication. The reporter is not justified, again except under the rarest of circumstances, in obtaining facts or materials by trickery. This is true for both ethical and pragmatic reasons. Not only is a news source entitled to know to whom he is talking, but so also is the reporter obliged to think beyond the particular story he is covering to the kind of reputation he is building up for his newspaper in the community. Getting one fact by trickery, he may lose a dozen that distrusting people will withhold.

Another kind of trickery, and another aspect of the conflict of the right to know with other rights, is illustrated by this incident:

Case 42. A newspaper had no photos of a murdered man. The family had no pictures except one, which the wife, for sentimental reasons, refused to lend to the paper. The reporter slipped the picture under his coat while no one was looking. After copying it, and keeping it a day so that the competing paper would have no access to it, he returned it. The wife's relatives said that the overwrought woman had been hysterical over the loss of the picture. The photographer said that her attitude was very unreasonable.

True. She was unreasonable. But what the reporter did was stealing. He would never be arrested or tried for it, but he was still both outside the pale of law and the limits of consideration to a shocked woman. The point that this illustrates is what has been happening to our newsgathering media in the last century.

Our news systems grew up under the severest restrictions from authoritarian governments. They were part of the great revolutionary movements which overthrew this authoritarianism in much of the Western world. In the democratic governments they were set up as the people's representatives to check on government, to see that authoritarianism did not return or that dishonesty or incompetence did not creep in. The newsgathering agencies therefore learned their business under the compelling demands of revolution and of a basic responsibility to represent the people's right to what was being hidden from them. Under these conditions they learned to get the news by whatever means they could. In general, the right to know and the need to know overrode all other considerations. They carried this same spirit over to the broader coverage of human events when the fight for governmental coverage was pretty well won.

But in the last hundred years they have learned that human

curiosity is boundless and that if the right to know is not somehow bounded it will ride roughshod over all other human rights. That is what has been happening and will doubtless continue as mass communications define their responsibility in a community: the news-gatherers have been re-examining their methods and re-drawing the limits of their legitimate interest. We have been trying to suggest the nature of these emerging boundaries in the foregoing pages.

THE RIGHT TO KNOW VS. THE RIGHT TO FAIR TRIAL

The coverage of a court trial brings together a whole complex of rights and responsibilities, some of which are not always fully compatible with one another. The accused individual has the right to a fair trial. The court has the responsibility of dispensing justice. The public has the right to know whether its courts are dispensing justice. And mass communication has the responsibility to represent the public.

Perhaps the best way to examine the nature of the press's responsibility in this situation is to look at a few cases.

Case 43. The press had a field day at the Hauptmann trial. For those readers who do not remember the famous criminal cases of the 1930s, it should be said that this was the trial of Bruno Hauptmann, a carpenter, for the murder after the kidnapping of the Lindbergh baby. The case was front page news for months, and was conducted and reported in a highly emotional atmosphere. The story was read avidly, but, after the trial was over, protests came in from a number of quarters that the way the story had been covered had been prejudicial to a fair trial for the defendant.

Mr. Walter Lippmann has stated very clearly the issues that confront us here, and we are going to quote him at length on the Hauptmann case:

We are concerned with a situation spectacularly illustrated in this case, but typical of most celebrated criminal cases in the United States, which may be described by saying that there are two processes of justice, the one official, the other popular. They are carried on side by side, the one in courts of law, the other in the press, over the radio, on the screen, at public meetings—and at every turn this irregular popular process interferes with, distorts and undermines the effectiveness of the law and the people's confidence in it.

Because there are two pursuits of the criminal, two trials and two verdicts—the one supposed to be based on the law and a thousand years of accumulated experience, the other totally irresponsible—the self-appointed detectives get in the way of the regular detectives, the self-appointed judges and jurymen and advocates for the prosecution and defense get in the way of the officers of the law, and the official verdict becomes confused with the popular verdict, often in the court itself, almost always in the public mind.

We can examine the problems best, I think, by examining a few concrete instances. Hauptmann was arrested on September 20, 1934, and within a week there was a headline in a New York paper saying that "clues build iron-clad case against Bruno, police claim," and a few days later it announced that "twelve men and women selected at random" by a reporter had decided, according to the headline: "Bruno guilty but had aids, verdict of man in street."

Here we find that the police, unless the newspaper was lying, which I doubt, made an appeal to the public to believe their evidence before that evidence had been submitted to a court of law. That was an interference by the police with the lawful process of justice. It is for the jury to determine whether a case is "iron-clad," and since juries have to be selected from the newspaper-reading public, such a positive statement on the authority of the police is deeply prejudicial. I do not for a moment think that Hauptmann was innocent. But that does not alter the fact that he had a right to be tried before a jury and to be tried nowhere else. Because he was tried in two places at once, thousands of persons came to believe that he was not tried fairly. But in the administration of justice it is of the highest importance not only that the right verdict should be reached, but that the people should believe that it has been reached dispassionately.

In the two headlines I have cited, and you will recognize them as being by no means exceptional, we see the police rendering a verdict on their own evidence and a newspaper establishing a verdict among the potential jurors.

Let us pass to the trial in Flemington. It had, of course, to be a public trial. But if it was to be a reputable trial, it had also to be a trial in which the minds of the judge, the jury, the lawyers, and the witnesses all concentrated on the evidence, were as little influenced as possible by excitement or prejudice. The court room at Flemington is said to have a maximum seating capacity of 260 persons. On January 2, according to *The New York Times*, the constables on duty admitted to an already overcrowded courtroom 275 spectators without passes. A few weeks later it was learned that attorneys for both sides were issuing subpoenas to favored friends in order to force their admission as spectators in the court room, more than a hundred having been issued for one day's session. The authorities permitted the installation of telegraph wires in the court house itself, and one of the telegraph companies alone had to have a hundred men on hand. Although it was forbidden to take pictures during the trial, pictures were taken, and the authorities took no action.

Now there is no use pretending that a case can be tried well in an overcrowded court room with every actor knowing that every word he speaks, every intonation of his voice, every expression of his face, will instantly be recorded, transmitted to the ends of the earth, and judged by millions of persons.

This brings us to the actual trial of the case outside the court room. As a sample from the press, we may take a report, in which it was said that Hauptmann on the stand '*made senseless denials!*' and he was described as '*a thing lacking human characteristics.*' This, let us not forget, was during his trial and before the jury had rendered its verdict. We should not delude ourselves into thinking that comment of this sort is of no effect simply because the jury is locked up and is not allowed to read the papers. The witnesses read them, the spectators read them, and no newspaper man needs to be told that the sentiment of a crowd communicates itself more or less to every one. There is no way of isolating a jury in such a way as to protect it from the feeling of the crowd.

We have next to consider the conduct of the lawyers. They began trying the case in the newspapers almost from the day of Hauptmann's arrest. The counsel for the defense, Mr. Reilly, appeared in the news reels two days after his appointment and declared his belief that Hauptmann was innocent. A few days after the opening of the trial he announced to the press that he would name the kidnapers and that they were connected with the Lindbergh household. Two weeks after the trial, while the case was set for appeal, he addressed the Lions Club of Brooklyn and denounced the verdict, and the next day he addressed a mass meeting at which, during the course of his speech, the crowd booed Colonel Lindbergh.

Hauptmann himself issued newspaper statements during the course of the trial, the statements being given out by his lawyers. The prosecution also tried the case in the newspapers. On January 3, Mr. Wilentz said at his press conference that Mrs. Lindbergh's testimony would be "loaded with importance"; on January 22, he told a reporter that he would "wrap the kidnap ladder around Hauptmann's neck," and so on and so on.

Finally, we cannot omit the Governor of New Jersey, who, on December 5, 1935, while the case was still pending before the Supreme Court of the United States, let it be known that he was conducting his own investigation. I do not criticize him for that. The governor of a state has a right and, I think, an obligation to satisfy himself that justice has been done in his state. But the governor, who is a member of the New Jersey Court of Pardons, a quasi-judicial body, proceeded to try the case not before the court but in the newspapers. On December 8 his investigators let it be known that rail 16 of the ladder had, in their opinion, been planted against Hauptmann, and the governor was quoted as saying that he thought so, too. He also gave his opinion about finger-prints and was reported as saying that his personal investigator was "convinced that Hauptmann is not the man."[4]

We have thus quoted Mr. Lippmann because hardly anywhere else could we hope to have the issues posed as vividly as this distinguished newsman has posed them. And only by thus describing the situation in a celebrated criminal case can the peculiarly difficult position of the newsgathering media be made clear.

As Mr. Lippmann says, there is one common denominator in all the events he has reported: the regular officers of the law acted irregularly. The press undoubtedly carried materials which were not conducive to a fair trial for the accused. But the press for the most part was given these materials by the officers of the law. The police revealed and commented on the evidence before the trial. The officers of the court did not provide an orderly courtroom. The attorneys on both sides, "by their public statements violated No. 20 of the Canons of Ethics of the American Bar Association." The Governor, acting in a quasi-judicial capacity, made ex parte statements to the press. It is clear that "without the connivance of the regular officers of the law the abuses of publicity would have been reduced to manageable proportions."[5]

Why do the police, the judges, and the attorneys connive, even take the initiative, in trying a spectacular case in the press? Obviously, because they are public figures dependent on public favor, because the attorneys are trying to gain every ounce of advantage for their clients, and would have to be strong men indeed to do otherwise. But here is where the responsibility of mass communication comes in.

As we have said, mass communication represents the right of the public to know that its courts are dispensing justice. Now there are two ways to look at this responsibility. On the one hand, it might consist of re-examining, re-evaluating all the evidence in the public media, and in effect conducting a second trial to check on the verdict of the court. Or, on the other hand, it might consist of checking on the performance of the judges, the other officials and lawyers as to whether they are doing their business in such a way as to dispense justice. Are they acting irregularly? Are they leaking facts and comments they should not leak? If we accept this second view, the responsibility of the mass media becomes a much more difficult one, for they must not only on occasion refuse to accept some of this proffered news, but must also attack the officials who proffer it. The question is, then, whether this second responsibility is not the more fundamental obligation of professional or responsible mass communications. Mr. Lippman thinks so. He says: "It is our duty, I believe, to make it plain to the regular officers of the law that we expect them to administer justice in an orderly way, that we shall attack them if they do not, and then we shall defend them if they do. Then let them choose between the yellow press and the reputable press, and let them find out whose favor counts the more."[6]

Obviously this does not mean that the news media should not report to the public on what happens inside courtrooms. The nature of the choice on what and how to report is illustrated by another example.

Case 44. The Sheppard case, which occurred in the 1950s in Cleveland, Ohio, was a particularly "juicy" case in that it involved the brutal and barbarous murder of a lovely young woman under mysterious circumstances. The family was prominent. The husband, who was accused of the murder, was a handsome young osteopath. There was "another woman" in the case. There was a mysterious man alleged to have been in the house on the murder night.

The newspapers made the most of it. Hordes of reporters and photographers descended on Cleveland. Many of the patterns of the Hauptmann case were repeated. Information was leaked. Notes were passed to reporters by the accused. Lawyers talked. Self-styled crime experts analyzed the evidence, even added evidence, in public print. Biographies of the accused were published.

The photographic coverage was extensive. The sex element was played big, and the crime described in gruesome detail.

There was, of course, great variation in the way the story was played in the papers. As Alan Gould, executive editor of the Associated Press, said: "You put a crime-and-sex story in the hands of 1,700 editors and you get every color in the spectrum. . . . Some papers are playing it big, with all the trimmings, photos, sidebars, purple phrasing. Others are dead-panning in the writing, but keeping the story on page one. Still others are keeping it inside. There is evidence that a few are ignoring it entirely, or nearly so. To the majority, it's a good news story—but only colossal, as they say in Hollywood."[7]

Dr. James Pollard, of Ohio State, said: "If in the years ahead the press, radio, and television find more states through their courts or by legislative action recognizing the right of privacy or strengthening it where it is now recognized, they will have only themselves to blame. And if this occurs, it will be because, as it seems in the Sheppard case, some of them have overstepped the bounds both ethically and legally."[8]

Every newspaper and broadcasting station in the country had to decide how to play the Sheppard story. The choice they had to make was essentially how much to play it as a good show. A good show it was, better than most "whodunits" or broadcast crime programs. The papers that sold the most copies on their coverage of the Sheppard trial certainly played it as an exciting crime drama. And one of the responsibilities of the media is to bring entertainment to their audiences. But let us again raise the question whether, in the case of a court trial, this is not a somewhat lower level of responsibility than that of seeing to it that justice is administered in an orderly manner.

Certainly the judges and the responsible mass communication spokesmen who have written on this topic have so thought it. Judge Philbrick McCoy, of the Superior Court of California, has this to say: "The primary misconception is that the courts are places of entertainment and that criminal trials are conducted for the purposes of satisfying the sadistic instincts of a large part of the public, including the relatively few who can crowd into the courtroom. The more sensational the offense or the defense, the more sordid the story which is unfolded, the greater is the demand for detail."[9]

Let us repeat again that it is often an extraordinarily difficult kind of decision for the mass media, particularly in a competitive situation. They represent the public's right to know. Obviously, great masses of people want to know all about the Sheppard trial and similar events. Many papers of great circulation have built their success on catering to such wants. Many attorneys and public officials are willing, even eager, to help in satisfying them. But what is the right to know in this situation? Is it the right to know whether the courts are dispensing justice, or the right to know the details of a good show?

In the case of a court trial clearly the first of these is the important right. And increasingly the responsible newsgathering media are measuring the advantage to be derived from this kind of legal "whodunit" against the ultimate disadvantage of contributing to unfair trial and miscarriages of justice.

Thus Sevellon Brown, editor of the *Providence Journal and Bulletin* says: "Almost any editor in almost any city on almost any week could go over his routine police file and pick out example after example of reporting that was clearly prejudicial. . . . [The Law] exists to serve and protect the individual. So does the press. And when the press instead sacrifices the rights of the individual, it is betraying itself—because the individual is both the why and the how of our freedom."[10]

Almost every nauseating example of coverage of criminal trials can be described in terms of a distorted or neglectful view of the individual—a neglect of the individual's right to fair trial in court, and a kind of "mass mindedness" that David Riesman and certain others write about—a measurement of results in terms of circulation and program ratings.[11]

Case 45. In the trial of Minot F. (Mickey) Jelke on a charge involving the procurement and sale of call girls, press and public were barred from part of the trial. Two news services and five New York newspapers brought an action to restrain the judge from carrying out this policy, and also to make public the court record of the portions of the trial from which the press was excluded. The defendant also petitioned for a new trial on the grounds that the exclusion of press and public militated against a fair trial for him. A new trial was granted, but on the petition of the defendant alone. The newspapers and press associations were not granted the right to open a trial in the name of freedom of the press.

The law seems to be that only a defendant may give up the right to a public trial. As the judge said, "Due regard for defendant's right to a public trial demanded at the very least . . . that he not be deprived of the possible benefits of attendance by the press. Its widespread reporting of what goes on in the court may well prove a potent force in 'restraining' possible abuse of judicial power. . . . It is for the defendant alone, for whose protection such rights are primarily designed, to determine whether, and to what extent, he shall avail himself of them."

The right of the defendant to insist on either a closed or an open trial is, at this writing, being tested further in California. But the law need not concern us at this point. Rather the problem before us, in terms of mass communication responsibility, is the meaning of closed trials, closed hearings, sealed documents, and similar obstructions to news coverage.

And here the mass media are clearly in the right in protesting any closure on their right to cover a trial or a hearing. Any precedent of this kind may be a dangerous precedent, for at the end of that road lies the star chamber court which England and America fought so hard against for so long. The public can never know whether a closed court is a just court.

At the same time, it must be recognized that there probably will always be judicial processes which will be closed to coverage. We have already mentioned that the defendant, in a trial which contains embarrassing evidence on sexual behavior or some such topic, can waive his right to an open hearing if he feels that an open hearing would be prejudicial to his chances for a fair trial. Similarly, it is the common practice of courts to seal the papers on certain legal proceedings, such as paternity cases, in order not to stigmatize the children of disputed paternity. In instances like these the rights of the individuals concerned will probably always override the public's right to know. But the mass media are justified in protesting nearly every closing of judicial doors against them, because by so doing they can protect the public against ill-considered closings and make each judge have a good and defensible reason for dispensing justice secretly when he feels he must do so.

It is equally clear that the more the mass media demonstrate their ability to handle judicial proceedings with a sense of responsibility to the right of fair trial, the less likely a judge or a defendant will be to close the court door against them.

This is clearly the way we must go. For we want to move neither in the direction of the star chamber where proceedings are secret, nor in the direction of the People's Court, such as we have seen in certain Communist countries, where the decision is rendered in an atmosphere of emotion by voice of the populace. Rather we want a situation in which both the courts and the media will exercise their responsibility to the fullest, and in which both rights—the individual's right to fair trial, and the public's right to know whether its courts are dispensing justice—will be protected as completely as possible.

THE SPECIAL PROBLEM OF MACHINE-INTERPOSED COMMUNICATION AND FAIR TRIAL

The machine-interposed media pose a special problem in court trials.

For one thing, people are less used to these machine media. They have grown accustomed to the presence of a reporter, but are embarrassed and inhibited by the knowledge that their every word and action is being carried to a vast audience.

In the second place, the presence of these machines—especially television and film cameras, flashbulbs and floodlights, and photographers moving around to get good camera angles—is more likely than the presence of reporters to result in a disorderly courtroom and distract attention from the serious attempt to administer justice.

Third, unless the television or radio is recorded for later broadcast, there is no middleman in the process to exercise judgment as to what should and should not go out. The newspaper reporter, on the other hand, can weigh his material, and exercise a sober second thought as to what it means, what should be restrained and what interpreted. But the machine media are open channels. They carry what they see and hear.

The courts, the investigative committees, and other public bodies have been keenly aware of these differences. As a result, we could cite a long series of "cases," in most of which the machine-interposed media have been excluded from the courtrooms and the hearing chambers—the record on court trials being almost 100 per cent. Public hearings, however, have been more willing to open their doors.

The Kefauver hearings were a dramatic demonstration of what television could do to meet the public's right to know about crime in the United States. In those hearings, when a witness objected to having his face photographed, and the cameras centered on his hands, what went on the air was some of the most eloquent news coverage ever made in a hearing room. When the Chicago City Council conducted public hearings of its crime committee in 1952, hearings that were of intense public interest, it first barred radio, tape recordings, and television from the hearing room, although the newspaper press was permitted to attend. After bitter protest, however, the hearings were opened to both radio and television, *except* when witnesses were being examined. The Army-McCarthy hearings were another effective demonstration of news coverage by television. On the whole, performances like these seem to have established a trend and a pattern, and it is likely that more and more hearings in the future will be seen and heard in the home.

In the matter of court trials, too, in spite of the record, there are straws in the wind. In Portland, Oregon, a presiding judge made news in 1954 when he permitted news photographers to cover the sensational Sack murder trial.[12] The judge specified that no flash-bulbs were to be used, and that the photographers were not to move around the courtroom, but should remain in their reserved seats in the front row of the spectators' gallery. Each Portland paper took more than 100 photos, and parts of the trial were also filmed for later television broadcast. No one complained about the trial being disrupted in any way. The judge expressed his great pleasure in the experiment, saying that the photography "was done honestly and decently without interrupting or bothering anyone." Television likewise has been tried, apparently successfully, in a trial in Alabama.[13]

It is our feeling that this is the beginning of a trend, and that time is on the side of the machine media.

It should be remembered that newspapers had to fight long and hard to get consistent access to such news sources as trials, hearings, and legislative assemblies. Not so many hundreds of years ago, the widespread use of print was regarded as a positive menace to society and government. That resistance was overcome, and so probably will be the resistance to these newer media.

New engineering developments are making it possible to cover a hearing or a trial or an assembly without disrupting or distracting it. Modern cameras can take interior shots without flashbulbs, and photographers can take good pictures without galloping around a courtroom and taking charge of proceedings, as so many news photographers still do when they have a chance. Modern television cameras require no more light than an average courtroom has; the day of hot and glaring floodlights is gone. Nor do the television cameras need any special room for maneuver. All they need is a clear shot at the principals to be photographed. It is thus technically possible, at least, for the coverage of a trial, a hearing, or an assembly by television, radio, and news photography to be unobstrusive and nondistracting.

It is reasonable also to think that people will get used to these devices as they have got used to court stenographers, reporters, and public address systems. Actually, the radio microphone is identical with the public address microphone. In future courtrooms built with photographic cubicles and windows, like the U.N. assembly hall, television cameras will be able to operate without ever being seen in the courtroom. And, as the Oregon trial proved, the presence of decorous flashbulbless photographers on the front row of the spectators' gallery is hardly noticed by any of the participants in the trial.

Likewise it is fully to be expected that improved recording methods will eliminate the objection of some deliberative groups that there is no responsible middleman in the machine-interposed media. Tape recorders are highly perfected, and we now have a commercial television recorder of high quality. These will permit editing of a program as needed. This kind of editing has made it possible for President Eisenhower, for example, to release portions of his press conference from time to time for rebroadcast on television and radio. It is not unlikely that similar methods will some day open the door of the United States Congress to radio and television.

And that will be a real victory for the public's right to know, because unquestionably these new media are capable of giving a new and important dimension to news coverage. Edward R. Murrow well said "I don't care whether it's McCarthy attacking, Owen Lattimore defending, Acheson explaining foreign policy, Lovett defending a defense appropriation—I would rather hear the eloquent excerpts of their testimony in their own voices, than read it or hear it after it has filtered through the minds of reporters and editors, whether in newspapers or on radio. No politician or witness ever claimed that his own voice misquoted him."[14]

The responsibility of the mass media is therefore clearly to represent the right to know by fighting for the right to cover public events with these new media as with the old. At the same time, the responsibility of the newer media—especially in this time of their probation—is to be scrupulously careful of the individual rights they might infringe upon, and the administration of justice with which they might interfere.

The problem of televising or broadcasting witnesses will probably represent a confused borderline of coverage for a long time. In the Chicago hearings mentioned above, the line was drawn at televising witnesses when they were being questioned. In the Army-McCarthy hearings, witnesses were televised. In the Kefauver hearings, a witness was allowed to keep his face out of camera coverage. The argument here is that in many cases witnesses are embarrassed at the thought of performing before a television or radio audience and are therefore inhibited and handicapped in telling their story. They are willing to talk to a committee, a judge, a jury, even a reporter, but not to the general public. As people become more used to these new media, and if the media do indeed remain unobtrusive, this objection will doubtless diminish. Meanwhile, the advice given to television by the Sigma Delta Chi Committee on Freedom of Information would seem to be sound: don't push; don't be in a hurry; show consideration of these rights; your ultimate victory will come quicker that way.[15]

It would seem that there are at least three kinds of responsibility involved here. One, as we have said, is the clear responsibility of the mass media to keep working to open the doors of news coverage to the machine-interposed media. This obligation to the right to know is no different for the newer media than for the press. At the same time, the newer media, as we have also tried to indicate, have a responsibility to the right of fair trial to behave with the utmost care and scrupulousness when they do gain access to these public proceedings. They should bend over backwards not to be disruptive, and to be fair and representative if they carry only a portion of the proceedings. And, finally, there is a real responsibility on the part of the lawyers, the committee members, the judges, the other public officials whose proceedings are going to be covered by radio and television.

We tried to point out that in the Hauptmann trial the lawyers and public officials did more than the press to turn the affair into a circus. This possibility will be doubly dangerous in broadcast coverage. A televised hearing or trial or assembly can be used or misused. The basic responsibility here is with the men in charge of the public proceedings. But the media also have an obligation—the same as the press has in the case of a trial—to check on the performance of these officials and to attack them if they are dispensing performances rather than justice. In the hands of a conscientious user, the sharp eye of television can report on "phonies" and manipulators and "show-offs" and bullies just as effectively as it can report on T-formation quarterbacks and dancing girls.

THE PROBLEM OF GOVERNMENT'S RESPONSIBILITY TO WITHHOLD

The mass communication viewpoint toward this problem can be stated by quoting James S. Pope, editor of the *Louisville Times*, to the American Society of Newspaper Editors in 1950.

Sharp and critical disagreement [he said] has been found to exist between the country's newspaper editors and the office-holders who contrive much of the news. How much should the people know? Of course, every newspaperman is used to a nominal tussle over news that reflects some discredit on elected or employed public officials. . . . That is a conflict as old as government and news of government. But the conflict has gone beyond that simple ceremonial. Only recently have most editors begun to realize that these familiar little guerilla skirmishes now are part of a broad-scale offensive against freedom of information—against the basic principle of the citizen's right to know, so that he may govern himself.[16]

There is no doubt that in the last few decades there has been a tendency on the part of government officials and bodies to increase the amount of secrecy in several important areas of news. One of these—and hardly surprising in view of war and cold war—is the spreading and intensification of security measures. Another—perhaps the chief of them all, in the opinion of Harold Cross, the distinguished newspaper lawyer—is the increase in secrecy covering financial dealings between government and citizens.[17] This includes information on what a citizen pays his government and what his government pays him—taxes, penalties, salaries, public assistance, settlement of claims, compromise of claims, et cetera. Another area of increasing secrecy is that of judicial proceedings and records involving family relationships, notably juvenile offenses, sex cases, matters of family support, and the like.

In all these matters, of course, the communication media represent the public's right to know—as Mr. Pope says, so that the public may govern itself properly.[18]

It is only fair to ask, then, what is on the other side? What rights is the government defending, and what responsibilities is it exercising when it withholds some of the information. In part, of course, it considers that it is upholding the right of privacy, and in part the right of fair trial. The first of these applies in such instances as the withholding of public records in which vital statistics and other "personal" bits of information are revealed; the second, to some cases of trials of family matters. But neither of these is central to the case. Rather, what seems to be involved is a generalized concept of the "public good." Government, when it withholds information of this kind, claims to be exercising its broad responsibility to act for the public good.

This is a "caretaker's" viewpoint and runs headfirst into the libertarian tradition which the press has been building for two hundred years. Thus here again we are in the process of redrawing the borderline between the authoritarian caretaker's responsibility and the Miltonian concept of a free market place of information and ideas.

Specifically, what are some of the component ideas in this broad and vague concept of public good? Without trying to define it or describe it completely, we can set down some of the theses on which it seems to operate in the area we are here considering. Among them:

1. Public interest is not served by opening all the deliberations of public bodies to the press and the public.

2. The public interest is not served by opening governmental records of a personal nature to the press and the public.

3. Publicity is thought to hinder, rather than aid, the rehabilitation of juvenile delinquents and the prevention of crime among young people.

4. A large amount of information about this country's scientific, military, and administrative capabilities, techniques, and plans must be withheld from public dissemination and knowledge because it would be more harmful in the hands of this country's enemies than it would be helpful in the hands of our own citizens.

5. The public good requires certain official information to be given the mass media for their own use but not to pass on to the public.

Let us take up these theses, one by one, and in terms of their relation to newspaper responsibility.

Secret Meetings

Consider these instances:

Case 46. The Mayor of Toronto convened the Board of Control at a meeting from which he excluded the press. Two members of the Board walked out, refusing to be a party to meetings which transacted the city's business without the press being present. Three reporters then entered the meeting room. Ordered by the Mayor to leave, they refused, saying that they were instructed by their editors to remain as long as the meeting continued. The Mayor argued and threatened, and finally adjourned the meeting rather than continue it with the reporters present.

Case 47. Reporter N came into possession of the purported record of a closed meeting of the City Council, containing news of significant public interest. He published the story, refusing to reveal the source although saying it was not a public official. Some of the Council protested bitterly to the paper, but the information was confirmed by later developments.

The typical situation here is that a council, a county commission, or a school board threshes out its business in closed or "executive" sessions. Then it convenes a public session and formally transacts its business—perhaps merely announcing its decisions. The news media argue that the reasoning and procedures leading to public decisions are as important to the public's participation in government as are the decisions themselves. In order to understand and evaluate the decisions, the public has to know how the decisions were arrived at. Therefore, newsgatherers have felt free, as did the Toronto reporters, to insist on open meetings wherever they can; and, if they can't force open meetings, to seek the information by indirect methods, as did Reporter N.

In the last ten years, many states, municipalities, and public bodies have become persuaded of the importance of open meetings and have passed laws or handed down directives to that effect—usually exempting sessions in which hiring or firing, or other personnel matters, were discussed. Nevertheless, there are still many closed meetings.

The views of a responsible mass medium in this situation have been well stated by the Sigma Delta Chi Committee on Freedom of Information, which can hardly be accused of failing to uphold the right to know.[19] This committee clearly recognizes the right of governmental bodies on occasion to have executive sessions for the public good. But it asks these questions of editors and broadcasters:

1. Is the star-chamber session actually one in which public officials are discussing things which belong in the public prints? For example: Premature publicity on a city council's plan to condemn private property for a street or parks project might artificially inflate the price of property under consideration. The council members feel an obliga-

tion to the taxpayers and hope to arrange a good deal for them. If the proposition they are considering is actually "on the up-and-up," they would not hesitate to tell the newspaper about it for background purposes. But do they have the assurance that the newspaper is as interested in acting with patience and restraint in the public interest as it is in obtaining a story and printing it—regardless of its implications?

2. Are public officials given enough protecton against inaccurate, adolescent, or outright malicious treatment of "sensitive" information? Do competitive pressures by two or more newspapers force reporters to betray confidence after they have been admitted to executive sessions of public officials? Are the stories the reporter writes published as written? Or are they "jazzed up" to his embarrassment and to the humiliation of his news sources when they come under the editor's eye on the city desk?

3. When news and information is withheld or suppressed, does the newspaper enter its complaint on sound ground and with clean hands?

(a) Does the paper have a consistent and generally unimpeachable record of having tried to cover the area of news in contention with intelligent, knowledgeable, and trustworthy reporters? Or is it asserting its traditional rights to information through personnel who are, in fact, demonstrably unfit to treat it with perspective, balance, and comprehension?

(b) Does the paper burden the source of information by spasmodic attention which demands time-consuming explanations of the obvious, the only alternative being a distorted and possibly damaging report?

(c) Is the information sought and published in an objective manner, or is it treated as an instrument of editorial policy preconceived by the front office?

4. Are objections to the suppression and withholding of information asserted and argued personally by responsible people in a manner that is considerate, logical, and convincing? Or do the objections take the form of personal recrimination, arbitrary criticism, or reckless insinuation?

5. Are newspapers alert enough and consistent enough in their insistence upon "all the news that's fit to print"? Or do some of them invite indifference to release of news through neglect of offices upon

which they are supposed to keep a sharp eye? Are not some newspapers guilty of encouraging news suppression that they may promote a certain candidacy, a pet project, or protect a special set of friends?

The news media must be eternally vigilant and aggressive, says the Committee, but it advises further:

There is nothing in the constitutional guarantee of freedom of the press which assures a newspaper the trust and respect of the people with whom it must live. Without that trust and respect, freedom of the press enters into direct conflict with freedom of information. Because the press does not manufacture most information, and only reports it, the newspaper must have the cooperation of those persons in whose custody the information is to be found.

That cooperation, in the main, must be freely given. Yet, because of conflicts between the impulses of political self-preservation which naturally rule most persons in public life, and the obligations of the press to print both the good and the bad, that cooperation must be assiduously cultivated. This is not to say that a newspaper should curry favor of any political regime. But certainly it must discharge its functions as the "fourth estate" of government with as much honor, consistency, and competence as are necessary to establish and maintain the complete respect of both public officials and the public.

Secret Records

As Harold Cross has well pointed out, so-called "public" records and proceedings are of many different degrees of appropriateness for publicity and differently related to the public's need and right to know:[20]

1. Some records, though kept by public officials in public offices, are not really "public" at all. For example, it could hardly be argued that the public interest would be advanced by opening diplomatic correspondence or FBI files to the press and the public. Tentative understandings or approaches are features of diplomacy that should not always be publicized—perhaps too often are. On the other hand, both press and public have the clear right, for example, to demand that their governmental representatives should not make secret agreements, as distinguished from tentative approaches and understandings.

2. Some records and proceedings, though "public," are not open to public inspection. Among these, in some states, are the records and hearings in juvenile courts, and in certain public assistance cases.

Here the borderline of responsibility is less clear. We shall discuss the matter of juvenile cases a few pages farther on. So far as such records as public assistance are concerned, the purpose in restricting them is apparently to defend the recipents' right to privacy, and to maintain the general morale of the community. It has been suggested that here there is a distinction between the newsgatherer's right to examine the records and his right to publish. He has a clearer right to check for graft and malpractice, and to publish what he finds along this line, than he has to publish a list of names which would accomplish nothing but further to destroy the self-respect of unfortunate people.

3. Some "public" records and proceedings are open to inspection or attendance, but restricted to persons who have a particular status, qualification, or purpose. For example, corporate tax reports in certain state offices, automobile accident reports, records of vital statistics, and records of salaries paid sometimes fall under this heading. Here the newsgatherer is on firmer ground in insisting on his right to know. His responsibility is obviously to be discreet, when deciding whether the public good of publishing a particular fact exceeds its public harm in invading the privacy of an individual. But he should certainly insist that his status as representative of the public's right to know does give him a special status for examining these restricted records. And he has every right to fight the recent tendency toward regarding the financial relationships of government and individual citizens as "privileged" material, unavailable to the public.

4. Finally, there are some records which are public, ostensibly unrestricted, but yet withheld at official discretion. For example, city books are officially open, but in practice are open only at the discretion of the officials concerned. Here the newsgatherer's right and responsibility are usually quite clear. He should take whatever legal steps are required to open the records.

Secret Judicial Proceedings

We can illustrate this problem area by using juvenile delinquency as an example. Consider this instance:

Case 48. In September 1948, and for eight months following, Hartford, Connecticut, had a crime wave. The crimes were solved by the arrest of eight high school students. They were secretly arraigned at night, and the proceedings were withheld from the newspapers. The judge made the somewhat unguarded statement that the names were kept secret because "the boys were from a good part of town and came of fine parents." This aroused wide resentment in areas where people considered that they were being considered "not quite so good." Furthermore, many rumors circulated as to the identity of the youths.

Finally, one of the Hartford papers, noting that the boys had not been arraigned in juvenile courts, where the proceedings were legally secret, took legal steps to secure the release of the names. It published the names. Then the boys were turned over to juvenile court, and the further proceedings were closed to publicity. It became known that the youths were suspended from school for the remaining six weeks of the school year; but, as far as could be found out, no other penalties were applied, although the cases involved car theft, safe cracking, and burglary. Several years later, one of the youths, 20 years old and in military service, strangled a girl in Texas while on a "date."

This case illustrates most of the problems that concern mass communication in the area of secret trials. In the first place, the responsibility for publishing or not publishing rests in some cases on the government side, in others on the communicator's side. Proceedings of juvenile courts, and a few other courts, are for the most part withheld from the news. Yet when a juvenile is brought before another court, his name is ordinarily not privileged. Some papers have the rule of publishing all the names of juvenile violators that can be obtained. Some refuse to publish names when the violators are under 18. Some publish the names only when the offense is unusually grave.

But the point is that this is a very difficult decision because no one knows for sure whether it is for the public good to withhold or to publish such information. If it were clear that the fear of publicity would deter youths from committing crimes, then the responsibility of the newsgathering media would be clear: they would be obligated to search out and reveal all they can of such cases. But it is not clear. If fear of being known were really a deterrent to crime, then juvenile delinquency would have ceased long ago, and our prisons would not be overcrowded as they are. There is no indication whatsoever that the Hartford paper's publication of the names of the teen-age criminals kept one of them from becoming a murderer—or, on the other hand, any proof that the secrecy of the juvenile court proceedings kept others of the youths from going on with a life of crime. It is an area of very great uncertainties, and one in which the newsgatherer must make the best decision he can on the best evidence he can find.

Therefore, it may be well to look at the arguments on either side. On the side of the freest publication, we have two main points.

The first is that the public has a right to know what is going on. If the public knows the extent and nature of the juvenile crime problem, then it is in position to seek out the reasons for it, and do something about it. This is a telling argument, although it has been argued in turn that the public can understand the delinquency problem perfectly well without knowing the names of offenders and their precise offenses.

The second argument is that fear of publicity will deter youths from committing crimes. Publicity will act as a punishment for those who have committed crimes. Furthermore, publicity will shame their parents into bearing their full responsibilities in these cases. It is necessary to admit that there is very little in the way of proof behind this argument. Psychiatrists, juvenile judges, probation officers, and social workers for the most part feel that it is not a good argument; in fact, that publicity would in many cases actually be no penalty and would have the worst possible effect on the rehabilitation of the youth.

They contend that children should not be treated like mature adults. Publicity, which would be thoroughly in order for mature criminals, would work against the rehabilitation of the child. For example, publicity may result in the child's being ostracized by his peer group, and even by his family, thus creating an almost impossible situation for rehabilitation. Furthermore, publicity may magnify the seriousness of the offense and thereby make it harder for the child to return to normal behavior. On the other hand, while publicity may ostracize one child it will glorify another. Many of the most dangerous of these juvenile offenders are children who are trying to gain some kind of recognition within a group or a gang. Publicity gives them the kind of attention they crave, and encourages them to go on and do more spectacular things in order to maintain their new reputations as "big shots." For this reason, Jersey City, among other places, has had the policy of bringing very few juveniles into court, but, instead, working with their parents. So it is argued that publicity is the worst possible way to try to end juvenile delinquency, and the purpose of an anti-publicity policy is to protect the young boy and the young girl in their chance to become normal, happy, useful citizens.

These are the grounds, then, on which the editor and the broadcaster must determine what is for them responsible conduct. On the one hand, they want to guard against what Russell Wiggins, of the *Washington Post and Times Herald,* calls "[sweeping] this whole problem of youth in crime under the community rug."[21] On the other hand, they have to decide, in close consultation with their consciences and with the most expert advice they can obtain, what procedure on their part, and on the part of the courts, the schools, and the homes, will be most likely to reduce delinquency and save young people for useful citizenship. Then their responsibility is obviously to see that these procedures are carried out.

To illustrate the problem as it appears to a thoughtful, public-spirited editor, here is a column by Robert W. Sink, of the *Champaign-Urbana (Illinois) Courier:*

[Says the sheriff]: "Suppose I do arrest them. You won't print their names. They've suffered no disgrace, and they can go right back and do the same thing all over again. . . ."

The sheriff is correct, of course, we don't print the names of law-breakers unless they are 18, or over. This is the newspaper's own rule. It is just a rule we have decided to adopt.

Because it is a rule of our own choice, we can select the exceptions, and in the last five or six years we have made two that I can recall. One concerned a teen-age burglar. When the police finally caught him, he confessed some 60 burglaries. We decided that this young man had lost his amateur standing and should be treated by professional rules. We printed his name.

The other exception was more recent and concerned one of the more monumental successes in juvenile vandalism. Nobody complained in either instance.

In general we adopted the rule because some very solid citizens convinced us that in the majority of cases the damage to the youngster might outweigh the social benefits of printing his name. First offenders, it is argued, should be given the opportunity to profit from the experience of an arrest, without having the public stigma of lawbreaker placed upon them.

Sheriff Hedrick thinks these kids need the public disapproval or their neighbors'. He also thinks that in some cases it would help to protect the neighbors.

"Let me give you a different kind of example," he explains. "There's one 15 year old boy that we've picked up twice for burglaries. In addition he's confessed breaking into a house and stealing a billfold. The neighbors ought to know that this kid does things like that, so that they can take the necessary steps to protect their property. But if the papers won't print the name, they don't know who it is, and there's no penalty on the boy. He isn't deterred by the disapproval of his friends and neighbors because they don't know about it. . . ."

What do you, gentle reader, think about this? We don't think all teen-agers are like this, so don't write us a letter, just to say so. There are plenty of law-abiding kids. We don't think prohibition is the answer, either. As an answer this is begging the issue.

Do you think we should drop our rule against printing the names of youngsters 17 and under when they are caught violating the law? Or should we print their parents' names? (One office wag suggested that we should print stories saying: "Driver of an automobile registered in the name of John F. Civicleader was arrested for parking without lights at 2 a.m. Tuesday on the Lincoln Avenue Road.")

Actually, we aren't going to take a vote, and do what the majority says should be done. This is something on which we have to make up our own minds.

It's something you have to make up your minds about, too.[22]

(At last report, the *Courier* was holding to its rule.)

Security Information

This country has had a tradition of clamming up in time of war, then releasing information quite freely in peacetime. Of late years, and notably during the "Cold War" period, habits of secrecy and censorship developed for war have tended to spill over into peacetime. Thus the media find themselves on one side bombarded by highly articulate spokesmen who warn that Communist spies are everywhere, and that security must be tightened; and on the other side by equally articulate spokesmen, who say that our security program is excessive, that it is not only destroying freedom of speech and of the press, but also covering up inefficiency and malpractice, and slowing the development of our science and technology.

No editor or broadcaster or film-maker would question the right and responsibility to withhold, for the public good, information which might help this country's enemies more than it would help us if released broadly. Furthermore, no one outside the security system is able to say just what is being withheld or to make a valid judgment on the wisdom of the policy. The responsibility of mass communications, representing the public's right to know, is clearly not to try to break the secrecy but to question carefully and attentively the way the secrecy is administered.

To put it in practical terms, the news organ is clearly being irresponsible, if not worse, when it does what a proud and prosperous American newspaper was accused of doing during World War II— publishing information on a Pacific Battle, in such a form as to reveal to the Japanese that the U.S. Navy had broken the chief Japanese code. It is just as clearly being irresponsible when it does not fight restrictions like this one in a Department of Commerce bulletin on advisory censorship:

> Information falling within the scope of this program includes *unclassi-fied* [italics mine] technical data on: advanced industrial developments, production know-how, strategic equipment, special installations.

This would extend secrecy beyond classified material. James S. Pope called this appropriately "a blunderbuss to shoot down all intelligence about our mobilization." It showed, he said, "little awareness of the dangers of public ignorance at a time of crisis."[23]

Off-the-Record Information

One of the best known instances of off-the-record information was this one:

> *Case* 49. Vice-President Nixon spoke off-the-record to the American Society of Newspaper Editors. In the course of his talk he dropped a bombshell by discussing the possibility of U.S. troops going into Indo-China. The editors published this story, attributing it to "a high administration source." The story created such a storm of comment and anxiety that the secret became known, and Mr. Nixon's authorship was admitted.

Hardly any newsman would argue that he should never accept any off-the-record information. He tries to establish a relationship of trust with his news sources. Frequently, he needs to know about a story before it can be published, or to know some background which will help him put the story into proper perspective. Information like this he will ordinarily accept gratefully, and keep it in confidence.

On the other hand, there are several uses of off-the-record information which make it suspect. One is the use of the off-the-record device to close a reporter's mouth on some information which he might legitimately obtain otherwise and publish. This is obviously unfair and against the public interest, and a reporter should refuse to accept such off-the-record information if he can recognize it. Another is the use of off-the-record channels to send up a trial balloon. There has been some suspicion that the Nixon speech was such a device, intended to find out how the country would react to the prospect of another war in Asia. The whole idea of making an off-the-record speech to several hundred people and expecting no word of it to leak out is somewhat unrealistic, but it is a matter of real doubt whether such a speech which makes big headlines (as did the Nixon speech) can legitimately be published without identifying its source. Is not the public entitled to know *who* said such an important thing? As Robert U. Brown said in *Editor and Publisher:* "If a top official is (merely) informative his off-the-record 'not for attribution' statement is okay; if he makes headlines, then a similar off-the-record stipulation is unwarranted."[24] One important aspect of the right to know is the right to know the source of a headline statement.

THE PROBLEM OF THE MEDIA'S RESPONSIBILITY TO WITHHOLD

In the preceding pages we have talked about the responsibility of the media to arbitrate conflicts between the right to know and the rights of privacy and fair trial, and about the occasional suppressions of news that will become desirable in view of those conflicts. Now we come to a somewhat harder problem, the responsibility of the media on occasion to suppress news for the "public good."

Vague as this standard is, it is clearly recognized. No reporter, no newspaper, no broadcaster, no newsreel is expected to be a perfect channel, offering no resistance and no interpretation to the news that becomes available. Elmer Davis once wrote a short story about a newspaper man who married a girl who was a perfect reporter. At first, this quality greatly attracted the man; then it began to bother him. Finally the girl wrote an accurate story of a speech which would destroy a public man, and the newspaper man divorced her. He couldn't live with a "perfect" reporter. And the rest of us couldn't live with one either.

The Oregon State Editorial Association adopted the following as one of its canons: It shall be one of our canons that mercy and kindliness are legitimate considerations in any phase of journalism; and that if the public or social interest seems to be best conserved by suppression, we may suppress; but the motive in such instances must always be the public or social interest, and not the personal or commercial interest.[25]

In the following pages we shall examine a number of instances by way of trying to draw a rough map of this territory which is affected by "mercy," "kindliness," "public or social interest," as opposed to the public's right to know.

Case 50. In San Francisco, in 1954, all local newspapers maintained 60 hours of silence about a kidnaping, because they were told by police that the man's life would be endangered by any publicity. The blackout of information was extended to the news services, the broadcasting stations, and the national networks. A major effort was obviously required to keep the blackout from being lifted somewhere in the country. Not until the man was freed and the kidnappers taken into custody was the public told about the crime.

This was a truly impressive example of the willingness of the mass media to suppress news in order to save a man's life. There would be no serious argument that the public right to know about a crime is more demanding than saving human life. But, on the other hand most of the San Francisco newspapers expressed serious reservations about the policy they were following. They recalled that full publicity had helped in solving other kidnapping cases. They went along with the police, who said that the man's life was truly at stake; and they would doubtless do so again. But, even after they had done so and the crime was solved, there was no proof that the news suppression had contributed to it.

The *San Francisco Chronicle* spoke for the others:

Suppression of information is certainly not our business: it is the opposite to the proper function of a free press. There are, of course, occasions when the public interest requires the suppression of news. News adversely affecting military security is an obvious example—but the fewer instances of suppression there are, the better off the American people are.

Publicity can greatly enlarge the power of the police by making an alert crime detector out of every newspaper-reading citizen; in general, publicity is the criminal's worst enemy. The police have the best of reasons to know this, and they will accordingly be well advised to avoid considering the voluntary cooperation given them by the press and radio in this extraordinary situation as something to be used as a precedent to be frequently invoked in the future.[26]

And on the other side of the record, of course, one can cite the Weinberg case. Here is a case of another kind:

Case 51. Near press time, there came to a newspaper desk the story of a baby which had strangled to death in an automobile. A young couple had left their child in the car, sleeping in a "snuggle duckie." The baby had apparently thrashed around, tightened the garment around its neck, and been strangled. The funeral director said the young couple was completely broken up, blaming themselves for the baby's death. He argued that printing the fact that the baby had been left unattended in a situation where it might strangle would only compound the couple's grief.

At first sight, this would seem like a case where news suppression would be justified on the grounds of mercy and kindliness. But looking a little deeper, it is seen to be something else. If this happens to one baby, it might happen to others. Is not the public entitled to this kind of warning? In this case, it would seem that the right to know overrides the motive of mercy. When we presented this case to a group of editors, they voted unanimously to print it, but some of them stated a wise caution:

This has to be checked carefully. Many papers, including ours, have run stories of unattended babies choking to death, only to find that a pathologist attributes the death to a disease, so swift in onset that it cannot be halted. If coroner has medical knowledge to back up his assertion, story should be printed. In our county, the pathological report is available many days later. We probably would wait for a definitive medical report before presuming to tell our readers what caused the child's death.

Let us look at another example where kindliness and mercy are involved:

Case 52. Jim Corbett died of cancer. His doctor told him he had heart disease. The newspapers cooperated and informed the public of the true cause of his illness only after he died. This was defended on humanitarian grounds.

In this case also, the public's right to know seems to have been forgotten in the warm and understandable impulse of the newspapers to show kindliness to a great public figure. Yet, when the true cause of the death was announced, how many readers would become suspicious that they might have cancer, and the true nature of their illness was being kept from them? The policy of not mentioning cancer in news has been much relaxed in the last ten years. It can be argued that the only way to get early diagnosis, best treatment, and adequate research on cancer is to bring the disease out into the open and talk about it as frankly as about the other great killers like tuberculosis. Therefore, in this case the impulse to be merciful was at least questionable.

There are a number of cases in which suppression of news is considered in order to save an individual's "good name." Let us look at a few examples:

Case 53. A number of newspapers always eliminate the name of a woman who has been the innocent victim of rape, even though the name of the victim is a question almost all local people ask about the story.

Case 54. Some newspapers have a rule that they don't mention the names of women in cases involving lack of chastity unless the woman is a prostitute or the case is important for other reasons. The argument is that a woman has a harder time regaining her reputation than a man does. On the other hand, it is argued that the sexes should be treated alike, and the amateur prostitute like the professional.

The question here in both cases is simply whether the public's right to know overrides the damage that publicity would do to the individual. In the first case, the decision of most news media would be as indicated: that the public's interest here is on the level of curiosity, and no real public interest is served by satisfying that need. The second case is less clear. Much depends on the circumstances of the case and the community. It could well be that the rumors which would circulate, if the matter were hushed up, would be more damaging than the facts.

There is another kind of case in which a doubtful reputation tends to "brush off" on someone. For example:

Case 55. A young woman of doubtful reputation is murdered. The police announce that they mean to question a prominent man in the case. There is no assurance that he has any connection whatsoever with the events. Should this fact of the questioning be published, in advance of whatever develops out of the questioning, even though some of the nastiness rubs off on the prominent man?

The strange thing in this case is that the police feel obliged to announce that they are going to question a suspect. Why don't they simply question him, and then, if he proves to have any connection with the case, take whatever steps toward publicity the case justifies at that point. There seems very little reason why the press need co-operate with the police in casting a shadow on a man who may be innocent. If he is arrested, if he confesses, if he is indicted—that is news. Otherwise it seems no more than Christian charity to leave him alone.

Case 56. A man's wife came to an editor, begging him not to publish the news of her husband's conviction for drunkenness. She said it would take away her last chance to save her husband and would ruin her children's lives. The editor said his rule on drunkenness was to ignore the first offense, but always to print the second one. Her husband had been caught once before.

This, again, is an instance that tempts any warm-hearted and sympathetic editor. Yet the question is, does sufficient reason exist here to tamper with the right to know? This is an adult, not a child. He has been given one chance: his first conviction for drunkenness has been ignored. Is there any assurance that to ignore another one would accomplish what the wife expects? Or would it merely make the man think he could get away with something? At some time the man will have to face up to his problem and decide whether to go all out to fight his alcoholic tendencies. As Herbert Brucker says, "newspapers shouldn't play God."[27] There is a limit to how far they can tamper with the flow of information. In this case, it seems that the line has been mercifully drawn at one conviction for drunkenness. Beyond that, there seems hardly enough evidence that it would be to the individual's benefit or the public good to keep the matter further from the public.

Case 57. A prominent businessman was killed in an auto accident late at night. The only passenger in his car, a young school teacher, was seriously injured and is unconscious. There were no other witnesses to the accident. A coroner's investigation revealed that the man had been drinking. The man is married and has several young children. The teacher's name is given the newspapers by the police. The question is whether or not (a) to publish the fact that a young woman was with the man in the car, and (b) if so to omit her name.

Newspaper editors, given this case, voted almost unanimously to print both the fact and the name. It was pointed out that in this case the rumors might be worse than the news story. In regard to the idea of mercy to the man's family, the general feeling was that a newspaper could hardly be expected to show more consideration to the man's family than he himself had shown. At the same time, a straight and careful coverage was indicated. But the fact that a man had been killed and a woman was near death made it almost impossible to quiet the news, even if the paper had been moved more strongly to do so.

Flint mentions a case in which cautious coverage was clearly both in the public interest and in the interests of mercy.[28] He tells of a superintendent of a Rescue Mission, a widely known evangelist, who was being sued by his wife for separate maintenance. The charges were sensational, including one that he had been the father of a child by his secretary at the Mission. Some of the members of the Mission Board believed the charges. The editors, however, says Flint, "considered the fact that the Mission had been a fine thing in the city and that many people had pinned their faith to its superintendent; also that the usefulness of the superintendent would be ended, however innocent he might be, unless all the facts could be presented at one time; also that such a case of scandal would do no good to the men, women, and children of the city." Therefore, the paper printed nothing until the trial, and then only extremely conservative items. This policy justified itself when the man was completely vindicated by the court, and the wife was shown to have been insanely jealous. At that time the paper printed the decision in full, and devoted a considerable amount of space to a full exposition of the case.

Another reason for occasional suppression of news is the maintenance of public order. Here are two examples:

Case 58. At a period in the antisegregation developments in the South when feelings were running high, a young white woman complained to a reporter that she had been insulted by a Negro as she went into a grocery store. The editor knew that even a spark like this might start a fire. He did not publish the story.

Case 59. Certain newspapers were said to have suppressed news of street fighting in New York between salesmen of Father Coughlin's paper and street crowds. The argument was that such news would arouse fanatics and make for more violence.

The first decision was doubly responsible because it is extremely hard to check up on the accuracy of such a story as this, at a time of high feeling. It may be asked why it is any more responsible to suppress news that may cause public violence than to suppress news that may make it harder to reform a criminal or a drunkard. The answer is, simply, that there is a good deal more evidence as to news causing fights or riots than there is about news affecting criminal or alcoholic habits. The editor is on firmer ground. He can confidently take action here to avoid violent conflict and try to keep the current controversy on the level of discussion.

Just as the newsman feels in some cases a responsibility for protecting an individual's good name, he feels also a responsibility for protecting civic good name. Without citing cases, let us look at some examples.

A few years ago the Chicago newspapers were accused in some quarters of suppressing the news of an amoebic dysentery outbreak until the Century of Progress Exposition closed. The newspapers vehemently denied this. But if it had been true, if the papers had suppressed this news on the theory that it might have ruined the Exposition's business, their conduct would have been particularly reprehensible, because in that case they would have been endangering human life and health. In this case clearly the public right to know was the overriding factor.

In some towns it has been strongly urged on news media that they should play down the news of vice or crime, because that kind of publicity is bad for the town. In other towns, where the Chamber of Commerce boasts of the healthful climate, papers have been said to play down the news of serious disease. A paper in a Western state was attacked for "lack of civic spirit" and "meddling" when it complained about sanitation at the city swimming pool and had the water tested, as a result of which the state health department closed the pool as a disease hazard. It is by no means contended that a news medium should not be concerned for the civic good name. In all these instances, however, the really responsible action seems to have been to improve the city's good name by improving the city. If there is crime and vice in the town, why not bring it out in the open and get rid of it? If the swimming pool needs a better sanitation system, why not work toward getting it? If there is serious illness in town, will it really in the long run help the town's reputation to ignore it?

On certain occasions, the news media have to make decisions as to whether to protect the good name or the interests of local business or industry. For example:

Case 60. There was an elevator accident in a downtown department store. Two people were slightly hurt. The question of whether to mention the name of the store came up at the news desk. On the one side, it could be argued that mentioning the name would keep customers away. On the other hand, someone argued, perhaps customers should be warned and store owners should be more careful about their elevators.

Newsmen divide as to what to do about this kind of incident (which is fortunately much less common now that elevators are more often inspected). The majority would print the name. As one of them said:

It seems to me this would simply be a routine coverage job. Certainly we'd name the store where the accident happened. Our readers want to know the full story. We don't attempt to set ourselves up as judge and jury. The story might keep customers away from the store, to be sure. On the other hand, a story not naming the store might keep the customers away from *all* stores that have elevators.

Another editor, however, introduces a useful distinction:

Use the name of the store where the store is at fault. We protect where a firm is not at fault, such as someone being arrested at a hotel, for instance, in which the hotel is in nowise at fault.

Another instance:

Case 61. A reporter got wind of a big real estate deal that was impending. It was very exciting news because it meant the opening of a whole new section of residences and the coming of several new industries. He checked back with the realtors. They confirmed the rumor but asked him not to publish, on the theory that publicity might kill the sale. He convinced himself this was true, received assurance that the rival paper would likewise not break the story, and did not publish until the formal announcement.

In this case, the newsman decided that the public right to know did not extend to knowing the facts a few days earlier, and that the public interest would be better served by seeing the deal on to successful completion than by early word of what was going on. The importance of competition can be seen in this case. This decision is easier in a one-newspaper than a multi-newspaper town. If the reporter had not been able to obtain assurance that his rival would cooperate, he would probably have felt obliged to break the story at once.

One more kind of problem. This occurs when a news medium has to decide whether it will be in the public interest to carry certain details of an otherwise legitimate story. Examples:

Case 62. A metropolitan daily published a feature story on a young burglar, arrested on his first attempted job. The story described the attempted crime in detail, telling how he proceeded like an "amateur," how he bungled the job, how with a little more skill he might have avoided detection and capture. The question was raised by the police whether this was not putting information of value into the hands of other potential criminals.

Case 63. The question arose whether to mention the means of a suicide. It was argued, on the one hand, that this was an important part of the news. On the other hand, mentioning the kind of poison used, or the method of violence, might well result in putting the idea into other disturbed persons' minds.

These cases are not easy because the evidence is not clear as to whether the news really does bring about the results anticipated. For example, it may be argued that if a young "punk" wants to go into burglary he has better means of learning the skills than from newspapers. On the other hand, the public's right to know hardly extends to details as to methods of committing crime. Here many responsible editors prefer to bend over backwards, in the hope that omitting such information may make it harder for potential criminals to take up crime. In the second case, editors divide as to whether to mention the means or not. In general, the majority practice seems to be to mention the means but not to give the details. As one editor said to us: "You don't have to be so specific as to make it easy. You can say a woman drank poison, or drank a disinfectant; but it's unnecessarily precise to say it was Lysol. The carbon-monoxide method is newsworthy, but you don't have to furnish a diagram."

In these, as in all the other cases in this chapter, the decision is not easy, and the borderline of responsible action is not always clear. The news media have to draw their own lines on their best definitions of their relative responsibility to the right to know, and to the right of privacy, the right of fair trial, and the general public good.

The Right to Know vs. the Media's Own Interest

We come finally to the interesting kind of case when the public's right to know is seen to be in possible conflict with the newspaper's idea of its own interest. Should the newspaper, for example, publish (for the public good) what might hurt the newspaper itself?

The Commission on Freedom of the Press had some hard words to say about that in 1947:

One of the most effective ways of improving the press is blocked by the press itself. By a kind of unwritten law the press ignores the errors and misrepresentations, the lies and scandals, of which its members are guilty. The retraction by John O'Donnell in the *Washington Times-Herald* and *New York Daily News* of his widely resented statement that the victim of General Patton's slapping incident was a Jewish soldier and that because of this the General's removal from area control in Germany was urged by prominent American leaders, also Jews, was mentioned by only one other daily newspaper in New York.[29]

It must not be forgotten that the mass media are business enterprises. As such they have the same need to fight for self-preservation as have other commercial and manufacturing enterprises. They have the same instinct to band together to protect each other. They have the same kind of trade associations. And we want them to be strong and prosperous, so that they can resist pressures. But what we are asking of the mass media, in effect, when we ask them to put the public's right to know above their own self-interest, is that they live up to a higher standard of public service than other businesses. Is that justified? I think it is, because the media are businesses of the kind they are.

The standard of performance in this respect has varied greatly with the paper, the magazine, or the station. On the one hand a certain newspaper chain is said to have refused to accept advertisements for "Citizen Kane" because that picture was thought to bear too close resemblance to the head of the chain. On the other hand, it is overwhelmingly the practice today to accept advertisements for books and pictures which are critical of the press in general. Thus George Seldes' book, *Lords of the Press*,[30] which was violently critical of the press, had very little difficulty placing advertisements. When a group of editors were queried as to what they would do if offered a Seldes ad, they voted 10 to 1 to accept it. "There's nothing illegitimate or questionable about the ad. Besides maybe some of the book's criticism of the press is warranted," said one editor. "Of course we'd accept the advertisement," said another. "Why not? The publisher who is afraid to run an ad like this—for the reason stated—has no business running a newspaper. It's guys like him who make Seldes look good."

Despite a few instances such as the "Citizen Kane" case cited above, there is a steadily lessening tendency among the media to protect their personnel or the personnel on other media from unpleasant news. Thus the divorces of several publishers have been treated as front-page news, in their own papers, although in communities where such news would be most unfavorably received. Queried about the custom of protecting personnel from uncomplimentary news, editors and publishers in 1955 responded overwelmingly that they would not and did not give such protection. "I wouldn't work for a newspaper that followed a custom of protecting the personel of other papers, or even its own personnel, from uncomplimentary news," said one editor. "Any policy of special treatment or exchange of courtesies is contrary to and in conflict with the public's right to know."

Similarly there are fewer and fewer reports of news being controlled by pinches on the pocketbook nerves of newspapers. Where such reports do come in, they are much more often about news being added than about its being suppressed. That is, papers are sometimes willing to go along with stories of a promotional character when an advertisement may be at least remotely connected. But it is rare, indeed, that newspapers or radio stations or news magazines will remove a story because the advertising department says it will lose some advertising if the story is run. Nevertheless, a medium is not anxious to give free promotion to a competing medium, unless the story is likely to get to the public anyway. Thus the newspapers carry stories on Oscars and such awards, and on the large giveaway quiz programs, because they are broadcast nationally anyway. But only a few newspapers in the United States carry the Benjamin Franklin Awards which compare with the Pulitzer Prizes and go to national magazines.

One of the most puzzling characteristics of American newspapers and broadcasting, however, is the extreme scarcity of good criticism of newspapers, radio, and television in these media, and their considerable sensitivity to criticism from any other quarter. The newspapers, some of them, have distinguished book, theater, and film criticism, but the number of distinguished critics of radio and television in the newspaper can be counted on the fingers of one hand. The number of radio and television critics of newspapers is now zero since Don Hollenbeck's program on the press has gone off the air. The newspaper has no critics of newspapers, and radio and television no critics of radio and television.

Furthermore, the performance of the press when criticism comes from outside is often skittish and resentful in the extreme. When the Hutchins Commission came in with their constructive criticisms of the press in 1947, the report was for the most part given silent treatment in the newspapers, and indignant treatment in their trade journal and meetings. One of the features of the Hutchins report most objected to was the suggestion that an agency be established to check on and criticize the press on a continuing basis. Why this should be so resented and resisted by the press is hard to understand, when the press itself is an outstanding example of an organization which continuously checks on and criticizes other social organizations.

But the suspicion remains that the majority of the press does not want to be checked on and criticized in the same way as, for example, the press checks on government. An interesting example of that occurred in the spring of 1956. This was the time when a committee of researchers, under the auspices of Sigma Delta Chi, proposed to a large foundation that they should make a thorough study of press performance in the 1956 Presidential campaign.

This idea went back to the 1952 campaign, when Mr. Stevenson, who was supported in that campaign by only 14 per cent of the newspapers with 11 per cent of the circulation, charged that America was developing a "one-party press." Experienced newsmen like Roscoe Drummond and Eric Sevareid expressed doubts that Stevenson was getting a fair break in the news columns.[31] Understand that this is not an objection to a newspaper favoring one candidate editorially, but to that paper giving its favored candidate favored treatment by its selection and play of news.

There was much talk of an impartial investigation of these charges. The newspaper trade weekly, *Editor and Publisher*, demanded an "exhaustive, extensive survey to reveal the exact degree of fairness or lack of it in this presidential campaign." For a time it looked as if a survey of this sort might be made under the auspices of Sigma Delta Chi, but it was decided that such a study would not be feasible *after* the election; it must be made *during* the campaign.

Therefore, in 1956, Sigma Delta Chi took up the idea again, assembled a distinguished committee of researchers to plan the study, and asked a foundation for a grant. It was felt that the support of at least a considerable segment of the press would be helpful, if not essential to such a study, and a "jury" of 76 publishers were asked to read and comment on the research proposal.

Of those publishers, 12 did not reply. Of the 64 who did reply, 35 were opposed to the study, two were noncommittal, eight were favorable with reservations, and only 19 were definitely in favor. Sigma Delta Chi dropped the proposal.

"In short," said Graham Hovey, editorial writer for the *Minneapolis Star*, in an indignant broadcast, "a majority of those responding reacted exactly as a majority of American newspaper editors and publishers have always reacted to criticism from any source. Some responded with bluster and abuse which thinly veneered the deep insecurity they invariably feel when anyone suggests that the press itself should answer to the public for its performance. Some admitted outright that they were afraid of such a survey and they should at least get credit for candor. Some of the editorial voices in this country who have bellowed loudest in the last year about the people's right to know plainly indicated by these answers that the people's right to know does not extend to the behavior of newspapers. Some publishers who pose as experts on the freedom of press guarantee in the First Amendment to the Constitution indicated clearly that they, and they alone, will decide whether the press is meeting the public responsibilities for which it was given that constitutional guarantee in the first place."[32]

The press, Mr. Hovey continued, was "singled out from all other private business institutions for special protection in the First Amendment to the Constitution. The press remains in private hands —and must remain privately owned, free from government control or coercion—if it is to do its job. But the press must never forget that it is charged with a public function. It is a quasi-public institution. And it should never object to public examination of how well it is doing that job. It should welcome—should always welcome— constructive evaluation and criticism of its performance."[33]

What did the newspaper trade paper, *Editor and Publisher*, have to say? It said that Sigma Delta Chi did the right thing to drop the whole project. "There will be shouts of protest from some people who have been promoting such a study since 1952," it said, forgetting that *Editor and Publisher* itself promoted the idea in 1952. But "the majority of responsible editors and publishers see little value in the study, regardless of its conclusions."[34]

One of the most encouraging things about this 1956 episode is that the "majority of responsible editors and publishers," as *E & P* characterized them, did not include the editors and publishers of many of the papers which are most frequently picked as the outstanding newspapers in this country. Not in that majority were the *St. Louis Post-Dispatch*, the *Louisville Courier-Journal and Times*, the *Christian Science Monitor*, the *Providence Journal and Bulletin*, the *Minneapolis Star and Tribune*, the *Washington Post*, the *Denver Post*, and the *New York Times* and *Herald Tribune*. The presence of newspapers like these on the side favoring a study of press performance leads one to hope that the newspapers' resistance to criticism is something they will outgrow.

The *Post-Dispatch* spoke very plainly about its colleagues who don't want the press criticized. "The newspapers of the United States," said the *Post-Dispatch*, "are strong for the unrestricted right to criticize public officials and individuals they do not like. But many of these same newspapers become suddenly allergic to the idea whenever criticism pertains to the press itself. . . . All stood strong for freedom of information until that free information began to concern the press. . . . The American press is storing up trouble for itself by this dog-in-the-manger strategy."[35]

8

Truth and Fairness

We have been talking about a kind of quantitative ethic: *how much*, under given conditions, is it the responsibility of mass communication to tell the public? But within these quantitative requirements there are qualitative responsibilities. One of these is the standard of truth and fairness we expect from the mass media. Another is the standard of taste and decency we expect. We are going to postpone the matter of taste and decency to Chapter 9, and take up the problem of truth and fairness here.

Charles A. Beard reminded the *St. Louis Post-Dispatch* symposium on freedom of the press that "in its origin, freedom of the press had little or nothing to do with truth-telling . . . Most of the early newspapers were partisan sheets devoted to savage attacks on party opponents. . . [To the editors of these early papers, freedom of the press meant] the right to be just or unjust, partisan or non-partisan, true or false in news column or editorial column."[1]

Conditions are different from what they were in those days, and our demands upon the press have changed with conditions. There is a very real doubt whether we can now permit our press the luxury of being deliberately untrue and unfair. For one thing, we doubt that the free market place of ideas will work as intended unless the individual units of the press are fairer in representing opposing viewpoints than they used to be. Again, we are impressed by the complexity of the world which the present-day press has to report to us, and by the possibly earth-shaking importance of a false picture and a wrong decision. For that reason we are inclined to put on the press certain safeguards of truth and fairness which have not always been there.

We shall consider this emerging code of new responsibility under half a dozen headings in the following pages: the separation of editorials from news, the nature of accuracy, the problem of objectivity, the meaning of balance, fairness, and reliability.

SEPARATING NEWS FROM COMMENT

One standard of truth and fairness is now so widely understood and followed that it is hardly new any more, but yet it represents a fundamental change since the early years of the libertarian press. This is the rule that news reports must clearly be separated from commentary. The news columns are as objectively accurate as possible; the editorial columns, as persuasive as possible.

President Eisenhower stated the rule while addressing the National Association of Radio and Television Broadcasters in 1955: "I once heard an expression with respect to newspaper standards," he said, " . . . the newspaper columns belong to the public and the editorial page belongs to the paper. And I find that an easy standard to follow and to apply as I examine a newspaper. I should think that some such standard could be developed among you."[2]

The same view was stated by the managing editor of *The New York Times* in connection with the 1952 election. Said Mr. Catledge:

> *The Times* is supporting General Eisenhower on its editorial page. It goes without saying, of course, that the news columns should offer no clue to this position. The editorial page is of no concern to *Times* reporters and news editors. It might be stressed conversely that bending too far in the other direction in an effort not to give any semblance of favoring the paper's candidate is also to be avoided. The rule—and this *is* a hard and fast one—is the same as they give the umpires: "Call them as you see them."[3]

This, as we have said, is fundamental to the emerging standard. The newspaper separates its editorials from the news space. The newscaster tells us when he begins to function as a commentator. This is clear and almost universally agreed upon. But beyond this lie several other problems where the line is not so sharp or clear.

ACCURACY

One of these areas is the apparently simple problem of inaccuracy. This has a superficial clarity: of course, the news media should be accurate; of course, a reporter should be accurate. And when glaring examples are gathered together, as they easily can be, it seems that mere carefulness and specificity might solve the problem. For example, here are some cases collected for *Editor and Publisher* by

Allan M. Lazarus, telegraph editor of the Shreveport, Louisiana, *Times:*

On Mossadegh's trial:

Wire A: "The ailing 73-year-old ousted dictator wore gray woolen pajamas and a gray bathrobe."
Wire B: "Mossadegh wore a brown, pin-striped suit under a grayish brown overcoat."

On the Korean prisoner exchange:

Wire A: "Anticommunist North Korean prisoners of war . . . walked peacefully into interview tents."
Wire B: "Kicking, screaming North Korean prisoners were dragged into interview tents."

On a man who threatened to jump from the fourteenth story of a New York hospital:

Wire A: [He was] "coaxed down" and "allowed two firemen to pull him to safety through a window."
Wire B: [Firemen] "pounced on him. They seized his arms and pushed him through an open window."

On a statement by Senator Knowland:

Wire A: "Senator William F. Knowland said today that we might not be faced with the present 'unfortunate situation' in Korea if the *Truman administration* had consulted with Syngman Rhee."
Wire B: "Acting Senate Republican Leader William F. Knowland blamed *President Eisenhower* today for the 'breach' with South Korean President Syngman Rhee."[4]

These quotations from our respected wire news services are rather shocking because they deal with facts which could readily be checked up. For example, did Mossadegh have on a brown suit or gray pajamas? And it is true that whenever an individual figures in a news story, he usually finds some parts of the report, major or minor, which are not in accord with the facts as he knows them. But news media have made great progress in this respect in the last hundred years and are constantly working to teach their newsgatherers to be as accurate as possible.

One of the great barriers to accuracy is what we can call:

The Dangerous Need to Be First

"There are scoops and scoops," said R. A. Farquharson of the Toronto *Globe and Mail*, "but the trend which has put the emphasis on being first, right or wrong, has been, I think, the most dangerous single road to irresponsible newspaper work."[5]

This is undoubtedly true. And yet time is of the essence on the newsgatherer's job. The reporter is often asked to do a considerable job of social research, involving complex economic, political, scientific, or psychological subject matter. He has to make decisions of the kind which ordinarily go into the report of a long-range investigation, a doctoral dissertation, or a scholar's book. But the reporter ordinarily can't afford to study the problem for months or years, as a scholar might. Over him hangs the demand of a deadline, and in many cases the threat that the opposition may get the story first or get a more interesting version of it.

These threats are somewhat less since competition between dailies has become less, and since radio has taken over much of the function for breaking news stories. But the time pressure is still there. Not often in our time, however, has it led to the kind of faking which it used to bring about. Flint quotes this description of the sinking of the *Titanic* which was published as an extra about the time that the rescue steamer arrived in port:

Stunned by the terrific impact, the dazed passengers, many of them half-clad, rushed from their staterooms into the main saloon amid the crash of splintering steel, rending of plates and shattering of girders, while the boom of falling pinnacles of ice upon the broken deck of the great vessel added to the horror. In wild confusion, men, women, and children rushed about the saloons and cabins of the great steamship as though driven out of their senses. . . . In a wild, apparently ungovernable, mob they poured out of the saloons to witness one of the most appalling scenes possible to be seen. . . . For one hundred feet the bow was a shapeless mass of bent, broken, and splintered steel and iron. . . . Then came the shudder of the riven hulk of the once magnificent steamship as she slid back from the shelving ice upon which she had driven and her bow settled deeply into the water. "We are lost! We are lost!" was the cry that rose from a hundred throats.[6]

This story was widely read at the time, but later proved to be mostly fiction. As all who have read the recent books on the event

will realize, there was little shock when the steamer hit the ice-
berg, little damage above the water-line, no panic. As Flint says,
"what a lesson in skepticism for newspaper readers!"

News-writing of this kind was not typical even in 1912 and has
become much less typical since. Much more typical of the current
kind of problem is the following, given to us by a reporter on a large
daily:

Case 64. At a public luncheon, a city official charged that the police
department had hired as officers a number of men the Army had discharged after finding them psychologically unfit for active duty.

A reporter covering the luncheon asked the official for more details
but received none. After hearing the story, a rewrite man contacted the
police reporter for a check on public personnel files. The police insisted
the files contained no pertinent information and said they were unable
to confirm or deny the charge.

With a deadline approaching, the rewrite man telephoned the city
official who had made the statement. The city official admitted making
the charge but refused to comment further.

The rewrite man decided the story in its present state was too flimsy for
publication. He reasoned that even if the charge were true, made without
malice, and involving a significant number of police, there was no evidence
that a man once unfit for military duty was incapable of serving later as a
police officer. He felt that the story might unjustifiably lower public confidence in the police department.

The city editor overruled the rewrite man. Seeking a local story for
banner play, the city editor argued that any statement by a police official
was adequate basis for a story.

A majority of newspaper editors and publishers would apparently
agree with the city editor. A group of them, polled on the question,
voted 4 to 1 to use the story. The typical response, however, advised
some caution. It went like this: "Run it, being careful not to point
finger at any individual officer or officers. If statement is true, public
should know, so situation can be corrected. If false, official should
be dealt with by public opinion."

This is an orthodox repetition of the "free and open encounter"
theory. But the fact that there was some difference of opinion on
the paper itself, and later among the editors polled, indicates at
least some disquiet with the principle. For instance, here is another
reply from an editor who was faced with the case: "No story for
this edition on basis of facts explained. I'd rather miss the story

for one edition than possibly get it fouled up. No reader really remembers that we had it first. It's better to get it right."

Here is another case recorded by a veteran reporter:

Case 65. It is important to have more than just quotes to support some stories. Take, for instance, the pneumonia situation they had at the Army camp south of here.

From a very reliable source I got "quote" material charging, first, that pneumonia was widespread among the men in basic training at the camp, and, second, that the camp hospital had insufficient supplies of medicine to treat the pneumonia cases. I suspected that the opposition had the same quotes.

I culled from several sources enough facts and figures to support the first charge, and even elaborate upon it. But I could not find any evidence to support the second charge. I figured it was a pretty dangerous charge to give publicity to, in view of how the families of the trainees might be made to feel, and even in view of its possible effect on the men themselves. So I let it drop and wrote my article about the incidence of the virus. A serious situation like that needs proof in every line.

The implication in this last case is that public figures making charges at each other do not automatically rate newspaper space for those charges, despite the theory of "free and open encounter" and despite the presence of deadlines and competition. It is better to look into the charges first. In other words, the news medium's responsibility for accuracy extends beyond merely reporting the accusation accurately.

Thus it seems likely that a concept of accuracy in fact is emerging beyond the concept of accurate presentation of charge and counter-charge in "free and open encounter." This is at least in part because competition for speed is less than it used to be. Newspapers seldom issue extras, and there is no longer such a pressure for firstness as there once was. The chief pressure today seems to fall primarily on the wire services, where a beat of two or three minutes may determine which service is used by newspapers and radio stations which subscribe to both. And it may well be that the public too is becoming more discriminating as between "getting it first" and "getting it right."

Here is an interesting case of "firstness":

Case 66. A small radio station without a newsman on regular duty habitually monitored a large network station in order to protect itself against news breaks of great importance. So doing, it thought it heard the large station give a bulletin to the effect that President Eisenhower had decided (in February 1956) not to run for a second term. An announcer interrupted the program to tell the listeners of the smaller station that the President had decided not to run. The station was flooded with calls of inquiry and protest. The announcer checked the story and went on the air with a correction. Thereafter, the station broadcast a correction and apology at fifteen minutes intervals for several hours. Asked why he hurried on the air with the erroneous bulletin, the announcer said that he didn't want to be scooped by the other stations. Stockholders of the station said that they felt this seriously affected the station's prestige and played a part in the later decision to sell the station.

If all inaccurate stories were so spectacularly inaccurate as this station's news bulletin on Eisenhower, there would doubtless be a swift subordination of the value of firstness to the value of rightness. But, of course, most stories are not so spectacular nor so easily checked up. And therefore the danger of hurry will remain. But the writing on the wall is clear. Newsgatherers are dealing with explosive material, whether nuclear or social. As the economic demands of competition continue to decline, their responsibility to be accurate will more and more override their responsibility to be quick.

The Problem of Quotes

On the surface this seems to be a simple matter. In dealing with a man's words and ideas a reporter should—then, if ever, it would seem—respect the source and reproduce it accurately. The trouble is that most of us do not speak literary prose. On many occasions we do not even speak grammatical prose, as the verbatim transcript of any informal meeting will prove. Even the Congress of the United States gives its members the privilege of correcting their statements before the *Congressional Record* is published, and the President of the United States may not be quoted verbatim on his news conference statements without his permission.

This creates a situation in which Christian charity, regard for human dignity, and the Golden Rule all bear on a newswriter to make him, in the narrow sense, inaccurate—that is, to clean up the speaker's grammar and smooth out his sentences. For example, this is the kind of case that arises:

Case 67. The new mayor, whom the paper has opposed, sounds illiterate when he is quoted directly, although he is a forceful and effective man. The paper's policy has been to quote directly wherever possible.

The city hall reporter inquired whether he should (a) abandon direct quotes in the mayor's case, (b) clean up his grammar, or (c) quote the mayor exactly as he talks and let the people see what they elected.

When that case was presented to 26 newspaper editors and publishers, 16 of them said they would instruct the reporter to clean up the grammar, and 6 said they would abandon direct quotes entirely in this case. One said that he would quote the mayor exactly as he talked, and the others said their decision would depend on other factors. "Some of our best government officials never got A in English," said one editor. "Why hold them up for ridicule?"

This is the advice of a reporter on a metropolitan newspaper:

I'll change a man's quotes when I write the story. How much I change them depends on the circumstances.

If his grammar is bad, I'll correct it if the changes do not alter the substance of the story.

If it moves the story, I'll rejigger the order of his statements. I often condense a number of quotes just to get the nut of the man's message.

The only thing about a man's quotes that is really sacred is his point of view. If you conserve that, almost any other change is perfectly proper. But on controversial or technical topics you've got to be careful and keep the quotes as close as possible to the original statement.

Let's face it. Unless you have shorthand—which every reporter should have and very few do—you cannot possibly get down accurately everything a man says. But you can listen carefully and avoid misinterpreting.

As the newsman says, there is a question whether a reporter who does not know shorthand should attempt direct quotes at all, except of a very short statement or one that can be checked back with the author. As newsgatherers are increasingly professionalized, we may look forward to a time when reporters will not be assigned to cover speeches unless equipped with shorthand to do so.

Most editors want direct quotes if possible, especially in speeches. Most reporters make an attempt to check their quotes back with the source. But more often than not, it isn't possible to check back. There isn't time, or the source can't be located at the crucial hour. If speakers will prepare for reporters such manuscripts as they have, if they will save a little time after the speech for reporters to check with them, and then tell the reporters where they can be reached during the reporters' writing time, there will be fewer complaints of being misquoted.

Incidentally, the entrance of radio and television into the reporting of speeches is helping to outmode the old complaint of misquotation. It is hard to maintain that one's own voice misquotes him. However, these new media are raising other questions: whether the frank give-and-take of a good press conference, or the candid interchange of a good council or board meeting is possible when every word is being broadcast. This we have discussed in the previous chapter.

However, there is one other dimension of the use of quotes which deserves mention here. That is the deliberate fictionizing of quotes. Occasionally a speaker reads strange and wonderful words in a newspaper, purporting to represent what he had said in public, but actually altogether strange and unfamiliar to him. The reporter, without shorthand notes, had simply taken the theme and elaborated it in his own words. Fortunately this quaint custom is now uncommon, and good riddance to it.

What Is an Accurate Photo?

News photographs are another component of mass communication which calls for a careful definition of accuracy. The difficulty is that many scenes at dramatic moments do not visually reflect the drama of the occasion, and that many individuals do not mirror the emotions or the characteristics which the news report is trying to illustrate. The photographer therefore poses his subjects in a stereotyped position—for example, the "cheesecake" photo of the actress arriving on shipboard, or the triumphant shouting picture of the athletic victors. In one way or another, therefore, it is the photographer, rather than the subject, that stimulates the action.

We are not talking about "faking" pictures. The composite picture of a Maryland candidate and a Communist official which was faked in the offices of the *Washington Times-Herald* has been indignantly condemned by the profession and can hardly be condemned vigorously enough. Similarly a newspaper was censured a few years ago when it used a picture of "wetbacks" crossing the Rio Grande, labeling it as Mexican families taking refuge against bandits who were overrunning the country. There is no question about this being irresponsible and unethical conduct. What we are concerned with here is the delicate line which the photographer must walk in trying to get a picture to "mean" what the news story will say.

Thus, for example, this case:

Case 68. A news protographer got an excellent picture by throwing a flashbulb into the crowd. Many people were frightened. The photographer was brought to the editor for praise or discipline. The photographer defended himself. He said there *was* excitement in the crowd, but it wouldn't show up in the picture without some special stimulus like the one he provided. Thus, throwing the bulb into the crowd resulted in a "truer" picture than he could otherwise have got. He thought he was justified in throwing the bulb.

This practice was condemned almost unanimously by a jury of editors and publishers to whom the case was put. "It's stuff like this that gives newspaper photographers a bad reputation and makes too many people, including a lot of judges (who won't permit pictures in their courtrooms as a result), afraid of them," said one of the editors.

But what about the less obvious case, in which the photographer merely reposes his subjects in more stereotyped positions because "the readers expect it"? What about the cases we have mentioned: the cheesecake photo of the actress and the shouting picture of the winning team? Here the growing tendency of the news media seems to be to play the picture in a lower key, and the growing tendency of the better photographers is to avoid the old stereotypes in favor of more candid reports. One of the best statements of this growing attitude was made by Milburn P. Akers, executive editor of the *Chicago Sun-Times*, to a conference of news photographers at Lawrence, Kansas:

Unhappily, news photos are not always honest and accurate. I am referring to the tendency of certain photo-journalists to paint the lily, to take liberties with the truth; generally, I might add, with no ulterior motive in mind except to produce a pleasant picture, full of grins, camaraderie and good fellowship.

I recall two bad examples. Several weeks ago, Senator McCarthy criticized a general who appeared as a witness. The next day Secretary of the Army Stevens, Joe McCarthy, and a few other Republican senators held a meeting to go over the situation. After their private confab, reporters and photographers were admitted into the meeting room.

A reporter for the *New York Herald Tribune* described the scene in this fashion, and I quote:

"At the end of two hours, the door was opened, and reporters poured into the room. Secretary Stevens was sitting alone on a green couch, silent and grim. The remnants of a fried chicken dinner lay on a wheeled table. Secretary Stevens refused any comment other than 'the statement speaks for itself.' *When photographers demanded it,* he managed a wan grin and shook hands with Senator McCarthy who was grinning broadly."

All of you here may remember that that photo and other similarly posed pictures, showing McCarthy and Stevens in "bosom-buddy" attitudes, were serviced to newspapers throughout the country.

Whatever the politics of each of us in this room, I believe we all agree on one point—namely, that the photos in question certainly gave a distorted view of what actually had occurred. They did not honestly and accurately report the facts.

Don't you think that the more honest—and yes, the more dramatic picture—would have been one of Stevens sitting silent and grim on the couch, the picked-over remnants of a fried chicken dinner in front of him?

All of us here are aware that the New York Yankees last year won their fifth consecutive pennant and World Series. But how many are aware that a great picture was overlooked—deliberately or otherwise—following the game that clinched the pennant for the Yankees?

According to sports columnist Red Smith, the Yankees did not engage in much hoopla after the game. They walked into the locker room, sat down on benches and began pulling off their socks. They looked and acted just like what they happened to be—polished professionals who knew they had done a good job, somewhat nonchalant about it all, as real champions should be.

Then the photographers came into the room. They demanded a 'celebration' picture. You know what I mean—the players throwing their caps into the air, shouting, pummeling each other. Even Casey kissing Yogi.

Now, which picture would you have preferred for your newspaper— the realism of the polished professionals matter-of-factly pulling off their socks, or the phony scene of synthetic bedlam?

I believe we would all demand the real thing. Not only is it the only honest picture of what actually took place, but it is the more dramatic photo.

Yet, not long ago an editor of a major news-picture organization told a member of the *Sun-Times* staff: "Newspaper editors want the phony picture because their readers won't accept the other. They expect to see a celebration picture."

I don't agree with that.[7]

We don't either!

The Problem of Headlines

The making of headlines is a process which, by its very nature, makes it hard for an editor to be accurate and completely truthful.

We are now talking mostly about newspaper headlines. Neither magazine article titles, film and television titles, nor cue phrases on radio which accomplish much of the same purpose as newspaper headlines, are either quite so important to the reader's choice or quite so hampering to the editor.

"Let me compose a newspaper's headlines, and I do not care who expresses its opinions," said Flint. And with good reason, for a newspaper's headlines are its showcase. A reader glances over them like a table of contents or a program and selects the items in which he wants to invest time.

But the process of building that table of contents is one of the most tortuous and demanding in the whole news process. The news editor must fit whatever headline he composes into an arbitrary letter count, which is usually very short. If the headline is in two lines, he must balance them for length. That is, what he can say in the story in anywhere from 50 to 5000 words, he must somehow condense into—for example—two lines of 13 letter-spaces each. And within this arbitrary restriction he must not only try to give the reader an accurate idea of what is in the story, but also, by position and size of the headline, he must give the reader an idea of the relative importance of the story.

Even beyond that, the headline writer has certain rules which he tries to follow. For example, he tries to make a headline with an action verb in it, on the theory that this makes the story seem more interesting. Also, he tries to avoid passive verbs: they are supposed to make the story seem dull. In fact, the headline writer is under a constant, if unspoken, pressure to create bright and interesting headlines, because everyone knows that unless the story has an interesting head it is unlikely to be read. Therefore, he is under pressure to play up the most sensational part of the story in the head, even to emphasize a feature angle which is foreign to the central meaning of the story. And all this he attempts to do under the arbitrary restrictions of line-length previously mentioned.

The obvious question is whether we are not in bondage to a system of headline writing that makes it hard for us to represent accurately and usefully what is in the story? And, if that is the case, is there any reason why we should not fundamentally change our approach to headline writing—perhaps to the use of label heads, or magazine-like heads not so arbitrarily restricted as to length and balance. The profession's concern with this problem may be illustrated by some words of R. A. Farquharson, the Toronto newspaperman whom we quoted earlier in this section:

Headline writing is a difficult, technical job, and because of the typographical limitations it is exceedingly easy to make mistakes. When the paper pushes a desk man for brighter and brighter headings, the number of mistakes increases, and it is not fair to blame the individual headline writer for what should be blamed on the paper's policy.

For years we have worshipped the action headline, but trying to put an action headline on a passive story is an almost impossible undertaking. I think it is time that we revised our whole approach to headings. It is definitely not enough to see that the point of the heading is covered in the story. Sometimes I have seen desk men write into the story an extra phrase to support the exaggeration they had dreamed up. I do not think it is too much to ask that the headline should be a fair interpretation of what the story is about and, if this cannot be done in one style of heading, the heading style sheet should be flexible enough to provide type in which it can be done.

There is nothing wrong with the label heading, and many times it tells the readers a great deal more about the story than the use of words full of sound, which so often signify nothing. In our search for action we often come up with a silly vagueness.[8]

Hoaxes

One of the great circulation builders in the history of American journalism was a hoax perpetrated by a New York newspaper describing a trip to the moon. That was more than 100 years ago, but at frequent intervals, ever since, editors and broadcasters have stuck tongue in cheek and passed along some improbable story to their readers.

In the last decades the growing responsibility of the media has led them to look hard at these hoaxes. The general line of distinction is whether the hoax is dangerous and potentially harmful, or merely funny; and whether it is concealed or frankly labeled.

All the mass media were somewhat startled by the tremendous reaction to Orson Welles' broadcast of *War of the Worlds* in 1938, in which a news bulletin format was used to tell the story of an invasion from Mars.[9] Even though the broadcast was several times labeled fiction, still many people panicked, some fled to the hills, and there was widespread concern and disturbance. The networks have been notably more careful since then about turning their news patterns over to fiction.

A few years ago in Hawaii a disc jockey made an apparently innocuous announcement in the early hours of April 1, to the effect that the Hawaii statehood bill had passed Congress, and that Hawaiians could therefore get refunds on their income taxes. Newspaper and radio switchboards were flooded with telephone calls, and when the hoax was discovered there was considerable indignation. As a result the *Honolulu Star-Bulletin* announced that its annual series of "April Fool" stories would be abandoned.[10]

It is undoubtedly true that hoaxes are potentially more dangerous on the broadcast media than in print, where they can be more easily re-examined and checked up. But even in the printed media, for example, there has been a decline in the stories of "ghosts" dug up in times of slack news. There was a unanimously disapproving reaction among editors and publishers to the following instance, reported by a foreign correspondent:

Case 69. A correspondent in Italy admitted frankly that most of his sparkling feature copy was, at best, doubtful in its authenticity. He pointed out that most of the hard news from Italy is handled by the wire news-agency correspondents and the representatives of a few large papers; he and other correspondents handle mostly feature materials. Lately he has come to suspect that most of the features his stringers [part-time correspondents, paid by the amount of copy they turn in] are sending him probably never happened. They are apparently mostly imagination. But they *could* have happened, for they are in the true spirit of the country. And they are entertaining. The question is, whether it is unethical for him to rewrite and send in some of these feature stories, even though he can't swear to their authenticity.

The reaction of newspapermen to this case, as we have said, was almost unanimously unfavorable. The question was asked why, if a paper has correspondents and stringers in Italy, it should not get stories of people that are real and things that really happened. It was also pointed out that these were not labeled as hoaxes or fiction but were presented as news, and therefore could cast doubt on all the rest of the news in the paper.

Here is another instance:

Case 70. A few years ago a rumor circulated in Muncie, Indiana, that a couple with a dead child had been given a ride to town by a kindly motorist. Hundreds of persons swore the story was true. Each said that others had positive proof. Checking around, however, the newspaper could not find the person who had the "positive" proof. The question was whether to print the story or not.

One hundred, or even fifty years ago, the story would undoubtedly have been printed. The fact that it was not printed in Muncie, even that it was made the subject for rechecking, indicates a development in the mass media concept of accuracy.

The least harmful and most acceptable of the hoaxes are undoubtedly the funny stories. For example, in the winter of 1953-54 the Associated Press carried a brief feature story about a woman motorist who tried to start a stalled car on the Merritt Parkway in Connecticut by ramming into it while going 30 miles an hour. It seemed that the owner of the stalled car had told the woman it was necessary to get moving 30 miles an hour before the automatic transmission would be activated. This story received tremendous play all over the country, but on sober second thought editors were not all so happy about it. While many admitted that the story "would be remembered when a lot of significant stuff is forgotten," others urged that the editor who let the story get on the wire ought to have his knuckles rapped. One AP member was "mildly concerned over the casual manner in which the AP apparently picked up a piece of gossip in a bar-room or newspaper column and serviced it as a feature story which later required a corrective item." The general verdict, however, was that no great harm had been done, and many readers had been given a good laugh. The *Providence Bulletin* said that "after warning the reader, it would have been selfish not to pass it along as a funny story." The AP internal publication summed up the reactions and concluded:

Well, no blood seems to have been spilled on this one, but we don't want the staff or members filing direct on the wire, to get the idea we want to compete with Joe Miller's Joke Book, or to think we enjoy handling correctives. Far from it. However, if we have any more, we hope: (1) the story is as funny and as universally appreciated; (2) it has as plain a warning in the intro: "A motorist from this city sheepishly swears this story is true—but even if it isn't, a newspaper would have to be pretty selfish not to pass it along as he tells it."[11]

Correcting Errors

Finally, the modern concept of accuracy clearly requires the prompt and full correcting of errors, whether or not the lack of correction might result in a lawsuit. This is so well accepted that it is unnecessary to cite any cases on it.

There are two real problems in administering this rule of responsible conduct, and only one of them is readily solvable. The one that is solvable relates to the manner and place of the correction. The common rule here is that a correction should be given as much prominence as the original error. This is not always easy to do. For example, a one-sentence correction of a one-sentence error on page one can be put on the same page and the same position as the original error. But is it really as prominent without the same size display head as the original story had? And no editor is going to give a one-sentence correction the same display head as a long story originally had. The radio station, facing this problem, has the same difficulty.

But the really insoluble problem is the fact that, by the very nature of the mass media, a correction never catches up with the original mistake. Not all the persons who received the original also receive the correction. Furthermore, the original item started a train of repetitions and elaborations, and the correction is unlikely to go down the same tracks or to travel as far. There is nothing to be done about this except to try to avoid making the error in the first place. Basically, the only effective correction for inaccuracy is accuracy.

OBJECTIVITY

There has for a long time now been a considerable debate as to whether news coverage should be objective or interpretive. It is obvious that not all contributors to that debate are talking about the same thing. For example, when William S. Paley says that "the goal of the news broadcaster or the news analyst must be objectivity,"[12] Ernest H. Linford argues that "objectivity is still a good thing, but it isn't quite enough any more,"[13] and sociologist William G. Mather declares that "interpretation or doctoring of the news by the reporter's typewriter or the editor's pencil is repugnant,"[14] it is obvious that they are not using the terms in quite the same way.

Therefore, to put the argument in perspective, let us recall that the development of a quality called objectivity has been one of the greatest accomplishments of American (and certain other) news services during the last hundred years. One hundred years ago news was usually filtered deliberately through the biases of the paper that carried it. A political figure whom the paper opposed could not expect a square deal in that particular paper, although he would probably have a paper on his side which would exaggerate his good qualities as much as the opposition paper exaggerated his bad ones. It was therefore understood that this kind of bias would exist, and newspapers were subscribed to and read with that in mind.

But when wire news service came into use, and papers began to exchange news, some of the dissatisfactions which readers had formerly felt with this kind of news coverage were magnified. A wire service, for example, might be serving papers of several political slants; it would be infeasible to prepare a differing story for each of them. A paper which belonged to a cooperative news service like the Associated Press might be exchanging news with another paper of opposite political persuasion. This difficulty, along with the very real dissatisfactions many people had felt in "slanted" news, led to a wide movement to "give us the news and keep your comments to yourself." Out of this came the separation of the news columns from the editorial columns. And anyone who has examined American papers of a hundred years ago cannot fail to marvel at the great change that has come about in this direction. For in most of those early papers comment was mixed indiscriminately with reported fact, and each paper tended to be a long editorial, illustrated with news details, and espousing one particular viewpoint from which all the the world was seen.

Let us record that progress gratefully. But it is recognized that the newsgatherer is fallible. And, as Wallace Carroll said, "the fundamentalist believes that bias is inseparable from human nature, and that reporters are at least as human as the rest of men."[15]

The question then is, how to take into account this human fallibility in trying to present the most useful news report to the public? Mr. Carroll sums up the two viewpoints in the following way: The fundamentalists in this controversy, because they do believe that bias is inseparable from the rest of human nature, say that reporters "should simply get the facts and present them with as much detachment as they can, but should not try to fill in the background, interpret or analyze, especially when they are handling an explosive subject. The reader can be left to figure out the meaning of the facts for himself, or the editorial writers can help him out in a day or two. The liberal interpreters (on the other hand) believe that this strict interpretation of objectivity leads to serious abuses. They argue that especially in times like these a newspaper is not doing its job if it merely gives the reader 'one or two dimensional reporting'; it must add a third dimension—*meaning*. Consequently, newspapers should encourage reporters to dig down through the surface facts and fill in the background, interpret and analyze."

There is no doubt that this latter interpretation has been gaining favor. Eric Sevareid, one of the leading news analysts of Mr. Paley's network, expressed himself as follows:

Our rigid formula of so-called objectivity, beginning with the wire agency bulletins and reports—the warp and woof of what the papers print and the broadcasters voice—our flat, one-dimensional handling of the news, have given the lie the same prominence and impact that truth is given; they have elevated the influence of fools to that of wise men; the ignorant to the level of the learned; the evil to the level of the good.[16]

Time magazine takes the view that its responsibility is to "evaluate" the news for its readers, even at the cost of objectivity. Says James P. Wood in his history of magazines in the United States:

. . . facts are aligned, joined, related, explained, and built toward an opinion ready-made for the peruser of *Time*. . . . The editorializing is an essential part of most *Time* stories. Far from hiding the attempt, *Time* boasts of it. From the beginning it said it would give both sides of a story but clearly indicate which side it believed to have the strongest position. Its editors have reiterated their conviction that it is the duty of the press to evaluate as well as report. *Time* has never claimed to be objective. In fact, it derides objectivity as impossible. . .[17]

Alan Gould, executive editor of the Associated Press, took a very important position in 1954 when he described the work of a news agency as "reporting the news fully and fairly" *and* "explaining the news." He said:

The dividing line between interpretation or explanation and a reporter's personal opinion is hard to define. It is a question of informed judgment which we try to keep clear of personal attitudes. To objectivity in covering the news we must adhere, but too often this connotes sterility in writing. The days are past when the superficial facts can tell the news. A strictly factual story can be distorted—it needs balance—it must also have background and analysis, the digging behind the facts for the essential truths.[18]

The late Douglas Southall Freeman, when he was editor of the *Richmond News-Leader*, made a striking suggestion for recombining news and comment.[19] Contending that the separation of news and editorial pages no longer fills the reader's need—for example, no news item which arrives at an afternoon paper after 9:30 A.M. is likely to be interpreted on the editorial page until the next day—he proposed that the editorial page be abandoned as such, that editorial writers be assigned to work beside the news writers, and that each story requiring interpretation or analysis be followed by a dash and then a paragraph or more of clearly labelled "Interpretative Comment" or "Editorial Comment." The *News-Leader* did not accept the proposal, but it shows how some leading editors have been thinking. This kind of problem was in the mind of the Commission on Freedom of the Press when it wrote: "It is no longer enough to report the fact truthfully. It is now necessary to report the truth about the fact."[20]

To see the import of this problem, let us review some of the cases which Wallace Carroll has cited:

Case 71. Reporters have been up against this for years covering the McCarthy story. It has been the chief headache of the press—how to deal with someone who breaks all the rules, who exploits the news conventions of objective reporting to distort the results. . . .

The one-man hearings brought this to its height. Then the readers were helpless. . . . When McCarthy came day after day to the door of a closed room in the Fort Monmouth hearings to say to the reporters who had not heard any testimony—Well boys. Espionage—Spying. Communism—they had to take it or leave it. Oh, some wrote in, "Senator McCarthy *said* today." And some remembered to put in parenthetically the contradictions from what he said yesterday or last week. But that doesn't matter very much in the local impact, and the headline slurs it all over.

In effect McCarthy had added himself to the staff of every newspaper in America. They took his story without check. . . .

I am sure that if a scholarly study were made of the part played by American newspapers in the rise of Senator McCarthy, it would show that the Senator understood the deadly virtues of the American press much more clearly than we do ourselves. Such a study would show, I am sure, that Senator McCarthy was able to exploit our rigid "objectivity" . . . in such a way as to make the newspapers his accomplices.

Well, what can a newspaper or a wire service do about that sort of thing? It can hardly label "false" a factual report given on the authority of a Senator of the United States. But it can check up. Actually, some of the New York and Washington papers and the *Christian Science Monitor* did send reporters to Fort Monmouth to check on the evidence. But it was several months before they got the facts to correct the original impression, and by that time most of the damage had been done. It isn't easy to try to cover news "interpretively." Obviously, it costs more. Only the larger and wealthier papers can afford a corps of experts to interpret the more complex questions. The problem of time is always demanding: if an interpretation follows several days after the original item, it will never fully catch up. And there is always the danger of substituting opinion for interpretation.

Elmer Davis, in *But We Were Born Free*, states this problem well:

The good newspaper, the good news broadcaster must walk a tight rope between two great gulfs—on one side, the false objectivity that takes everything at face value and lets the public be imposed on by the charlatan with the most brazen front; on the other, the "interpretive" reporting which fails to draw the line between objective and subjective, between a reasonably well-established fact and what the reporter or the editor wishes were the fact. . . .[21]

What can be done about it? Even a small newspaper without a corps of experts can realize that bare facts may not be the truth, that a factual news story may be distorted news. It can therefore permit —urge—its reporters to dig into the meaning and the background of the news presented. It can even hold up news occasionally until more can be found out about it. Certainly it can demand of its wire services that they provide this kind of service. And at the same time it can maintain the most rigorous safeguards against editorializing under the name of news.

It is worth mentioning also that not all the responsibility for this situation lies on the press. Those who try to misuse the press are also responsible. And the public shares the ultimate responsibility for what it demands, or neglects to demand, of its media.

Let us take another of Mr. Carroll's examples:

Case 72. Several months ago our county held a referendum to decide whether voting machines should be acquired and used in future elections. On the day before the referendum, and shortly before the deadline for our afternoon paper, two of the county commissioners released a statement that if the vote went in favor of voting machines the county tax rate would have to be raised. We printed the story in the afternoon paper under a headline about the possible increase in the tax rate.

In the referendum the next day, voting machines were rejected by a margin of about 100 votes. The people who had favored the machines said that our story had swung the election. I think they were right. Now what was wrong with that? We had merely reported the statement of the commissioners, and we had reported it "objectively."

The trouble was that the commissioners had raised a new issue on the very eve of the election, and, as you know, not even atom bombs will scare voters as thoroughly as an increase in the county tax rate.

So I think there were two things we might have done if we had wanted to be truly objective. The first would have been to get together as quickly as possible some information on the other side of the case; this could have been used in a balanced story under a balanced headline. If time did not permit this, we might have held the story for the morning paper and presented a balanced roundup of the arguments on both sides, including the tax-rate issue together with what people on the other side would have said about it. Actually, we did print such a story in the morning paper, but the afternoon paper did the damage.[22]

Flint cites a case in which the *New York Times* rendered a noteworthy public service by refusing to report a story "objectively."[23] It happened that the War Department distributed to the newspapers a list of alleged draft evaders with the request that these names be published. It was explained that the Department desired both to help run down the actual evaders and to clear the names of those unjustly accused—for example, those who, after registering for the draft, had volunteered for military service, but had never so notified their draft boards. It was obvious that printing the list was going to work a great injustice on many people. Therefore, some papers printed it "objectively" as issued, some declined to print it at all, and a few, including the *Times*, treated it as raw material to be investigated. A number of men were assigned by the *Times* to check on the names in the list. As suspected, it was found that the list included the names of many who were already serving, some of them with conspicuous gallantry, in the armed services. It also included the names of some who had died since registering. Finally the list became so long that even the *Times* with its great resources could not check all of it. But in the meantime the *Times* had established clearly for all its readers the idea that the list was not accurate in the sense of being made up entirely of draft evaders. And in due time the War Department exonerated many of the men who were on the list.

This is the argument for an enlightened kind of interpretive reporting. On the other side we have the danger of mixing comment with interpretation, opinion with explanation. Let us take a few homely cases which illustrate some of the practical problems. This one was given us by a reporter:

Case 73. It is so easy to say, "Let's background that story." But what is background, and what is a knife? For instance: A big man in the shipping business made a statement last week that the United States should have the greatest merchant marine fleet in the world. It was a routine story until I checked the morgue. Just the month before, this man's firm had sold a number of ships to a Greek firm. I mentioned the fact in the paragraph after his quote. He telephoned the editor and charged that I had "knifed" him.

This very likely was a case in which the well-planned public relations policy of the magnate ran into an embarrassing fact dug up by the newspaper. Certainly, however, the background fact was useful information by which to evaluate the speech. The only question that isn't answered in the case is whether there were some additional facts about the sale of the ships that would help relate that policy to the policy enunciated in the speech. Possibly the reporter should have dug a little further.

Several problems were reported to us regarding the objectivity of sports news. They can be illustrated by this case:

Case 74. As sports editor I am constantly expected to ballyhoo the coming games and fights. Coaches and managers regard it as the paper's obligation to furnish that kind of service. Fans seem to expect the editor to take the side of the home team, and to support it in every way. I am treated very well until I criticize the team. Then people get hurt and angry. They complain to the publisher. They say that I have no sense of loyalty, no sense of civic pride. I am hurting the sports program. Take the game this weekend. It is probably going to be a stinker, but if I don't beat the drum a little, I'll be blamed for being disloyal to the program and helping to ruin athletics here. I'm expected to be a kind of unpaid promoter.

This may well be put beside another case from another department of the news. The following is reported by a society editor:

Case 75. I sometimes wonder how right we are in giving with the adjectives. For instance, we always write of socially prominent people as the *charming* Mrs. Smith, or President Jones and his *lovely* wife. The adjectives are just a part of the protocol.

The last sentence gives a clue to this kind of behavior: this is just a part of the protocol. Society and sports are not news at all in the sense that politics, business, health, and foreign relations are news. They share many of the features of entertainment. The parade of the athletic heroes with their bulging muscles and their gay colors, the parade of the society leaders with their graceful manners and their lovely costumes, fulfill a certain vicarious function for different groups of readers. They can identify. They can enjoy the triumph. They can imagine *themselves* crossing the goal line or being presented in the debutante's cotillion. They can feel real anger at what looks like a poor decision called by an umpire they have never seen against a youngster they have never met. And therefore their expectation of sports and society writing may be somewhat different from that of front-page news.

But yet it may not always be so. In many of the better papers now, the sports columnists' kind of writing is clearly separated from the sports news, and most of the extravagances of vocabulary and imagery and hero worship which used to characterize sports writing have disappeared. Many people have begun to realize that the extravagances of the sports pages were not unrelated to the excesses in athletic subsidization and recruiting which have lately caused us so much trouble. And so also with society news. Some of the gushing is on the way out. Some of the almost medieval pageantry previously credited to the "400," or whatever number of social leaders the community has, is being given the daylight treatment.

To sum up, then, the emergent line of responsibility for the news media is somewhere around that slender borderline Elmer Davis described as lying between the objectivity that takes everything at face value and reproduces it accurately, and the extreme of interpretive reporting which fails to distinguish between analysis and commentary. A careful kind of interpretive reporting is what is most wanted.

But let us be clear about one kind of "interpretive" reporting that is *not* wanted. That is what most people would call slanted news. Slanted news, as John Crosby says, is "something the other guy does. There's probably not a news program on the air that doesn't strike somebody or other as viciously slanted. . . . No two guys view or report a news story exactly alike." But, he says, there are limits, and he told, in his radio and television column, of one broadcast that overran these limits:

On September 27 the Watkins committee issued its report recommending censure of Senator McCarthy. It certainly seemed to all the newspaper editors to be the story of the day and they played it that way.

But not the "Three Star Extra"* men. They didn't even include the day's biggest story in their preliminary "headline" reports. When they did get around to it, they backed into the story—not with a report that the committee recommended censure—but with the statement from Martin Dies of Texas that he doubted whether censure would hurt McCarthy. "The committee recommended that McCarthy be censured on two counts only." (I love that "only.") It was all over in about thirty seconds and not once did the boys see fit to mention that the committee called McCarthy's conduct "contemptuous, contumacious, and denunciatory," which struck every one else as eminently newsworthy.

The following day, when the Watkins report was still pretty hot news, "Three Star Extra" dismissed it with a single sentence: "Republican National Chairman Leonard Hall said today that the American people are sick and tired of the McCarthy issue and it will not have any effect in the November election."

"Well, "Three Star Extra" is sponsored by Sunoco, which sells a product that oozes out of the ground in Texas, and Texas oil millionaires—some of them, anyway—are notoriously partial to Senator McCarthy. They're entitled to their opinions on McCarthy, but not to let them creep into a straight news program. It isn't as if "Three Star Extra" were a commentary-type program like, say, Fulton Lewis, Jr., where you expect a large measure of personal opinion. It isn't; it's billed as the "newspaper of the air" and it's supposed to be straight factual news.

* A radio news program.

And I'll bet every editor in the country—pro-McCarthy, anti-McCarthy or neutral—would support me in saying that that was hardly adequate coverage of the McCarthy censure report.[24]

BALANCE

We must depend on our mass media for a true and balanced picture of that part of our environment with which we do not have direct contact. That we do not always get that true and balanced picture goes without saying, and we may infer that it is to be expected in any except the perfect society. Yet this is a matter of concern to media and audiences alike, and certain principles of responsibility are emerging.

Phil Kerby, editor of *Frontier* magazine, cites a case in which balance was apparently violated in reporting political campaigns. This is Mr. Kerby:

Case 76. General Eisenhower landed at our International Airport, whence he paraded, with his entourage, to the Coliseum, the scene of a speech which it was advertised would be nonpolitical, but nevertheless would be a major address of some importance to the nation. (This was during the 1952 campaign.)

Later that night in listening to a news broadcast I was rather intrigued to learn that only some 15,000 persons, which included delegates to the Veterans of Foreign Wars convention, had heard the talk. Confessing to a bit of malicious interest, I turned to the papers the next morning, not to read the speech, but to get a look at the spectacle of some 15,000 persons lost in a stadium seating 105,000.

I looked in vain.

There were pictures of Eisenhower, with the crowd looming up behind him, but nary a glimpse of an empty seat. While musing over the kindness of editors, it seemed to me there was a similar event in the news four years ago, but with dissimilar results.

President Truman spoke on that occasion in Omaha before an audience that filled only one-fifth of a large auditorium. This fact, it seemed to me, was recorded in the press across the nation, along with graphic illustrations showing the empty auditorium.

I checked my recollection with newspaper files, and, sure enough, there was the picture, big as life, and, in fact, in *Life*, and on the front pages of many other publications, including a morning Los Angeles newspaper.

Four years ago, a picture of 8,000 empty seats was news, but today a picture of 87,000 empty seats isn't news. When is a picture a picture?

Perhaps newspaper techniques have changed in four years. Or could it be that news values are somewhat flexible, depending on who it is who speaks to empty seats.

How were the two events covered in words?

A newsmagazine which specializes in sharp, timely reports had this to say on Truman's appearance in Omaha:

"That night he had an evening of pure horror . . . Although his trip had been well advertised and admission was free, he had drawn an audience of only 2,000. . . .. One of Truman's aides reported 'We had to chop a hole in the ice to get him out.' " A caption on the picture of the almost empty auditorium read "Campaigner's nightmare: 8,000 empty seats in Omaha."

Now let's take a look at the report in the pages of this same newsmagazine after General Eisenhower's Los Angeles speech.

"Ike's advisers were worried when they found out that the VFW meeting was to take place in Los Angeles's vast 105,000 seat Coliseum, which they knew would not be filled. In the TV age, such huge crowds, unless they are carefully drummed up in advance, have become rare. Since his appearance was nonpolitical, Eisenhower did not allow any interference with the veterans' plans, or any attempts by the Republican Party organization to drum up spectators. Only 14,925 seats were filled."

Then the magazine goes on in the same kindly vein:

"Despite the empty seats, it was perhaps Eisenhower's most effective speech. It seemed to get across not only the man's principles but the man's heart. . . ."

This magazine was a little less kind to Truman after Omaha on his western trip four years ago. Quoting a newspaper editorial, the newsmagazine said: "Then it called the pitch on his western trip: 'It's politics, but not smart politics.' "[25]

As Mr. Kerby suggests, the last remark might be paraphrased: "It isn't smart reporting." For a more attentive public—and the American public is becoming more aware of its needs from the mass media —will demand a more balanced picture.

Mr. Kerby cites another case:

Case 77. The discharge of General MacArthur was a dramatic event that excited controversy to a fever pitch and deserved the most careful handling by the press. In many newspapers that was exactly the way it was reported, but in others it was a different story.

When General MacArthur testified in Washington, the "lead" news story of a Los Angeles chain newspaper published this report: "General MacArthur today not only vindicated himself with documentary evidence before the Senate Committee probing his removal, but offered a dynamic blueprint for ending the Korean War and keeping Russia from taking over the Pacific."

Other, more confused, minds had to await the completion of testimony before trying to reach a decision on this involved matter, but not the writer of this dispatch. He settled it in a brief 35-word distorted paragraph that was passed along to his readers in the guise of news.

Several days more, this same correspondent pictured General Marshall more as a culprit brought to dock than as a man who had rendered distinguished service to his country. He wrote of Marshall's then forthcoming appearance before the Committee in these words:

"Defense Secretary Marshall, author of the multi-billion dollar giveaway plan for Europe and active participant in the Red China appeasement program, will have considerable to explain tomorrow before the Senate Committee probing the dismissal of General MacArthur."[26]

A better illustration could hardly be cited of the difference between a responsible and an irresponsible kind of interpretive writing. But even to cite these cases may give an unfair impression. These are on the unlovely side. We could cite many more instances from the desirable side: instances where newspapers have bent over backwards to represent fairly the point of view they disagree with.

Unquestionably, there has been a great improvement in the American press in this respect. "Press lying," about which the Commission on Freedom of the Press talked a great deal, seems to be a relatively uncommon phenomenon. Much more bothersome is the presenting of truthful material out of balance.

The principle of responsibility which has emerged is that the news media should adequately represent all sides of a controversy. This does not mean that the editorial page should be balanced, only that the news column should fairly represent both sides. As President Eisenhower said, the editorial columns belong to the paper, the news columns to the public. It does not mean that the news columns should be edited by a foot-rule, or the newscasts by a stopwatch, to assure that each side of the controversy gets precisely the same space or time. Some papers do give opposing parties equal space on battle pages, and some stations do allocate equal time for opposing sides. But if Party A or Candidate B makes more news than Party X or Candidate Y, there is no good reason why the amount of news space or time should not reflect that fact. The important things are (a) that the arguments of each side are *ade-*

quately represented, (b) that the news presentations of the campaign are as fair and accurate as the paper can make them.

A memorable broadcast by Edward R. Murrow, three years ago, raised in a vivid way some of the problems of fairness and balance.

Case 78. Edward R. Murrow devoted one program of his *See It Now* series to Senator Joseph R. McCarthy. He began by offering the Senator free and equal time to answer. Then, with a skillful combination of film clips, tape recording, and his own commentary, Mr. Murrow put together a devastating attack on the Senator and his methods. In effect, the Senator was used as a witness against himself. In a closing editorial, Mr. Murrow summarized his indictment and called for "a reaffirmation of basic concepts of fair play and particularly the elementary right of dissent."

Vigorous objections were made to this program, despite the fact that Senator McCarthy took the proffered free time for answer. It was charged that Mr. Murrow's partisanship was contrary to the kind of balance expected of television. It was charged that television had the power to destroy, and that this power was too dangerous for television to be permitted to use it against an individual. On the other side, Jack Gould wrote that "for once television was a leader, not a passive camp follower, in the realm of public opinion."[27]

So far as the problem of balance is concerned, television, like the newspaper, is permitted to editorialize, although it must give equal time for rebuttal. There is no requirement that each editorial program need itself be balanced pro and con: only that an equal opportunity be furnished for the other side to be heard. In fact, often it works better for both sides to have separate broadcasts on which to present their views coherently and without interruption. Note, now, that we are talking about *editorial* broadcasts, not news broadcasts. We expect news items to be full, fair, and balanced. But so far as editorial programs are concerned we ask of radio and television more than we ask of newspapers; newspapers have no obligation to represent more than one side on their editorial pages, but radio and television do. And it is clear that Mr. Murrow, by offering his target free and equal time to reply, was fulfilling this obligation.

But is this a misuse of the power of television? Is it fair to let the great weight, the overpowering authority of television, fall on one man? This is indeed a disturbing question, despite what one may think of the merits of Mr. Murrow's program on Senator McCarthy.

For if television has the power to destroy a public figure, that power must be guarded zealously. Television might fall into the hands of unscrupulous men who would have as much skill as Murrow in the use of the medium, but none of his social conscience. Television, in other words, might become a bridge to demagogy and dictatorship.

This is one of the points where a high sense of responsibility is required of the medium. For, on the one hand, we don't want television to give up its opportunity to take a stand on an issue; if equal opportunity for rebuttal is given, this is one of the most vivid ways we have to get an issue out in the open and stimulate public discussion. On the other hand—let us quote Jack Gould again—"if Mr. Murrow with his firm and measured presentation can overnight stir up strong public reaction, what could the hypnotic, reckless, and charming firebrand achieve in like time?"[28] The only answer to this is judgment, balance, care, and responsibility on the part of the television industry. It is a dangerous, useful power they have. The danger must not keep us from using it, nor must the heady drug of the power blind us to the danger.

It is always harder to administer a fair and balanced policy than to administer a biased one. This is true, whether in the dramatic current of national politics with Mr. Murrow, or in the more modest level represented by the following case:

Case 79. A hot controversy over fluoridation is raging in the town, and the newspaper is receiving many letters to the Editor about it. The only trouble is that the paper is receiving about three times as many on one side as on the other. The question is whether to publish three times as many on one side, or to give equal space in the letters column to both sides of the controversy.

When this case was presented to a group of editors and publishers, they voted overwhelmingly for printing all the letters, regardless of ratio, if space is available. If the number exceeded the space available, some editors said they would run only those that raised new points, restated old ones most effectively, and answered opposition arguments best—in other words, a selection on basis of quality. Some said they would run also a box score on numbers received favoring each side. Some said they would take all the letters out of the column and summarize them in a pro-and-con front-page story. Whatever the device, though, the objective these responsible news executives were trying to reach was to put all the important arguments, on both sides of a controversy, before the public, fairly and accurately. This is obviously a vastly different purpose from the one which was being served by the writers of the political news items we quoted at the beginning of this section.

The responsibility of the mass media is to bring us not merely a true and balanced report of political controversy but rather a true and balanced picture of *all* noteworthy aspects of our environment. How do the news media stack up against that test? Are we learning enough to understand our foreign relations? Are we learning enough to get a balanced judgment of the implications and requirements of the nuclear age? Are we getting an adequate picture of our own national government, our educational system, or our labor-industry relations?

When you tell a mass communicator that the average local newspaper devotes less than a tenth of its stories to all the world outside the U.S. and our relations with the rest of the world; that only if one reads one of half a dozen metropolitan newspapers in this country can one get anything like an adequate picture of what happens at the President's press conferences; or that the media have succeeded rather in confusing than in clarifying the present controversy over education—if you accuse him of these things, he answers quite rightly that the news channels carry what they think the public is interested in.

He is absolutely correct. One of the first things a reporter learns is a list of behaviors which the public is supposed to enjoy hearing about. These include sex, conflict, children, animals, et cetera. And the real nub of the problem is whether the portrait of man which is held before our newsgatherers is adequate for us in the present stage of our civilization?

For it is this concept of man—reading and listening man—which is chiefly responsible for the flood of trivial features which crowd out solid news in our media; for the casting of every possible behavior in terms of conflict, so that we invariably read of diplomatic conferences in terms of a sort of international athletics in which there is a clear victor for every race, and of international athletics in terms of warfare between countries; for the glorification of sex which brings us to know about Hollywood show-girls even to the minutest details of their private lives, whereas even the public lives of our public servants are far too often unreported. Is this a fair picture of the nature of man and a fair estimate of what he needs for a picture of his environment?

One example. The following item was plucked from a great and respected West Coast newspaper. It attracted my attention doubtless because it was datelined Marietta, Ohio, which happened to be the town where I was born. It came from a wire news service and had been given a two-column head. This was the item in its entirety:

Marietta, Ohio, June 17—Are you man or mouse? In case of an atomic attack, says Marietta College physics professor Winston Love, you had better wish you were a mouse.

Love told a science club here that a mouse's body can withstand a much higher radiation level than a man's and would be "much more comfortable" in the radiation "fallout" area.[29]

I mused on this item, because it was probably the only story from Marietta that would make this distant newspaper for months, perhaps for years. As I recall, the last news Marietta made was of a juicy murder. And I asked myself: is this a true and balanced picture of what is happening in Marietta? Was this the most important part of Professor Love's talk on atomic energy, or was there some other part which would more clearly justify 2,000 miles of leased-wire travel and a two-column head? This souped-up lead paragraph, this "man or mouse" twist—is this all that the great newsgathering organizations can find of interest in the oldest town in the Northwest Territory and in an old and honorable college? And if so, what concept of the interests of the Pacific Coast must the newsgatherers have?

Another example: All this week, as I have been writing in a California town, the National Education Association Convention— the big education meeting of the year—has been going on a few hundred miles away in Portland, Oregon. All week I have been waiting for a report on what is happening at that meeting with its hundreds of talks, section meetings, forums, et cetera. This evening, after five days of the convention, it finally broke into the very good local daily paper. What managed to break in? Here is the lead:

A wild-cat floor fight—with charges of "subterfuge" and "dilatory tactics" enlivened closing sessions of the usually serene sessions of the National Education Association.

What they decided about the several great issues now before education, what new ideas came out of the research papers and forums, we don't know. But we do know that they had a fight on the convention floor. That is what the newsgatherers think we are interested in.

The most worrisome feature of the "true and balanced" picture is not the sins of commission, but the possible sins of omission. For we can see the imbalance that occurs occasionally in political news, but we can only guess what news from the NEA meeting, from Marietta, from Southeast Asia, from Washington, from our schools, laboratories, factories, and farms is not being reported to us, supposedly because we aren't interested in it.

What is the source of this concept of news interest? It is partly in the lore of newspapers, partly in the readership studies which have now shown for several hundred papers how many readers read what items. In either case, it is based on a doctrine of massness—that the more people who can be brought to read an item, the better public service it is. This is at best doubtful, for it reduces news choice to seeking a common denominator. The items that will be universally read will indeed be a sexy story (with picture), a sensational murder trial, a cute picture of a child, a bitter conflict of one kind or another. But how about what the minorities want to read?

The news media recognize some of these minorities. They carry a lot of sports news for the largely-male minority of sports fans. They carry a lot of society and home feature news (and the radio a lot of soap operas) for the largely-female minority which is interested in that kind of stuff. They carry a lot of comics (and children's programs on the radio) for the largely-youth group which cares for these things. They carry a lot of business news for the business minority, a lot of agriculture information for the farmer, et cetera.

But how about some of the other minorities which may not be so directly related to advertising? And how about the many people who would like some material on religion?

The Rev. Everett Parker, director of the Congregational Christian Churches' Office of Communication, told the Bricker Committee that NBC devotes only 30 minutes a week, less than one per cent of its time, to religion. And this time has to be divided among Protestants, Catholics, and Jews, with such a fine line that "during 24 weeks of the year not a single minute on the NBC network is devoted to Protestant Christianity." The American Broadcasting Company, he added, gives no TV time at all for religion. CBS is now the only network which regards religion a public service obligation and "demands no payment for what little time it does allocate to religious matters."[30]

Says Gerald:

The labor point of view, and the place of the working-men in society, for example, are seriously under-represented in the mass media of communication. Whereas in England two of the biggest newspapers, with a total of nearly 7,000,000 daily circulation, speak for politically moderate or conservative labor, only small newspapers perform that function in America.

Some of our writers and leaders assert that each community needs a number of newspapers devoted to different political points of view in order to obtain full discussion of controversial issues. However, an industrial society produces newspapers in its own image. It is said truthfully that as the newspapers become larger in response to the public's demand for a variety of information and entertainment, and as their circulations grow to great size, they take on more and more of the aspects of large factories disseminating information and entertainment.[31]

And how about the minorities that are interested in news that would make them better citizens? The minorities, that is, which would like more than the seven foreign news stories they get in an average day from their hometown newspaper? Those who would like to know more about developments in nucleonics, or automation, or education? In other words, how about the minority which has had more schooling than the 9th-grade average assumed for the mass, which has more sophistication than is represented by the 8th-grade vocabulary level which many of our most successful media try to reach, who have more intellectual curiosity than many of the age, sex, and occupational groups who are already served? Is it not the responsibility of the mass media to serve this minority too?

A news medium which so recognizes its responsibility will probably find something more newsworthy in Marietta, Ohio, than that man-or-mouse story.

From the critics' side have come horrible examples of how the media have at times not lived up to their responsibility for balance. For example, here are two that John Oakes cited in *Nieman Reports*:

There was a Montana newspaper which offered its readers a report of the National Plowing Contest in Minnesota, at which both candidates delivered major addresses. The paper gave a full account of the speech of General Eisenhower, whom it was supporting for the Presidency, and then added at the bottom of the story: "Governor Stevenson also spoke."

Then there was the evening newspaper in West Virginia that didn't print a word about the fact that the President of the United States was going to make a whistle-stop there that day. The editor explained later: "I saw no reason why I should help the Truman crowd."[32]

Responsible performance in single-ownership communities is not attained without effort. Here is part of Paul Block Jr.'s account of what single-ownership has meant to his *Toledo Blade*:

On the *Toledo Blade*, we have found it necessary to adjust our approach and some of our news techniques to this "one voice" psychology. One of the first of these adjustments has to do with the story that would ordinarily be rejected because it will interest too few readers— in other words, is not "newsworthy." Where there are competing newspapers, the rejection would be accepted as a matter of judgment. Where there is single ownership, rejection frequently brings the charge of discrimination. It's hard on the well-trained city editor at first, but standards of what is "newsworthy" have to change in cities with but one newspaper "voice."

Some techniques adopted under single ownership will seem to the newspaper in competition to be leaning over backwards to avoid even the most foolish accusation of unfairness. Good journalists would squirm at the way the *Toledo Blade* edits political news during election campaigns. It's done with a ruler—partly in deference to the political prejudices of readers, partly to protect the *Blade* from that type of post-election survey which implies that a newspaper was grossly unfair because the speeches of one party's candidate received more space than those of the other.

Then there's the matter of letters to the editor. Competitive newspapers as a rule carefully screen them, printing only the better ones. Where there is only one "voice," the newspaper can't be so fastidious. The *Blade* cheerfully prints letters that are merely illiterate or idiotic, drawing the line only at blasphemy, pornography, or sedition.

Another way single-ownership newspapers may do things differently is in the use of syndicated columnists, who offer a chance to present conflicting political points of view. On the *Toledo Blade*, these columnists are used without regard for their popular appeal, solely in the belief that its politically variegated readers are entitled to every viewpoint that can be had, provided it is an honest one. Contrary to the practice of appraising each column on the basis of what it has to say, and how well it says it, recognizing that no writer can be good every day, the *Blade* carries its hands-off policy to the point of refusing to edit or omit the copy of any of its regular columnists (however much forbearance it sometimes may require).

Single-ownership newspapers can demonstrate their concern with the public interest in the most practical pecuniary way. Public appeal advertising and that of charities gets the lowest possible rate in the *Blade* (the same rate earned by those retail stores which do the largest amount of advertising in a year's time). The *Blade* also keeps its rate for political advertising low, in contrast with the rather general practice of charging a premium rate. In a single-ownership field, it is more important to encourage the fullest expression of political opinion than to set a high price on it, even though political advertising—being irregular and uncertain—will not otherwise carry its share of the cost load.

These are only a few of the ways single ownership newspapers may use to vary their approach and change their techniques. More will be developed as publishers are willing to stand up for the journalistic advantages of single ownership.[33]

One of the interesting developments in the efforts of newspapers to maintain the free market place of ideas has been the "battle page." The *Indianapolis News* became aware that, amidst all the heated controversy which the Bricker Amendment was generating, many of their readers—in fact, even learned editors and college professors, explained the editor of the *News*—could not state the provisions of that Amendment. Therefore, the *News* devoted its editorial page on a Monday to presenting the Bricker Amendment, explaining it as carefully as possible, stating pro and con arguments with the utmost balance and care. The page became a reference sheet for local club and school discussions and was very favorably commented on by readers.[34]

In following weeks, the *News* devoted Monday editorial pages to such topics as the Eisenhower farm program, the St. Lawrence Seaway, and "Are the people of America moving toward hard times?" For the last of these pages the *News* called on Senator Homer Ferguson of Michigan and Senator Paul Douglas of Illinois to write pro and con articles.

The battle-page idea has been used on many other papers, and is one example of what can be done to obtain full and balanced presentation of ideas on a controversial subject.

What has just been written suggests some of the problems which are raised by the responsibility of being alone. Basically, the problem is that this situation requires of an editor or a broadcast executive a rather special degree of initiative. The energy and imagination which in a multiple market he might devote to beating the competition he must in a single market devote to maintaining the market place of ideas. He can no longer wait for the opinions to flow into and through his paper or his station; he must actively seek them out and be sure he is representing them, and in some equitable balance. He can no longer wait for the circulation figures to give him a quick tab on how well he is meeting the needs of his readers, or on the latest edition of the opposing paper, to give him an idea of the standard he must meet. He must actively seek out the needs of his readers and figure out ways to meet them.

A number of cases and problems have been reported to us, growing out of this peculiar responsibility of being alone. Here let us cite three of them as examples:

Case 80. A single-ownership paper vigorously opposes a candidate for national political office. One of its regularly syndicated columnists writes a column vigorously in favor of the candidate the paper opposes. The decision is, whether to print that day's column or not. If it is part of the editorial offering, the editor reasons, you have every right to omit it for disagreeing with your editorial policy. On the other hand, he asks, does not the paper have an obligation to represent the other side on its editorial page as well as in its news columns?

Ten to one, the editors and publishers to whom this case was presented said that the paper did indeed have an obligation to present the column; indeed, should actively seek out such contrary viewpoints and expose its readers to them. On the one hand, the newspaper surely has the right to omit a column or any other part of its contents which it feels does not measure up to its readers' needs or interests. On the other hand, as one editor said, "We certainly wouldn't do it in this case. Our columns are open to all kinds of political thinking, and we encourage opposition to our own views. The charge of a 'one-party press' would certainly be true if we forbade anything in our papers that didn't agree with our political thinking."

Here is another problem:

Case 81. A paper is offered an editorial advertisement which follows a line that the paper opposes and advocates public action which the paper feels would be detrimental to the community. The paper can do one of three things: (a) accept it, (b) accept it and say nothing about it, (c) accept the ad and comment on it on the editorial page. The publisher gets conflicting advice. His advertising department doesn't want an editorial written in opposition to the ad. Some of the editorial staff feel the ad should be rejected outright; others that it should be accepted and commented on.

By about the same ten to one margin, editors and publishers believe the ad should be accepted. This is a view with which it is hard to quarrel: the newspaper offers its space for private messages, whether or not it agrees with them; a single-ownership newspaper would be on doubly dangerous ground if it refused an ad except on specific grounds of public interest (for example, patent medicines, games of chance, et cetera). But, by the same token, the newspaper is not obligated to remain silent about the ad. Rather, it should welcome a chance to state its own side of the argument, and thus get both sides before the public and stimulate the functioning of the "free market place."

Another interesting case reported to us really was a variant of this last one.

Case 82. A "well-heeled" group has been buying advertising attacking G., a school official. G. bought one advertisement to reply but apparently cannot afford to buy more. The question is, what obligation, if any, has a newspaper in this single-ownership town to represent G.'s case?

The obligation, it seems to us, is simply to see that G.'s side is fairly represented. This can be done through letters to the editor, through editorials, through a "battle page," through interviews with G. It is not necessary to "edit with a ruler" so that G. gets as many column inches as the opposing group buys. But a single-ownership paper has a responsibility not too unlike the responsibility of a network to give an attacked person the right to reply. A network will ordinarily grant the attacked person the same amount of time and at the same hour as his attacker had. The paper at least can see to it that G.'s side of the story is adequately told.

FAIRNESS

It is easier to be fair to a big man than to a little man. It is easier to be fair to someone who can hit you back. It is easier to be fair to someone whom you like. The mass media, like other organizations or individuals, therefore face most of their severe problems of fairness in dealing with the little men of this world and with their own enemies and opponents.

What do we mean by fairness? We mean giving justice. Is it the responsibility of newspaper and broadcasting stations and films to mete out justice? Of course it is. For every case tried in court, one hundred are tried in print, on the air, and on film. These are not often cases in law. More often they are cases involving what society is going to think of one of its members—whether he has written a good book, whether he is a conscientious and efficient public official, whether his speech made sense, whether he is at least ordinarily good-looking or ludicrous, whether he is someone to look up to or someone to sneer or laugh at. The mass media have the power to try cases like that, and they do it every minute of the day with the news and comment they carry, and the pictures they present.

By fairness we mean seeing the other fellow's position and presenting it adequately. We mean charity and kindness in the Judaeo-Christian tradition, with handicaps and foibles.

For example, take this problem:

Case 83. The paper I am on now does not mention the fact that a man is a Negro unless there is some special reason to—almost never does, in fact. The last paper I was on identified a criminal as a Negro when he was, although it did not identify a criminal as a white man when he was.

Question: Which is better practice?

The responsible answer here, and the one to which both newspapers and broadcasters are trending, is that if knowing that the man is a Negro is essential to understanding the case, the fact should be mentioned; otherwise, not. Why should the mass media give themselves to creating separateness among humans? Why should they, even by inference, imply inferiority or greater criminality among human beings of one color? Prejudice is a deep and hard-to-change trait, and if any change is to come about, the mass media and other educational institutions of society will have to be in the foreground of change. This same responsibility applies obviously to identifying people as Jews or of any other race or natonality to which prejudice is sometimes attached.

Here is an instance involving the "little man." A reporter on a metropolitan newspaper gave it to us.

Case 84. Sometimes the little man gets it in the neck. Just yesterday a motorman operating a street-car hit a pedestrian who was jaywalking between Twelfth and Thirteenth avenues.

The story carelessly reported the accident at Twelfth and Broadway giving the impression that the victim had been in a pedestrian crosswalk zone. There was no libel because the reporter mentioned that the motorman had not been cited.

But the motorman's neighbors got an impression of the accident that was all wrong. The story had emphasized the sob angles. The victim was an elderly lady with a bouquet of flowers in her hand. All the drippings.

Let's say that instead of a motorman one of our socialites had driven into the old lady under the same circumstances. Instead of just stating the driver was not cited, the reporter would have explained exactly how the accident had happened. And he would have been accurate in reporting the facts.

That doesn't leave us much comment to make. Obviously the reporter had let the entertainment value of the scene crowd out accuracy; he was in effect contributing entertainment rather than news to the paper. And he was obviously being unfair to the little man who, unlike the socialite, would not be able to hit back.

One of the hardest tasks of a newsgatherer is to be fair to sources he doesn't like. Take this case, given us by a reporter.

Case 85. I can't stand the school superintendent. Frankly. He is superior and scornful and "fake" culture. I suspect he's a "phony." But he's news—two or three times a week. The problem is how to keep that feeling out of the stories I write about him.

Because this reporter recognizes the problem he probably will be able to keep his bias from showing. He is under no obligation, of course, to withhold any news which will show up inefficiency or malpractice on the part of the school superintendent. But here he must be doubly careful—both of his sources and his evidence, and for the right of the superintendent to state his side of the case. In general, a "phony" will reveal himself, and straight news reporting will ultimately get the idea over. Meanwhile, the reporter's problem is to keep it straight.

Another problem is fairness to one's professional competitors. This is easier because one's competitors are usually not "little" men. Here is what one man who covered a metropolitan news beat for many years and now works for a broadcasting station has to say about how he handles this problem:

Case 86. We all have to decide how far we'll go in cooperating with a rival reporter. Every reporter has his own rules of conduct, but in my experience rules of conduct are forgotten when the story gets big.

As a rule, there is no obligation toward a competing newsman. We are in a very competitive business. In some circumstances, however, I feel it is all right to help out a rival. Sometimes it is a matter of friendship. Sometimes it is a matter of common decency. Usually, I believe it is a matter of safeguarding yourself for the future.

Take press conferences. I'm happy to fill in a rival reporter who arrives late for a press conference. But if he misses an important quote after he has come, that's too bad for him.

Every story has its own ethical problems, I suppose. I just play it by ear. If I had to state an overall principle, I suppose I'd have to say that my first loyalty is to my paper. I like my fellow reporters, but they don't pay my bills.

Many of the complaints that mass media get about fairness have to do with their reviews and criticisms. Here the main principles are fairly clear and have been set up by a long tradition of book, theater, and music reviewing. The reviewer should be an expert in the subject matter he is reviewing. He should have no axes to grind with the author. He should tell enough about the book or performance or play—and tell it accurately—so that the reader can make up his mind whether the critic is justified in what he says. And he should review the book, not the man, except as one must know the man to understand the book.

A different and more disturbing problem of fairness was raised by Paul Butler, Democratic national chairman, when he attacked the CBS coverage of the first night of the Democratic convention.

Case 87. Early on that first night, the Democrats presented a film in documentary style. The first half of it was somewhat less than breathtaking. CBS turned away from the film during the second half in favor of interviews with prominent personalities on questions related to the convention. The other two networks stayed with the film. Chairman Butler attacked CBS for unfairness to the Democratic Party, and telegraphed a demand that CBS carry a complete showing of the film on all stations which had carried the substituted interviews. Frank Stanton, president of CBS, answered that the network, in covering an event, was entitled to its own judgment as to what was worth covering. "Those who make the news cannot, in a free society, dictate to broadcasters . . . to what extent, where, and how they shall cover the news. Television and radio . . . are not mere conduits which must carry everything which the newsmaker demands. . . . We insist . . . that we are, and must remain, free to exercise our news judgment."[35]

It is hard to feel that Mr. Stanton is not, in this case, in the right. The networks are not common carriers. We do not want them to be common carriers, for that would give them responsibility only to deliver what is handed them. We expect them to exercise some responsibility for what goes into their channels. And therefore they clearly have the right to turn their cameras away from one aspect of a convention to cover another aspect. Undoubtedly some of Mr. Butler's irritation stems from the fact that his convention planners had been trying to "manipulate" the media a bit—that is, to use the convention coverage to get a political film, free of time charges, to a huge audience. But, even though CBS was clearly within its rights in doing what it did, still the question of fairness remains. By showing only half the film, was it fairly covering the convention? No one can answer that without reviewing all the coverage and the action that was there to be covered. The difficulty of the question illustrates what a complex and mature responsibility is being placed on the media which report to us on our environment. The wisdom and discernment that it takes now to be fair in news presentation is something completely beyond any public service ever asked of the party press.

RELIABILITY

Let us look at three aspects of the reliability problem which especially trouble the media—their relations with sources, their responsibilities in giving advice, and their responsibilities for advertising.

Relations With Sources

One of the most important services a news or information medium can provide is to state frankly and fully the sources of its information. This is clearly a part of its responsibility.

But this principle runs into trouble when news comes, as it often does, off-the-record or without clear attribution. Here are examples cited by newsmen:

Case 88. About once every two weeks we get a story which we know to be a trial balloon. It has an indefinite source and has to do with a policy which the state government will or will not adopt, probably on the basis of public reaction. Are we justified in playing our part in this little game? That is, ought we tell the people what the situation is, or just go on printing the stories?

Case 89. We can't help getting a lot of good material without permission to quote. That is, we can use the material but not the name. We usually publish the story, crediting it to "usually reliable sources" or "an official spokesman" or "a member of the Administration who declined to be quoted." But I wonder whether we are justified in printing something whose spokesman won't stand up and be counted?

There is no simple answer to either of those questions. Suffice it to say that there has been a marked tendency on the part of all news media during the last half-century to try to state sources. Many news media, when they know a story to be a trial balloon, will say so. Many reporters will refuse to hear material "not-for-attribution," if it turns out to be something on which the source *should be* willing to stand up and be counted—for example, an attack on someone or something. On the other hand, it is obviously necessary, considering the complex news being made today and the demands of government security, that reporters be given certain background information off the record, and that they be given certain stories in advance of release date in order to handle them properly. These confidences are respected by the responsible media.

There was recently a much publicized case involving release dates which it may be well to put into the record at this point.

Case 90. A certain Mutual Broadcasting System commentator broke the release date on the Atomic Energy Commission's summary of the Oppenheimer hearings. The documents were in the form of a 992-page

book in 8-point type. They were made available to the press at 6 P.M.
June 15, subject to release date of noon June 16. This particular commentator, however, revealed the contents of the documents on his broadcast during the evening of June 15. Defending his action he said that
he was "tired of the phony business of reports and documents being
leaked to a selected, if motley, collection of the left-wing press, while
the rest of the news world toddles along behind."

The newsmen themselves reacted vigorously. Typical is this statement to *Editor and Publisher*:

Any news man who accepts a release voluntarily assumes an obligation
to respect the release date. He violates that obligation at the expense of
his personal honor and the respect of his fellow craftsmen. Breaking
the release on the Oppenheimer testimony was also a national disservice.
By forcing the news services into a hurried analysis of a stupendous
amount of material it deprived morning newspaper readers of a properly
evaluated presentation of an important case.[36]

How about unsigned letters? Most papers say they will not print
letters that come to them unsigned. This is necessary and justified;
otherwise the paper would be flooded with crack-pot, irresponsible
material. But on the other hand, a responsible paper will sometimes
publish a letter from which it has withheld the signature. As Flint
says, "Sometimes persons not without courage, and actuated by the
best motives, may write unsigned letters. Circumstances may render
such a proceeding their only avenue of attack upon evil. Of course,
in so doing they are asking the newspaper to shoulder all the responsibility. This may or may not be a fair request. But the editor
may be expected to decide the question without assuming the easy
attitude of contemptuous indifference toward all such communications."[37]

Case 91. We always have a few qualms (says an editor) about printing *made* news—stuff the press agents figure out. For instance, the
picture of the midget on J. P. Morgan's lap; or the story of the hippo-
potamus with the stomach-ache. These stories and pictures are apparently
highly interesting to a large number of people, but so contrived!

The instances cited are harmless, except insofar as they take space
or time which might be given to more important items. But what
editor was really proud, a week later, of having published a press
agent's photo of a midget on J. P. Morgan's knee? And what editor

was really proud, when he thought it over, of delegating the editing of his circus coverage to the press agent who dreamed up a gigantic stomach-ache for the hippo?

Here is an instance reported by a wire service correspondent overseas:

Case 92. This reporter feels the lowest point of American press policy in Korea was the decision to black out the news of the first truce talks at Kaesong in July 1951. This refusal to disclose even the slightest developments in armistice negotiations forced the UN correspondents into conversations with Communist "newsmen," who freely briefed the reporters on the proposals of each side.

As a result, this reporter and the others covering the armistice negotiations used Communist sources to supply the core of their dispatches. Although each statement was clearly attributed to one or the other of the two Communist newsmen (Alan Winnington, of the *London Daily Worker*, or Wilfred Burchet, of *Paris Ce Soir*), there was a vague but disturbing sense of guilt that the stories might be, indirectly, a product of the Communist propaganda machine. By its silence, the UN Command prevented the free press from presenting the Allied side of the story. This fact was of tremendous torment to this reporter. I wanted to boycott the Communist newsmen, but that would give the opposition all the play. If the opposition agreed to a joint boycott, then some special (a correspondent for a single American newspaper or magazine or network) would have taken over, or one of the non-American agencies.

There was no choice—the story was too competitive for any finer ethics.

Fortunately, when the armistice negotiations were resumed at Panmunjon the UN Command reversed its press policy and commenced full briefings after each session.

Here is another problem of source relationships:

Case 93. An advertiser buys space for editorial advertising, but does not want to include his name as the advertising source. In other words, he wants to publish a kind of anonymous editorial in advertising space. The publication ruled that he had to publish his name as the source of the advertising. Right?

Clearly the source of editorial advertising is something the public has a right to know, and the publication a responsibility to divulge.

These variations on a theme might be spun out indefinitely, but the pattern has at least been suggested. The ideal is a full and frank statement of sources. That is for the public's protection. In a few cases, responsible news handling requires that the principle be violated in the public interest. Responsible media will keep those exceptions as infrequent as possible.

The Problem of Advice

We are going to talk briefly about the responsibilities of giving advice.

Giving advice might seem to be about as far from the standard of objective news reporting as one could get, and yet all the news and opinion media are increasingly being asked to give advice of one kind or another. "How to do it" articles are increasingly popular in magazines. Hardly a newspaper, now, can be found without one or more advice columns: advice to the lovelorn, advice on bringing up children, advice on health and dental matters, advice on legal problems, et cetera. In short, the mass media are observing a great deal of the advisory function which used to be handled only through person-to-person channels in the smaller community.

Now what is dangerous about that? Simply that the mass media give great status to the people who write regularly for them, and, if such a person is not giving reliable advice, his bad influence is likely to be spread out of all proportion to what it would be if he were merely advising individuals face-to-face.

Therefore, the responsibility of a mass medium is obviously to hire the most expert persons it can find to give advice, and, secondly, to limit their advising to such topics as may properly be treated in the channels of mass media. No *individual* case of medical or dental illness can properly be diagnosed or treated through a mass medium; that is a matter for consultation between a patient and his physician or dentist. There is very grave doubt that most problems of individual family relationships, child rearing, or love affairs can be adequately handled by advice columns; these, too, require more complete knowledge and are of a more personal nature than can be carried by letter and print or broadcast. There is a curve of danger rising from advice about how to cultivate gardens, how to repair furniture and build homes; through advice on how to make out an income tax return, and how to interpret the law; up to how to prevent and cure illnesses and maladjustments. The media are on safer grounds at the low end of the curve. They are on safer grounds, wherever they are on the curve, if they stick to generalized materials as opposed to individual problems—for example, how to keep food sanitary on a picnic is a safer subject than how to explain or cure a pain in the stomach; and what to expect, in general, of the child between 4 and 6 is a safer subject than what to do about a particular 5-year-old child's particular problem. Finally, they are on safer ground when they deal with advice derived from the "wisdom of the race," from practical experience as opposed to professional expertness. For example, magazines may be doing a positive service in telling a teen-age girl some of the common-sense advice which she might have got from her mother if the mother had not been too busy or too uninterested. Publications are certainly performing services in helping to guide amateur gardeners, cabinet makers, et cetera. Professional and occupational groups, such as farmers, have every reason to be grateful for the advice they get from their special publications. But when a publication or a broadcasting station begins to take over the duties of a physician, or a dentist, or a marriage counselor, or a lawyer, or a psychiatrist, then it is in danger of acting irresponsibly.

Responsibility for Advertising

We are going to talk briefly about responsibility in regard to advertising, because advertising has been a favorite whipping boy for many of the most articulate critics of the mass media.

But let us take pains to point out here that advertising, if it is one of the aspects of the media most vulnerable to criticism, is also one of their strong points. For it is advertising that chiefly makes press, broadcasting, and magazines strong and self-supporting and independent of government support and control. If it were not for advertising, we could never have a strong privately-owned communication system. And advertising is more than a necessary evil; it is a service to millions of people who shop in the ads and read them as a nonauthoritarian kind of purchaser's news service.

Frankly, the critics who yearn toward a U.S. broadcasting system wholly without commercials, or toward printed media wholly without advertising support, are mostly day-dreaming. The problem is rather to focus on the responsibility of the media which carry the ads.

It is exactly the same responsibility as for news or opinions they carry. The media are responsible for the advertisements they carry.

Now what does that mean? For one thing, it means that the media are responsible for the *amount* of advertising they carry. In a newspaper, the advertising commonly fills a little less than half the space and brings in a little over two-thirds of the income. In a magazine, the advertising may run from one-fourth to one-half the space and bring in as much as three-fourths of the income. On radio and television, the amount of commercial time is carefully controlled by FCC regulations, but these regulations are often circumvented by irresponsible stations. "Some radio stations," said Robert E. Lee, chairman of the FCC, "crowd as many as ten commercials into a half-hour program. The disc-jockey show is a notable offender. A prevalent practice at some stations is to turn up the volume during the commercial lest the deafest member of the audience fails to note that Smiling Joe's appliance store is practically giving away television sets."[38] This kind of thing is clearly irresponsible conduct.

On the part of newspapers and magazines, responsible coduct in this regard consists in keeping the relation of advertising space and news or entertainment space in some reasonable relationship. And if half the space is to go into advertising, then the publisher has a rather special responsibility as to how he uses the remainder. The less space he has for news and other public information, the more carefully he should handle that news and public information, and the more careful he should be to present a true and balanced picture, an adequate coverage and a well-edited and easily usable presentation. One of the great objections which many readers find to most American newspapers is that they really contain very little news. The reason is that the editor's "news hole" (the part of the paper he can use for news) is very small—that is, the advertising, comics, entertainment material, feature material, society, and sports, have pretty well crowded foreign, national, and local public affairs news out of the paper. Actually, the space devoted to public affairs news in many papers is less than 20 per cent. It may well be asked whether this is the most responsible use of space.

But, more important, the media are responsible for the content of the advertising they carry—not for the words, unless those are offensive, but for the reliability. Let Mr. Lee, previously cited, give another example:

The wife of a Navy combat flyer saw a commercial on a television station advertising a rebuilt sewing machine at a bargain price. When she went to the store, the salesman talked her out of buying the bargain by explaining it was junk, and talked her into signing a contract for another machine at $144.85 with $44.00 down. Soon afterward, she discovered the machine would not work properly and was a Japanese import of inferior quality. When she tried to get a refund on her purchase, two hoodlums came to her house. While one beat and kicked her, the other took the machine.[39]

This is the kind of thing that Fairfax Cone, president of the large advertising agency of Foote, Cone, and Belding, was talking about when he proposed to the American Association of Advertising Agencies in 1954 that they "throw the hucksters out of our own association" as well as "among our advertisers"; and that Mr. Lee was referring to when he said that "the pitchmen and the gandy dancer do not belong on the air."[40] The responsible media have grown up beyond the time when they can afford to carry "bait" advertising of the kind that led the Navy wife to buy the sewing machine, and the kind of advertising copy that Mr. Cone described as made up of "mealy, weasel words that make it at once both legally truthful and utterly dishonest."

Let me cite another example, this one reported in the *Encyclopedia of Classified Advertising*:

The following advertisement appeared in classified columns:

> Earn easy money at home, addressing envelopes. The work is simple and pleasant, Write XXX.

Respondents to this ad received a letter extolling the ease with which money could be made and a request for $5 for complete details and necessary equipment. The people who fell for this bait were said by the *Encyclopedia* typically to be widows, physically handicapped persons, and others who could ill afford any monetary loss. When they sent in the five dollars they got in return a bottle of ink, a penholder and a pen point, worth altogether perhaps 50 cents. They also received a letter of instructions, advising them to contact their local mail order houses which do an abundance of direct-mail advertising. Seldom, if ever, says the *Encyclopedia*, did any respondent secure work.[41]

Slowly the Better Business Bureaus and the Federal Trade Commission catch up with some of this dishonest, unreliable advertising. They are doing a fine job, but still inevitably too slow. Slow methods will not catch the worst offenders. They spit their ugly messages like grasshoppers and move on. If advertising is to be cleaned up, the media themselves must take an active part in doing so and must force the agencies and the advertisers to cooperate. It is neither necessary nor possible in all cases to give a "Good Housekeeping Seal of Approval" or its equivalent, but, at the least, questionable products, offers, and arguments should be caught before they reach the public.

It is good to be able to report that this is increasingly being done. Most newspapers have an unwritten code as to what advertisements are acceptable, and for a written code they can turn to an extensive set of rules in the *Encyclopedia of Classified Advertising,* which we have been quoting. The Chicago *Tribune* spent thousands of dollars capturing and convicting a criminal who used a classified ad to exploit a woman. Some magazines guarantee their ads. *Sunset* is an example, and has on occasions reimbursed readers who have believed themselves cheated.

This is not only good ethics; in the long run, unreliable advertising is ineffective advertising. In France, where advertising has not been policed, large numbers of readers don't believe it. Result: not much advertising is sold, and the media have a much less solid basis of support.

Without trying to cite more examples in an area where examples are already knee-deep, let us instead try to state the principle in another way and leave it. One hundred years ago, an accepted principle in advertising (which was then largely in the barker and pitch-man stage) and in much of commerce itself was *caveat emptor,* let the buyer beware. American mass media have now grown up beyond that slogan. It is no longer possible to operate with it. The meaning, for media advertising, of the new age of responsibility is that the media must be as responsible for the truth and accuracy of their advertising as for their news, their informative articles, and their comments.

9

Popular Art

The areas of news and comment we have been dealing with in the last two chapters are old and familiar ones within mass communication. Now we come to an area that is relatively new: mass entertainment. And it may well be that future historians will decide that the most important development in mass communication during the first half of the twentieth century has been the emergence of popular art to replace folk art.

Lyman Bryson,[1] Gilbert Seldes,[2] and others, have written insightfully of popular art, and there is no need for us to devote any great time to defining or explaining it. After all, we are surrounded by it. But let us at least point out here that, whereas popular art is to some extent an extension of folk art, the folk element has very little to do with the form it takes. Folk art, as Dwight MacDonald says in his standard definition, is "a spontaneous, autochthonous expression, shaped by the people themselves, pretty much without benefit of High Culture, to satisfy their own needs."[3] Popular art, on the other hand, is handed down from above. It is manufactured commercially by technicians employed by the moneyed groups of society. Whereas folk art was the common people's own institution, largely independent of the more formal art and culture of the society, popular art is provided to the common people for a price (either direct purchase of admission or copies, or indirect support through purchase of advertised goods). It is therefore an extension of the vaudeville stage and the circus, rather than of the folk dance, the folk-ballad singer, and the cracker-barrel story teller. It is important to note that whereas folk art encourages individuality and differentness—a dance for this part of the country, a pattern for this family of weavers, a version of a ballad known only in this region—popular art encourages similarity or uniformity. That is, popular art encourages people everywhere to hear and sing the same popular songs, to enjoy the same Ed Sullivan vaudeville at the same time, to laugh at the same jokes told by the same comedians, and to read the same stories. To any student of society this is obviously a fundamental and terribly important change, and it is not surprising that it raises a number of problems of media stewardship.

For the most part, folk art policed itself. The artist was in such direct contact with his audience, and the audience was so comparatively small and compact that the artist was able to know almost at once whether his performance did or did not please the audience for which it was intended. Popular art has no such feedback, although its success or failure depends just as clearly on the audience. As broadcasters are in the habit of saying, they have the job every day of coming into almost every American home—and after getting into the homes, pleasing most of the people most of the time and *hardly* ever displeasing *any* of them.

Therefore, the manufacturer of popular art has been driven into a situation where he has had to make maximum use of such feedbacks as he has had. These have been of two kinds: the size of his audience (judged from box office, or sales, or audience surveys), and such specific comments as have come from the more articulate portions of the audience. These more articulate portions are likely to be pressure groups, anxious to see that popular art does not weaken their positions or kill any of their "sacred cows." To guide and protect themselves from these pressures, most of the makers of popular art have established codes and created offices to administer the codes. Therefore, the popular artist has been in the not altogether enviable position of having to observe a code made up largely to avoid offending articulate groups in the society, and at the same time to reach and please as many (different kinds of) people as possible.

This description simplifies things too much, as will become evident on the following pages, and yet it points toward the essence of the problem which this time of change is bringing to the makers of popular art. For they face a certain revolt in their audience. The boiler-plate product, made to be as inoffensive as possible and to reach the largest numbers possible, is entirely too pallid to interest parts of the audience who are looking for the insights and frankness of fine art or the differences and freshness of folk art. A few years ago, audiences were staying away from movies. For several years now, television has experienced an acute shortage of new material. And, to make it worse, an articulate segment of the audience has begun to question the social effect even of the "inoffensive" code-approved product. They raise disturbing questions about the effect of scenes of violence in the mass media, of what they choose to call the "unreality" forced on the art in order to avoid offending pressure groups, and of the general level of taste and thought which popular art appears to represent.

✓Therefore, the nub of the problem is something like this: The maker of popular art, in most cases, has been able to use as standards (a) a somewhat artificial code of content, and (b) the commercial success of a given kind of content. These standards obviously represent outside judgments. Now, in line with the broad change that is taking place in mass communication, the question is asked whether the maker of popular art should not himself bear more of the responsibility for his product, and whether he should not be freed or free himself from the demands of these two great leveling forces in order to make more different kinds of products for different kinds of people, and in every respect to raise the artistic level of his product.

In this section we shall need to explore the kind of responsibility which the maker of popular art might be asked to assume. In general, we ask popular art to be pleasing, to be decent and in good taste, to provide an adequate service, and in defining that service to make use of an adequate concept of man. These things we can ask glibly, but to define them in terms of specifics is a serious problem for the film maker, the broadcaster, and the publisher. Perhaps the best place to dig into that problem is in terms of the relationship we expect popular art to maintain with its audience. Here the typical question is, "Should the public be given what it wants?" This is as good a place as any to begin.

SHOULD THE PUBLIC BE GIVEN WHAT IT WANTS?

The question as stated is probably unrealistic. It is hard to believe that anywhere in the mass media this question could be answered entirely on a yes or no basis. The media can never move very far from what they conceive to be the demands of public taste, and yet they can never establish such a perfect connection with public taste that their own artistic standards, their own aspirations for the art form they are creating, their own feelings as to what constitutes truth in the subject matter they are dealing with, do not enter into the shaping of the product.

Yet this question is so widely put that we must face up to it. For example, the Hutchins Commission is widely quoted as advocating giving the public what it should have, and among Mr. Hutchins' critics there is a kind of after-image of the chairman of the Commission on Freedom of the Press sitting with Mr. Mortimer Adler on his right hand decreeing that this week the public should be taught Thomas Aquinas. The typical reaction to that idea was expressed by Dwight Bentel somewhat more vigorously than elegantly:

American journalism is strewn with the dead bodies and bleaching bones of newspapers that tried to operate on the Hutchins' "what the readers ought to have" approach.

There have been a lot of mighty fine guys down through the years who set out to give the readers "what they ought to have." Good family men, too, who paid their dues at the Elks and went to church on Sunday. But their confounded readers wouldn't cooperate.[4]

But this, too, is knocking down and trampling on a straw-man. As the British Royal Commission said, the standard of the responsible press is "compounded partly of what it thinks its public wants to read about, and partly of what it thinks the public ought to read about."[5] Or, as William Allen White used to say, the editor tries to give his readers "a little better paper than they know they want."[6] This is the general attitude I have observed among responsible newspaper and magazine editors, broadcasting executives, and film makers. And there are many cases on the record when men in all these fields have taken courageous and dangerous steps to exceed the ceiling of public taste as they understood it to be.

Let us analyze that question a little more closely.

It isn't a sharp question, for a number of reasons. For one thing, our knowledge of what the public "wants" inevitably looks backward. Take an example. A motion picture producer discovers by a survey or other means that his potential audience is interested in pictures of refugees' escape from the Communist-dominated countries of Eastern Europe. He gets a story written, a picture made. It is probably a year before the picture can circulate in the theaters. Meanwhile, public interest may have shifted to another subject. What the producer would really like to know is what the public *will* want one year from now, and there is no sample survey technique to determine that. That is what Ben Hibbs, editor of the *Saturday Evening Post*, was talking about when he entitled an article, "You Can't Edit a Magazine by Arithmetic."[7]

Furthermore, there is a very real question whether the public can know what it wants. It knows what it prefers among alternatives it has already experienced; it can decide, that is, whether it prefers the concert it heard Tuesday or the concert it heard Thursday. But the very essence of art is newness. And the public can't know whether it wants what it hasn't experienced. Did the public "want" Shakespeare before it saw any of his plays? Did the public "want" Bach before he became known, or Brahms before the First Symphony? The evidence is rather on the other side. Very often, the artists who come to be most popular have the hardest time establishing their popularity. For example, Edgar Dale recalls that during the lifetime of Brahms a sign in a Boston auditorium read, "Exit, in case of Brahms."[8]

And what is this public we are talking about? Isn't it really many publics? When we make a costly film, we expect it to reach large audiences in many parts of the world. Does that mean that its public is the two and a half billion people in the world, or, in this country, the 170 million people now resident in the United States? Certainly not. There are many publics within these great masses of people. As Dale says, there is a public for a soap opera and a public for a symphony.[9] There are few "majority" publics. Even the farthest-reaching of our mass entertainment productions usually reaches only a small minority of the total "public." The number of people who attend a feature movie in this country is usually 13 to 15 million—less than one tenth of our people, one sixth of the adults. It is no paradox, therefore, to say that any piece of mass programming is really minority programming. Therefore, when we talk about what the public wants, we are usually talking about what *some segment* of the public *will* want, or rather *would* want if it had experienced the kinds of choice it will have some time in the future.

Then why is this question so often asked and argued today? For one thing, because of the new demands on the media for responsibility. Also, because of the tremendous economic pressure which bigness and fewness of units exert on the makers of popular art. Consider the enormous capital resources and investments required of the popular art media: ability to take an initial 3 to 5 million-dollars loss in order to start a popular magazine; ability to bet 1.3 million dollars on a fairly ordinary Class A picture; ability to cover recurring costs of up to $100,000 for 30 minutes of national television. This indicates the incredible cost of making a bad decision in popular art. A bad decision, of course, means misjudging what the public will buy. The pressure of corporate ownership is an additional weight on the artist and the manager, and the very ponderousness of the system tends to substitute corporate or managerial decision for what, in a smaller medium, would be the artist's decision.

Therefore a certain amount of anxiety has been generated. The critics who look from the outside wonder whether the media are going to prostitute themselves by pandering to the very lowest denominator of public taste. The media men who look from the inside out wonder whether the critics and the commissions are going to force them to ignore public taste and "go broke." Some of the critics have still another angle of approach: they fear that some of the media are actually moulding public taste into the form which is most advantageous commercially, the easiest and simplest to service.

Here are some examples of how the relationship between public taste and standards comes in a practical form to be decided by the mass media.

From newspapers:

Case 94. Today we played big a murder, two accidents, and a society divorce. The UN and the new bond issue got secondary play. We say, "but that is the stuff people are interested in. That's what sells the paper." But is it right? (Reported by a midwestern editor.)

(As Flint says, everybody knows that the burning of a bridge is bigger news than the building of a bridge, and yet which is the more important for the public?)

Case 95. Some people say our comics are cheap, and I'm not very fond of them myself. But, the devil! Every readership survey has them right up at or near the top readership. They're what the people seem to want. Who am I to censor the public will? (Another editor.)

Case 96. All of us wrote about the Olympic games as an international conflict—U.S. vs. Russia. Now we hear that it's false to the spirit of the Olympics to do that. It's not sporting. I say, that makes the stories more interesting. That's the way people want it, and they ought to be able to get it. (A sports editor.)

From the magazines:

Case 97. A magazine could obtain an article by one of the world's greatest historians, discussing eruditely the philosophic choices which are before the human race as a result of developments during the last century. The article was expensive, it was difficult, and it was unquestionably important. In an editorial conference, the editors estimated that perhaps only 5 per cent of their readers would really understand it. Yet it would start discussion, and the ideas ultimately would permeate much more than 5 per cent. After considerable thought, the magazine bought and published the article.

From broadcasting:

Case 98. A network had to choose a new master of ceremonies for a forum program. It had the choice between a man who was known for his ability to conduct a clear, orderly, and penetrating discussion, and a man who was known for his ability to generate heated controversy. It chose the latter, because it said frankly, that is what the people want. Perhaps clear and temperate discussion might teach them more about the subject, but they really want entertainment out of their forum programs—or so the network said. They want the participants to lose their heads and shout at each other. As Frederick C. Gruber says, that's the kind of forum they call "terrific."[10]

From comics:

Case 99. Some members of the comic industry have given thought to the possible effects of a number of comics like *Superman, Steve Roper,* and some of the crime strips which feature a hero doing superhuman deeds to right wrongs and bring criminals to justice, without often calling on the forces of organized law enforcement or showing any of the ordinary weaknesses of human beings. But, on the other hand, they say, if we would change the nature of these strips, the public would have a fit. They want the heroes as they are, the more supermanish, the better.

From motion pictures:

Case 100. A studio bought rights to a novel which had received high critical acclaim and hired the author to come out and prepare a movie script. When the author arrived, he was somewhat surprised to be told gently and over the space of some weeks that the public would not accept a film which carried the very frank message of his novel. What the producers really wanted out of his novel was the romance and the well-advertised title. Even the romance would have to be cooled down, he discovered. Not that the public wouldn't want it, but the Code said they shouldn't have it.

Apparently, he told friends later, what goes into a film is compounded of what the original author thinks the public should have and wants, plus what the studio thinks the public wants, minus what the studio thinks the public doesn't want, minus what the Code says they can't have. Ultimately it was discovered that the original author couldn't write a satisfactory script for shooting, and other writers were brought in. At the end, the story was so different from the novel that it seemed to demand a new title, so even the title was dropped.

These cases are all built around the theme that the media could give the public better stuff, if something would only let it. If public taste itself would permit. Or the economic situation. Or the Code.

One hundred years ago, this matter would not have been so important as it is today. At that time, there was a little better balance between serious art for the "high hats," folk art for the little people and the separate groups, and popular art for anybody. A medium could be a great success, by the standards of those times, in serious as well as in popular art; in fact, perhaps more easily so. And there were no national voice-and-picture media to make people dissatisfied with their own story-tellers, their own dancers, their own ballad-singers. But the great wave of popular art, the coming of mass circulations and mass audiences, has tended to obscure these distinctions. In a very real sense, every medium has tended to become an entertainment medium. Few communication services have been able to continue to exist solely for an enlightened minority. Folk art and artists have been outshone by the popular artists on television, radio, and film. And Hanns Eisler laments the fact that a "kind of merger" is taking place between popular art and fine art:

The old distinction between serious and popular art, between low-grade and refined autonomous art, no longer applies. All art, as a means of filling out leisure time, has become entertainment, although it absorbs materials and forms of traditional autonomous art as part of the so-called "cultural heritage." It is this very process of amalgamation that abolishes aesthetic autonomy: what happens to the *Moonlight Sonata* when it is sung by a choir and played by a supposedly mystical orchestra now actually happens to everything.[11]

And so even in the newspaper. Here is what Helen McGill Hughes says in her penetrating study of the coming of the human-interest story to newspapers:

. . . These practices point to the nearly complete conversion of certain dailies from bearers of news into pastime reading engaged in for the pleasure it gives. The simultaneous concentration of the press, the movies, and the radio upon sensational events like certain love affairs and murder trials affirm, too, that the newspaper is duplicating the role of the two other industries which have never been anything but agencies of entertainment. And so the American newspaper has largely ceased to be solely the informant of small active publics and has become primarily a medium of mass entertainment.[12]

That was what Charles Cooley was talking about when he described the new form of the newspaper as "organized gossip," which "fosters superficiality . . . , is the antithesis of literature . . . and stands for diffusion as opposed to distinction."[13]

There has been some bitterness among the social scientists as they observe the growing dominance of popular art. For example, Dwight MacDonald:

There seems to be a Gresham's Law in cultural as well as currency circulation: bad stuff drives out the good, and the worst drives out the bad. For the bad is more easily enjoyed than the good—in fact, it is this facility of access which at once sells it on a wide market and also prevents it from achieving quality. . . . The success of *Reader's Digest* illustrates the law: here is a magazine which in a few years has attracted an enormous circulation simply by reducing to even lower terms the already superficial formula of commercial periodicals. Where *Harper's* treats in six pages a theme requiring twelve, *Reader's Digest* cuts the six pages to two, making it three times as "readable" and three times as superficial.[14]

The question such critics raise is really the question of dynamics: has the great trend toward popular art come about because public taste has shaped the media in its own image, or because the media have manipulated public taste into a pattern which they can most easily and profitably serve? As I have indicated above, this seems like a chicken and egg question. There must be some of both: the media are the way they are partly because of what the public wants and will buy, and partly because of what the media want and feel they can produce. But the question, nevertheless, has some weight because of its implications concerning responsibility.

For example, if the media are really manipulating public taste to fit their commercial purposes, as a certain group of critics contend, then we could expect a vastly greater change if the media were to behave more responsibly, but we should have a harder time persuading them to behave responsibly. On the other hand, if the media are merely following the demands of public taste—if the public itself is the motivating factor—then we can expect relatively less change as a result of more responsible behavior by the media, but there will be less difficulty bringing about that change.

I stand rather on the side of the people who think that taste shapes the media. Not wholly, for it is obvious that people can choose only from the alternatives they have at hand. They cannot be sure that they would or would not like what they have not seen or read. Therefore, there is unquestionably a certain amount of conditioning of the public taste in the direction of what the media offer them.

What governs what the media offer? First, it seems to me, a careful effort to anticipate the demands of public taste, illustrated by the tremendous amount of audience research, media research, and attention to mail and telephone calls. In the second place, the economics of the industry which forces them to try to meet the taste of a very large number of people and to engage in all this audience studying activity in order to find out what those tastes are. And finally, the standards of the media executives, which unquestionably result in a better product than a mere parroting of taste would make possible.

My observation has been that there are far more leaders in the popular art media who are trying to raise standards of public taste than there are leaders who are trying to manipulate public taste for cynically commercial ends. Why does CBS maintain such a superlative news service? Why do *Life* and *Look* publish the courageous and thoughtful articles which seem not at all to be aimed at the same common-denominator audiences as many of the picture stories in the same magazines? Why does Hollywood take such a real pride in a picture which wins acclaim for its artistic validity?

I believe, therefore, that we can count on a certain amount of free will and willingness on the part of media executives to raise the level of popular art, if they are convinced it should be raised. True, this amount of freedom is seriously restricted both by public taste and by the economic ponderousness of the industry. But we can realistically ask the media to face the hard questions which the emerging age of responsibility is posing.

When Is Popular Art a Success?

The following instance is reported by Hortense Powdermaker, the anthropologist who studied Hollywood:[15]

Case 101. The successful Broadway play, *The Voice of the Turtle*, could not be made into a movie without changing its basic theme. The play was a quite moral tale about two young people who had "been around" and whose love life had been based on the principle of "love them and leave them." In the play, for the first time they find with each other a love that is lasting and know happiness and life at its best. The moral of the play is that a permanent and monogamous love brings greater happiness than temporary, illicit affairs. In the movie, the whole point of the play and its moral theme is lost, and the picture really has no point beyond that of depicting a very immature and adolescent girl falling much in love with a returned soldier who is at first not attracted to her, but later falls for her and proposes marriage.

This "case" is interesting for a number of reasons. For one thing, it illustrates one of Hollywood's most pervasive moral taboos: that sin must be punished. And furthermore, that some kinds of sin should not be talked about. Adultery is one of them. The word "adultery" is not to be mentioned on films. The fact that the hero and heroine of *The Voice of the Turtle* had "been around" is to be no more than dimly hinted at.

But this taboo structure is itself only a phenomenon. The question that really interests us is, what lies behind it? Obviously, an official morality of this kind is adopted in order to protect the viewers of the film. How are those viewers envisaged? What kind of person is Hollywood making its pictures for? This, indeed, is the basic question for all the popular arts.

✓ But behind that is still another question: By what criteria do the makers of popular art propose to judge whether their work is having a desirable effect on their audiences? When is popular art a success?

Let us begin with the latter question: when is popular art a success? The answer of the media, their basic rule, is: when it is a *commercial* success. Such a test is not always necessary for fine or high art. Many a fine artist has not been appreciated in his own time. For fine art to be a success it is merely necessary (a) that it please the artist, and/or (b) that at some time in human history it receive approval from the critical elite. But not so with popular art. It cannot afford to have approval withheld until the next generation or the next century. It must make money for its makers.

✓ That is the basic economic reality. Popular art will be judged first according to the number of people who will pay money (in the case of films, magazines, and books) or time (in the case of television and radio) to experience it. Now, what will bring in these large audiences? The media approach this question from two sides: by trying to put in what *attracts* audiences, and trying to leave out what will *repel* audiences.

Behind the makers of popular art, as we indicated a few pages back, are always the cost accountants, the owners, and the stockholders, reminding them of the tremendous costs of popular art, the tie-up of talent and equipment and time, and the frightening cost of making a mistake.

The effect of all this is obviously to restrict what can be done in popular art. The maker will depend on the tried and proved patterns —Boy Meets Girl, Loses Girl, Wins Girl (or vice versa); the attractions of sex; the excitement of conflict; the themes of love, hate, loyalty, sacrifice, etc. He will fill his medium with fiction; even factual articles and biographies must be told like stories. He will be exceedingly cautious about trying something new. Faced as he is with a medium which demands unbelievable amounts of new material, surrounded by owners and executives who warn him against misjudging public taste, he lives in a sort of occupational schizophrenia. In actual practice, he seeks gadgets, gimmicks, tricks that will make the old seem superficially new. When a maker discovers a new slant that proves successful, all his competitors jump in to copy it—always adding a gimmick to make it "new." Thus the same joke makes the rounds of broadcast comedians, the same situations repeat themselves in different comic strips, several movies of the same kind (e.g., the recent series of movies on Egypt) tend to come out near together.

But the maker of popular art must also avoid what will antagonize potential audiences. This is an enormous universe of material. Especially in the case of the movies, which are international in scope, are the complaints constant, and the resultant restrictions almost as broad as human experience. For example, writes Leo Rosten in his lively book on *Hollywood*:

The Japanese censors . . . strongly objected to a Hollywood version of *Madame Butterfly* because Sylvia Sidney, in kissing Lieutenant Pinkerton (the scene was handled with pathetic caution), placed her arms around his neck in such a manner that her elbow was bared. This, apparently, was tantamount to nudity in Japan. A national billiard association voiced hot protest because pool rooms, in the movies, are shown as unkempt places where disreputable characters congregate. The late Polish Government barred *Show Boat* because the song "Ol' Man River" was "proletarian propaganda" likely to incite the Polish masses to rebellion (the date of Rosten's book was 1941). The American Newspaper Guild objected to the prevalence of impolite, intoxicated, or unscrupulous reporters on the screen. The British regularly censor those movie scenes in which animals so much as *appear* to be suffering, even though Hollywood's studios offer affidavits from humane societies proving that the effects were achieved quite without pain to our Darwinian cousins. The Glass Bottle Blowers Association complained that the movies were giving free advertising to canned beer, and a group in the canning industry insisted that the movies are spreading the gospel of bottled beverages. France (1939) compelled Hollywood to change the villain of *Beau Geste* from a Frenchman to a Russian. An organization of silver fox breeders expressed their indignation because in one picture a Negress was seen wearing a silver fox. The Audubon Society voiced a complaint concerning a story which was being considered by a studio because the plot required an eagle to carry off a child. It is easy to extend this Domesday Book to chilling proportions, but let us end this array of hurt feelings by citing the letter which denounced a movie because it "maligned and burlesqued" the Master Plumbers of America, a group, it was insisted, "which has done more to promote the health and comfort of the American people than any other group or industry."[16]

All these objections are important to the makers and custodians of popular art because they threaten to pinch them in the pocket-book nerve. Probably the most articulate and effective pressure group in the United States, so far as its influence on movies is concerned, is the Roman Catholic Church, which operates by film rating, by protest, and by boycott. The makers of popular art have to consider constantly not only the need to *please* but also the need not to *teach* anything which would offend effective segments of the audience and make for failure of the program, the picture, or the publication.

The objections Rosten quoted above are, in the broader sense, moral. That is, they are objections to what people may be taught by popular art—the kinds of opinions and behaviors they might learn. And the more one thinks about this, the more evident it becomes that Lyman Bryson was thoroughly right in beginning his essay on "Popular Art" (which makes as much sense as any writing on the subject) with Plato and Aristotle, whose ghosts, he says, stand constantly at the elbows of the critics of popular art. Imagine Plato and Aristotle in a modern movie theater, he says:

> We can imagine them, disguised by darkness, watching a vividly photographed and competently acted modern story. It makes little difference what the story is. They would both be wondering what was happening to hundreds of men and women and boys and girls who sat together in the magic darkness seeing themselves do deeds of courage and cleverness, sweeping up rewards of honor and romance. Plato, I think, would be wondering if it was good experience. Aristotle would be wondering if it was good art. . . .
>
> So Aristotle in the movie theater would be looking for a work of fine art. He would be judging the movie by its logical consistencies; the balance of character elements. He would be seeking something to respond to emotionally, but it would not be the obvious vicissitudes of the heroine. . . . One can be reasonably sure that Aristotle would not consider the laughter and tears of his companions the kind of purgation that makes art a noble experience.
>
> Plato, being an older and sadder and quite possibly a wiser man, is unhappy for a different reason. He takes it for granted that the imaginary life that is enjoyed with tears and laughter by the people around him is precisely the purpose of the whole institution. People have come to the theater to be absorbed for a time in the affairs of imaginary persons, and they are quite properly letting themselves be swept on by the story. Plato's unhappiness would be because he would, as he listened and looked, pass judgment on all the moral implications of what was happening on the screen.[17]

✓These are the only two ways to judge popular art, outside of the purely commercial test. That is, is it good art, and is it good teaching? The aesthetic critics blame popular art, in effect, for not being fine art. But it is exceedingly hard to lift popular art—with its enormous scale of production, its need to turn up so much new material, and its need to reach and attract vast audiences—to the level of logical balance, fresh insight, and subtlety of meaning which we expect of fine art. It is much easier to make popular art fit moral standards. And certainly this is a key to the understanding of what goes out under the name of popular art. For it goes out in the spirit of Plato—a timid and cautious Plato—rather than the spirit of Aristotle.

✓The maker of popular art is constantly forced to measure his product against moral standards: what is it going to teach its audiences? Where does he get his standards? Not merely from the society in which he lives. Rather, from the pooled standards of all the societies and groups he wants to be in his audience. From the Master Plumbers who care what picture people get of their members; from the Japanese who don't want their youth to be corrupted by seeing a girl's elbow; from the Roman Catholic Church which doesn't want the media to inform audiences about birth control. From all the groups which are articulate enough and potent enough, in a box-office sense, to deserve his attention.

The popular art media have institutionalized their consciences. They have created Codes of Conduct, of which we shall talk at greater length later, but which all have roughly the same origin in the sensitivities and moral dislikes of audience groups. Thus, the maker of popular art is not only restricted to a relatively small number of plots, forms, and character relationships which he can count on to please without fail a very large number of different people, but he is also restricted to having them do and say only what will not offend the Codes.

And so, after a long time, we come around to the questions with which we started: what is the media image of the person whom popular art is serving? And what is the expected relationship of art to that person?

THE NATURE OF MEDIA MAN

✗ Obviously, the makers of popular art, as well as their critics and the thousands of protesting organizations and individuals, feel that popular art is deeply influential on the individual. He identifies with characters, copies them, adopts some of their mores as his own. Popular art both pleases and teaches. As the Motion Picture Production Code says, "the MORAL IMPORTANCE [capitals and italics are the Code's] of entertainment is something which has been universally recognized. . . . Entertainment can be of a character either HELPFUL or HARMFUL to the human race. . . . So *correct entertainment raises* the whole standard of a nation. W*rong enter-*

tainment lowers the whole living conditions and moral ideals of a race."[18]

Now what manner of man is this upon whom popular art is thought to have so much influence?

Man as viewed by popular art is what we might call *generalized man,* or *common denominator man.* The major attention of the entertainment media naturally must be directed to the tastes and interests on which people agree, rather than those on which they disagree. This is, of course, true to a different extent in different media.

The large popular magazine has a considerable amount of latitude in choosing its contents. It can present one story or article which will appeal primarily to one kind of man, another story or article which will appeal to another kind. It doesn't expect that every reader will read every article. Television and radio have perhaps less latitude than the magazine, because after all there are only four radio and three television networks—therefore only three or four network choices at a given time. But, on the other hand, TV and radio have more latitude than films, for they can afford to program for women in the afternoon, children at 5 p.m., families in the evening, intellectuals who like "Invitation to Learning" or the "Chicago Roundtable" on Sunday mornings, and sports fans Saturday afternoon. Motion pictures are the most restricted of the media, for a much larger proportion of their resources is tied up in one film, which must be seen over and over in as much of the world as possible.

But all these media are clearly interested in the aspects of human taste which are common throughout most of the human race and in presenting the kind of ideas and behaviors which will offend as few of the human race as possible. Do three per cent of the potential great audience like Bach, 50 per cent like jazz, 80 per cent like Stephen Foster? Then obviously, jazz is safer than Bach, Foster safer than either. Is a large audience group going to be advised not to go to a picture in which an adulterer is allowed to work his way back to a happy, normal, proper life? Then obviously, that subject is out of bounds. Popular art man is simple undifferentiated man, dwelling in the fenced-off territory where the stones of protesting pressure groups cannot reach, and where life and its problems are kept as simple as possible.

In the second place, popular art man is envisaged as a person who comes to radio, television, and films (and to the entertainment parts of magazines and newspapers) chiefly for relaxation, excitement, escape. "Theatrical motion pictures. . . ," says the Production Code, "are primarily to be regarded as ENTERTAINMENT. Mankind has always recognized the importance of entertainment and its value in rebuilding the bodies and souls of human beings." To be sure, the movies are more purely an entertainment art than either broadcasting or magazines. Radio and television recognize a responsibility for informing their audiences through news and other treatments of public affairs. Magazines, in varying degrees, feel a responsibility to devote part of their content to material which will stimulate rather than divert, encourage rather than discourage critical thought.

But, as far as popular art is concerned, all these media look at man with the eyes of an adolescent Plato, rather than the eyes of Aristotle. They think of him as coming to the movies, or sitting before the television screen, not in a mood to think about the artistic form of the product before him, but rather in a mood to suspend his critical facilities, to give himself to the story, to identify with the characters and experience vicariously what they do, to forget for a while the problems of his daily life and the aspirations which he may hold for art or society.

And, by the same token, popular art conceives man to be rather immature in his reactions to the teaching content of entertainment, and highly susceptible to corruption of morals. This is not the time to discuss the several media codes in detail, but anyone who reads the code of the American Society of Newspaper Editors, in contrast to the motion picture, radio, television, and comic codes, cannot fail to be impressed with the difference between the newspaper code and the others in this respect.

The newspaper code treats man as a rational being, able to discover truth and to separate right from wrong by the power of his reason. It follows John Stuart Mill in the point of view that all beliefs and customs should be subjected to vigorous challenge in order to preserve their vitality and prevent their being held as dogma. It goes along with John Milton who argues in the *Areopagitica* that to learn the difference between good and evil one must know both good and evil; that a man can scarcely be called truly moral if he has not been subjected to the temptations of evil.

Insofar as the radio and television codes deal with news, they follow approximately the line of the ASNE code. But all the entertainment media codes, so far as they deal with entertainment, vigorously turn their backs on the libertarian position and contend that the beliefs of society should *not* be questioned; that the showing man evil is *not* a necessary or desirable part of helping him to be good; and that the audience for the machine-interposed media is altogether less able to keep up its defenses and its critical attitude than are the readers of print.

Radio and television recognize certain special obligations for themselves because they are "guests in their audiences' homes." Motion pictures recognize a special obligation because theaters are "built for the masses," and it is therefore "difficult to produce films intended for only certain classes of people." Some are more susceptible than others, for example, "the immature, the young, or the criminal classes," and persons in "small communities remote from sophistication and from the hardening process of larger cities"; but in general these media feel the need to program for audiences which are at the least easily influenced by the content of entertainment material, and at the worst infantile in their reaction to it.

Now this is not to say that all films appeal only to the infantile members of society, that all broadcasts discourage rather than encourage thought, or that no popular art has the earmarks of fine art. That is obviously not so. There are films that do not hew to the line of the common denominator, stimulating broadcasts, popular art of many kinds that catches some of the aesthetic perfection and fresh insightfulness we look for in fine art. But what we have been describing is the broad central stream of popular art. And, viewing it as we have from the standpoint of its basic economics and its basic assumptions, we can perceive some of the challenges which the emerging concept of social responsibility in mass communication presents to the makers of popular art.

1. Is the concept of *generalized audience* an adequate one? In other words, how far can the media go in meeting the art needs of different groups within their audiences, without endangering the media's economic position? How can the media avoid the artistic straitjacket of programming for all and offending none? As we have suggested, this problem is severest in the motion pictures. With large magazines, it is least. With radio, which has lost some of its mass audience, group programming is now smart policy. Television can reach different segments at different parts of the day and occasion-

ally can afford to satisfy the "high-hats" with a program or two. But movies, as Ruth Inglis says, "in order to maintain mass audiences . . . have subordinated other considerations and have submitted to moralistic and other demands. Now the problem is to reconcile these with a more meaningful content. The industry finds itself between the Scylla of moral reform groups and the Charybdis of the growing liberal resentment against stifling the freedom of the screen."[19]

The Motion Picture Code recognizes this problem and suggests a possible way out: "If there should be created a special type of theatre, catering exclusively to an adult audience, for plays of this character (plays with problem themes, difficult discussions and maturer treatment), it would seem to afford an outlet, which does not now exist, for pictures unsuitable for general distribution but permissible for exhibitions to a restricted audience." However, says the Code, the "practice of using a general theatre and limiting its patronage during the showing of a certain film to 'Adults Only' is not completely satisfactory."

2. Is the concept of *immature, susceptible man* at too low a level? It is a very serious and fundamental question whether the concept of news-reading and news-hearing man as a rational being, able to distinguish between truth and error and make up his own mind, is compatible with the concept of entertainment-receiving man as unable to distinguish between truth and error, and dangerously susceptible to whatever doctrine appears in the popular art he experiences. It is hardly necessary to say that the latter of these concepts is an authoritarian one which puts the media in the role of caretaker of the people; whereas the former concept is a libertarian one. Yet these two exist side by side in the codes and the practice of the mass media.

But, in order really to judge whether this concept of media man is too pessimistic, it is desirable to look in more detail at the kinds of content he is to be protected from—that is, the kinds of content which are regarded by the custodians of popular art as corrupting to his taste and morals and dangerous to his social behavior.

What Is a "Bad" Picture?

Once again we are speaking in the language of Plato rather than the language of Aristotle. We mean something that is *morally* bad.

When we talk about a "bad" picture, program, story, or comic book, we mean one that teaches undesirable behavior, whether irreverent, indecent, in poor taste, or criminal. In other words, a bad piece of popular art, in the Platonic sense, is one that threatens or goes against the current mores and values of the society.

In order to understand the struggles and gyrations which popular art undergoes in order to avoid violating the mores, one has to consider the almost impossible situation in which popular art finds itself. What is "bad" in one culture is not necessarily so in another, but the wider the audience the more cultures it will embrace, and the more kinds of behavior that must be avoided. Stories that would be all right in a traveling salesmen's or luncheon club's culture are not all right in the home culture into which television enters. The treatment of cows which is perfectly all right in American movie theatres is taboo in India, where Hollywood wants to sell the same films. A treatment of divorce which might be quite all right in an American Protestant culture is not all right in an American Catholic culture. And so the wider the audience the fewer the kinds of behavior that popular art may teach without violating the mores of some important group within the audience.

Furthermore, the larger the audience the more pressure groups feel a need to act as caretakers. Many a play that runs without complaint on Broadway could never be televised or filmed without substantial changes—moral, that is, rather than aesthetic changes. Salty language which is all right for a public speech is dangerous for radio.

Even in book circulation, the rule applies. Dan Lacy cites the case of *Catcher in the Rye*, which sold about 40,000 copies in its original hard-backed edition, was purchased by public libraries throughout the United States, was a choice of the Book-of-the-Month Club (where it sold 155,000 more), and was widely and favorably reviewed as a "sincere, thoughtful, and sensitive treatment of adolescence"; but it had a quite different history when it went into paper-back and began to circulate from magazine racks, stations, and drug stores.[20] Its paperback edition was bitterly attacked before various state and city commissions, and was banned from sale in a number of cities. The same thing has happened to Nobel Prize winners, Pulitzer Prize winners, National Book Award winners. As long as they stayed in hard covers and sold at three or four dollars, they were not regarded as threatening even though they had very large circulations. But, as soon as they went into paper backs at a low price, then the objectors, the caretaker groups, the police, and the censorship boards went into action.

Why? Obviously to protect the mores of society; to shield the younger and more corruptible members of society. There is an implicit assumption here that the person who can afford to pay three dollars for a book is less corruptible than one who can pay only 50 cents; that the person who can afford to go to a Broadway play is less corruptible than one who has to get his drama at the neighborhood movie house or from his television screen. It is interesting to realize that the shocked reaction of censors and objectors to a book like *Catcher in the Rye* in its paper-back edition, as Lacy points out, was due in large measure to the book's exposure to "large masses of people previously habituated only to carefully industry-censored magazines, movies, and radio programs, and unaccustomed to the greater latitude always enjoyed by books."[21]

The large producers of popular art, as we noted before, have institutionalized their consciences and codified their practices, so as to avoid offending the mores of the societies to which they sell. These codes, of course, are guides to media-making for the larger audiences. More correctly, perhaps, they are guides as to what content to avoid if one also wants to avoid attack and loss of patronage from offended groups. As such, they are the industry's own definition of what constitutes good or bad popular art, and we may well begin by looking at what they enjoin and proscribe.

The Newspaper Code. Unlike the other industry codes, the ASNE code has very little to say about decency, morality, and the other concerns of popular art. It is concerned with information rather than entertainment, and it assumes a free, self-righting process in society, and a public able to distinguish between good and bad, truth and error. Insofar as it makes any assumption about morality, it is the Socratic one that the intelligent man prefers a moral to an immoral society. The topics of the "Canons," therefore, are responsibility, freedom, independence, sincerity, truthfulness, accuracy, impartiality, fair play, and decency. Only the last one, "decency," covers the ground which most concerns popular art. Says this canon: "A newspaper cannot escape conviction of insincerity if, while professing high moral purpose, it supplies incentives to base conduct, such as are to be found in details of crime and vice, publication of which is not demonstrably for the public good."

The Motion-Picture Code. The newspaper code is essentially a series of *positive* directions: what the newspaper *should* do. The motion-picture production code, in contrast, is essentially negative. Paying little attention to positive ideals of performance, it lays down a number of general and specific prohibitions and says in effect that these things do *not* constitute ethical conduct.

Ethical conduct as suggested by the movies code consists of conforming to what the drafters of the code believed to be public standards of morality—"principles which are present in all established religions," as Shurlock puts it. Here the movies code differs from the newspaper code. The latter emphasizes the public good; the former emphasizes public morals, a narrower concept.

The ethical movie-maker, in general, will deplore sin and respect patriotism in his productions. Some sins, the code observes, are inherently repellent—murder, for example, and cruelty. But others—sex, crimes of apparent heroism, for example—tend to attract. This latter group needs more "care in treatment."

Specifically, what moral principles should the ethical movie-maker follow?

(1) The ethical movie-maker in his films must respect law, natural and human. The code defines natural law as "the great underlying principles of right and justice dictated by conscience," and human law as that "written by civilized nations." Respect for the law means many things. Movies, for example, should not depict crime so as "to throw sympathy with the crime as against law and justice." They should not inspire potential criminals with the desire for imitation, should not teach the methods of crime, and should not cast doubt on justice as administered by the courts of the land.

(2) The ethical movie-maker should respect "pure love" as exemplified by marriage and the home, and should shun "impure love," that which "society has always regarded as wrong and which has been banned by divine law." Even movies about pure love should not include scenes of excessive passion. "Impure love" evidently includes sex out of wedlock, homosexuality, lesbianism, and miscegenation, to judge from the code. It must never be made to seem permissible, "attractive or beautiful," must never be the subject for farce or comedy, and must never be detailed in method or manner.

(3) The ethical movie-maker must seek to curb the passions of his audience. He must not portray scenes of complete nudity, of suggestive dances, of lustful love, and so on.

(4) The ethical movie-maker must avoid vulgarity, obscenity, and profanity. Vulgarity, the code says, consists of "low, disgusting, unpleasant though not necessarily evil subjects." The code spells out profanity in great detail. It bars, for example, such words and expressions as "broad" and "tart" as applied to a woman, "S.O.B.," "louse," and so on.

(5) The ethical movie-maker must respect religion. He must treat the ministers and the ceremonies of the various faiths with dignity.

(6) The ethical movie-maker must respect national feelings. "The history, institutions, prominent people and citizenry of all nations," the code says, "shall be represented fairly." Moreover, films shall not employ such derogatory racial designations as "Chink," "Wop," "Dago," and so forth.

(7) The ethical movie-maker must show good taste in his choice of subjects. For example, he must show no scenes of brutality to human beings or animals, no scenes of excessive bloodshed, no scenes such as surgical operations or childbirth.

The Radio Code. The radio code is both positive and negative, perhaps more the former than the latter. It does state general ideals of performance, but it also outlines proscribed content. Further, it represents a move from a pure code of ethics toward a code of ethics including a statement of trade practices.

The code visualizes radio as a medium of both enlightenment and entertainment. Perhaps for that reason, it combines features of both the ASNE and the movies codes in its delineation of ethical behavior. And since, unlike the ASNE code, it recognizes the commercial aspects of broadcasting, it has an additional proviso for ethical conduct.

Ethical behavior as defined implicitly by the code consists of (1) promoting the democratic process by enlightening the public; (2) promoting accepted standards of public morality by presenting wholesome entertainment; and (3) maintaining a proper balance between enlightenment and entertainment on the one hand and contributions to the economic welfare on the other hand, as well as maintaining high standards of advertising.

The code reflects some trust in the self-righting process. Radio can expedite the process by presenting news from reliable sources; by clearly distinguishing commentary from straight reporting; by "willingness to expose its convictions to fair rebuttal"; by insuring equality of opportunity "in allotting time for the presentation of public issues"; and so on.

Yet broadcasters seem to doubt that the process is literally self-righting. Reading the code, one senses that they have reservations about man's rationality, that they do not want discussion to be *too* controversial, and put narrower limits to it than do newspaper editors. The newspaper code positively and purposely states that the area of discussion should be large: "It is unquestionably right to discuss whatever is not explicitly forbidden by law. . . ." No such statement appears in the radio code. On the contrary, the radio code sets itself the difficult task of respecting "the rights and sensitivities of all people," which, if adhered to literally, would impose severe limitations on what is discussible. Moreover, participation in the presentation of public issues should be limited to "qualified, recognized, and properly identified groups or individuals whose opinions will assist the general public in reaching conclusions."

The public good for the broadcaster also embraces a concern for public morals. In all operations, broadcasters should "observe the proprieties and customs of civilized society." In news programs, they should not present "morbid, sensational, or alarming details." In entertainment, in children's programs especially, they should hew to accepted standards. Programs for children, the code notes, "should convey the commonly accepted social and ethical characteristics of American life. They should contribute to the healthy development of personality and character."

Therefore, the ethical broadcaster will respect certain moral principles and institutions which the ethical movie-maker also will respect. First, law and order. He will not make crime attractive, for example; will not encourage listeners to imitate the activities of criminals; and will not disparage law enforcement. Second, he will respect what the motion-picture code calls "pure love"; he will, as the code stipulates, "honor the sanctity of marriage and the home." Third, he will respect all religion.

In contributing to the economic welfare, too, the ethical broadcaster shall be judged by "high standards of performance," for he has a "responsibility to the public." One measure of performance is how well he keeps advertising in proper proportion. The code specifically suggests the maximum time to be used for advertising by a single sponsor at various periods of the day. But the "quality and integration" of advertising are as important as its quantity. Therefore, the ethical broadcaster will make sure that advertising meets certain minimum standards, some of which are specifically set forth in the code.

The Television Code. The television code is as heavily negative as the motion-picture code, which indeed seems to have been a model for some sections of it. More than any of the other codes, it embodies a statement of good business practices.

The TV code acknowledges the duty of television to promote the democratic process by public enlightenment. The responsible telecaster, for instance, will offer a well-balanced and adequate news presentation which must be "fair, factual, and without bias." He will "seek out and develop with accountable individuals, groups, and organizations, programs relating to controversial public issues of import to . . . fellow citizens; and . . . give a fair representation to opposing sides of issues which materially affect a substantial segment of the public."

But over-riding the telecaster's duty as enlightener is his duty to make program content conform to the accepted beliefs and behavior of the majority. "Education via television," the code states, "may be taken to mean that process by which the individual is brought toward informed adjustment to his society."

The ethical telecaster, then, will keep discussion within rather narrow bounds. He will make sure that the views presented are "responsible" ones, and he should evaluate requests for discussion time "on the basis of their individual merits, and in light of the contribution which the use requested would make to the public interest, and to a well-balanced program structure."

The code closely links promoting the public good with promoting public morals. Even news and analysis must be offered with concern for public morals. "At all times," says the code, "pictorial and verbal material for both news and comment should conform to other sections of these standards, wherever such sections are reasonably applicable."

As propagator of public morals, the ethical telecaster has obligations similar to those of the movie-maker. In his programs, he must respect law and order. Although the code recognizes that crime is a part of the world at large, the ethical telecaster will not lead the young to believe that crime plays a greater part in life than it actually does. He will portray criminality as "undesirable and unsympathetic." He will uphold law enforcement and the dignity of the law. He will not inspire his viewers to engage in crime, nor will he furnish them with information on criminal techniques.

The ethical telecaster will maintain respect "for the sanctity of marriage and the value of the home." By implication, he will uphold what the movies code calls "pure love" and will not portray "impure love." Thus he will not depict divorce with levity or as a "solution for marital problems." He will not portray illicit sex relations or sexual perversions.

The ethical telecaster will seek to hold in check the baser emotions of his viewers and to shield the viewers from temptation. "The presentation of cruelty, greed, and selfishness as worthy motivations," says the code, "is to be avoided." The ethical telecaster will transmit no scenes involving lascivious dances, indecorous costumes, excessive horror, cruelty to animals, and so forth. He will respect sobriety. "Drunkenness and narcotic addiction are never presented as desirable," the code says; and another section forbids the advertising of hard liquor and requires that ads for beer and wine be "in the best of good taste." Gambling can be depicted only when essential to plot and then only with discretion and moderation.

The ethical telecaster will respect religion. He will emphasize "broad religious truths" rather than "controversial or partisan views." He will respect national feelings by avoiding words, especially slang, derisive of any nationality or national derivation. He will not permit profanity of any sort.

The television code acknowledges that advertising enables telecasters to make available programs of enlightenment and entertainment. Nevertheless, the ethical telecaster must keep advertising in proper proportion and must exercise unceasing care to supervise the form it takes. Nearly half of the code deals with advertising; this part amounts to a statement of good trade practices.

In general, the ethical telecaster will try to make the advertising carried by his station conform to the standards of his programs of enlightenment and entertainment. Just as he should present news which is truthful and labeled as to source, for example, so should he

THE MEDIA CODES*

	When and How Adopted	The Code's View of Man	Its View of the Medium	View of Function of Medium	Principles of Ethical Behavior
Newspapers	When newspaper was almost 300 years old, and newsmen spoke of a "profession," of journalism. No pressure on papers to adopt code	Primarily a rational being, able to discover truth and separate right from wrong by power of reason	Appeals to the intellect—to the critical sense	Primarily enlightenment	Promoting democracy by enlightening the public (expediting the self-righting process). Independence, accuracy, truthfulness, impartiality, fair play, decency, no invasion of privacy, no opinion in news reports, no incentive to base conduct.
Movies	Fairly early in history and few years after advent of sound —against background of organized criticism and official censorship	Much of audience will be immature and highly susceptible to corruption of morals	Capable of suspending critical faculties	Primarily entertainment, though it can contribute to "correct living," presumably by indoctrination	Promoting public morals (in general, by respecting the home and the sanctity of marriage, religion, law, and justice, national feelings; by curbing the base emotions; by avoiding violence, vulgarity, and profanity).
Radio	After about decade and a half, amidst public criticism, government regulation, and threat of further government intervention	Much of audience will be highly susceptible to corruption of morals	Capable of suspending critical faculties	Enlightenment, entertainment, service to economic system	Promoting democracy by enlightening the public (expediting self-righting process); promoting public morals (in general, by respecting the sanctity of marriage and the home, religion, law and justice, national feelings; by avoiding vulgarity and profanity); keeping advertising in proportion and maintaining high standard for it.

Television	Very early in history. No serious threat of further government intervention (but code may have helped to forestall it)	Much of audience will be highly susceptible to corruption of morals	Capable of suspending critical faculties	Enlightenment, entertainment, service to economic system	Promoting democracy by enlightening the public—but not at expense of the media task of promoting public morals (in general, by respecting the home and the sanctity of marriage, religion, law and justice, national feelings; by curbing base emotions; by avoiding vulgarity and profanity); keeping advertising in proper proportion and maintaining high standards for it.
Comic Books	At end of first decade—against backdrop of public criticism, official censorship, and threat of further government intervention	Immature, highly susceptible to corruption of morals	Capable of suspending critical faculties, if any	Entertainment	Promoting public morals (in general, by respecting the home and the sanctity of marriage, religion, law and justice; by curbing base emotions; by avoiding violence, vulgarity, and profanity; by teaching that good must triumph).

* Prepared by Theodore B. Peterson for this volume.

carry only advertising which is free of misrepresentation. Just as discussion should be conducted by responsible persons, so should advertising be that from firms of integrity. Just as other programs
should avoid offending the majority by profanity, indelicacy, and so
on, so should advertising avoid being "objectionable to a substantial
and responsible segment of the community."

The Comic Book Code. Ethical conduct for the publisher of comic
books, the code suggests, consists of avoiding "violations of standards
of good taste, which might tend toward corruption of the comic
book as an instructive and wholesome form of entertainment." The
test of his ethical behavior, then, is how little he offends public
morals.

The comics code, like the motion-picture code (on which it may
have drawn in part), is primarily a negative code. It says, in effect,
that certain things constitute violations of ethical behavior, without
formulating ideals of performance.

Like the movie-maker and broadcaster, the ethical publisher of
comic books must respect certain moral standards and American
institutions. As the code puts it, "Respect for parents, the moral
code, and for honorable behavior shall be fostered."

First, the ethical publisher must respect law and order. "In every
instance," the code says, "good shall triumph over evil. . . ." Therefore, comic books should never engender sympathy for crime and
criminal; on the contrary, crime shall be depicted as "a sordid and
unpleasant activity." The books should not teach criminal methods,
nor should they disparage "policemen, judges, government officials,
and respected institutions."

Second, the ethical publisher must respect marriage and the home.
He should never treat divorce as a subject for humor or as desirable.
He should respect what the movies code calls "pure love." Says the
comics code: "The treatment of love-romance stories shall emphasize
the value of the home and the sanctity of marriage." On the other
hand, he shall avoid references to "impure love": he shall not refer,
explicitly or by innuendo, to "illicit sex relations," to "sexual ab-
normalities," or to "sex perversion." The ethical publisher will try
to restrain the passions of his readers. "Passion or romantic interest,"
the code says, "shall never be treated in such a way as to stimulate
the baser or lower emotions." Comic books will not run pictures in-

volving nudity, suggestive postures, or "exaggeration of any physical qualities" of the female.

The ethical publisher also will respect religion. And he should keep his books free from profanity and vulgarity; indeed, he should even have them use "good grammar" whenever possible.

The standards of the advertising carried by comic books also should be a concern of the responsible publisher. "Good taste" is his guiding principle in accepting or rejecting advertising. In general, "good taste" means rejecting advertisements for products which promote crime, gambling, drinking, and sexual vice.

Let me not leave an erroneous impression concerning what I think of these codes. High-minded men have helped to make them. They are not the censorship arm of any single pressure group; I do not buy the charge that the Motion Picture Code is a Roman Catholic document; actually it expresses the taboos and prohibitions of many churches and groups. And undoubtedly the codes have helped to avoid some of the excesses which otherwise would have characterized popular art during its rapidly growing years. The questions I have to raise concerning the codes are rather these: (a) are the assumptions behind the codes adequate to their purpose? and (b) could the industry afford to operate without the protection of these taboos in return for the freedom to program according to its own lights?

THE ASSUMPTIONS OF POPULAR ART

Behind all these codes that deal with popular art there is an implicit assumption that popular art has a great and unique effect on its audiences. It is evident, for example, that a great many things which are widely observable in actual life are "bad" in popular art: for example, the Bronx cheer, the word "Madam" referring to prostitution, the sight of a baby's sex organs, any expression of passion or sexual desire even between husband and wife, all of which are explicitly proscribed by the Motion Picture Production Code. Likewise, many subjects that can freely be talked about in news or in print are "bad" in popular art. This extends even to advertising, for the same audience which is not permitted to see hard liquor advertising on television can turn to large circulation magazines and be urged to emulate "men of distinction" drinking whiskey. Therefore, we need to examine this assumption about the dangerous power of popular art.

The Assumption of Effect

We have already had something to say about the effects of mass communication. Here let us repeat that it is very difficult to demonstrate a causal relationship between mass media and any of the criminal or perverted behaviors which are sometimes blamed on the media. On the other hand, it must be admitted that when audiences go to popular art they seem to have a rather different attitude and expectation than, for example, they have as they turn to the evening news or observe a street scene. They are much readier, in a motion-picture theater or in a comfortable chair before the television set, to suspend their critical facilities. They are more likely, someone has said, to feel than to think about what they receive. They go to popular art, not overtly to learn or be informed or even to undertake the responsibilities of a conversation or a buying-selling relationship. They go, for the most part, to be entertained. They go with their guard down. They go relaxed. And the most evident feature of their behavior as listeners or viewers or readers is that they *identify* with the characters in the story.

Everyone who has explored the psychology of the popular-art audience has noted the fact of identification. Thus Waugh, writing about the comics, says that "people read comics because they find themselves reflected in them."[22] Orwell, writing of boys' magazines, notes that "the characters are so carefully graded as to give almost every type of reader a character he can identify with."[23] Herta Herzog says in regard to soap operas: "In identifying themselves and their admittedly minor problems with the suffering heroes and heroines of the stories, the listeners find an opportunity to magnify their own woes. This is enjoyed if only because it expresses their 'superiority' over others who have not had these profound emotional experiences."[24]

But Miss Herzog notes further that the soap operas which are so profoundly identified with "are liked because they 'explain' things to the inarticulate listener. Furthermore, they teach the listener appropriate patterns of behavior. 'If you listen to these programs and something turns up in your own life, you would know what to do about it' is a typical comment, expressing the readiness of women to use these programs as sources of advice."[25] Arnheim, studying the same relationship, commented on the female listener's identification with the strong, helpful, efficient woman in the case, and suggested: "One might speculate whether the ideal type of a helpful woman does not act partly as a substitute for religion."[26]

Be that as it may, there is no doubt that people do accept some advice from the media. I saw a homely example last week. One of the large magazines for women came out with a reducing diet which was in fact only an infant's feeding formula, although intended in this case for adults. Within a few days, drug-store counters were full of the dextrose which went into the formula, evaporated milk and corn oil were selling at a great rate, and apparently large numbers of people were on the "formula diet." In a more subtle way, too, people get "help" and advice from the soap operas and similar sources.

Likewise, there is no doubt that people imitate some behaviors from the characters with whom they identify. The way phrases and gestures from Hollywood and Broadway go around the country is more than coincidence. It is hardly possible that the young people of America would have decked themselves out in coonskin caps and Davy Crockett shirts without exposure to certain popular art. And it is still rather shocking to remember how many people in the radio audience accepted uncritically Orson Welles' fiction of an invasion from Mars.

Furthermore, some people are clearly more suggestible than others. And all people are more likely to accept suggestions they are looking for. If a boy is rather planning to run away from home anyway, he may be more swayed than others by Huckleberry Finn's adventures. A disturbed person, whose aggressions or criminal tendencies are already well developed, may find a crime program useful in a way it was never intended—for example, as a demonstration of how to burglarize a second story, or strangle a victim, or avoid the police.

Joseph Klapper, in a careful memorandum for the Bureau of Applied Social Research at Columbia, reviewed the chief concerns of parents, psychologists and psychiatrists, teachers, and such groups as the P.T.A., concerning the effects of television on children.[27] He mentioned the fear that television will divert time from more important aspects of growing up; that the crime and violence in the medium will have a bad effect on personality and behavior; that the experience of seeing so much adult conflict on television will have unhealthful psychological effects; that it will make difficult problems for schools; and that it will excite the children without providing for any release except a vicarious one. Reviewing the evidence, he demonstrated quite accurately that none of these effects is proved beyond question, or at least no injurious effect is proved, and that there is considerable difference of opinion even among the experts.

This is all true. The substance of the situation, as we now understand it, is that we don't entirely understand it. There is no doubt (a) that audiences approach popular art in a less critical way than the way they approach the news and public affairs content of the mass media; (b) that because of the large and diverse audiences which are attracted to popular art, these audiences unquestionably contain more uncritical and suggestible persons than, say, the audiences of fine art; (c) that many people will identify strongly with the characters of popular art, and therefore become more suggestible; and (d) that some people at some time under some conditions will accept advice and imitate behaviors from popular art. What is not known is the extent of this effect—how many people under what conditions will accept what kind of advice or imitate what kind of behaviors.

So it isn't proved and isn't disproved. What does popular art do about that? Gilbert Seldes expresses himself strongly on that question. He says it would be criminal to take a chance. "As meager an ethical standard as can be imagined," he calls it, to make the standard of acceptability that "as long as no positive proof of harm is presented, the program may be transmitted." And certainly one can understand why Hollywood and New York, and all the groups and individuals who have put pressure on them to frame the codes as they have done, should bend over backward in order to avoid doing individual and social harm.

But this problem has a positive as well as a negative side. The codes have proscribed a number of kinds of conduct which, it is feared, might be injurious. When you eliminate these large parts of experience from popular art, are you getting what you want out of what is left? Have you possibly cut out something important? Have you got an imbalance? In other words, is this expurgation, this negative approach, the best way to insure the responsibility of popular art? To approach that question we shall have to look at some other assumptions that seem to lie behind the popular art of today.

The Assumption Regarding Sensation, Crime, and Violence

The codes say that violence is never justified for its own sake. With that we can hardly argue. The question is, then, how does popular art justify the enormous amount of violence, crime, and sensation it carries. And the answer seems to be that it makes a further assumption of considerable importance. It assumes that a great amount of such material may be justified if the audience is carefully informed that crime never pays, that evil-doing is punished, and that accepted social mores have a way of enforcing themselves.

This results in a kind of eat-your-cake-and-have-it-too ethic.

For example, when some newspapers—functioning more as entertainment media than as information channels—sensationalize such a case as the Sheppard trial, their theory is that nothing destroys an infection like sunlight. But I wonder whether the result is not, rather, that everybody wallows in the filth and has a grand old time without any sense of moral guilt?

Again, consider the way power is treated in popular art today. Attention to power is nothing unusual. Folk and legendary heroes since the beginning of time have tended to be men of great power. Remember Hercules, Roland, Robin Hood, Lancelot, and Paul Bunyan? And so in comic strips, the crime dramas, and the Westerns, some of the leading characters tend to be men of great power, engaged in adventures of great violence and danger.

For the most part, these power characters take one of two forms. They may be villains. Such, for example, are many of the men Dick Tracy pursues so relentlessly. They are men of great canniness, strength, and daring. True, they are always captured, sometimes after they have strewn their way with corpses, and they are suitably punished. But in the meantime I wonder whether the reader has not tended to identify with the character who is willing to dare such adventures, has so much skill, and makes fools of the cops? Orwell remarks on the tendency in American popular art to tolerate crime, even to admire the criminal so long as he is successful. It is this attitude, he says, "that has made it possible for crime to flourish upon so huge a scale. Books have been written about Al Capone that are hardly different in tone from the books written about Henry

Ford . . . Lord Northcliffe, and all the rest of the 'log cabin to White House' brigade."[28] It is perfectly all right with the codes to write of the power and skill of this kind of criminal, so long as his ultimate fate is disposed of according to rule. But *is* it all right?

"The MPAA," says Hortense Powdermaker, "gave its seal of approval to a picture in which the two leading characters committed adultery and then murder, and, of course, were finally punished for all their sins. What the MPAA ignored were the implications of a sexy-looking, beautiful woman and a strong handsome he-man, both popular stars, irresistibly drawn to each other, committing adultery, and finally murder. That they are punished at the end would not necessarily destroy the identification of the preceding sixty or eight minutes."[29]

A second form these power characters take is that of great heroes who settle the problems of society without needing the help of the usual agents of justice. Such, for example, are Superman, Steve Roper, Mr. and Mrs. North, and all the successors of Robin Hood and Sherlock Holmes. These are individuals of great charm and power, all of whom fall into one general pattern. Martha Wolfenstein describes it thus: "The hero, the self-appointed investigator and agent of justice, is able to set things right independently. The world, which is not effectively policed, does not need to be policed at all.[30]

I wonder whether this is a satisfactory implication to leave with the audiences of popular art—that, come a crisis or danger or crime, it can be taken care of by a Superman or an almost-Superman, and in any case there is precious little you can expect out of the police?

Still another form which this eat-your-cake-and-have-it-too ethic takes is the device of false appearances, chiefly in films, but also to some extent in broadcast drama. By false appearance I mean a situation that only *seems* to be morally wrong. It *looks as though* the girl is breaking the sex code, or the boy is breaking the criminal code. They aren't, of course. Everything comes out all right in the end, and we see that we suspected them wrongly all the time. But meanwhile we have gone through some of the experience which otherwise would be forbidden us by the code. Miss Wolfenstein pays her respects to this device, too. It is in false appearances, she writes, that "the forbidden wishes are realized which the hero and heroine so rarely carry into action. In a false appearance the heroine is promiscuous, the hero is a murderer, the young people carry on an illicit affair, two men share the favors of a woman. This device makes it possible for us to eat our cake and have it, since we can enjoy the suggested wish fulfillments without emphatic guilt; we know that the characters with whom we identify have not done anything."[31] But, it may be asked, is this any way to keep forbidden fruit out of the view of the susceptible?

In fact, it may be argued that there is a basic dishonesty about the practice of popular art in this whole area. A man of great power can operate outside the accepted channels and the realistic patterns of society, provided that he does it for a good cause—for example, if he does what the police should be doing. A criminal may be depicted as powerful, smart, successful, attractive, just so justice catches up with him at the end. All kinds of sexy and violent ideas may be written into popular art, provided that we are told at the end that it is all a mistake: it didn't really happen.

But perhaps the most interesting of all these basic dishonesties is the way that the codes enforce and the producers produce a kind of popular art which is moral in the little things, but still full of crime, cruelty, and violence. An example: it is required that kisses in entertainment films be given with closed lips, not an open mouth. The word adultery, as Hortense Powdermaker found when she made her anthropological study of Hollywood, is not mentioned. Prostitutes in the script are changed in the film to dancing girls. Yet what happens? Still movies are openly sexy. Let us quote Miss Powdermaker again: "The hero is a virile he-man, and the heroine has obvious sex appeal, enhanced by every device of make-up, by accenting of bosoms with 'falsies,' by provocative clothes. An immediate and obvious sexual attraction between hero and heroine is part of the theme of most movies. Whether the story be a murder mystery, farce, musical, or serious drama, the sensual nature of the leading characters is always accented. This is carried still further in boldface type in the advertisements, such as 'Alluring, Seductive, Wicked!' "[32]

In other words, although a picture may observe meticulously every rule of the Code and every ruling of the Code Administrator, it does not observe the spirit of the Code, and the question is whether it has the opposite of the intended result of the Code? This is what happens when you tell a maker of popular art what *not* to do. It is much harder, perhaps impossible, to tell him what *to do*.

The result of these restrictions, and their occasional circumvention, is to create a kind of unreality about popular art, which raises another serious question we must look at.

The Assumption Regarding Reality

It would seem that another implicit assumption of popular art is something like this: that if a person is exposed to popular art in which desired mores are demonstrated in a somewhat unreal and simple world, he will learn desirable behavior for a much more complicated world.

When Wolcott Gibbs resigned his post as motion picture reviewer for the *New Yorker*, he characterized the world of the cinema as "an astounding parody of life devoted to a society in which anything is physically and materially possible, including perfect happiness, to a race of people who operate intellectually on the level of the New York *Daily News*, morally on that of Dayton, Tennessee, and politically and economically in a total vacuum."[33]

It is a dangerously simplified world. The need of writing for the enormous, undifferentiated audience makes it difficult, if not impossible, to deal with the subtleties of life. The need of producing such a mass of new material each year makes it difficult, if not impossible, to create new characters, different from each other in the subtle ways that human beings are. Instead, we have types and stereotypes. Take national types, for instance. The Frenchman is likely to be excitable, to wear a beard, to gesticulate. Spaniards, Mexicans, Arabs, Chinese are likely to be sinister and treacherous. The Chinese is differentiated from others by the fact that he wears a pigtail. The Swede and the Dane are usually kindhearted, usually stupid. The Negro is comic and faithful.

But even beyond this, the moral code, which is made necessary by the fact of the enormous audience, makes a mental and moral type even of a character who is not a physical type. Right has to triumph. Wrong must always be punished. A character must always be good or bad; the blends and combinations that one sees in life are not very frequent in popular art. For a long time, it was impossible even to expiate sin on the screen; the wrongdoer relentlessly had to be carried to a sad end. That is to say that the Christian doctrines of repentance and forgiveness and the theory of penal rehabilitation simply didn't enter into the world of the cinema. How, however, the Code Administrator will permit a suitable amount of "remorse" to replace the more absolute punishment; after being remorseful enough, a wrong doer can have some hope for happiness, provided he has not done too much wrong.

The Institute for Propaganda Analysis listed the following which it called examples of dubious value judgments in the movies:

That the successful culmination of a romance will solve most of the dilemmas of the hero and heroine.

Catch the criminal and you solve the crime problem.

War and the preparation for war are thrilling, heroic, and glamorous.

The good life is the acquisitive life, with its emphasis upon luxury, evening dress, swank, and suavity.[34]

"Only rarely does a movie-goer have the experience of seeing real human beings in a complicated world," wrote Miss Powdermaker. "Instead, he is treated to static characters not unlike the symbolic personifications of sin and virtue in medieval miracle plays. It is only the exceptional movie which portrays any human being, member of majority or minority group, with truthfulness and understanding. The reality of most movies usually consists only in the photography, the setting, the curve of a star's leg, the friendly or handsome looks of the hero and heroine, and other surface characteristics. Seldom is anyone concerned with the reality of emotions and with truthfulness of meaning."[35]

To get some idea of what this means in practice, let us look at a few instances from the popular arts:

Case 102. A certain newspaper has the practice of using "disrobe" for "undress," when reporting that a woman takes off her clothes. The theory is that this is more dignified, less offensive.

Case 103 (reported by Hollis Alpert).[36] "In the film 'From Here to Eternity' a Honolulu brothel was called the New Congress Club and was converted into a place where soldiers could dance with hostesses and could even hire an upstairs room for private conversations. Only the most naive would have assumed that soldiers use their hard-earned pay to rent a room for a chat with a strange girl. . . . The New Congress Club resembled no social or sexual institution known to man since Adam (certainly nothing an enlisted man would have found in Honolulu) and inexcusably injected one small sour note into a powerful but realistic movie."

Case 104 (also reported by Alpert).[37] In "Slightly Scarlet" Rhonda Fleming "is seen as an expensively dressed and groomed girl employed as secretary of a rich and prominent businessman. On her secretary's wages, and with no sign of other income, she manages to live in a $50,000 house (from the looks of it), drive a spanking new convertible, dress in clothes that might put Grace Kelly to shame, and apply all the latest California-style decorative features to her home, patio, and large-sized swimming pool. One might be pardoned, then, for assuming that she is being kept by the businessman. But just in case any of us does take such a view there is provided an illuminating scene between Miss Fleming and her employer. He tells her he loves her and pleads with her to marry him. But Miss Fleming has standards. She informs her employer that she can't marry him because she doesn't love him. Obviously she is just a girl with a fantastic ability to make ends meet."

Case 105. A scene in a television play was deliberately vague about what, if anything, had transpired between a young couple during the night. But the director was careful to have the girl enter the apartment in the morning, not from the bedroom, but from the balcony.

These cases all have a similarity in that they are concerned with the details rather than with the broad meaning of the art. And, to one degree or another, all result in an abortion of reality.

Miss Wolfenstein analyzed several hundred entertainment films from several countries and came up with what she feels is the typical pattern of British, French, and American films.[38] British films, she says, evoke the feeling that "danger lies in ourselves, especially in our impulses of destructiveness. . . . The essential plot is the conflict of forbidden impulses with conscience. Either one of the contending forces may win out." In French films, "human wishes are opposed by the nature of life itself. The main issue is not one of inner or outer conflicts in which we may win or lose, be virtuous or get penalized. It is a contest in which we all lose in the end, and the problem is to learn to accept it." As for American films, the major plot configuration is like neither of the others: "Winning is terribly important and always possible though it may be a tough fight. The conflict is not an internal one; it is not our own impulses which endanger us nor our own scruples that stand in our way. The hazards are all external, but they are not rooted in the nature of life itself. They are the hazards of particular situations with which we find ourselves confronted. The hero is typically in a strange town where there are apt to be dangerous men and women of ambiguous character and where the forces of law and order are not to be relied on. If he sizes up the situation correctly, if he does not go off half-cocked but is still able to beat the other fellow to the punch, once he is sure who the enemy is, if he relies on no one but himself, if he demands sufficient evidence of virtue from the girl, he will emerge triumphant. He will defeat the dangerous men, get the right girl, and show the authorities what's what."

Now, of course no such "typical" plot as that could ever represent all American films, but the fact that this psychologist so contrasts American films with those of two other countries is, at the least, interesting. If this is indeed a fair comparison, which of the three pictures of life would you say would be least helpful, least "moral," in helping to prepare a young person to take his place in life?

There is something about the cabined, restricted, mechanical, unreal pattern of much of our popular art that is deeply disappointing. It is almost as though we were unwilling to spend enough on it. Enough in money, for we are lavish with the cost of film, the cost of television, the cost of thick, slick magazines, and all the rest; but not with the cost of emotion and the cost of penetrating inside the human mind. William E. Hocking, in an eloquent passage, talked about this. "The most available emotion is the laugh, and the most external; it has become the habitual American sign of enjoyment, because it is cheapest in terms of sympathetic understanding. The moral emotions are most costly, the indignant response to injustice, pity toward misery, the expansion of one's being in presence of an element of human greatness. Readers are not prepared to spend lavishly in these costly terms. . . ." And the mass media, Mr. Hocking continued, "must deal with entertainment, with the 'funnies,' with a crime, catastrophe, and adventure, because these involve the common emotion of semi-physical 'reaction'; they make no heavy drafts on either thought or conscience or faith."[39]

This is one of the respects in which our popular art seems to me to fall dangerously short of reality—in that it refuses to deal, except in rare cases indeed, with the more profound and moving experiences of man. Instead, it presents for the most part a rather shallow and externalized picture of a life that moves like a copy-book or a mechanical soldier, by rule, by blueprint, by code. Do the kinds of insights which emerge from it really make better men, a greater respect for morality, and a more Christian world? Or does it merely divert one from the problems of living a moral life in a complex world, and grant a bit of respite in a life where the rules are simple and the results all predictable?

A second respect in which popular art seems to fall disturbingly short is in the range of the behavior it reports. The world of Grandma Malone and Gary Cooper and September Bride and Mr. Botts is smaller than the world their audiences have to live in. Alpert quoted a movie screen writer as asking what would happen if someone told the movies, "Try it. Don't play it safe. What have you got to lose?" Then the script writer answered his own question:

"Do you know what could happen?" he went on. "There'd be motion pictures in which a married man would have an affair with his secretary and return to his wife with his marriage enriched; a husband and wife would quarrel, get a divorce, their friends would conspire to get them together again, and it wouldn't work, because the couple genuinely disliked each other; an unmarried woman would fall in love with a man, live with him for two years, and leave him because she'd met someone else, and the left-behind lover would go out and celebrate with his friends because he'd been tiring of her; a married man would visit a call-girl one night and nothing—but absolutely nothing, not even pangs of conscience—would happen later; a married couple would decide they didn't want children, and they wouldn't have any, and they'd be quite happy; a fortune hunter would have a choice between a lovely but poor young girl and a bitchy but rich heiress, and he would marry the heiress, fade-out the end; a doctor would give up his small-town practice to become a Park Avenue doctor, meet a rich girl, build up a lucrative practice, never go back to the home-town, and become one hell of a happy man. The possibilities are endless!"

"As endless as life," Alpert comments.[40]

The Assumption Regarding the Nature of Man

Now we can turn to the question we raised in the last section: whether the concept of the dignity and worth of man which lies behind our popular art is adequate to our needs?

Let us hasten to point out that popular art is not all of one piece, or on one level. Many examples of popular art are less codebound, less restricted in their concepts of man and their deference to taboos, than the broad mainstream of popular art we have been describing.

But so far as that mainstream is concerned, we can say that

Popular Art Man is somewhat more developed than Pithecanthropus or Peking Man, but not so much more as you might think. He cannot be trusted with a true and realistic picture of the way men live, the problems they face, and the way those patterns are settled. He cannot be trusted to distinguish good from evil, at least when the choice is presented in popular art. The only safe thing, therefore, is to show him a world in which human beings are pretty clearly divided into a good class and a bad class (although some who are *really* good *seem* bad, and vice versa), and in which right always wins and wrong is always punished. It is unsafe to show him in popular art many of the behaviors which he must see around him in life.

Especially is it unsafe to let him see or hear anything in popular art which might arouse elemental emotions. It is dangerous to expose him to anything which might test his faith in the sanctity of marriage or the home, or in his religion, or in law or justice; he might fail the test. It is dangerous also to let him hear anything profane or vulgar: he might pick it up. More important, it is useless to expect him to respond to any very deep and insightful treatment of human nature and human life; instead he must be expected to respond only at a superficial level, only on the level of what is funny, what is scary, what is physically powerful, et cetera.

In these respects, Popular Art Man is a child. In other respects he is a fool. For the media seem to assume that they can attract him by violence and sex ("Alluring! Seductive! Wicked!") and then cover up the sex and punish the violence in the show so that he won't see it, or at least won't find it in any way attractive.

Now, obviously there are many high-minded men in the popular art industry who do not appear to hold this view of man. A few examples out of many: Some of our large magazines do not seem to be edited with that kind of man in mind; John Huston's pictures are not made that way; *Omnibus* is not prepared that way. But the picture we have painted is the dead-center picture: the level of the majority of the entertainment films, of the crime dramas, the serials, and most of the variety shows on radio and television, and of much of the content of entertainment magazines.

And if we now ask whether that concept of man is adequate for today, I think we have to answer that it is not. At least it is not adequate for a very large part of our population. There are certainly children among us, adult and juvenile children. There are undoubtedly fools among us. But in programming for these more susceptible elements of our population, is not popular art selling us short?

If we ask whether a popular art which had higher aspirations—which, as Gibbs said, would show us something other than "a society in which anything is physically and materially possible, including perfect happiness, to a race of people who operate intellectually on the level of the *New York Daily News*, morally on that of Dayton, Tennessee, and politically and economically in a complete vacuum"[41]—if we ask whether a popular art that strove to do better than that would really be dangerous to the mores and values of society, then I think we should have to answer frankly that we don't know. But everything we have seen leads us to believe that the great majority of humans could take that in stride, and that the danger would lie only with the more susceptible few, the children and the fools and the disturbed.

Is there not some way to program so that the majority will not have to operate at the level of the susceptible few? There is plenty of room for initiative, change, and imagination even within the bounds of the codes. Is there not room within the demands of the undifferentiated audience, the hungry media, the pressure groups, and the economic arrangements of large entertainment industry? That is the challenge of this emerging age of social responsibility to the makers of popular art. And there are enough encouraging examples—fine drama, music, dance, pictorial art, and fiction—to indicate that it is a challenge within our power to meet.

THE PROBLEMS OF AN ADEQUATE SERVICE

We have said that the popular arts seem to us to be operating, in considerable part, on an inadequate concept of man and to be furnishing a service inadequate to the needs and capacities of large segments of their audiences. Now, if that is the case, why should it be so, and what can be done about it?

In the first place, this situation has come to exist because of the economic realities of very large investments which require very large audiences in order to return the cost. In the case of popular magazines, these are subscribing audiences partly, but to a certain extent they are measured in terms of readers among subscribers; for an advertiser obviously cares whether his ad is next to a much-read story or article.

In the case of movies, these are box-office audiences. In the case of radio and television, these are listening and viewing audiences; the entertainment is buying these audiences for the advertiser who foots the bill for both entertainment and advertising.

Because these audiences must be so very large in order to pay the bills, they tend to be undifferentiated. They tend to include all kinds of people. They include children and adults (the children often are among the supposedly "adult" audiences, and adults among the audiences for supposedly "children's" fare). They include people with twelve or more years of education, and people with four years. They include people from what we called a Dayton, Tennessee, culture, and a New York City East-Central-Park culture. They include representatives of many religious groups, many political groups, and many social groups. In the case of movies and to a lesser extent magazines, they include people from forty or more countries, each with their own culture traits, values, and taboos. This is the kind of miscellaneous and diverse audience for which the makers of American popular art have to program.

The obvious result of these restrictions is that popular art—to varying degrees in different media and under different stewardship—tends to appeal to common tastes in a very large and diverse audience, which means that it tends to appeal to the less subtle, less cultivated, less penetrating, and less discriminating tastes. More important, it has to avoid any number of kinds of content which might offend and repel large segments of the possible audience. Therefore, it tends to take over as its own the taboos of the cultures it wants to serve. When these cultures are various enough, their combined taboos leave surprisingly little room for maneuver.

Finally, the popular arts have a gargantuan hunger for new material which makes all the other problems more difficult. Some media are hungrier than others. Motion pictures have to come up with the fewest new stories per year. Magazines are somewhat hungrier, and most editors complain bitterly about the shortage of good material. But it is on television and radio that the popular arts reach their climax in demanding new material. A play that would run for a year in the theater plays itself out in a night on radio or television. A vaudeville act that would last a comedian for most of his professional lifetime expends its audience in one broadcast performance. A lecture that would take a man around the country or serve a professor for many classroom years, can be heard but once on the broadcast media. And television in this respect is more demanding even than radio, for it must fill in all the sights that are imagined on radio. As a result, a situation comedy like the weekly Jack Benny program on radio is too much effort to produce oftener than every two weeks on television.

Therefore, the makers of popular art are caught between millstones. Although they must be infinitely careful not to drive away any considerable part of their possible audience and thus fail to meet the economic demands of large media operation, they are constantly harried about material. Although desperate for new material, they are constantly warned not to make a mistake. The only possible result of this is to make change difficult. A producer can't afford to experiment much in that situation. He has to play it safe. He seeks innovation in the unimportant aspects of his productions, but not in their basic qualities. Audiences can't say very clearly what changes they would like if they have no chance to see the alternatives. Thus, success tends to be imitated, and the same pattern of common-denominator popular art repeats itself over and over again.

These are truly formidable obstacles in the way of change. Reviewing them, one confesses to a sense of surprise and pleasure that the best of American popular art is as good as it is: that Hemingway and Churchill and "The World We Live In" can appear in *Life*, or Murrow and Mary Martin and *Omnibus* and first-rate Shakespeare on television, or the Philharmonic and "Invitation to Learning" on radio, or the six most original and imaginative pictures per year— you name them—out of Hollywood.

On the other hand, there is no reason to think change can't be brought about. You change the situation by altering any of the factors just mentioned. To discuss these in detail would be to forecast what is going to be said in the remaining chapters of this book. But let us here point out, for example, that if you can change the economic base of the popular arts, you can make a considerable change in conditions. Frankly, there isn't any very satisfactory way to do this. It is highly unlikely, and to our mind not desirable, that American broadcasting should now get into a pattern of government support, which would mean that the cost would be transferred from advertising to tax money. We shall have to talk about this in the following chapters, wherein we can weigh the pros and cons of limited government support, and try to estimate what a series of noncommercially supported media as educational television and radio stations could contribute if used to maximum efficiency.

And there are other ways in which the economics and the control of the popular arts might conceivably be changed to make the task easier for those who would furnish a more diversified and imaginative service. For example, motion-picture theaters might conceivably be divided into different groups, showing different levels of films—one, perhaps, for young people, one for the bang-bang and kiss-kiss audience, still another for the audiences who like art films and realistic treatments of life. And, if these categories were clearly named, and if children were kept out of adult theaters until they were ready, it might be a good deal easier to serve adequately each of these different groups. Similarly, if broadcasting were to divide its programs by level—as the British Broadcasting Corporation does, for instance, with its Popular Programs, its middle-level Home series, and its "high-hat" Third Program—it might conceivably be possible to serve each of these more adequately. It is hardly necessary to point out, however, that to do this would raise severe economic problems for a private enterprise system and would not avoid the objection that each of these programs goes into the home where its audiences are supposedly unrestricted, and where immature or susceptible individuals must be protected from "damaging" or offensive material. Still another possibility would be deliberately to reduce the demand for new material on such a medium as TV by broadcasting less than a complete day.

It is common practice to blame the ills of the popular arts, and especially of motion pictures, on the codes. This is a little short of nonsense. Two things enchain us to the codes. One is what has been called the "code mentality." This is taking the codes in minutia, as a series of tiny rules of conduct, rather than as a guide to the spirit of conduct. This is what happens when Hollywood bans open-mouth kisses and still makes its pictures as sexy as possible. There is a tendency to be concerned with the trivial in the aspects of censorship, whether imposed by governments, or by industry-organized authorities (such as the Motion Picture Association of America), or by media themselves (as, for example, by the program acceptance offices in the networks).

There is a game played with a large map, in which one player challenges the other to find within a certain number of seconds a certain name on the map. A new player as challenger will choose a name in very small type, but the old experienced player will choose a name that is in very large type with the letters spread far apart. This, he finds, is less obvious than the small compact names. Censorship typically works with the small compact items. Smart writers have driven many censors crazy by giving them trivia to correct, while slipping the message through in the generalities. This kind of thing is characteristic of popular art censorship, too.

For an illustration of the difference between the trivial and the significant in self-censorship, let me cite two cases quoted by the acceptance department of a broadcast network:

Case 106. A character in a dramatic script was supposed to say, "I followed the first commandment: 'Live it up.'" This was cut out of the script, on the ground that it would offend Jewish and Christian religious groups.

Case 107. A network was considering a sponsored religious program to be called something like "Men in Black," and to feature each week a different clergyman. The program was to be sponsored. The network liked the sample scripts and was given to understand that a sponsor was available. But the head of the network, after considerable thought and consultation, said no to the idea. He asked, "Where would you put the commercials?" He said that it would be improper and irreverent to sell goods when the audience is in the mood for looking at men of God.

These cases illustrate radically different levels of judgment. The first judgment was on a triviality. It was not contended that the character might not say such a thing; or that such a statement would be presented as a favorable character trait; or that it would necessarily corrupt a hearer—but merely that it might offend a religious group, and result in a protest. By definition, it was therefore "irreverent." The other case is a different kind of attention to reverence and religion. Without passing on the rightness or wrongness of the decision—which one could hardly do without seeing the scripts and the commercials—still, it is clear that the network head was concerned with the spirit of the program, rather than the details. He was asking not whether a phrase would be picked up and protested but whether the total result of the program would be to contribute to the spirit of reverence in the audience. If the codes were always interpreted in this spirit, we would not have the contrast of sexy films with behavior on the screen that is carefully, even unreally, circumspect, or very attractive criminal behavior that is carefully punished at the end.

The second circumstance that chains us to the codes is that we treat them as chains, rather than guides. The popular art codes, for the most part, were introduced as protection and adopted out of fear. They were not so much to represent the conscience of the industry as to protect it from audience disaffection; not so much to make good programs as to make programs which would offend audiences as little as possible. As far as one can see from outside, the codes have been treated as a necessary evil, just as censorship has been treated since the beginning of time. At best, censorship is a sporting proposition to be outsmarted and circumvented wherever possible. At worst, censorship is a negative guide to conduct, a spelling-out of things one may not do; one can surrender his conscience to it, avoid carefully what it proscribes, and then freely go about doing what he wishes except for the specified "don't." This is an inadequate concept of religious behavior, and an inadequate concept of the kind of responsibility we expect of the mass media. And yet one sees evidence of both these kinds of attitude toward the codes on the part of some of the popular art makers.

Many of the custodians of popular art, particularly of entertainment films and entertainment broadcasting, and particularly in the early stages of those arts, have tended to come from the ranks of business rather than the ranks of fine arts. Whether they were financiers or entrepreneurs (spiritual descendants of Barnum whose exploits and legends they in many cases surpassed), they tended to bring to the new arts the ethics of nineteenth-century business, which—as Powdermaker puts it—"is basically unconcerned with morality, but . . . has to take on a moral system from powers outside and foreign to it."[42] Therefore, they accepted the codes—too often—as morality. They followed meticulously—and too often—the details of the codes, and neglected the spirit. In short, they used the codes as a negative guide, but not as a positive one. And the positive guide turned out, more often than not, to be the voice of economics: this art must be a success, i.e., make money. Will the people flock in to see sex? Give them sex, but keep out the provocative kisses. Will the people flock in to see violence? Give them violence, but be sure to tell them that crime doesn't pay. Will the people flock in to see an old formula? Give it to them again, don't risk a change.

If the makers of movies want to lift their concept of man, there is room within the code to do it. If they want to lift their idea of Plato a bit, so as to take account of how *important* the subjects are on which their art tries to be "good teaching," there is nothing in the code to keep them from doing it. If they want to introduce a little of Aristotle's test to try to make their popular art better art as well as good teaching, there is still room within the code. There is nothing really to stop them except the voice of the producer saying, "this film must make money." And there have been superior films—in both Platonic and Aristotelian series—which have made money. There have been superior broadcasts and superior magazines which have packed in the audiences.

The point is, even within the existing limitations, more can be done in the direction of responsibility than is being done. Let me give you an example from broadcasting, which indicates that children's programs need not necessarily be based on the low-common-denominator concept of man to which the serials, adult and children, have accustomed us. They need not necessarily grind along on their old rusty track of violence and infantilism. This is a memorandum from network officials to the production staff of a new children's program:

TO: "CAPTAIN KANGAROO" PRODUCTION STAFF

The following are some random thoughts for your general guidance —not necessarily in order of importance.

1. The child viewer of TV can enjoy a clever game or a baby raccoon more than a pie thrown in a face.

2. No child should be called such names as "fatty," "shorty," or "string bean," by his school chums as a result of a character skit or anything appearing on this show.

3. A behavior hint can sound to a child like a common-sense idea or an irritatingly coy preachment from his prissiest aunt—depending on how it is handled.

4. When choosing the show's music, remember that it's to be played not for a small, tone-deaf animal, but for a young human of potentially great taste.

5. We think that our audience can enthusiastically admire a character without our providing any evidence that he can beat someone up.

6. It's possible for a child's oft cited "innate aggression" to be worked off without the aid of a villain on our show for him to hate.

7. We have heard no psychological theory stating that a child's attention span is increased by loud noise and chaos.

8. In regard to props—we would rather a child learn from us that

he can use his imagination and a kitchen chair to make an airplane than that he see a real superjet on this show.

9. The widespread TV tradition, that if it's tasteful, kids won't like it, is one we reject entirely.

10. In general, the fact that children are imitators outlines our scope and our limitations. If you're writing or planning anything that can create an undesirable model for a child to imitate in action or thought —throw it out, there's a better way to entertain him.[43]

We have said that the communicator can raise his sights if he has the will and the ability to do so. How about the audience itself? Does not the public itself have some responsibility in this situation?

It is clear that the public has some responsibility to react to the media's image of it and to make its reaction known to the makers of popular art. This we shall talk about in the last section of the book. But does not the public have some obligation in regard to dividing the audience so that the old concerns about "everybody sees this film," or "this program goes into the home where it can be seen by children as well as adults," will not apply? For example, has not the family some responsibility as to what programs children see? Has not the family some responsibility as to whether their children go to films which are made for adults? And, finally, have not the pressure groups and their spokesmen some responsibility as to what they object to—whether to the details or the spirit of a program, whether to the minute items that may give an erroneous impression of a particular group or the large items that may give many groups an erroneous impression of life?

So it seems to me that both the makers and the receivers of popular art have responsibilities that they are not fully meeting, even within the narrow limits of the situation in which popular art works. If these responsibilities were fully met, then I think popular art would come nearer to the goals we most want for it: that is, to be a service which will fit the needs, tastes, and wishes of different kinds of people, rather than lumping all people together; and a service which is based on a higher concept of man than the infantile creature for whom much of this art seems to be tailored—for a creature dignified and discriminative, able to distinguish between good and evil, and between art and life.

PART IV

Responsibility
in
Mass Communication

Abuses of the freedom of speech ought to be repressed, but to whom dare we commit the power of doing it?
—Benjamin Franklin

10

The Government

In the first two parts of this book we described the development of an age and a situation in which social responsibility has become an increasingly important element in mass media performance. In the third part we followed through some of the patterns of responsible performance as we saw them developing. Now in the next pages we must ask, *whose* responsibility is it?

There are only three great instruments which society may use to encourage or prod the mass media to responsible performance. These are government and its various regulatory bodies, national, state, and local; the media themselves, their individual personnel, and their formal and informal associations and administrative organizations; and the general public, with its formal and informal organizations and associations.

If we ask where, among those, responsibility lies for the kind of mass communication we have in this country, and for any change we want to bring about in mass communication, then quite clearly the answer is that responsibility is shared. Neither government, nor the media, nor the public can be counted on to do the job alone, and on the other hand, none of them is exempt from responsibility for doing it. What we are looking for in these chapters, therefore, is a desirable balance of responsibility among them. And let us start with government.

When I said in the first chapter of this book that the chief responsibility of government in regard to mass communication is to keep its hands off, I was not being cute or whimsical or paradoxical. For government to keep its hands off mass communication will require the greatest self-restraint and devotion to principle. Yet hardly anything government can do will be so important as this act of restraint.

It will be a very difficult behavior pattern. We have got used to big government, and to counting on government to set things right. This is only natural. We have been faced with gigantic problems and have felt that no force except government was big enough to cope with them. In other parts of the world we have seen centralized authoritarian governments overcoming great difficulties and doing great deeds, although not always in a way we admire. In this country, too, we have seen government move into areas where it has never been before, simply because of the size and urgency of the need.

It is undoubtedly true that many Americans now feel that mass communications have grown so big, so powerful, so removed from the public, that no force except government is big enough to control them. There must be a vast difference between the way an American now perceives his relation to a large newspaper or a television network or a motion-picture studio, and the way an American must have perceived his relation to one of our tiny newspapers a century ago. Today he feels a kind of helplessness when he wants to register his needs or wishes with the rich and powerful media. And therefore, when he is dissatisfied, when he feels a change should be made, he typically turns to some power center which is better able than he to cope with the power of the media.

This is the kind of pressure that is constantly on Congress, on regulatory commissions such as the Federal Communications Commission, and on the state and local licensing authorities and punitive bodies. They are forever being exposed to the worries, the dissatisfactions, and the indignations of the public, and to the alleged shortcomings of the media. Religious and socially-minded spokesmen among their constituents are forever pointing out to them instances in which the media may be endangering the morals of youth, or contributing to crime, or offending minority groups, or breaking down religion. Political groups among their constituents are forever pointing out instances in which the media are presenting less than a clear lens to political realities. And public officials are moved to action by some of their own contacts with the media. If they are judges, they may become dissatisfied with the way a trial is handled in the press. If they are elective officials, they may feel they are being misinterpreted or misquoted or neglected in favor of their opponents. If they are members of regulatory bodies, they may look at the media with special thought to their own children or their neighbors'.

They may sincerely believe, as many government officials and many individuals outside government do, that the mass communication system is getting out of hand: that it is serving one political master rather than others, that it is moving away from the free market place of ideas, that it is becoming monopoly-ridden, plagued by bigness, or insensitive to the needs of minorities. And whatever the reason, there is every incentive to take the direct, the obvious, the simple way to remedy the trouble. Use the police power, the regulatory power, the legislative, judicial, or administrative power of government. Just as we built up the media to check on government, now that the media have grown so big, let us use government to check on them. What other force at our disposal is powerful enough to do it? Invoke the licensing power against a film. Order a book or magazine "banned." Remove the reporters from the court-room. Put a public relations man between a public official and the reporters who would see him. Make a broadcasting station put on good programs or deny it a license. Call a Congressional investigation of a doubtful practice. Use the antitrust laws to break up big units in the industry. Prohibit multiple ownership or cross-media ownership. Do it simply: let the government do it.

This is a beguiling argument, an apparently simple and direct way of solving certain continuing problems. But this argument should be resisted with every bit of wisdom and influence at our command.

Why? Because it is too dangerous. The cure is more deadly than the illness.

This is the point at which we should decide what we believe. Do we, or do we not believe in a democratic political philosophy? If we no longer do, if we believe in some form of authoritarianism, then we can properly call on our government to act as a caretaker of our mass communications. But the assumption of this book is that we still believe fundamentally in the kind of democracy which was reflected in our Constitution and our Bill of Rights, and developed over the years as new conditions required; that the changes which have taken place in our attitudes toward the media and our expectations of them are mostly results of changes in the media and the generally increasing complexity of life around us; and that all we want of the media is a high degree of social responsibility so that we can maintain the flow of information which is essential for a democracy. If that is a fair assumption, then we must exercise the greatest caution and restraint as to how we encourage government to enforce responsibility on our media.

We are not contending that government should have nothing to do with the media or that it bears no responsibility for their performance. It seems to us that Hocking was essentially correct when he called government a "residual legatee" of this responsibility.[1] That is, it inherits such responsibility as is not adequately absorbed by the media themselves or by the public. And our theme in these chapters is going to be that fundamental responsibility for checking on the media and making any socially desirable changes rests primarily with the media themselves, secondarily with the people, and only tertiarily with the government.

Why is it dangerous for the government to police mass communication? One hundred years ago it would hardly have been necessary to ask that question. But because the media have become so large and somewhat withdrawn from the people, we sometimes forget that they were set up as they were, and given special privileges, primarily to check on government. They were the people's media. They still have that function. Therefore, if we use government to police communications, we are really giving to the agency which we want checked the power to control its checker. This is obviously an awkward, if not an impossible, situation. The more control we give government over mass communication, the less confident we can be that mass communication is giving us an accurate and fair report on government.

Furthermore, we have an old and justified suspicion of what happens when government tampers with social and business relationships. This is what Arthur Garfield Hays was talking about when he testified against the right of government to forbid newspapers to own radio stations. He began by recognizing that most people who want government to crack down on the media do so with good intentions. "Of course, everybody who starts out with the idea of denying these (democratic) principles does it with good motives," he said. "The purpose, unquestionably, is to bring about a desired end. But the theory of government is that, if you let people alone, they will get farther by their own efforts, so long as you treat them alike, and that no government can safely lay down methods that will bring about as beneficial results as giving people equal rights under the law."[2]

It takes real courage to let people alone, to refrain from correcting by governmental action what seem like social abuses. But that is just what we are asking government to do. And we give it a rule by which it can determine whether in any given case it should intervene. This is the rule stated first by Mr. Justice Holmes and echoed by the President's Committee on Civil Rights: "Only where the danger to the well-being of society is clear and present."[3] In other words, we are asking government to let mass communications alone except where a situation presents a clear and present danger to society.

It may be useful to remind ourselves again of the actual wording of the "clear and present danger" doctrine as it has been stated by Justices Holmes and Brandeis and Chief Justice Vinson. The classical statement of the rule was by Mr. Holmes in the case of a California pamphleteer named Schenck who had been accused of wartime sedition for opposing the World War I draft. Mr. Holmes said, for a unanimous court:

The question in every case is whether the words used are in such circumstances and are of such a nature as to create a clear and present danger that they will bring about the substantive evils that Congress has a right to prevent. . . .

He added:

It is a question of proximity and degree. When a nation is at war many things that might be said in time of peace are such a hindrance to its efforts that their utterance will not be endured so long as men fight and that no Court could regard them as protected by any constitutional right.[4]

Five years later, in the period when this doctrine was being interpreted and applied, Holmes helped to clarify it:

. . . when men have realized that time has upset many fighting faiths, [he wrote] they may come to believe even more than they believe the very foundation of their own conduct that the ultimate good desired is better reached by free trade in ideas—that the best of truth is the power of the thought to get itself accepted in the competition of the market, and that truth is the only ground upon which their wishes can safely be carried out. That at any rate is the theory of our Constitution. It is an experiment, as all life is an experiment.[5]

Mr. Brandeis further amplified the doctrine in 1927 in a sedition case:

Those who won our independence by revolution were not cowards. They did not fear political change. They did not exalt order at the cost of liberty. To courageous, self-reliant men, with confidence in the power of free and fearless reasoning applied through the processes of popular government, no danger flowing from speech can be deemed clear and present, unless the incidence of the evil apprehended is so imminent that it may befall before there is opportunity for full discussion. If there be time to expose through discussion the falsehood and fallacies, to avert the evil by the processes of education, the remedy to be applied is more speech, not enforced silence. Only an emergency can justify repression.[6]

In the case of one of the Communist officials tried in 1951, Mr. Vinson stated the doctrine in probabilistic terms:

Chief Justice Learned Hand, writing for the majority [in the lower court], interpreted the phrase as follows: "In each case [courts] must ask whether the gravity of the 'evil,' discounted by its improbability, justified such invasion of free speech as is necessary to avoid the danger." . . . We adopt this statement of the rule.[7]

That is, to be sure, a difficult line to draw. Where one man sees a danger, another man may not. Where one sees "gravity" and "probability," another may not. But the impressive thing is how careful and conservative the United States Supreme Court has been about declaring a clear and present danger to society, and how vigorous the court has been in keeping the mass communication system free of government. For this we should be deeply grateful.

Let us take an example or two of how the line is being drawn between what is and what is not the responsibility of government.

One situation into which government is constantly invited to enter is the case where some individual or group believes media content to be offensive. Perhaps it is believed to be offensive to a religious or political group. Perhaps it is thought to be such as to teach children criminal habits or to disturb their personalities. There are countless such reasons given, all more or less convincing, why a given kind of program should not be permitted to come into the home, why a movie should not be allowed to show at a neighborhood theater, why a given comic book or magazine should not be permitted to circulate, why a book should not be sold on the bookstalls, et cetera. And the demand goes to one or another branch of government: shut off this flow of offensive material; keep it away from people it might injure.

Now, to what extent is this a field that government should enter? The apparatus is there: state and local censorship boards, ordinances regarding offensive material, a Federal Communications Commission instructed to see that radio and television broadcasts are in the public interest, and court precedents for punishing obscenity. And, if it is true that the media are leading society to spawn criminals or mentally disturbed persons, and committing offenses against human dignity and matters of conscience, then the situation has the sound of a clear and present danger.

Most such actions have originated in state or local commissions charged with censorship, or in local courts where charges have been brought. And the interesting thing, despite the willingness of states and municipalities to censor and despite the indignant and well-organized complaints against the media, is how very loath the Supreme Court has been to admit the existence of such a clear and present danger. Indeed, it has moved, case by case, to strike the ground out from under almost all such charges on which a governmental body might censor media content.

In the *Esquire* case, it forbade the Postmaster General to take a publication out of the mail on the charge, as he said, that it "failed to contribute to the public good and the general welfare." Said the court: "To withdraw the second-class rate from this publication today because its content seemed to one official not good for the public would sanction withdrawal of the second-class rate tomorrow from another periodical whose social or economic views seemed harmful to another official."[8]

In the *Miracle* case the court forbade New York to censor a film on the charge that it was "sacrilegious."[9] In the Winters magazine case, it forbade the censorship of cheap magazines on the charge that they were "principally made up of criminal news, police reports, or accounts of deeds of bloodshed, lust, or crime," and were therefore "vehicles for inciting violent and depraved crimes."[10] It refused to admit that the constitutional protection of a free press applies only to the exposition of ideas. Mr. Justice Reed said that "the line between the informing and the entertaining is too elusive for the protection of that basic right."[11] In fact, in only one situation has the court acted to permit censorship of media content. This is in the case of obscenity —smut for smut's sake. Even here, frank treatment of sex is not necessarily considered obscenity. For example, the novel *Ulysses* was ruled not to be obscene; the sexual details were adjudged to be part of the novelist's description of the world as he saw it, part of an idea he was trying to convey.[12] In the case of real obscenity, precensorship (e.g., licensing of a picture) or punitive action after publication (e.g., in the case of a magazine or comic) has been permitted. But the remarkable feature of this story is how loath the Court has been to let the government get its fingers on media content, and how in every case it has weighed the possible damage to society through suppression of free ideas against the possible damage to society through offending or corrupting, and come out with the conclusion that very few such dangers are so clear or present or frightening as to justify the government in interfering with the flow of ideas and information through the media.

The Commission on Freedom of the Press recommended that the government "maintain competition among large units through the antitrust laws."[13] The motive for taking action in this area is clear and defensible: we want competition in our mass media. We want to come as close as possible to a free market place of ideas. But for the last fifty years we have been faced with economic forces that have made for fewer communication units and larger ones. We have described this trend earlier in this volume. No one has been able to prove that this development has made for poorer communication content; indeed, there are signs pointing to just the opposite conclusion. But the development is troublesome in theory, because it tends to make it harder for a true clash of ideas to exist; and whether it is really having this effect is something that is difficult to measure.

The Commission itself was somewhat troubled by its recommendation and added a word of caution, recommending "those laws be sparingly used to break up such units, and that, where concentration is necessary in communications, the government endeavor to see to it that the public get the benefit of such concentration."[14] *Where concentration is necessary* is another line that is hard to draw.

Nevertheless, the government, as we previously pointed out, has been diligent in using its well-tested antitrust laws against the growing communication centralization. It forced the Radio Corporation to sell one of its two radio networks. It secured a decision forbidding studios to undertake the distribution of films. The Associated Press was forbidden to exclude membership applicants whose acceptance would put them into competition with present members. The *Kansas City Star* was flagged down on some of its practices which would use the double ownership of the newspaper and a radio station to advantage over other stations or papers. Radio and television networks and chains were severely limited in the number of stations they could own. All of these decisions were hard fought, but upheld.

However, the Federal Communications Commission decided it did not have the case to justify it in refusing newspapers permission to own radio stations or vice versa. The recent Congressional committee hearings into alleged monopoly in the television networks have so far come to nothing. And this fact illustrates the great difficulty which we experience in trying to establish a line on how far the government shall go in manipulating communications. The question is not whether concentration in the industry is bad *per se*, but rather *how much* concentration is bad. As Morris Ernst said, "Nobody would favor having all of the radio stations owned by the newspapers. . . . The only dispute is at what point should we be frightened, at what point should we stop—300 out of 800, or should we wait until 700, 600? There can be honest differences of opinion as to just where is the frightening point. I am telling you my prejudices. I am frightened when I see *one*."[15]

And so are many other people frightened when they see one newspaper buy out its competition in the same town, or when six studios make a large part of all the films which are seen on American screens, or when a television allocation plan is adopted which leaves room really for only two strong national networks, or when a magazine like *Collier's*, with four million circulation, is still forced out of business. But to resist those developments is to go against economic and electronic realities. The costs of modern mass communication and the tastes which people have developed for mass communication demand larger and fewer units. The television spectrum, unless we use an entirely different set of wave lengths, simply does not have room to cover the whole country with a larger number of networks.

Furthermore, there is little assurance that greater decentralization would make for better service. Take the example of the television networks, which are currently under attack. If the networks were forced to sell their wholly-owned stations, their ability to serve their affiliates would almost certainly be reduced. The reason is that the network business itself brings little profit; most of the profit of the network comes from the stations it owns. Likewise, if the networks were forbidden to demand an option on some of the choice time of their affiliated stations, then there is no certainty whatsoever that the program level would be better. In fact, it might very well be worse—not only because the networks claim they need that time to make things attractive to their sponsors, but also because a very high percentage of the good programs on the air come from networks rather than from local stations, and local stations are notably averse to taking high-quality sustainers from the network—for example, less than one third of CBS affiliates take "Invitation to Learning."

There is another disturbing possibility which John Crosby, the *Herald Tribune* broadcast critic, writes about:

Of course, NBC and CBS with their control of key stations in key markets are in the drivers' seats, and their control of what you and I and 100,000,000 other Americans are going to see or not to see has not always been used wisely or even scrupulously. But who is to control it, if not the networks? For years the networks were under attack not for controlling what was on their air, but for abdicating control to the ad agencies and the package producers, whose moral and intellectual and artistic standards were far lower than those of even the sleaziest network vice-president.

. . . Well, if the networks are going to be divorced from control of their broadcasting, who will rush in and fill that power vacuum? The ad agencies again? The package producers? The very threat of government intervention has kept the networks in line in the past. But there is almost no threat you can hold over an ad agency, and none at all over a package producer. What would keep *them* in line?[16]

This illustrates the narrow line that government intervention has to walk in the area of mass communications, even using tools which are so well tried and so favorably regarded as antitrust laws.

The Hutchins Commission recommended also that the government should, where necessary, supplement existing mass communications.[17] The Commission suggested this might be done in cases where existing private media are unwilling or unable to present the government's policies or the purposes behind those policies, or where private media are unwilling or unable adequately to represent this country to foreign countries. This the government has usually been willing to do. It has established the United States Information Agency, with an annual budget bordering on 100 million dollars to help speak for this country abroad. The government has published pamphlets, white papers, etc., to explain its policies, both here and abroad. Increasingly national and state governments have become publishers and broadcasters of useful information to farmers and homemakers; and very few voices have ever been raised in objection to the Agricultural Extension Service. So far, so good.

But there is clearly a point beyond which government should not go in a system like ours. It is unthinkable, for example, that our government should operate a wire news service, as a large number of the world's governments do. *The Stars and Stripes* for servicemen overseas is quite permissible, but a government-owned national newspaper of fact and political opinion would be a violation of all that we believe about a free press. Similarly, a state university may properly own a radio or television station to extend to a wider audience the advantages which the university offers on its own campus, but not to take part in politics. In all these respects there are limits beyond which we are not willing to let the government go. These are seldom written down, and not always clearly understood, but they can be established by the kind of give-and-take that precedes the making of a regulation or a decision.

Said the Commission on Freedom of the Press: "We recommend that government facilitate new ventures in the communication industry."[18] The Commission noted that "in the communications industry it is difficult to start new units because of the large investment required and because of the control of the existing units over the means of distribution. Little can be done by government or any other agency to reduce the cost of entering the industry except to adjust governmental charges, such as tax laws and postal rates, to facilitate new enterprises, and to prevent established interests from obstructing the introduction of new techniques. Tax laws and postal rates should be restudied with a view to discovering whether they do not discriminate against new, small businesses and in favor of large, well-established ones."[19] It is worth noting that federal corporation income taxes have been lowered for businesses whose annual incomes are less than $25,000, and also that newspapers now circulate free in the first postal zone. So far as new techniques are concerned, it may now be too late to do much about FM, which once looked a shining possibility for increasing the number of local radio stations. But the ultra-high-frequency band holds out a corresponding hope for television. If the engineering problems of using this band could be conquered, and if the transition could be managed without too great economic difficulties, then many more channels might be opened for television in the UHF band, resulting in better network service and more opportunity for local stations. This is clearly the kind of area in which the Federal Communication Commission can properly work.

Concerning distribution, the Commission recommended that government should act to stop "the attempts by existing units of the press to monopolize distribution outlets. The types of governmental action called for range from police protection and city ordinances which would make it possible for new newspapers and magazines to get on the newsstands to antitrust suits against motion picture companies which monopolize theaters."[20]

The chief difficulty in getting new publications on newsstands is simply the size of the stands. After World War II, the new crop of veteran-edited magazines overcrowded these stands, and many bundles were returned unopened by the stand operators. We have seen what has been done in the way of the antitrust suits forcing the motion picture companies to get rid of their distribution outlets and the efforts of the FCC to make it easy to get into FM. The problem of altering tax laws and postal regulations is one of those where we want and expect government to make haste slowly. This is the kind of case which Arthur Hays was talking about when he said, as we quoted him a few pages back, that our system works better when all people are given equal rights under law, not when *some* people or groups are protected. But the interesting thing here is the emphasis by the Commission on facilitating, rather than restricting, the flow of communication. "The main function of government in relation to the communications industry is to keep the channels open," said the Commission, and this is indeed one key to the kind of government activity which we consider desirable and permissible.[21] We want government to be most restrained and careful in any action it takes which restricts or controls content. Any action which facilitates flow, or makes it easier to enter the field, is much more likely to be a desirable one.

The government faces most directly up to the question which and how many new entrants should be permitted to mass communication in the case of broadcasting. Every new radio and television broadcaster must have a license from the Federal Communications Commission. Every three years or so, the successful applicant comes back for a renewal. This is a necessary service on the part of the government because otherwise broadcasters would clog the channels and make it impossible for listeners to get any decent reception. Therefore, there is no argument as to whether the FCC should have this power, only as to what tests it should apply in deciding between applicants. Let us review and expand what we have already said on this point.

Obviously *some* standards must be considered. We do not have enough channels to give them out by lot, or on the basis of first-come first-served. It is therefore necessary to consider how well equipped the applicant is to perform the public service for which he is to be granted property rights in the electronic spectrum.

Few people would disagree that the FCC has the right to ascertain that the applicant has the experience, the financial backing, the technical facilities, and the operating plans to put a good station on the air. But what is really important about a "good" station? Isn't it the quality of the program? A technically skilled and experienced station might broadcast only trash. A financially profitable and competently managed station might broadcast only commercials. Therefore, is it not in the public interest that the FCC give some attention to the question whether the applicant plans to program in the public interest? And when he comes back for a renewal, whether he *has been* programming in the public interest.

This is the nub of the problem: should the Commission have anything to say about the kinds of content that go on the air? In theory, no. In practice?

What are the alternatives to that? One would be vastly more channels, so that there would be room for everyone on a desirable frequency, and the public would have its own opportunity to decide what kind of service it wants. Another would be such a high standard of responsibility on the part of broadcasters that any applicant could be counted on to furnish excellent public service, and it would therefore be unnecessary for the FCC to take account of programming in making its decisions. A third might be a much more alert and aggressive participation by the public in the judgment of broadcast performance, so that public criticism and objections and suggestions could guide broadcasters, advertisers, and the FCC alike. The last of these alternatives is not immediately in evidence; the second has not yet been proved to everyone's satisfaction; and the first is infeasible without considerably re-arranging the electronic spectrum.

The Commission itself has been more than circumspect in handling this issue. True, it frightened the broadcasters with its "Blue Book," but the action it has taken following that famous report has been mostly to examine the amount of public service a station said it would do or has done, the proportion of commercials to programs, et cetera. For example, take the case of station KIEV. This station petitioned for a channel in a Southern California town, arguing that the town was being deprived of local programming, and promising to make major use of local talent and give major attention to local issues. On this promise KIEV was given a license to broadcast, and, to clear room for it, another station on the same wave length was restricted to limited time on the air. Three years later KIEV came up for a license renewal. In preparation for the hearing, FCC engineers recorded several days of KIEV's programming. It was found that the programs consisted entirely, or almost entirely, of records, mostly popular, some semi-classical. There was a high percentage of commercials. Local talent and local issues were conspicuously absent. On that evidence the Commission refused to renew the license, and restored the time it had taken away from the conflicting station.[22] It is very hard to find anything wrong with this kind of action. If an applicant asks time from another station on the basis of a promise to give certain important public service, he should put up or shut up. (It should be added that KIEV is still on the air, and that the FCC's function has proved to be rather to frighten stations than actually to withdraw a license.)

And yet somewhere in the shadowy territory just beyond this kind of decision is a line over which we should be loath to see the FCC go. In fact, the whole arrangement is one we live with most uncomfortably. The FCC itself is uncomfortable and very cautious with it. The argument for taking some account of a station's programming is very hard to counter. And still everyone is jittery about the kind of value judgments the FCC may make, and looking for a way out—perhaps a new arrangement of the spectrum to provide more room, or something like a nongovernmental body to speak for the public and advise the Commission on matters of programming.

There is one area in which we are quite sure we want a minimum of government intervention. This is in the channels which carry government news. A recent book by Russell Wiggins, of the *Washington Post and Times Herald*, gives ample evidence of how alarmed the newsgatherers are over the barriers that are being put in the way of government news coverage. But even here there are encouraging signs. The White House is more open to newsgatherers than it has been in some administrations. More officials are willing to submit to the give and take of a press conference.

Let us sum up. Our kind of mass communication system will be more healthy if the government keeps its hands off as much as it possibly can. The time it is justified in interfering is when there is a clear and present danger of the kind which Congress (or the FCC or another governmental body) is legally entitled to handle. This is very seldom. It is more often justified in interfering where it can facilitate the flow of information than where it restricts the flow or censors some of the content. In other words, its primary job is to help keep the channels of information open. And this applies to its own news channels too.

The record of the United States government in this respect is better than almost any other government one might cite. A foreign observer came to me in amazement some years ago, asking how one of our national administrations could show such restraint when two-thirds of the newspapers, representing more than three-fourths of the circulation, were actively against it. In that situation, he said, any authoritarian or semi-authoritarian state would not have hesitated a moment. It would have coerced the newspaper. That failing, it would have seized a wire service or published its own papers. Yet the U. S. administration in question did no such thing, and it stayed in power a considerable length of time, and the administration, the communication system, and the country all came through the crisis.

But it is worth remembering that government always tends to do the jobs other units of society don't do for themselves. If the public is ineffective in expressing its wishes of the mass media, then the government will tend to step in to act for the people. If the media are irresponsible, and there is no other force to call them to responsibility, then the government will feel it should enforce responsibility on them. We are not saying government *should* step in. On the contrary, even a considerable degree of irresponsibility in our media would be preferable to government interference. But ultimately a system like ours today requires responsibility of its mass media. Our mechanism for maintaining that responsibility is a delicate balance among the forces that bear on it. If the media do not act to weed out irresponsibility, then some other force will. If the public cannot make its will felt, then the government will step in. Government is the "residual legatee." Therefore, if we want government to have as little as possible to do with mass communication, the best way to prevent it is for our media to give as responsible a performance as they possibly can, and for the general public to be alert to media performance and vocal in expressing its needs and judgments.

11

The Media

Let us, then, talk about the communicator. What is his responsibility? Basically it is to turn out the highest quality product he can. To be aware in depth and breadth of the needs and interests of his public. To maintain the free market place of ideas and the self-righting process of truth despite the growing concentration of voices. To do for his own product by responsibility what many outsiders think can be done only by the government "cracking down." No small assignment.

There are two chief patterns in which the communicator organizes his sense of responsibility. One is self-regulation—the provision of codes of conduct, administrative machinery, and penalties for infractions. The other is the pattern of education, improvement of personnel, self-criticism, and setting of standards, which we shall call, for want of a better term, professionalization.

SELF-REGULATION

We have already paid our respects to the media codes in some detail. Of necessity we have talked about them in a somewhat negative manner, because it has seemed necessary to make clear just how far we can count on the codes to do the job that needs to be done. Therefore, let us say again at this point that there is a great deal the codes can do and, indeed, have done. They were made by well-intentioned men and are administered by careful and scrupulous men. Especially in the case of motion pictures and comic books, the codes and the industry "czar" have contributed to cleaning up a mess that no one was very proud of. In radio and television the codes have undoubtedly succeeded in generalizing a pattern of desirable trade practices. Radio and television have benefited also from another form of self-regulation—the network acceptance offices which exercise a benevolent censorship established by the networks, so that scripts can be read and sanitized if necessary before going on the air. Unquestionably these network facilities have been able, in a large number of cases, to screen out commercial and entertainment material which would have offended many listeners or viewers. Therefore, let us not undervalue the machinery of self-regulation as it exists in mass communication. It has done a great deal for the industry and can continue to do a great deal.

The danger in the codes is simply that we may count on them to do more than they can do. There is a tendency in the industry, and among some organized groups which have been critical of it, to see a code established and then rest secure in the confidence that they have fulfilled their responsibility—that the code will take over. This, it seems to us, is very far from the case. And therefore, we must try to understand just what the codes can do, and what they cannot do, toward insuring responsible mass communication.

We have earlier pointed out a fundamental difference between the newspaper code and the other codes. The American Society of Newspaper Editors' code, the Canons of Journalism, is a positive, eloquent document, couched in general terms, and based on a concept of rational man and the libertarian philosophy of the free market place of ideas. The other codes are rather more negative documents, highly specific in nature, based on a caretaker-philosophy, and on a concept of man as a suggestible and malleable being, in need of protection from moral and political ideas that might be harmful to him. Furthermore, the ASNE code is made and subscribed to by employees—editors, who work for publishers; the other codes are subscribed to by the men who own and publish or broadcast.

The ASNE code has not demonstrated that it has any teeth. Only one charge has ever been brought under the code, and that charge was dropped; however mitigating and qualifying the circumstances may have been, still it looks as though that particular newspaper was too tough to handle, and since that time no attempt has been made by ASNE to enforce the provisions of the code. Nor is there any mechanism set up for its enforcement. The code is therefore a statement of objectives and standards which new members of the editorial group or future members can read with enlightenment and inspiration. It does not have the force or mechanism of regulation.

The other industry codes are set up with varying degrees of enforcement in mind. The radio and television codes are administered by staffs which investigate complaints and sample the offerings of networks and stations. These staffs call violations to the attention of the broadcasters concerned, and have the power to recommend expulsion from the National Association of Radio and Television Broadcasters. This is not a penalty likely to be invoked very often, nor a penalty which is likely to terrify a real sinner. But it is combined with other powers: the publicizing of undesirable practices within the industry; the advantage of having such trade practices as the permissible amount of advertising in a program of given length discussed and decided upon by a group of leaders within the industry (whose recommendations were then written into the code); the additional enforcement by network acceptance offices, and the constant threat of FCC action on undesirable practices which are not corrected. Therefore, the self-regulation of the broadcast industry may have a considerable amount of influence on programs. The comic book publishers appointed Judge Charles F. Murphy as their "czar" with an independent code authority to examine the books and, so the code says, with "strong powers of enforcement." The motion-picture industry maintains a staff usually totaling about nine persons to administer the code. They read scripts in advance of shooting, view films before release, and have the power to withhold or give the MPAA seal of approval.

It may help to understand the nature and limitations of these codes, if we recall that, with the exception of the newspaper code, they grew out of fear and were designed to protect the industry against damage from public criticism or official action.

The Canons of Journalism seem to represent what might be called the newspaper man's quest for professional status. As might be expected in a libertarian system, newspapers had long attracted men with high moral responsibility, and some of these men—for example, William V. McKean of the *Philadelphia Public Ledger*—wrote codes of ethics for their own staffs. From 1900 on, newspapermen spoke often about the "profession of journalism." Schools of journalism appeared, some of them, like the Pulitzer School at Columbia, endowed by publishers. When Will Irwin wrote his much-discussed series on American newspapers for *Collier's* in 1911, he said he could detect an unwritten code of ethics among good reporters. The formation of the American Society of Newspaper Editors itself was a sign of the newspapers' striving for professional status. The ASNE adopted the Canons of Journalism at its first annual meeting in 1923. Since then the ASNE meetings have been notable for discussions of ethics and press freedom. But the code, as we have said, has never been enforced, and is now certainly no more than morally binding on members, if that. It has never been formally subscribed to by the men who are in command of the policy of newspapers, the publishers. But it is helpful in understanding what kind of code this is to recall that the document was adopted in a period of professionalization, without any special pressure on the industry to "reform" or "clean up," and by employees rather than owners or top executives.[1]

The motion-picture code grew out of threats to the industry and honest concern over what might be evil effects of its products. After World War I the industry was caught in two social currents which were not exactly congruent. On the one hand, movies began to reflect the freer moral standards of the times, notably the freer discussions of sex and family. On the other hand, they met a tendency on the part of the American people to try to correct social evils by law. (Prohibition was an example.)

The motion picture industry faced both boycott and official censorship. From 1918 to 1921 several voluntary organizations had scrutinized the content of movies and declared much of it evil or worthless. Religious and civic leaders spoke against the indiscretions of movies. Magazines and newspapers editorialized against them, and the daily press carried the juicy scandals of the Hollywood folk. Notable among these was the disgusting story which ended the enormous popularity and the highly profitable movie career of "Fatty" Arbuckle. Although Arbuckle was never convicted of the manslaughter with which he was charged, the story was sufficient to dramatize countrywide the charge that Hollywood was a modern Babylon. More and more, people turned to law to correct the alleged abuses in the films, as they had turned to law to correct the abuses of the saloon. Between 1909 and 1922, eight states and a number of cities established legal censorship of motion pictures.[2]

Caught between public indignation and consequent threats of boycott and the increasing need to pass censorship in many places, the movie makers became alarmed for their investments. They formed the Motion Picture Producers and Distributors of America in 1922. This association passed a resolution discouraging the purchase of questionable books and plays as plots for movies. The resolution had little effect, however, and the movie makers decided that they had to put teeth into their self-regulation for their own protection. They called on Martin Quigley, a Catholic layman and publisher of motion-picture trade papers, to help draft a code of standards. He sought assistance in turn from Daniel A. Lord, S.J., a professor of dramatics from St. Louis. The resulting code was adopted by the MPPDA in 1930 and has remained essentially the same ever since, although parts have been clarified or slightly changed. Will H. Hays, a member of the Coolidge cabinet, had been employed in 1922 to head the association office, which soon became known as the "Hays Office." A seal of approval was created, and fines were established as a result of the Legion of Decency campaign in 1934.[3]

Ever since 1930, then, the motion-picture code has done exactly what it was set up to do. It has served as a guide to the studios in avoiding material which might bring on boycott or censorship, and it has served to represent the good intentions of the movie makers to the public, to receive complaints, and to explain and defend the kind of movie practice which bears the code seal of approval.

Broadcasters drew up their code of radio practice in 1937 in the context of government regulation and threatened intervention. Broadcasting has always been a child of mixed parentage: public interest and commercial profit. For a long time radio was unrestrained by government. Radio signals clashed and crossed as stations ranged up and down the spectrum. So chaotic was the situation that the radio industry itself wanted some government intervention to establish wave lengths. It got it with the Radio Act of 1927, which created a Federal Radio Commission (later the Federal Communications Commission) to regulate channels and to police radio practice. In 1934 Congress passed the Communications Act which embodied major principles of the Act of 1927, but extended them. This Act established the Federal Communications Commission and the standard of "public interest, convenience, and necessity," which has ever since hung over the broadcasters as a threat of what government might do concerning broadcast content.

Meanwhile, the broadcaster's idea of the functions of radio had been changing. At first, radio was thought of as purely a public service from which the industry would benefit through the sale of sets and equipment. This was David Sarnoff's principle when he put the Radio Corporation of America into the broadcasting business in 1920. But advertisers quickly recognized what the new medium might do for them. By 1922, there was a rapidly rising curve of radio advertising, and many people, including some broadcasters, were looking askance at the development. The new Federal Radio Commission in 1927 began to study "advertising excesses." The National Association of Broadcasters reacted in 1929 with "standards of commercial practice," which sought to keep the air free of "commercial announcements" between 7 P.M. and 11 P.M. If this has a quaint and old-fashioned sound today, it is not surprising, because the "standards" did very little good. Noting the "domination" of radio by advertising, Congress in 1932 considered a resolution inquiring into the feasibility of government ownership and operation of broadcasting.

This was the setting in which the radio code was drafted. On the one hand, broadcasters recognized the possibility of government intervention—even ownership—as a real threat, and, furthermore, they recognized their obligation to operate in the public interest. On the other hand, they recognized that advertising was their financial life's blood. Therefore, content had to meet government standards and avoid antagonizing the public, in order to avoid severe government intervention; but it also had to avoid antagonizing advertisers and potential purchasers of advertised goods and services. The code, therefore, was a statement of trade practices designed so as to walk the fence between these two dangers. The first code was then adopted, after long discussion, in 1937, and revised in 1945, 1948, and 1954.[4]

Television inherited the traditions of radio and the same general pattern of government regulation. It recognized the possibility of some of the troubles radio had experienced. Many people were already talking about the power and the potential dangers of the new medium, and the allocation plan was focusing attention on the importance of government regulation. Therefore, the television code was adopted in 1952, and revised in 1954. Even more than the radio code it is a statement of acceptable trade practices. Nearly half of it deals with the handling of advertising.

Comic books grew into an important medium of communication during World War II. Much of "comic" content came to consist of picture stories dealing with crime, sex, and romance, war, mystery, adventure, the West, and violent behavior in general. These were themes which the pulp magazines had treated for years, but the comics treated them vividly and often without much restraint, and made them highly accessible to children. Consequently, in the 1940's comic books became a favorite target of parents, educators, government officials, and clergymen. One of the most vocal critics was Frederic Wertham, a psychiatrist. He said, in words which gained weight from his professional standing: "The comic books, in intent and effect, are demoralizing the morals of youth. They are sexually aggressive in an abnormal way. They make violence alluring and cruelty heroic. They are not educational but stultifying."[5]

Critics named several instances in which comics were alleged to have incited children to crime, even to murder. By 1948, more than 50 cities had tried to regulate the sale of comic books, some by local ordinances, others by censorship committees. Thirty-two bills or regulations to curb the sale of comics were introduced in state legislatures in 1949, although none were passed. In many cities, formal and informal voluntary associations held meetings to complain about the danger of comics, and in many cases descended on dealers threatening boycotts and other action unless they "cleaned up" their shelves of comic books.

To protect their investment, 14 publishers of comic books formed the Association of Comics Magazine Publishers in 1948 as a self-policing body for the industry. Henry Schultz, an attorney and member of the Board of Higher Education in New York City, was retained as executive director, and a code for comic-magazine content was adopted. This was not effective in abating the criticism. The Gathings Committee of the House in 1952 investigated comic books, along with pornographic books and magazines. At least one state legislature gave the books critical attention. Vigorous criticism continued to appear in the press. In 1954 the Association retained the well-known judge, Charles F. Murphy, as code administrator and elicited the aid of a public committee in drafting a new code. This succeeded in eliminating some of the practice which had brought the criticism.

This, in brief, is how the later codes came into being. They were chiefly protective measures, aimed at blunting the edge of public criticism, avoiding government intervention, and helping the communicators to avoid material which might bring boycott, censorship, or other such trouble on their product.

As such, they told the communicators what *not* to do, to avoid trouble. As an example of how a code administration works, consider this letter sent by the Motion Picture Code administrator in 1940 to a producer who had submitted a script for review. The administrator said that the script had been read and approved under the Production Code. However, he said, the producer's attention should be directed to the following points:

Scenes 32, 35, 36, and 44: Please bear in mind that the Code prohibits the showing of gun battles between criminals and law-enforcing officers. We recommend that a line be inserted to indicate that N—— is trying to shoot the *tires* of the police car, and that N's shooting be held to a minimum and that he use but one revolver.

Scene 218: We presume that there will be no gruesome details as to the injured boys.

Scene 287: We believe it would be well to have M—— wounded rather than killed by the police, and, in Scene 288, contd. Page 130, he would be shown conscious, but perhaps limping, when he gets into the police car. This will change the dialogue at Scene 309, contd. page 139, from indicating that M—— has been killed to his being wounded.

Scenes 291 *et seq.*: We assume that there will be no unacceptable exposure of A's person.

Scene 33, contd. Page 140: Please amplify L's speech to indicate that G—— has been arrested and will be punished also.

You understand, of course, that our final judgment will be based upon the finished picture.

Cordially yours,
Joseph L. Breen.[6]

Whereas the mechanisms in the different media are quite different, this is a good example of the level at which code authorities operate. The broadcasters' code administrators may point out to a station that it is carrying six minutes too much commercial time in a certain program and therefore violates the code, or that criticisms are coming in regarding a certain performer's comments on religion. The comic-book authority may point out that a particular treatment of violence or sex will not be given the seal of approval. But in general they all work at the level of acceptability, rather than at the level of responsibility. As the Commission on Freedom of the Press said, the standards are minima, not goals of adequate or ideal performance. The codes are to keep communicators out of trouble. They do not tell what to do to meet audience needs for quality. They could not be expected to do that. You can legislate acceptability, but not responsibility.

Therefore, at the same time as we record our appreciation of what the codes have done, we must record also an estimate of what they have not done. They have succeeded in eliminating a number of undesirable and offensive practices and materials from motion pictures, broadcasts, and comic books. They have enforced a degree of surface morality, although in an arbitrary and mechanical way. They have not enforced and cannot be expected to enforce quality. They have not necessarily made for any aesthetically better pictures. They have not even made for any more truthful pictures or programs—that is, production in which the answers to problems are honest, not "phony," or in which the characters are real people rather than robots moving about in a rather artificially delimited world. Truthfulness is a part of morality, and in that sense they have not even been able to legislate morality; in fact, they may have done just the opposite by making it impossible for producers to treat certain problems and certain behaviors which are important parts of life and understanding.

All this we have talked about in an earlier section of this book under the question whether the assumptions in the codes are adequate. Our conclusion was that the assumptions are not entirely adequate; but they could hardly be adequate when the codes were constructed to avoid potential criticism from each and every source. This is the strength of the codes but also their limitation. They will meet the most vocal criticism from the greater part of the critics. They will perform, in a negative way, to reduce offensiveness and broaden acceptability. They will tell the communicator how to avoid some of the things he should avoid, but not how to put in some of the things he should put in: truthfulness, insight, material to serve the diversity of needs and interests in his audiences. In other words, what the codes do we can respect, but we cannot equate what the codes do with the responsibility of the mass media.

It would doubtless be possible to improve the codes. Ruth Inglis, in her book, *Freedom of the Movies*, advances a good idea for a national advisory board of distinguished citizens to review and propose changes from time to time in the Motion Picture Code, to take account of criticisms of the screen, to report annually to the public on the use of the code, and to contest the decisions of censor boards which request changes in addition to those made under the code, and which the advisory board feels are unwarranted.

The first duty of such an advisory board, said Miss Inglis, would be to "produce a realistic code in which obscenity is prevented, and which at the same time allows the screen to realize its full potentialities." "Why," she asks, "should the consequences and social implications of the white-slave trade, venereal disease, or miscegenation not be depicted in movies? Why should judges or the clergy receive blanket protection against indirect censure or ridicule? Why must script-writers invent 'compensating moral values' in films, when often they are lacking in real life? Should history be perverted as it was in the case of the movie *Conquest*? Is it not a fraud upon the public to release movies bearing the same titles as plays such as *The Voice of the Turtle* or novels like *Forever Amber*, but with the contents drastically altered?"

All these things can be avoided in a properly drawn code, she feels, without nullifying the restriction upon obscenity. Having drawn the code, the board would then proceed to observe its use, reporting annually to the public on the number and kind of rejections and changes which are made in pictures during the production process. "Without public review," she points out, "the work of any private regulatory agency is open to abuse." Finally, the board would be in a position to defend the freedom of the films against what it considers unjustified legal attacks. This does not seem an infeasible kind of adjunct to the motion-picture code authority, and it might make a great improvement in the effect of that agency. And, if it would work in the case of films, it would also work in broadcasting, and, if desired, in comic books.[7]

But with or without such public advisory boards and such code reviews as they might make, codes by themselves will never give us the kind of mass communications we need in our society. The responsibility of mass communicators is a great deal more than can be taken care of by codes of conduct.

PROFESSIONALIZATION

Self-regulation is a quick way. Make a code, hire an administrator, establish mechanism for enforcement, and you can very quickly make a difference in the media product. Professionalization is the slow way. It requires a long process in which change takes place in people before it takes place in the media. But we are inclined to have more hope over the long run for the slow process than for the fast one.

When we talk about professionalizing mass communication, we do not mean to require of it all the characteristics and trappings of law and medicine. By any of the traditional definitions, mass communication (journalism, or broadcasting, or film-making, or even writing) is not a profession. A profession is regarded as an occupation which exists to perform certain types of important public service. A large proportion of its members are self-employed. They usually maintain a confidential relationship with the members of the public whom they serve. In general, before they are admitted to practice the profession, they are required to show mastery of a substantial body of knowledge which is unique to the profession. In order to acquire this knowledge, a candidate for the profession usually spends a long time in a professional school, which is a center of research and criticism as well as teaching. The profession has a conscience which is usually expressed in a code (for example, the oath of Hippocrates). The new member accepts responsibility for maintaining the profession's standards when he enters membership. If he fails to maintain them, an authority, usually acting on the advice of his peers, has the power to debar him from further practice. And there is a tradition about the profession that the member will perform needed public service regardless of the income from it. That is, the physician will treat a patient in the most ethical way, even though he might make more money by "quack" practices; he will minister to a sick man even though the man cannot pay his fee, et cetera. These are among the characteristics of a true profession.

Mass communication and its branches obviously do not meet all these qualifications. No occupation has a higher public service to perform than to serve man's need to know. And there is a trace of a confidential relationship between newsgatherer and source of news. But the parallel begins to break down at that point. The practitioners of mass communication, except a few, are employees. Consequently, the ultimate responsibility for their actions and the quality of their public service rests not on them, but on their employers. Many mass communicators now go to quasi-professional schools of journalism or communications, but these schools have no substantial and unique body of knowledge, like law or medicine or various other generally recognized "professions," to teach their students. They can, of course, introduce the students to some of the skills required. They can prepare them to go understandingly into the occupation by exposing them to the history of the craft and discussing its social responsibilities, its relationships to other social activities, and the way it works.

But the really substantial body of knowledge which the mass communicator needs is not so channeled or specialized; it is a complex of whatever helps him to understand the world around him. That is, he needs some psychology to help him understand the people around him; some sociology to help him understand social relations, organization and disorganization; some political science to help him understand the workings of government; some economics to help him understand business and finance; some anthropology to help him see his culture in perspective; something of the broad and illuminating sweep of history; some of the humanizing insights of literature and art; some introduction to science, so that he can at least understand its language and method, and be prepared to look through its window into modern life. In other words, he needs, not a specialized education in a body of knowledge unique to his occupation, but rather the broadest possible education so that he can understand and interpret what he is going to see and write or talk about.

Furthermore, the very nature of our system makes it unlikely that entrance to mass communication would ever be restricted by such a professional examination as determines what candidates become practicing physicians or lawyers (or clergymen or teachers or engineers). Even if the subject matter of such an examination could be decided upon, still the restriction of entrance into the "profession" would almost inevitably be interpreted as a restriction on the freedom of expression.

The idea is in many ways attractive, and in certain European countries the licensing of journalists has been done. But from our viewpoint the dangers would outweigh the advantages. To give either the government or any nongovernmental organization the right to say who enters the profession is tantamount to giving that authority the right to say who can use the mass-communication system. And, whereas that right of restricting entrance might be exercised most scrupulously and always with the public interest in mind, still the suspicion would be that some of the decisions might be influenced, consciously or unconsciously, by political bias. Therefore, the idea of a license or an entrance examination for professional journalists or other communicators has always been rejected in our society, and probably will continue to be rejected. And by the same kind of reasoning the possibility of expelling a communicator from the profession for malpractice would have to be approached most carefully, if at all.

Let us agree, then, that mass communication is not and probably can never be a profession in the traditional sense. To try to pour it into that mould would be a wasteful activity. But the fact that mass communication does not fit the pattern of a traditional profession is no reason why we cannot expect professional standards, attitudes, and behavior from it. Indeed, we can argue that an occupation which is organized, as mass communication is, around a very high concept of public service is necessarily a profession, and its members must be professionals. A profession develops, not by asking how another profession is organized, but by asking what kind of behavior is necessary in order to carry out the public service obligations of the craft. This is certainly a legitimate question for mass communication. If that question is seriously asked and thoughtfully answered and acted upon, then certainly communication is on the road to professionalization.

That is what we are talking about under the term "professionalizing" mass communication.

And specifically, what might the communication industry do toward professionalizing itself?

It could personalize the professional responsibility which the industry feels, and which its clients expect of it. This is a vague, slow process, altogether different from making and enforcing a code. It is something that people have to do themselves; it can't be done to them. And yet what we are talking about is perfectly clear and can be understood by every member of the communication industry.

As we have already noted, most members of the industry are employees. Legal and administrative responsibility for what they do therefore rests with their employers, and ultimately with ownership. But that is not the way a newspaper or a broadcasting station or a publishing house operates. That is rather the way an army operates; if a superior officer orders a soldier to kill a prisoner, he kills the prisoner. But in Part III of this book we have cited instance after instance in which employees of mass communication have acted according to a code of ethics quite apart from any instructions given them by their employers. The relationship to the source of news is one example. Furthermore, this kind of action is something which can be and is discussed by members of the profession, and in which desirable behavior is quite freely specified, even though in such terms as "I would do this" or "That isn't the right way to do it."

Nothing is farther from the truth than to say that mass communication is at present ruled entirely by a principle of *caveat emptor*, or by an amoral code which extends down and out from the business interest of the owners. Almost everybody in mass communication realizes he is engaged in a public service and has special responsibilities for that reason. In some cases, these responsibilities are put on a high moral basis; in others, they are expressed merely as a need to give the public what it wants. But, in any case, the greatest step toward professionalizing the mass-communication industry would be simply to emphasize the *individual* sense of responsibility rather than merely the corporate sense—that is, the responsibility of the communicator as a public servant and a professional, as apart from but not fundamentally contrary to his obligations to the business he works for. Pull these unwritten codes of ethics out into the open. Make them the subject of discussion. Shift a little of the emphasis in the industry's trade papers and conventions away from the problems of meeting the economic challenge to the problem of meeting the public service challenge. Let the employers encourage their employees to behave like professionals, and support them when they do so. Let the employees, on their part, take their own responsibility very seriously and cease to hide behind the fact that they *are* employees and that someone else pays their salary and determines policy.

What we are talking about is therefore the building of professional attitudes. This isn't something you can legislate or buy. But it is something that the members of the mass communication industry have it in their power to accomplish if they will.

We mean the building of such attitudes from top to bottom of the profession. We include the owners, whom we expect to distinguish between good business practices and public responsibility, and the youngest cub reporter, whom we expect to be accurate and fair and free of corrupting influences even on his first assignment. We include the advertising men and the management personnel, the writers and the "talent." We expect them all to perform somewhere above the level of a Barnum, who would have looked at the enormous audiences of mass communication and rejoiced that "one is born every minute." We expect them to operate somewhere above the level of a pitchman, but somewhere below the level of the angels. We want them to try to live up to the peculiar responsibility of informing free citizens of a free country, and thus to help to keep it and them free.

One of the convincing signs of such a developing professional sense would be the development of lively self-criticism within mass communication. The scarcity of mutual criticism in communications is one of the features of the industry an outsider finds hardest to explain. In part, it may be due to the evanescence of some of the products. In the case of books, plays, and films, for example, a widespread and effective pattern of criticism has been built up. These media are not so evanescent: the play continues, the book is on sale. But a radio or television program is on the air today, gone tomorrow. Many, if not most, news stories are completed in one or two editions of the newspapers or on one or two broadcasts. The media have no hesitation in criticizing fleeting phenomena outside the fields of the industry, as for instance the arguments of a political speech, the unethical action of a lawyer or a physician. Yet self-criticism is not entirely wanting. Even in an organization like the American Society of Newspaper Editors it has become common practice to discuss the performance of the press and its members. The *Nieman Reports* are full of honest self-questioning by thoughtful young newsmen. And the media do now in a few instances criticize one another. Don Hollenbeck kept a lively criticism of the press on CBS radio for a time. A. J. Liebling twits the press every once in a while in the *New Yorker*. Jack Gould and John Crosby write sharp criticism of radio and television for two of the New York papers. It can be done.

Some say this kind of thing is of no use. It is argued that if an offending member cannot be expelled, as he can from such professions as law or medicine, it is of no real use to criticize his conduct. But this argument hardly holds water. Public and professional opinion can be a powerful punishment, goad and teacher.

The real reason for the scarcity of mutual criticism seems to relate rather to hypersensitivity on the part of some members of the industry, notably the newspapers. In this respect the pocketbook nerve seems to be close to the freedom of the press synopsis. But newspapers rarely criticize each other, except to argue political views. Even in flagrant instances like the Illinois or New England payroll scandals, the newspapers reported them late and left them early. Newspapers handled the Commission on Freedom of the Press like a live rattlesnake. Schools of journalism seldom make any public criticism of newspapers. Trade papers give little space to such materials. The publishers' meetings are concerned with the business and administrative, rather than the ethical or public service problems.

And the question is, why need this be? It is unlikely that any grave misdeeds are being hidden, but as long as the protective silence exists there will always be suspicion. There will always be charges of "press lying" or "one-party press." There is everything to be gained by encouraging a lively mutual criticism and discussion of practices within the profession. Whatever one thinks of the medical profession, one is confident that the doctors will make some collective effort to root out malpractice and police their own backyard. There is no such confidence about the press or broadcasting. That is why there is a constant call for government intervention or censorship or new regulations or boycott. Nothing would do so much to reduce this activity as some frank and live mutual criticism within the industry.

One thing the employers can do to help professionalize the industry is to upgrade their staffs in every way possible. We hope that our newsmen will prepare for their calling by obtaining such a world-view in breadth and depth as few college graduates ever get; yet we start them at salaries considerably below what we pay employees with good scientific or business training, or even merely some technical skills. This is one reason why we get so many reporters who are technicians only, who are smart but not informed. This is one reason why we have to worry about whether the social problems of a community are being adequately reported to us, whether our science is being covered with sufficient understanding, whether politics and economics are being covered in depth rather than as combat and human interest, whether speeches and interviews are understandingly reported.

We have no intention of claiming that all the ills of mass communication would be solved by raising the pay scale a bit. The communication industry is no longer notably low-paid, and Guild contracts usually include severance pay which helps to encourage tenure. The reason for the high turnover in the writing part of the industry may be partly low pay, but must stem more largely from other causes. The newspaper men whom I have talked to when they were leaving the profession have usually mentioned reasons other than pay: they thought their job didn't give them the chance for creative expression and initiative they wanted, or they didn't like the ideals of the publisher they were working for, or they wanted to start a magazine of their own, or they thought their health wouldn't take the "rat race" much longer, or something of that kind. The writers I have talked to in Hollywood were usually frustrated by not being permitted to do the job they thought they ought to be doing, and actually somewhat ashamed of the high salaries they were drawing. Therefore, it seems that when we go about professionalizing the industry we must go beyond the salary problem. We want to reward able employees, not only with money, but even more with professional recognition for jobs well done, with initiative and freedom and responsibility they can act on.

Another way to upgrade staffs is with in-service training programs. We do not mean that newspapers should do more about teaching their reporters to write leads and copyread stories; training on that level is being competently handled now. But the training which results in a deeper understanding of the world they write about is not being handled except in the day-to-day experience of covering a beat or the day-to-day discussions of the city room. What is needed is more experience of the kind represented by the Nieman Fellowships, which permit a newspaper man to go back to Harvard for a year, study what he feels the need to study, and participate with other Niemann Fellows in a highly stimulating seminar on the responsibilities and practices of the press. The Nieman program is expensive. A great deal could be accomplished if newspapers and other communication units would finance shorter and less costly courses at universities: for example, intensive three-months courses for newsmen which would provide an overview of the social sciences, a kind of systematic start to a lifetime of reading. Courses of this length would be relatively inexpensive either in employee time or in money to the sponsoring newspapers, and would immensely upgrade the level of understanding with which difficult and important stories were handled. Similarly, many a newspaper or radio newsroom could and should afford to help a newsman prepare himself by advanced study to write about natural science or mental health or education or any of the crucial topics which are now so poorly understood.

By the same token, mass communications could help universities set up really adequate professional or quasi-professional training for future members of the profession. I think it could be argued now that the influence of the industry on schools of journalism has been to make them vocational, rather than professional. That is, the over-riding obligation of the schools has been to prepare a young man or woman to go to work without a large amount of additional training from the industry. The industry has not been wholly consistent here. It has talked about the need for broadly trained employees, and yet its general influence, whether in advice to the schools or in choosing graduates, has been to emphasize the practicality of their training.

If the industry really wanted the universities to train their future employees in the manner of what one newspaperman called "Junior Niemans," it could accomplish this. If it really wanted schools of journalism to emphasize a deep understanding of the social sciences and history, and a concern for the social responsibilities and social performance of mass communication, it could act through the accrediting program of the Association for Education in Journalism to accomplish this. Similarly, if it wanted more centers of research and criticism in this field comparable to the centers which exist in medical and law schools, it could soon persuade, help, and encourage a number of first-rate universities to set them up. In the next chapter we are going to argue that the provision of suitable academic training and academic research for mass communication is primarily the obligation of the public, but here let us point out that it is partly also the obligation of the profession. And it is a part of any real program of professionalization.

As we began this little discussion by suggesting that the industry's responsibility should be personalized and individualized by all its members, so let us end it by returning to the institutional responsibility.

Just as every employee of the mass communication profession should feel a responsibility for his own acts, for his dealings with news sources or his communications to an audience, so also should every member of the profession feel a responsibility for the institutional activity of the newspaper, the broadcasting station, publishing house, or film studio which he represents. Primarily, of course, this responsibility rests on ownership and top management, but it is shared beyond that, just as a lawyer feels responsibility for the activities of his firm or a doctor for the operation of his clinic or hospital.

There is a great deal of temptation in a communication organization to dodge responsibility—to say that this program is as it is because the advertising agency made it that way; or that this story is as it is because the wire news agency didn't do any better; or that a certain set of inaccuracies were carried because a certain commentator is responsible for them and must be given freedom to say what he thinks; or that a picture is no better than it is because the code washed it out. None of these is an adequate explanation, of course. In each case, the communication unit is responsible for what it carries.

The television industry is taking a great step toward responsibility by having its programs done in its own studios or in packaging houses rather than by advertising agencies. Associations of managing editors have already shown what can be done by periodic review and criticism of a wire service. An inaccurate commentator is no better or more sacred than an inaccurate reporter. And the old canard that it is impossible to make an insightful and artistic picture under the code has been disproved again and again. It is simply a question of what degree of responsibility the communication unit feels.

What we are arguing for, therefore, is really an attitude of deepened responsibility throughout the industry, personally and institutionally. This, it seems to us, is the *sine qua non* of a real professionalization and of the kind of social improvement which we want in mass communication. As the Commission on Freedom of the Press said, "the outside forces of law and public opinion can in various ways check bad aspects of press performance, but good press performance can come only from the human beings who operate the instrumentalities of communication." There are encouraging signs that this kind of attitude of responsibility is penetrating through mass communication, downward from some of the leaders, outward from performers whose accomplishments are a credit to the industry, and is beginning to show results.

12

The Public

The Commission on Freedom of the Press concluded that the more the media and the public are willing to do toward insuring a free and responsible communication system, the less the government will have to do; and that in general the "outside forces" of law and public opinion can check bad aspects of media performance, but only the media themselves can bring about good performance.[1]

It is hard to disagree with these statements, but I depart somewhat from the Commission's emphasis. It seems to me quite clear that the media have the chief responsibility. If they do not assume it, if they do not voluntarily provide us with the public service on a high professional level which our society requires, then I do not see how our communication problem can be solved without to some extent going out of bounds, as we have defined the bounds of desirable action.

What the media do not do for us they invite the government to step in and do or cause to be done. This, in our view, is a dangerous, an ominous kind of action. For that reason, I have urged that the government "keep its hands off" wherever it can, that it put down the temptation to step in and set things right, that it set strict limits on the kind of actions it will take with reference to mass communication, and that these actions should be chiefly facilitating, rather than restrictive ones.

I have therefore tended to put somewhat more responsibility on both the media and the public than did the Commission. Whereas the media must assume the central responsibility and do the job, I envisage the public as being prime movers in the communication dynamic. It is my firm belief that the public can come pretty close to having whatever kind of mass communication system it wants. Of course, this requires that it know what it wants and say what it wants. I do not accept the old idea that the mass-media public is a vegetable. I think that the "great audience" can be active rather than passive, that it can assay its needs and be articulate in getting them. Granted those assumptions, then it seems to me that the people hold the balance of power in determining the shape of their system and the service it gives them.

The listening, viewing, reading public underestimates its power. The media heads do not underestimate it. I have seen very few media men who look on the public as a mass to be moulded and say, "This year we shall teach them to like thus and so." Rather, they are deeply concerned with what the public will be interested in, what the public wants and *will* like, and one of their greatest problems is trying to find out these things.

Anyone who looks at mass communication as a social institution cannot fail to note the tremendous push and pull of public interests and tastes on the institution. The program pattern of the networks vibrates like a windharp to the breeze from the monthly program ratings. New films go out to "sneak" previews, sample public reaction, and go back to the cutting room. One hundred letters to a network will often bring a review of policy; even fewer letters to a station will lead it to review a program or a program structure. One visit of a serious committee to a newspaper editor will make him think hard about what he is doing, even though he will be crusty about making promises. The motion picture industry has been in greater fear of boycotts than of censorship. Its code is spotted throughout with "special legislation" intended to appease this or that group and avoid boycott or public criticism.

In an earlier part of the book we mentioned how a comparatively slight outpouring of public indignation forced a network to take a well-known personality off the air because he had offended the friends of "Silent Night." Letters to the Federal Communications Commission get into station files, and they have a way of turning up embarrassingly in hearings. Listeners' councils have been able in many cases to exert a real and salutary influence on the kind of programs a local station carries. And underneath all this is the great groundswell of audience and attention, which none of the media can ignore. A newspaper publisher, who may resist what he considers a special interest group or special pleading, will pay attention if his circulation begins to fall off. A network or a station will perk up when the ratings begin to drop. A film studio is keenly aware what kind of business its pictures are doing. A magazine is compelled to worry when its newsstand sales fall off, or its readership studies indicate little interest in a certain part of its content.

Ultimately, therefore, the audience calls the tune. The people hold the trumps. And the only question is whether they will play their cards.

Is it realistic to hope that the public, the great audience, will seize this opportunity? This, of course, is the fundamental problem posed by the coming of bigness and fewness to the media. When media were many and audiences were small; when only a small percentage of the population could read, and only a small elite group formed the reading audience for most newspapers, magazines, and books; when the entertainment media were small and intimate—then there was a close connection between the men who made the media and their audience. There was a quick and vigorous feedback of demands and judgments. The audiences themselves felt the closeness of their relationship and took a lively interest in what the media were doing. The readers knew the editors. The performers knew some of their audiences. But now that audiences have grown so large that they include almost the whole population, when a great anonymity has settled over them, and they become known to the media only in terms of program ratings or percentages of readership or circulation figures —is there a realistic hope that some of this liveness and intimacy can be recaptured?

Of course, CBS or Metro-Goldwyn-Mayer or the *Reader's Digest* is unlikely ever to recapture the relationship which the *Dial* maintained with its audience when that influential magazine had 200 subscribers, most of them known personally to the editor, Margaret Fuller. It is certainly unrealistic to expect that situation to recur except in the case of a little magazine subsidized to serve a coterie. But between that situation and the far end of the scale, at which audiences are a kind of anonymous mass, I think it is clearly realistic and possible for the audience of mass communication to move a long way up the scale from anonymity toward personality. It seems to me clearly possible for the great audience to become a live, responsive, discriminating audience, to make its opinions and wishes known to the media, and in its own quiet way to enforce those opinions and wishes on the media. And if it should appear that in this audience there are a number of levels of taste and kinds of need, then I think it is clearly possible for the audience to insist that the media serve those different tastes and needs, instead of ladeling up an insipid common-denominator broth which appeals somewhat to each and satisfies none.

The basic responsibility of the public, therefore, is to make itself, as far as possible, an alert, discriminating audience. This may require a somewhat different habit of mind from the one we most commonly see on the part of many individuals who by virtue of position or education might be expected to be the leaders of and spokesmen for the public in their demands upon the media. This common attitude —"Oh, I never watch television except when there's something like a political convention on—it's just trash!"—is fundamentally an irresponsible attitude. It neglects the fact that television doesn't *have* to be all trash, if indeed it is. Television is potentially one of our greatest windows on the world. It is one of the best ways in which we could expand our horizons, bring a sense of reality to faraway events, make a more informed judgment on public figures, share the lectures and demonstrations at our greatest universities, see the kind of opera, ballet, drama, museums, and concert artists formerly available only to a few fortunate people, most of them in great cities. If television isn't being used that way, what a great social waste it is! What a loss we are suffering! And whose fault is it? Basically, it is the fault of the people who don't watch it and don't do anything about improving it.

The greatest newsgathering services man has ever devised are connected to our home-town newspapers. Through wire services these newspapers are connected to every corner of the world where news is being made. A statement by Nasser in Egypt is perhaps twenty minutes away from each of our newspapers. An incident beside the Iron or the Bamboo Curtain is, at the most, thirty minutes away from our newsrooms. A full interpretation of Mr. Dulles' latest statement is available if a few persons in Washington or New York or on a university campus are given a few hours to think about it. In that situation, have we any right to say, as so many of us do: "I can't get any picture of what's happening in the world from our paper; it carries only six or seven foreign news stories a day"? Or, "I can't understand what's really going on in national politics or this international situation. We never get any background." Have we any right to say that, if we never complain to the editor? He has the space to put in more world news, more background, if he thinks his audience wants it. He is putting that space into sports, or features, or society, or some other news. If he thought there was a serious demand for more world news or background, he would carry it.

The first requisite, therefore, is an alert, interested audience. This implies that we pay some attention to our media. We read, view, listen. We find out what is in the media. We don't wash our hands of the media in the supposition that they are being patterned for somebody else.

Then we try to make ourselves a discriminating audience. We give some thought to what the media *might* be giving us. We talk about the media with our friends. Perhaps we organize listeners' councils or readers' groups to talk about what we find in the media. We try to see that our schools give some attention to the question how to use the media intelligently; there are good textbooks now on such subjects as "How to read a newspaper," and many schools are helping their students to make best use of the mass media, just as they prepare them to make use of other parts of human experience. After all, these young people will be giving perhaps five hours a day, or nearly a third of their waking time, to mass media. This is too large a segment of life to use wastefully. And so we try to see that our young people have a systematic introduction to the media. We try to read newspaper or magazine criticism of the other mass media, just as we read book reviews. And in every way we try to build into ourselves some standards for judgment of what we see, hear, and read.

Another way in which we can develop discrimination is by controlling our attendance upon the media. If we don't want all movies to be made as though for children, we can keep our children away from *some* movies. If we don't want all television to be filtered out so as not to be above the sensibilities and sensitivities of *any* member of the family, then let us exercise some discrimination about what members of the family watch television at a given time. This is partly our responsibility. We can't expect the media to serve the interests of all kinds of people and displease or offend none unless we do something about getting the right kind of people to the media at the right time.

Then the next step in our responsibility is to make our views known to the media. One way to do this is simply by reflecting in our patronage our discrimination in what we subscribe to, what we attend, what we view or listen to. If enough of us do this, it will have an effect. But this method sometimes cuts off our nose to spite our face. For example, if we stop buying our home-town newspaper because it carries only seven foreign news stories a day, that will lose us *all* the local news. The big stick is not the best way. A better way is to tell our media what we do and don't like about them, and what would make us like them better.

This we can do through letters—to the editor, to the station, to the network, to the theater, or to the studio. The more individual these letters are, the better. The media tend to fill their wastebaskets with letters which are all written in about the same words and therefore reveal that they are inspired by some pressure group. But individual letters are read and valued. So are individual contacts, when those are possible. These help to tell media employees, and especially media heads, what you think of their product. If you feel seriously enough about it, you can call on the editor or the station manager or the theater owner. You can certainly take advantage of meetings or social events or casual contacts to talk to media people. They appreciate these little feedbacks, and over the course of weeks such contacts add up to a picture of what the public wants and thinks.

Things like this you can do informally and individually. Or you can organize and go about it more formally. We have occasionally in this book said unkind things about pressure groups, but there is nothing in our political philosophy to keep audiences from organizing whenever and however they wish, to communicate more effectively with the media. Listeners' councils, where they have been organized, have been very effective in this way. Organizations like the League of Women Voters or the Association of University Women have sometimes made the media their chief discussion topic and have sent delegations or resolutions to represent their opinions and needs to media heads. Sometimes community groups, or student groups, or church groups have arisen spontaneously because of dissatisfaction with some aspect of the media. Often these groups have asked newspapermen or broadcasters or theater operators, or magazine salesmen, to speak to their meetings, in order to get their side of the story and convey the feelings of the group.

There are already a number of well-organized groups active in the field, many of them with professional staffs watching the media, trying to keep out of them material offensive to the particular group. Such are, for example, the Legion of Decency, the Chamber of

Commerce, the American Legion, et cetera. There is nothing wrong with this. Any group has a right to organize and tell the media what it thinks of them. But remember that our communication system is built on the theory of a free market place of ideas. It will not work right unless *all* viewpoints on a controversial question are freely presented.

Therefore, there is a kind of pressure-group activity which is as clearly out of bounds as is government interference with the media. I mean the kind of informal censorship which tries to remake the shape of the media in the image of one group's needs and sensitivities, at the cost of all other groups. The news about Christmas time, 1956, contained what may be an example of this kind of activity. Station WGN-TV, of Chicago, canceled the world première showing on television of the film *Martin Luther*. The station said the film was canceled because of the "emotional reaction" of the public to its plan to show the picture. This "emotional reaction," said the *Christian Century*, took the form of a telephone blitzkrieg "organized by Roman Catholics to keep WGN telephones humming with protests."[2] The Chancellor of the Chicago archdiocese said that the Church had made no official representations to WGN-TV whatsoever, and that if any Catholics had protested it was an individual matter. It was claimed that the film was "down-right insulting" to Catholics.

Now I have neither investigated behind these facts nor seen the picture. It is a fact, however, that the film was shown in many theaters without any substantial opposition. If the facts are as suggested—an organized campaign by members of one religious sect to keep off the air a film about the founder of other religious sects—then this is a questionable kind of pressure-group activity. There could be no possible objection to one church exerting discipline over its own members and keeping them away from a theater or from watching a television program. But when such a group acts to deprive other groups of opportunities they very much desire in the mass media, and which are not obscene or otherwise clearly censorable, then it would seen that this is restricting the free market place, and should be resisted both by the media and the public.

As I say, the Chicago incident may or may not be an example of this kind of action; I have not thoroughly investigated it. And the particular religious group mentioned is by no means the only group, religious or political, which has been accused of such activity. But whoever does it, it doesn't fit into our system.

Pressure groups, like government, are usually on less dangerous ground when their activity is facilitating, rather than restrictive. That is, they are more helpful when they try to represent the needs of the public than when they speak for the sensitivities of particular groups. But even here caution is needed. We can't expect mass communication to meet all our needs if we depend on a few well-organized groups, each with a special interest, to speak for us. These groups may keep the media free of material which disturbs, and encourage the media to present material which pleases, the Legion, the Chamber, the Roman Catholic Church, or some other organization; but they will not necessarily be concerned that the media carry what the rest of the public wants or needs. The remedy for this situation is not to complain about "pressure groups," but to organize groups to represent our own interests, if these are not being represented. And when the media heads see the full spectrum of public needs and wishes, they will be better able to plan their product.

A further responsibility of the public, it seems to us, is to encourage intelligent criticism of the media. This is not an attack on the media; it is rather a service to media and public alike. Book reviews, for many years, have served not only to sharpen the standards of taste on the part of writer, reader, and editor, but also to call the attention of the public to new books of interest. It is amazing that so little criticism of broadcasting and newspapers has come into being. The influential daily critics of radio and television number less than a handful. No sustained regular criticism of newspapers has ever proved feasible. Yet criticism of this kind is surely a part of the professionalizing and general growing up of the media.

The Commission on Freedom of the Press recommended that "a new and independent agency" should be established to "appraise and report annually upon the performance of the press."[3] By *press* the Commission meant all the mass media. This proposal was received with undisguised horror by the newspapers, and was equated with all sorts of dire threats to press freedom. Yet it is hard to see how such an agency, given a board of distinguished citizens and a competent staff, could really threaten freedom of the press. And it might do a great service, both in scrutinizing the media for the public and in representing to the media the dissatisfactions and unmet needs of the public. Such an agency would, of course, have no governmental connection and would represent the public in general rather than any segment of it. The Commission listed a long series of services such an agency might undertake, among which were the following:

• Helping the media "define workable standards of performance";
• "Pointing out the inadequacy" of media service in certain areas;
• Investigating areas and instances "where minority groups are excluded from reasonable access to the channels of communication";
• Examining the "picture of American life" presented abroad by the media;
• Investigating charges of "press lying," with particular reference to the persistent misrepresentation of the data required for judging public issues;
• Appraising "governmental action affecting communications";
• appraising the "tendencies and characteristics of the various branches of the communications industry";
• Encouraging the "establishment of centers of advanced study, research, and criticism in the field of communications at universities";
• Encouraging projects which give hope of meeting the needs of special audiences;
• Giving "the widest possible publicity and public discussion" to all its findings.

For any one agency, this might be an overambitious assignment. Yet the objective of all of it is simple enough—an agency to represent the interest of the public as a whole, as distinguished from the special interest of groups; to speak for the whole public in a way that the public could never speak as individuals; to observe the work of the media and think about it in terms of the needs and interests of the American public; and finally to report both ways, to the media and to the public, and thus to serve as a valuable communication link between them. To choose the board and staff of such a public agency would be difficult. To outline and restrict its tasks to realistic goals and limits would take a great deal of thinking and some trial. But the result might be very salutary, might result in a much better mutual understanding between the media and their publics, and on the whole would be an excellent project on which a foundation might bet some money.

If such an agency of communication and observation is ever established, it is a responsibility of the public to do it. It should not be established by the government nor by the media, although it should counsel with both the media and government. It should represent public interest at the highest level. So far as the newspaper objection is concerned, it is a good guess that, after the first mechanical reaction of resistance, most of the newspapers and the other media would respect and welcome the new agency.

We said in the preceding chapter that it is a responsibility of the media to help in the establishment of adequate schools for prospective members of the profession, and also university research centers in mass communication. It is certainly a responsibility of the media to concern themselves with these problems and help with them, but the basic responsibility is the public's. The public has to found such organizations at universities, and send able young people to them. Over the next two or three decades the schools of journalism and their related training and research centers can make a profound difference in the level of media personnel. They can do so, that is, if they are used at their full potential which, as we tried to say in the last chapter, is not for vocational training, but for training of a breadth and depth which very few other occupations require.

Another way to say it is that journalism school and other mass communication curricula are not best used when they train students for the first six months of their employment; they should rather prepare their graduates for the years that follow the first six months: not in the skills which enable the young employee to do well at first, but rather in the understandings which enable him to do well throughout his career. There is no reason why he should not learn some skills, too; but, whenever there has to be a choice of time between learning the vocational skills and gaining the broad understanding of society and mass communication's place in it, the time should always be used for the broader and less immediately useful studies. The schools should aim for the long, not the short term; for on his job the new man can much more easily learn the skills of his job than he can learn to understand human beings, social organization, government, economics, and science.

Schools of journalism have been moving in this direction, but they are handicapped by a tradition which began in the land-grant colleges under the example of service to agriculture, and the early leadership of weekly newspapermen who wanted employees they would not have to train. Even now the schools of journalism are unlike other professional or quasi-professional schools in that *they* do not necessarily train the new members of the profession as do medical or law schools; their graduates have to compete on a level with graduates of every other curriculum in the university and with nongraduates of universities. Indeed, the fact that university graduates expect more salary gives an advantage to nongraduates on smaller papers and other media. Therefore, the school of journalism has felt some need to stress, by teaching journalistic techniques, its uniqueness in the university and its close relationship to the newspapers and the broadcasters. Even so, the best schools now build their curricula on a broad grounding of liberal studies in other departments, and this is a tendency which the public should certainly encourage.

Another healthy development is the establishment of research centers and programs in connection with a few schools of journalism and elsewhere in a few universities. This is a long step on the road to professionalization. Without strong research programs in connection with and feeding into schools of medicine, we should still be letting blood for various diseases and treating mental diseases with chains and dungeons. It should be pointed out that both the schools and the research centers in mass communication are essentially a public responsibility.

Another important way in which the public can demonstrate its discriminating concern with mass communication is in the encouragement of new ventures. It is increasingly hard to start anything new in mass communication because of the costs involved. Yet there is increasing need for new ventures, not only to provide a variety in viewpoint, but, more important, to serve the needs of groups within the great audience who are not sufficiently served by "common denominator" media content. If the public, or segments of it, want these special services they must make their wants known, and be alert to support, or at least try out, new ventures when they come.

There could be more newspapers covering public affairs in somewhat the way *The New York Times* does, but in other parts of the country, if publishers thought people in sufficient numbers would buy them. There could be more and better community television stations, covering local public affairs and carrying the best in local entertainment and information, if audiences would give them a few dollars per viewer per year. The university radio and television stations would furnish a better service—indeed, they could give a very exciting service—if the public made known to administrations and legislatures that they wanted these activities adequately supported with budgets. There would be more theaters specializing in high-quality films, and more studios making such films for such theaters, if the public would patronize them. The possibility of endowed newspapers or broadcasting stations is a fascinating one, but it is not necessary to have financing from a foundation or a wealthy man in order to bring about superior communications. The thing most needed in order to have new ventures in mass communication is assurance that there is a discriminating public waiting for them, willing to support them.

In another way, too, the public has a peculiar responsibility in regard to mass communication. More nonprofessional members of the public must learn to use the media. There is no excuse for religious broadcasting being less skillful than entertainment broadcasting. There is no reason why the public should permit educational broadcasting to be any less skillful than entertainment broadcasting; yet the educational stations are starved for funds and are therefore unable to train and keep skilled performers. There is no reason why local broadcasting, radio or television, could not be more of a force than it is; for leaders in any community to acquire the basic skills of broadcasting would not be a great task. This implies also that more members of the nonprofessional public should come to understand the media—to learn what can be expected of the newspapers and the broadcasters especially, and how to work with them and make use of their media in the best way.

All this comes back to the question whether we can realistically expect to have a live, articulate, discriminating public concerning itself with mass communication. If so, great things are possible. If not, progress will be slow. For, as I have tried to indicate, responsibility in mass communication is a delicate balance between the media, the government, and the public. The chief responsibility for doing what needs to be done with mass communication is that of the media, but in a sense the basic obligation is with the public. The public's responsibility is to be an active, discriminating audience, to make its needs known to the media, to be helpful as the media try to meet these needs—in other words, to be full partner in the task of making the kind of communication society needs. To the extent that the public is less than a full partner, government and media will fill the gap, and we shall be less sure that we get what we want. For it is the public's own responsibility that is controlling in this case, and if we do not exercise it we deserve only what we get.

In a radio address to America in 1931, and in his usual salty tongue-in-cheek manner, George Bernard Shaw startled some of his listeners with the following proposition. "Every person who owes his life to civilized society," he said, "and who has enjoyed since his childhood its very costly protections and advantages should appear at reasonable intervals before a properly qualified jury to justify his existence, which should be summarily and painlessly terminated if he fails to justify it."

I am not advocating such summary justice. But I should like to suggest that all of us who enjoy the protections and advantages of a free communication system do indeed have some obligation to justify our existence under it. I have been suggesting what that obligation consists of. And if we are not doing enough to justify such protections and advantages, then we certainly face the possibility in this fateful century of having our existence under them summarily but not painlessly terminated.

Acknowledgments

Literally hundreds of people have helped with this book, and if I could, I would now thank each of them personally. For what is good about this book, they are doubtless responsible; for what is not good, they are probably blameless.

There is space to mention only a few of these people by name. Chief among them is my advisory group:

Chester I. Barnard, former president of the New Jersey Bell Telephone Company and former president of the Rockefeller Foundation and the General Education Board.

David W. Barry, executive director of N. Y. City Mission Society, and co-author of the recent study of religious broadcasting.

Robert J. Blakely, now an executive of the Fund for Adult Education, and formerly on the editorial page staffs of the *Des Moines Register* and *Tribune*, and the *St. Louis Star-Times*.

Herbert Brucker, editor of the *Hartford Courant*, and author of much trenchant writing about the press, including the volume *Freedom of Information*.

Lyman Bryson, of the Columbia Broadcasting System, Columbia professor emeritus, author of some of our best writing about broadcasting and popular art, and editor of the distinguished collection, *The Communication of Ideas*.

Gardner Cowles, of the Cowles newspaper, magazines, and broadcasting stations, editor and publisher of *Look*.

S. Franklin Mack, executive director of Broadcasting & Film Commission, National Council of Churches of Christ in the U.S.A.

Kenneth Underwood, professor at Wesleyan University, chairman of faculty for Institute of Ethics and Politics, Wesleyan University.

Surely no one has ever had a more helpful advisory committee. These busy men have been generous and kindly with their criticism and suggestions, ever willing to give time for a meeting or a personal talk, or to read a big chunk of manuscript hot out of a typewriter. No one should think for a moment that each member of this committee agrees with everything in this book. The fact that they recognize that an honest difference of opinion or judgment might exist is one of the qualities that have made them such an extraordinary group of advisers.

Then I should like to mention a few of my colleagues and former colleagues who have helped greatly in one way or another. Fred Siebert and Theodore Peterson, of the University of Illinois, each wrote two memoranda for this project which have been of great help. Three of their four memoranda and one of mine went into a little book, *Four Theories of the Press*, which was published last November as a kind of by-product of this project. Some of my colleagues were kind enough to join my advisory committee in reading the manuscript and making detailed criticism. Among these were Chilton R. Bush, of Stanford, and Bruce Bliven, of Stanford, former editor of the *New Republic*. A large number of persons read sections of the book and commented. Among these are a few I should like to mention, for one special reason or another: Professor Alex Inkeles, of Harvard; Richard Dyar McCann, of Hollywood and *The Christian Science Monitor*; Howard Wilson, of the Educational Policies Commission; Professors Paul Lazarsfeld, Harold Lasswell, Dan Lerner, and other scholars in our field who commented on some of the ideas and concepts of this manuscript when it was in an earlier form; Dean Frank Mott, of Missouri; and Professor Raymond B. Nixon, of the University of Minnesota. Among my colleagues who have taken time to remember back over their own mass media experience and dredge up instances and generalizations that would be of help to me are Chilton R. Bush, Clifford F. Weigle, James M. Brinton, Lloyd Churchill, all of Stanford; Donald Brown, Joseph Sutton, and the late John T. Trebilcock, of Illinois; Fred Pownall, of Iowa; Robert Hudson, of the Educational Television Program Center and formerly of Illinois; and Paul Deutschmann, of Michigan State.

Mr. Robert Gibson, of the Associated Press, was of great help, while he was a graduate student at Stanford, in interviewing members of the profession and gathering some of the "cases" which appear in this book. Miss Lillian Williamson, also a graduate student at Stanford, worked hard and long searching the literature and copying out parts that sometimes got used and sometimes didn't.

Numerically the largest group of people who have helped have been members of the profession—working press, broadcasters, and film-makers. A very large number of these have been willing to remember back over their recent working days and try to recall the ethically-weighted decisions they had to make or saw made, and thus to contribute a realistic frame of reference to this book. I wish I could mention all the media men who have talked to me candidly about responsibility in the profession. My experience with these men was encouraging and illuminating. They are far more aware of the need for responsibility in the profession than many of their critics make them out to be. Among the generous and helpful things done for me by the media men, I remember especially how Frank Stanton opened the doors for me to talk freely to anyone I wanted to talk to, at CBS. Among the many media men from whom I got useful insights during the period of incubation of this book were

James Reston of *The New York Times*; Ben Gedalecia, of Batten, Barton, Durstine, and Osborne; Melvin Goldberg of the Westinghouse Broadcasting Company; Gerhard Wiebe of CBS; the late Frederick Lewis Allen of *Harper's*; Leo Rosten of *Look*; Jonathan Daniels, editor of the *Raleigh Observer*; Norman Isaacs of the *Louisville Courier-Journal*; W. W. Waymack, formerly of the *Des Moines Register*; Irving Dilliard, of the *St. Louis Post-Dispatch*; Francis Harmon, the former vice-president of the Motion Picture Association; John Ellwood, formerly of NBC and RCA; and many others. Let me repeat: these men are in no sense to be blamed for what is said in this book; in some cases they did not know such a book was contemplated; but they contributed, nevertheless.

My intellectual debts to books are to many, rather than a few chief ones. But I should like to mention two magazines: *The Nieman Reports*, which is one of the best places now to read the self-appraisals and the questionings of thoughtful newspapermen, and *Editor and Publisher*, through which most of the newspaper world moves week by week.

The National Council of Churches financed this study, for which I am, of course, grateful. But I am most deeply grateful because the Council gave me complete freedom to write the book as I wished and at no time tried to impose a philosophy or a political viewpoint on it. The chief representative of the Council, during the long period of making the book, was F. Ernest Johnson, the director of the series of studies of which this is one. Dr. Johnson was an adviser, a reader, a stimulator, a friend and aider, and in every respect a good example of what a Christian gentleman should be. And while we mention Dr. Johnson, we should also mention Mrs. Barbara Solomon, his secretary, who pounded out hundreds of thousands of words on her typewriter as a result of this project, who wrote and mailed hundreds of letters and kept notes for meteoric committee meetings, always in a state of good humor.

Betty Schramm, my wife, had more to do with this book than she realizes. She too kept her good humor, although the typewriter often clicked on after midnight, and although the manuscript took precedence over vacations and trips and dinners and other things that are dear to a family.

And finally, when one looks back over the years and asks how a book like this really came to be, one usually remembers a few men and a few incidents far back of the actual writing. Here tonight I remember the first newspaper editor who took me in as a cub reporter so many years ago that I rather hesitate to mention it. His name was J. Dudley Chamberlain, and he taught me more than he thought he did. I remember a teacher at Harvard, Alfred North Whitehead, who stirred me to think about some of these things. And I remember one afternoon when

I stood with my fellow staff members of a little daily newspaper and read on the bulletin board that the paper was suspending publication as of that day—bought out by the rival paper in the pattern of fewer papers and larger papers we described early in this book. That bitter day taught me that mass communication was more than a business, and in that spirit I have tried to write this volume.

For Further Reading

Growth and structure

BRYSON, LYMAN, ed. *The Communication of Ideas.* New York, 1948. A remarkable group of lectures, including Lasswell on the functions of mass communication and Bryson on popular art.

GRAMLING, OLIVER. *AP: The Story of News.* New York, 1940. An AP man's highly readable story of news agencies, with AP in center focus.

HUETTIG, MAE. *Economic Control of the Motion Picture Industry: A Study in Industrial Organization.* Philadelphia, 1944. A careful account of the situation before the distributors were split off from the film makers.

INGLIS, RUTH A. *Freedom of the Movies.* Chicago, 1947. One of the Commission on Freedom of the Press books. Valuable both for history and structure, and for its discussion of performance and responsibility.

JACOBS, LEWIS. *The Rise of the American Film.* New York, 1939. The most readable history of films, though it stops in the 30's.

LANDRY, ROBERT J. *This Fascinating Radio Business.* Indianapolis, 1946. Lively account by a radio executive.

MANVELL, ROGER. *Film,* London, 1944.

———. *The Animated Film.* New York, 1955. Keen and insightful commentaries.

Members of the Staff of The New York Times. *The Newspaper: Its Making and Its Meaning.* New York, 1945. Newspapermen on newspapering.

MOTT, FRANK LUTHER. *American Journalism: A History of Newspapers in the United States Through 250 Years.* New York, 1941. Standard text by the leading historian of the press.

———. *Golden Multitudes: The Story of Best Sellers in the United States.* New York, 1947. The most popular books in our history.

———. *History of American Magazines.* 3 vols., Cambridge, Mass., 1931-1938. Pulitzer-prize-winning history. First three volumes bring record up to 1885.

McMURTRIE, DOUGLAS C. *The Book: The Story of Printing and Bookmaking.* New York, 1942. By a famous type designer and printing scholar.

ROSTEN, LEO C. *Hollywood: The Movie Colony, The Movie Makers.* New York: 1941. A lively and readable look around the movie capital.

SCHRAMM, WILBUR, ed. *Mass Communications: A Book of Readings.*

Urbana, Illinois: 1949. The first section of this book is a usable brief history of mass media. Later pages deal with structure and function.

SMITH, HENRY L., and EMERY, EDWIN. *The Press and America.* New York: 1954. Readable and accurate history.

UNESCO. *World Communications,* Paris, 1956.

————. *News Agencies,* Paris, 1954. Basic data on mass media in all countries and on wire news agencies.

WHITE, LLEWELLYN, and LEIGH, ROBERT D. *Peoples Speaking to Peoples.* Chicago: 1946. A Commission on Freedom of the Press book useful for brief historical account of international communication facilities and wire news services.

WHITE, LLEWELLYN. *The American Radio.* Chicago: 1947. Commission on Freedom of the Press book, with good historical material as well as discussion of freedom and responsibility.

Process and effects

CANTRIL, HADLEY, *et al. The Invasion From Mars.* Princeton, N. J.: 1940. Analysis of the panic caused by the Orson Welles radio broadcast.

———— and ALLPORT, GORDON. *The Psychology of Radio.* New York: 1935. Out of date, but stimulating effort to systematize research on radio.

CHARTERS, W. W. *Motion Pictures and Youth.* New York, 1933. Main report of the Payne Fund studies of motion pictures.

HOVLAND, CARL I., LUMSDAINE, ARTHUR A., and SHEFFIELD, FRED D. *Experiments on Mass Communication.* Princeton, N. J.: 1949. Careful studies of effect or orientation films in the Army.

————, JANIS, IRVING, and KELLEY, HAROLD. *Communication and Persuasion.* New Haven, Conn.: 1955. Report of laboratory experiments on effect of persuasive communication.

LAZARSFELD, PAUL F. and STANTON, FRANK, eds. *Radio Research, 1941.* New York: 1941.

————. *Radio Research, 1942-1943,* New York, 1944.

————. *Communications Research, 1948-1949,* New York, 1949. Important research on mass media process, content, and effects.

MERTON, ROBERT K, FISKE, MARJORIE, and CURTIS, ALBERTA. *Mass Persuasion: The Social Psychology of a War Bond Drive.* New York: 1946. Analysis of effect of Kate Smith's radio war bond sales.

RUESCH, JURGEN, and BATESON, GREGORY. *Communication: The Social Matrix of Psychiatry.* New York: 1951. Psychiatric theory of communication.

SCHRAMM, WILBUR, ed. *The Process and Effects of Mass Communication.* Urbana, Illinois: 1954. Collection of major research in this area.

THE PHILOSOPHY OF MASS COMMUNICATION

INKELES, ALEX. *Public Opinion in Soviet Russia.* Cambridge, Mass.: 1950. Best book on the Soviet mass communication system.

LOPEZ, SALVADOR P. *Freedom of Information, 1953.* Report to the United Nations Economic and Social Council, New York: 1953. Evidences of surviving authoritarian control.

MILL, JOHN STUART. *On Liberty.* New York: 1947 (also other editions). Basic document in libertarian philosophy of mass communication.

MILTON, JOHN. *Areopagitica.* New York: 1951 (also other editions). Another basic document for libertarianism.

MOTT, FRANK L. *Jefferson and the Press.* Baton Rouge, La.: 1943. Jefferson's kind of libertarianism.

SIEBERT, FRED S. *Freedom of the Press in England.* Urbana, Ill.: 1952. Account of the passage from authoritarianism to libertarianism.

————, PETERSON, THEODORE B., and SCHRAMM, WILBUR. *Four Theories of the Press.* Urbana, Ill.: 1956. Brief, clear statement of the four main philosophies—authoritarian, libertarian, Soviet Communist, and social responsibility—of what mass communication should be and do.

THE RESPONSIBILITIES OF MASS COMMUNICATION

BECKER, CARL L. *Freedom and Responsibility in the American Way of Life.* New York: 1945. A historian's informed and illuminating view.

BRUCKER, HERBERT. *Freedom of Information.* New York: 1949. Eloquent and informed book by editor of Hartford *Courant.*

CHAFEE, ZECHARIAH JR. *Government and Mass Communication.* 2 vols. Chicago: 1947. Commission on Freedom of the Press book by a constitutional law scholar.

CHENERY, WILLIAM L. *Freedom of the Press.* New York: 1955. Highly readable book by former magazine editor.

Commission on Freedom of the Press. *A Free and Responsible Press.* Chicago: 1947. Principal report of the Commission on Freedom of the Press—what they think can be done by the media, by the public, and by government to maintain free and responsible media.

Communications Media: Legal and Policy Problems, Lectures delivered at the University of Michigan Law School. Ann Arbor, Michigan: 1954. Discussion from the legal point of view of many problems of control and regulation.

CRAWFORD, NELSON ANTRIM. *The Ethics of Journalism.* New York: 1924. Somewhat high-minded essays by a magazine editor.

CROSS, HAROLD L. *The People's Right to Know*. New York: 1953. The legal rights of the press.

ERNST, MORRIS L. *The First Freedom*. New York: 1946. Ernst feels freedom is "evaporating" because of monopoly and irresponsibility.

FLINT, L. N. *The Conscience of a Newspaper*. New York: 1925. A discussion of "cases" in newspaper ethics.

GERALD, J. EDWARD. *The Press and the Constitution, 1931-1947*. Minneapolis: 1948. The recent cases in which freedom of the press has been defined.

HAIGHT, ANNE LYON. *Banned Books: Informal Notes on Some Books Banned for Various Reasons at Various Times and in Various Places*. New York: 1955. Interesting notes on censored books.

HOCKING, WILLIAM E. *Freedom of the Press: A Framework of Principle*. Chicago: 1947. The philosophic background for the Commission on Freedom of the Press's conclusions.

LIPPMANN, WALTER. *Liberty and the Press*. New York: 1920.

——. *Public Opinion*. New York: 1922.

——. *The Public Philosophy*. Boston: 1955. Lippmann's penetrating conclusions on how the press functions and the responsibilities it has.

MACDOUGALL, CURTIS D. *Newsroom Problems and Policies*. New York: 1941. Frank discussions of newspaper ethics.

MEIKELJOHN, ALEXANDER. *Free Speech and Its Relation to Self-Government*. New York: 1948. Statement of basic relationships.

MOTT, FRANK L. and CASEY, RALPH D. *Interpretations of Journalism*. New York: 1937. Collection of many famous and illuminating comments on press freedom, function, and ethics.

NEWMAN, EDWIN S. *The Freedom Reader*. New York: 1955. Includes selections from court cases and other writings on the First Amendment.

PARKER, EVERETT C., BARRY, DAVID W., and SMYTHE, DALLAS W. *The Television-Radio Audience and Religion*. New York: 1955. Study of viewers of religious television and implications of results.

Problems of Journalism: Proceedings of the conventions of the American Society of Newspaper Editors. Published annually (except 1945) since 1923. Washington, D. C. Annual volumes of speeches and discussion at ASNE meetings. Contains many discussions of newspaper ethics.

REID, RICHARD. *The Morality of the Newspaper*. South Bend, Ind.: 1938. Essays on newspaper ethics by a Roman Catholic priest.

SELDES, GILBERT. *The Seven Lively Arts*. New York: 1924.

——. *The Great Audience*. New York: 1950. Insightful comments on performance and shortcomings of mass media.

SIEPMANN, CHARLES A. *Radio, Television and Society*. New York: 1950.

Interesting for its discussion of broadcasting's responsibility and its relation to the Federal Communications Commission.

SHAYON, ROBERT LEWIS. *Television and Our Children.* New York: 1951. Impressionistic, but stimulating discussion of what television may be doing to young people.

SVIRSKY, LEON, ed. *Your Newspaper: Blueprint for a Better Press.* New York: 1948. Essays on press performance by Nieman Fellows.

"What Every Newspaper Reader Should Know," *Social Action Magazine,* Vol. 15, No. 5. Entire issue of magazine, issued by Council for Social Action of the Congregational Christian Churches, deals with the state of the press and ethical standards to be applied to it.

Notes

CHAPTER 2

[1] David Riesman, *The Lonely Crowd* (New Haven: Yale Univ. Press, 1950), see especially Chap. I.

[2] Claude E. Shannon, "The Mathematical Theory of Communication," *Bell System Technical Journal*, July and October 1948. Reprinted as a book (Shannon and Weaver, *The Mathematical Theory of Communication* [Urbana, Illinois: 1949]).

[3] This famous essay is now most readily available in the collected papers of Robert Ezra Park, Vol. 3, *Society* (Glencoe, Illinois: Free Press, 1955), pp. 89-104. It was originally published in Park, Burgess, and McKenzie, *The City* (Chicago: Univ. of Chicago, 1925).

[4] Park, *op. cit.*, p. 96.

[5] Quoted in Park, *op. cit.*, p. 97.

[6] Walter Lippmann, *Public Opinion* (New York: Macmillan, 1927, 1944), pp. 331-32.

[7] It is only fair to point out, however, that whereas the number of *general* newspapers (both daily and weekly) has notably decreased in the last 40 years, the number of *special* newspapers and other publications has greatly increased. Many of these are the publications of corporations, trade unions, trade associations, community organizations, and similar groups and organizations which have a need to communicate frequently among their own members. Much of the news in these publications used to get into the local newspapers, but it has been crowded out as the newspapers have grown larger and a larger proportion of their space has been given over to wire news and advertising. These house organs, organization bulletins, and private newspapers sometimes reach a very high circulation and are often highly valued and influential with their audiences.

[8] Estimates for television (4:06) and radio (2:12) are from A. C. Nielsen 1955 figures. The figure of 40 minutes a day for newspaper reading is the average of several estimates made in connection with readership surveys. For example, see Schramm and White, "Age, Education, and Economic Status as Factors in Newspaper Reading," *Journalism Quarterly*, v. 26, (Spring, 1949) pp. 149-59. The most recent national survey (by Sindlinger and Company, in 1957) came up with an average of 34 minutes.

CHAPTER 3

[1] Standard sources of these figures are *Editor and Publisher Yearbook* (for daily newspapers); N. W. Ayer, *Directory of Newspapers and Periodicals* (for weekly newspapers and magazines); *Broadcasting and Telecasting Yearbooks* (for radio and television); the *Film Daily Yearbook* and *Motion Picture Almanac* (for films); and publications of the American Book Publishers Council (for books).

[2] See *Editor and Publisher*, April 16, 1955, pp. 7 ff.

[3] CBS, *Network Practices*, prepared for the Senate Interstate and Foreign Commerce Committee, June 1956.

[4] For an excellent development of the first three of these functions, see

Harold D. Lasswell, "The Structure and Function of Communication in Society," in Lyman Bryson, ed., *The Communication of Ideas* (New York: Harper, 1948).

[5] For the classical description of a day in a newspaper office, see Henry Justin Smith, "The Day," published as Chap. 1 of his book, *Deadlines* (Chicago: Wash. Book Co., 1922).

[6] One of the best documentations of the complexity of television production is the story of how a commercial was filmed for a program sponsored by General Electric: "Producing a Three-Minute Spectacular," *General Electric Review*, September 1956.

[7] A good sense of the atmosphere of movie-making can be gotten from Leo C. Rosten, Hollywood, *The Movie Colony, The Movie Makers* (New York: Harcourt, 1941). An excellent description of the making of a particular film is Lillian Ross's *Picture* (New York: Rinehart, 1952), which originally appeared in the *New Yorker* magazine and is an observer's account of how John Huston made *The Red Badge of Courage*.

CHAPTER 4

[1] John F. Kennedy, "Courage and Politics," republished as Chapter 1 of his book, *Profiles in Courage* (New York: Harper, 1955), p. 18.

[2] A. C. Spectorsky, *The Exurbanites* (New York: Little, Brown, 1955), p. 8.

[3] Richard T. LaPiere, *A Theory of Social Control* (New York: McGraw-Hill, 1954), pp. 518-22.

[4] Paul F. Lazarsfeld and Robert K. Merton, "Mass Communication, Popular Taste, and Organized Social Action," in Lyman Bryson, ed., *The Communication of Ideas* (New York: Harper, 1948), pp. 95-118.

[5] Robert K. Merton, *Mass Persuasion* (New York: Harper, 1946).

[6] See Hadley Cantril, *The Invasion from Mars* (Princeton: Princeton Univ., 1940).

[7] For a study along this line, see Matilda White Riley and John E. Riley, Jr., "A Sociological Approach to Communication Research," in W. Schramm, ed., *The Process and Effects of Mass Communication* (Urbana: Univ. of Illinois, 1954), pp. 389-401.

[8] Eunice Cooper and Marie Jahoda, "The Evasion of Propaganda," *Journal of Psychology*, v. 23, (1947) pp. 15-25.

[9] Kurt Lewin, "Group Decision and Social Change," in Newcomb and Hartley, eds., *Readings in Social Psychology* (New York: Holt, 1947).

CHAPTER 5

[1] In writing this chapter, I have had the aid of memoranda prepared especially for this project: "The Authoritarian Theory of the Press," by Fred S. Siebert; "The Libertarian Theory of the Press," by Fred S. Siebert; "The Social Responsibility Theory of the Press," by Theodore B. Peterson; "The Soviet Communist Theory of the Press," by myself. These memoranda have recently been gathered and published under the title, *Four Theories of the Press* (Urbana: Univ. of Illinois, 1956), by Siebert, Peterson, and Schramm.

[2] See Alfred Zimmern, ed., *Modern Political Doctrines* (New York: Oxford Univ., 1939), pp. 3 ff.

[3] Siebert, Peterson, and Schramm, *op. cit.*, pp. 10 ff.

[4] Robert MacIver, *The Web of Government* (New York: Macmillan, 1947), p. 322.

[5] Zimmern, *op. cit.*, p. 3.

[6] This is in an appendix by the Secretariat of the International Press Institute to an ECOSOC report: Salvador P. Lopez, *Freedom of Information, 1953*, submitted to the Economic and Social Council of the United Nations, 16th session (Document E/2426).

[7] Ernst Cassirer, "The Enlightenment," in *Encyclopedia of the Social Sciences* (New York: Macmillan, 1935), Vol. 5, p. 547.

[8] Robert L. Heilbronner, *The Worldly Philosophers* (New York: Simon & Schuster, 1953), pp. 13-14.

[9] Arnold J. Toynbee, "Man Owes His Freedom to God," *Collier's*, Vol. 137; pp. 7, 82.

[10] John Milton, Areopagitica (ed. George H. Sabine [New York: Beacon, 1951]).

[11] Erskine's defense of Paine will be found in Thomas B. Howells, compiler, *A Complete Collection of State Trials* (London: 1704), Vol. 22.

[12] *The Writings of Thomas Jefferson*, ed. A. A. Lipscomb (Washington: Thomas Jefferson Memorial Association, 1904), Vol. II, pp. 32-34.

[13] John Stuart Mill, *On Liberty*, ed. Alburey Castell (New York: Crofts, 1947), p. 16.

[14] Siebert, Peterson, Schramm, *op. cit.*, p. 41.

[15] The quotation is from the *Communications Act* of 1934.

[16] Carl L. Becker, *New Liberties for Old* (New Haven: Yale Univ., 1941), p. 93.

[17] Joseph Pulitzer, "The College of Journalism," *North American Review*, Vol. 178 (May 1904), pp. 641-80.

[18] See Siebert, Peterson, Schramm, *op. cit.*, p. 73.

[19] The book, of course, was *Das Kapital*. (We have used the Chicago: Chicago Univ. Press, 1909, edition.)

[20] See Siebert, Peterson, Schramm, *op. cit.*, p. 107.

[21] Herbert Muller, *The Uses of the Past* (New York: Oxford Univ., 1952), p. 310.

[22] Crane Brinton, *The Shaping of the Modern Mind* (New York: New American Library, 1953), p. 204.

[23] Marx, *op. cit.*, p. 25.

[24] Friedrich Engels, *Writings* (New York: 1915-21), p. 410.

[25] V. I. Lenin, *Collected Works* (New York: International Publishers, 1927), Vol. 4, p. 114.

[26] Margaret Mead, *Soviet Attitudes toward Authority* (New York: McGraw-Hill, 1951), p. 21.

[27] Lenin, *op. cit.*

[28] A. Vyshinsky, *Law of the Soviet State* (New York: Macmillan, 1948), p. 617.

[29] For a comparison of Soviet communication theory with that of Hitler and other totalitarians, see Siebert, Peterson and Schramm, *op. cit.*, pp. 139 ff. Also Schramm, *The Soviet Concept of "Psychological" Warfare* (Washington: 1955).

[30] Will Irwin, "The American Newspaper," 15 articles in *Collier's* between January 21 and July 29, 1911.

[31] Siebert, Peterson, Schramm, *op. cit.*, pp. 78-79.

[32] Charles A. Beard in *St. Louis Post-Dispatch Symposium on Freedom of the Press*, St. Louis, 1938.

[33] See Frank L. Mott, *American Journalism* (New York: Macmillan, 1950).

[34] Pulitzer, *op. cit.*

[35] See Siebert, Peterson, Schramm, *op. cit.*, p. 84.

[36] *Ibid.*, p. 73.

[37] *Ibid.*, p. 74.

[38] Commission on Freedom of the Press, *A Free and Responsible Press,* (Chicago: Univ. of Chicago, 1947).

[39] *Ibid.*, p. 22.

[40] Elmer Davis, *But We Were Born Free* (Indianapolis: Bobbs-Merrill, 1954), p. 175.

[41] Norman Isaacs, "A Small Town Paper Has One Supreme Ethical Duty—To Print the News," *Quill*, Vol. 41 (December 1953), p. 15.

[42] Siebert, Peterson, Schramm, *op. cit.*, p. 90.

[43] *Ibid.*, pp. 99-100.

[44] *Ibid.*, p. 100.

[45] William Ernest Hocking, *Freedom of the Press: A Framework of Principle* (Chicago: Univ. of Chicago, 1947), pp. 182-93.

[46] *Ibid.*, p. 54.

[47] See Commission on Freedom of the Press, *op. cit.*, p. 113.

[48] Siebert, Peterson, Schramm, *op. cit.*, p. 98.

[49] Commission on Freedom of the Press, *op. cit.*, p. 121.

CHAPTER 6

[1] William O. Douglas, "The Manifest Destiny of America," *The Progressive*, February 1955.

[2] John B. Wolfe, "Man's Struggle for Freedom against Authority," In *Social Science and Freedom: A Report to the People* (Minneapolis: Univ. of Minnesota, 1955), p. 3.

[3] Zechariah Chafee, Jr., "An Outsider Looks at the Press," *Nieman Reports*, Vol. 7, (January 1955), p. 5.

[4] See *Hannegan vs. Esquire*, 327 US 146 (1946).

[5] J. Edward Gerald. "Freedom in Mass Communication," *Social Science and Freedom*, *op. cit.*, p. 9.

[6] 326 US 1 (1945).

[7] Robert Lasch. "For a Free Press." *Atlantic Monthly*, Vol. 173 (June, 1944), p. 6.

[8] 343 US 495 (1952).

[9] 333 US 507 (1948).

[10] *Ibid.*

[11] Walter Lippmann, *The Public Philosophy* (Boston: Little, Brown, 1955), p. 127.

[12] Lippmann, *op. cit.* pp. 130-131.

[13] Quoted in Ruth Inglis, *Freedom of the Movies* (Chicago: Univ. of Chicago, 1947), p. 17.

[14] Inglis, *op. cit.*, pp. 19-20.

[15] Inglis, *op. cit.*, p. 20.

[16] *Public Service Responsibility of Broadcast Licensees* (Washington: 1946).

[17] See note 8.

[18] See note 9.

[19] Commission on Freedom of the Press, *A Free and Responsible Press* (Chicago: Univ. of Chicago, 1947), p. 18.

[20] Commission on Freedom of the Press, *op. cit.*, p. 59.

[21] Lasch, *op. cit.*

[22] Quoted in Commission on Freedom of the Press, *op. cit.*, pp. 60-61.

[23] San Francisco *Chronicle*, Jan. 11, 1956.

[24] Michael Bradshaw, "Slanting the News," *Atlantic Monthly*, Vol. 174, I (July 1944).

[25] A. J. Liebling, *The Wayward Pressman* (New York: Doubleday, 1947), p. 103.

[26] Quoted in *Editor and Publisher*, June 26, 1954, pp. 13 ff.

[27] Bradshaw, *op. cit.*

[28] *Editor and Publisher*, Nov. 6, 1954, p. 32.

[29] John Drewry, address on "Newspaper Advertising and Ethics," before Circulation Clinic of Georgia Press Association, 1954.

[30] Bradshaw, *op. cit.*

[31] *Report of the Royal Commission on the Press* (London: 1949), p. 143.

[32] *Editor and Publisher*, April 24, 1954.

[33] *Ibid.*

[34] Quoted in *Editor and Publisher*. April 17, 1954.

[35] *Editor and Publisher*, Nov. 20, 1954.

[36] Charles E. Swanson, "Midcity Daily," *Journalism Quarterly*, 26, I (March 1949).

[37] A. Gayle Waldrop, letter to *Nieman Reports*, Vol. 9 (July 1955), p. 18.

[38] Commission on Freedom of the Press, *op. cit.*, p. 58.

[39] Hortense Powdermaker, *Hollywood, the Dream Factory* (Boston: Little, Brown, 1950), p. 71.

[40] Edwin S. Newman, ed., *The Freedom Reader* (New York: Oceana, 1955), pp. 129-130.

[41] John B. Oakes, "The Dangerous Obligations of a Newspaperman," *Nieman Reports*, Vol. 7 (October 1953), p. 6.

[42] Quoted, *Editor and Publisher*, March 19, 1955, p. 44.

[43] *Ibid.*

[44] *Editor and Publisher*, March 26, 1949.

[45] *The New York Times*, January 5, 1956.

[46] Gerald, *op. cit.* pp. 12-13.

[47] J. C. Schneider, *The Golden Kazoo* (New York: Rinehart, 1954).

[48] Stanley Kelley, Jr. *Professional Public Relations and Political Power* (Baltimore: Johns Hopkins, 1956), p. 35.

[49] Kelley, *op. cit.*, p. 228.

[50] Walter Lippmann, *op. cit.*, 96-101.

[51] Walter Lippmann, *op. cit.*, pp. 96-101.

[52] For summary, see Kelley, *op. cit.*, pp. 107-143.

[53] Edward L. Bernays, *Propaganda* (New York: Liveright, 1928), p. 92.

[54] "Business Is Still in Trouble." *Fortune*, May 1949, p. 69.

[55] American Library Association and American Book Publishers Council. *The Freedom to Read: Statement of Policy* (New York: May 1953).

CHAPTER 7

[1] S. D. Warren and L. D. Brandeis, "The Right to Privacy," *Harvard Law Review* (1890) Vol. 4, pp. 193 ff.

[2] *Harper's*, July 1955. Quoted, *Editor and Publisher*, July 2, 1955, p. 34.

[3] Terence O'Flaherty, in the *San Francisco Chronicle*, October 9, 1956, p. 21.

[4] Walter Lippmann, address in *Problems of Journalism* (proceedings of the American Society of Newspaper Editors), 1936, pp. 154-56.

[5] Lippmann, *op. cit.*, p. 157.

[6] Lippmann, *op. cit.*, 158.

[7] Quoted in *Editor and Publisher*, November 20, 1954, p. 10.

[8] *Ibid.*

[9] Quoted in *Editor and Publisher*, March 13, 1954, p. 84.

[10] Sevellon Brown, address to American Society of Newspaper Editors, in *Problems of Journalism*, 1955.

[11] David Reisman, Nathan Glazer, Reuel Denney, *The Lonely Crowd*, (New Haven: Yale Univ. Press, 1950).

[12] The trial of George Sack, before Judge Frank L. Lonergan, in Portland, Oregon. See *Editor and Publisher*, October 9, 1954, p. 62.

[13] *Ibid.*

[14] From his CBS commentary. Quoted in Report of Sigma Delta Chi Committee on Freedom of Information, 1953. In *Quill*, January 1953, p. 20.

[15] *Ibid.*

[16] Address to the American Society of Newspaper Editors, in *Problems of Journalism* (proceedings of the ASNE), 1950.

[17] Harold L. Cross, *The People's Right to Know* (New York: Columbia Univ., 1953), pp. 12 ff.

[18] See note 16.

[19] Report of Sigma Delta Chi Committee on Freedom of Information (see note 14), p. 7.

[20] Cross, *op. cit.*, p. 6 ff., also p. 63 ff.

[21] Quoted, *Editor and Publisher*, July 17, 1954, p. 34.

[22] Robert W. Sink, in *Champaign-Urbana (Illinois) Courier*, March 14, 1955.

[23] See Cross, *op. cit.*; Also James S. Pope, address to the American Society of Newspaper Editors, in *Problems of Journalism*, 1951, p. 175.

[24] *Editor and Publisher*, April 24, 1954, p. 76.

[25] *Canons of the Oregon State Editorial Association*, Portland, no date.

[26] Quoted, *Editor and Publisher*, January 23, 1954, p. 13.

[27] Herbert Brucker, "Newspapers Shouldn't Play God," *Saturday Review of Literature*, January 1, 1955, pp. 9ff.

[28] L. N. Flint, *The Conscience of the Newspaper* (New York: Appleton, 1925), p. 88.

[29] Commission on Freedom of the Press. *A Free and Responsible Press* (Chicago: Univ. of Chicago, 1947), pp. 65-66.

[30] George Seldes, *Lords of the Press* (New York: Messner, 1938).

[31] Graham Hovey, broadcasts over Station WHA, Madison, Wisconsin, February 5 and February 19, "Background of the News" (mimeo.), pp. 1-2.

[32] *Ibid.*, p. 6.

[33] *Ibid.*, 2, p. 3.

[34] *Ibid.*, p. 7.

[35] *Ibid.*, p. 8.

CHAPTER 8

[1] *St. Louis Post-Dispatch, Symposium on Freedom of the Press* (St. Louis: 1938), p. 13.

[2] Address to the 1955 convention of the National Association of Radio and Television Broadcasters. Quoted, *Editor and Publisher*, May 28, 1955, p. 9.

[3] *Times Talk* (internal publication of *The New York Times*), September 15, 1952.

[4] *Editor and Publisher*, January 2, 1954, p. 12.

[5] Quoted, *Nieman Reports*, Vol. 5 (October 1951), p. 5.

[6] L. N. Flint, *The Conscience of the Newspaper* (New York: Appleton, 1925), p. 44.

[7] Milburn P. Akers, address to conference of news photographers at Lawrence, Kansas. Quoted, *Editor and Publisher*, May 8, 1954.

[8] *Nieman Reports, op. cit.*, p. 5.

[9] See Hadley Cantril, *et al.*, *The Invasion from Mars* (Princeton: Princeton Univ. Press, 1940).

[10] See *Editor and Publisher*, April 17, 1954, p. 68.

[11] From the AP *Log*. Quoted, *Editor and Publisher*, March 13, 1954, p. 66.

[12] William S. Paley, address to the National Association of Radio and Television Broadcasters, May 25, 1954 (typescript).

[13] *Nieman Reports*, Vol. 9 (October 1955), p. 8.

[14] Address at State College, Pennsylvania, Quoted, *Editor and Publisher*, April 23, 1955, p. 100.

[15] Wallace Carroll, "The Seven Deadly Virtues," *Nieman Reports*, Vol. 9 (July 1955), p. 25.

[16] Quoted, *Nieman Reports*, Vol. 9 (October 1955), p. 8.

[17] James P. Wood, *Magazines in the United States* (New York: Ronald, 1956), pp. 205-206.

[18] Quoted, *Editor and Publisher*, November 20, 1954, p. 7.

[19] See *Editor and Publisher*, June 19, 1954, p. 64.

[20] Commission on Freedom of the Press, *A Free and Responsible Press* (Chicago: Univ. of Chicago, 1947), p. 22.

[21] Elmer Davis, *But We Were Born Free* (Indianapolis: Bobbs-Merrill, 1954).

[22] Carroll, *op. cit.*

[23] Flint, *op. cit.*, p. 20.

[24] John Crosby, "Radio and Television," New York *Herald Tribune*, November 8, 1954.

[25] Phil Kerby, "How Free Is the Free Press?", *Nieman Reports*, Vol. 6 (October 1952), pp. 21-22.

[26] *Ibid.*

[27] Jack Gould, "TV and McCarthy," *The New York Times*. March 4, 1954.

[28] *Ibid.*

[29] San Francisco *Chronicle*, June 18, 1956.

[30] Quoted, Washington *Post and Times Herald*, June 12, 1956, p. 10.

[31] J. Edward Gerald, "Freedom in Mass Communications," in *Social Science and Freedom*, (Minneapolis: 1955), pp. 10-11.

[32] *Nieman Reports*, Vol. 7 (October, 1953), p. 4.

[33] Paul Block, Jr., "Facing Up to the Monopoly Charge," *Nieman Reports*, Vol. 9 (July, 1955), p. 7.

[34] See *Editor and Publisher*, March 13, 1954, p. 40.

[35] For a discussion of this, see Gilbert Seldes, "Politics, Freedom, and Madison Avenue," *Saturday Review*, August, 1956, p. 36.

[36] Message to *Editor and Publisher* from Walter Lister of the *Philadelphia (Pa.) Bulletin*, quoted from issue of June 19, 1954, p. 12.

[37] Flint, *op. cit.*, p. 154.

[38] Quoted, *Editor and Publisher*, September 25, 1954, p. 15.

[39] *Ibid.*

[40] Quoted, *Editor and Publisher*, May 1, 1954, p. 7.

[41] F. Towle, ed., *Encyclopedia of Classified Advertising* (New York: M. S. Mill, 1950), pp. 255-84.

CHAPTER 9

[1] Lyman Bryson, *The Communication of Ideas* (New York: Harper, 1948).

[2] Gilbert Seldes, *The Great Audience* (New York: Viking, 1950).

[3] Dwight MacDonald, "A Theory of Popular Culture," *Politics*, February 1944, p. 20.

[4] Dwight Bentel, "A Critic? Hit Him over the Head with History." *Editor and Publisher*, July 16, 1955, p. 46.

[5] *Report of Royal Commission on the Press*, 1947-49 (London: 1949), p. 108.

[6] Personal reminiscence of men who knew White.

[7] Ben Hibbs, "You Can't Edit a Magazine by Arithmetic," *Journalism Quarterly*, Vol. 27 (1950), pp. 369-77.

[8] Edgar Dale, "Can You Give the Public What It Wants?" *The News Letter*, November 1956, p. 1.

[9] *Ibid.*, pp. 2-3.

[10] Frederick C. Gruber, "Radio and Television and Ethical Standards," *Annals of the American Academy of Political and Social Science*, Vol. 280 (March 1952), p. 120.

[11] Hanns Eisler, *Composing for the Films* (New York: Oxford University, 1947), pp. ix-x.

[12] Helen MacGill Hughes, *News and the Human Interest Story* (Chicago: Univ. of Chicago, 1940), p. 183.

[13] Charles Horton Cooley, *Social Organization* (New York, Scribner, 1911), p. 84.

[14] MacDonald, *op. cit.*, p. 21.

[15] Powdermaker, *op. cit.*, p. 63.

[16] Rosten, *op. cit.*, pp. 356-7.

[17] Bryson, *op. cit.*, chapter on "Popular Art," pp. 227ff. See also the *Saturday Review of Literature*, May 30, 1940, p. 14.

[18] Motion Picture Association of America, *The Production Code*, adopted 1930, and occasionally revised since that time. In writing these pages on the contents of the codes I have made close use of a memorandum by Theodore Peterson, written especially for this project. The other codes are: *The Canons of Journalism*, adopted by the American Society of Newspaper Editors in 1923; *Standards of Practice for Radio Broadcasters of the United States of America*, adopted by the National Association of Broadcasters (now the National Association of Radio and Television Broadcasters) in 1937, and several times revised in part; *The Television Code of the National Association of Radio and Television Broadcasters*, adopted 1952, and since revised in part; *Code of the Comics Magazine Association of America, Inc.*, adopted 1954. Further quotes in this chapter from these documents will not be footnoted.

[19] Ruth Inglis, *Freedom of the Movies* (Chicago: Univ. of Chicago, 1947), p. 61.

[20] Dan Lacy, "Freedom and Books," *Nieman Reports*, Vol. 8 (January 1954), p. 29.

[21] *Ibid.*

[22] Coulton Waugh, *The Comics* (London: Macmillan, 1947), p. 352.

[23] George Orwell. *Dickens, Dali, and Others.* (London:), pp. 90-91.

[24] Herta Herzog, "What Do We Know about Daytime Serial Listeners?" *Radio Research, 1942-43*, eds., Paul F. Lazarsfeld and Frank Stanton (New York: Duell, Sloan & Pearce, 1941), pp. 24-25.

[25] *Ibid.*

[26] Rudolf Arnheim, "The World of the Daytime Serial," in Lazarsfeld and Stanton (eds.), *op. cit.*, p. 61.

[27] Joseph Klapper. *Children and Television: A Review of Socially Prevalent Concerns.* New York (Bureau of Applied Social Research, Columbia Univ.), mimeo., no date (approx. 1952).

[28] Orwell, *op. cit.*, pp. 214-15.

[29] Powdermaker, *op. cit.*, p. 74.

[30] Martha Wolfenstein, *Movies: A Psychological Study* (Glencoe, Illinois: Free Press, 1950), p. 300.

[31] *Ibid.*

[32] Powdermaker, *op. cit.*, p. 73.

[33] Wolcott Gibbs in the *Saturday Review of Literature*, quoted in Inglis, *op. cit.*, p. 8.

[34] Quoted, Inglis, *op. cit.*, p. 10.

[35] Powdermaker, *op. cit.*, p. 72.

[36] Hollis Alpert, "Sexual Behavior in the American Movie," *Saturday Review*, June 23, 1956, p. 10.

[37] Alpert, *op. cit.*, p. 38.

[38] Wolfenstein, *op. cit.*, pp. 293-307.

[39] William E. Hocking, *Freedom of the Press: A Framework of Principle* (Chicago: Univ. of Chicago, 1947), pp. 44-5.

[40] Alpert, *op. cit.*, p. 40.

[41] See note 33.

[42] Powdermaker, *op. cit.*, p. 80.

[43] Mimeo, in possession of the author.

CHAPTER 10

[1] William E. Hocking, *Freedom of the Press: A Framework of Principle*, (Chicago: Univ. of Chicago, 1948), *passim.*

[2] Arthur Garfield Hays, in *Freedom of the Press*, a selection of testimony of witnesses before the FCC Newspaper-Radio Hearings (New York: 1942), p. 66.

[3] *To Secure These Rights*, Report of the President's Committee on Civil Rights (Washington: 1947), pp. 8-9.

[4] *Schenck vs. United States*, 249 U.S. 47 (1919).

[5] *Abrams vs. United States*, 250 U.S. 616, 624 (1924).

[6] *Whitney vs. California*, 274 U.S. 357 (1927).

[7] 341 U.S. 494 (1951).

[8] *Hanegan vs. Esquire*, 327 U.S. 146 (1946).

[9] *Burstyn vs. Wilson*, 343 U.S. 495 (1952).

[10] *Winters vs. New York*, 333 U.S. 507 (1948).

[11] *Ibid.*

[12] *United States vs. One Book Called "Ulysses"* 5 F. Supp. X 182 (1933).

[13] Commission on Freedom of the Press, *op. cit.*, p. 83.

[14] *Ibid.*

[15] Morris Ernst, *The First Freedom* (New York: Macmillan, 1946).

[16] John Crosby, "The Monopoly Question," *New York Herald Tribune*, May 13, 1956.

[17] Commission on Freedom of the Press, *op. cit.*, p. 89.

[18] *Ibid.*, p. 83.

[19] *Ibid.*, pp. 83-84.

[20] *Ibid.*, p. 84.

[21] *Ibid.*

[22] Llewellyn White, *The American Radio* (Chicago: Univ. of Chicago, 1947), p. 87.

CHAPTER 11

[1] I am indebted to Bruce Bliven for a historical note, on the ASNE code, which should be preserved. He recalls that while he was chief editorial writer for the old *New York Globe*, the editor of that paper, H. J. Wright, wrote the principal draft of the Canons of Journalism in the *Globe* office, and discussed it at great length with some of the staff.

[2] For more material on the adoption of the Motion Picture Production Code, see Ruth Inglis, *op. cit.*, pp. 62-65; and Geoffrey Shurlock, "The Motion Picture Production Code," *Annals of the American Academy of Political and Social Science*, Vol. 254 (November 1947), pp. 140-145.

[3] Mr. Quigley has added some notes of his own to the story of the making of the code, in *America*, March 10, 1956, pp. 630ff.

[4] For the adoption of the broadcasting codes, see Charles A. Siepmann, *Radio's Second Chance* (Boston: Little, Brown, 1946), pp. 142ff.; and also his *Radio, Television, and Society* (New York: Oxford Univ., 1950), pp. 13ff. Also Llewellyn White, *The American Radio* (Chicago: Univ. of Chicago, 1947), *passim*.

[5] Frederic Wertham, *Seduction of the Innocent* (New York: Rinehart, 1954), p. 22.

[6] Inglis, *op. cit.*, pp. 157, 164-65. This is material cited by Francis Harmon, then vice-president of the Motion Picture Association, before a Congressional hearing in 1940.

[7] Inglis, *op. cit.*, pp. 185-187.

CHAPTER 12

[1] Commission on Freedom of the Press, *op. cit.*, pp. 79, 105.

[2] *Christian Century*, Vol. 74:1 (January 2, 1957), p. 4. "TV Station Yields to Catholic Pressure."

[3] Commission on Freedom of the Press, *op. cit.*, pp. 100-104.

Index of Names

Adams, Charles F., quoted, 20
Akers, Milburn P., quoted, 226
Alpert, Hollis, reporter, 303-4, 306
American Book Publishing Council, quoted, 163-5
American Broadcasting Company, 122-3
American Library Association, quoted, 163-5
American Medical Association, campaign, 158
American Newspaper Guild, 278
American Society of Newspaper Editors, 104; code, 88, 282, 283, 336
American Tobacco Company, 131
Associated Press, 109-10, 142, 231, 233
Association of Comic Magazine Publishers, 340
Association of University Women, 358
Atlantic Monthly, 176; quotations from, 125, 127, 136
Atomic Energy Commission, release date broken, 258

Beard, Charles A., quoted, 88, 217
Becker, Carl, quoted, 76
Bell, Alexander Graham, 15
Bentel, Dwight, quoted, 269
Bernays, Edward L., quoted, 160
Better Business Bureau, 264
Block, Paul, quoted, 250-1
Bowen, Howard R., ix
Bradshaw, Michael, 136, 139
Brandeis, L. D., cited, 167; quoted, 323
Breen, Joseph L., quoted, 175, 341
Brier, Royce, 127
British Broadcasting Company, xviii, 311
British Royal Commission, 3, 89, 140; quoted, 269
Brown, Robert U., quoted, 144-5, 203
Brown, Sevellon, quoted, 186
Brucker, Herbert, quoted, 207
Bryson, Lyman, cited, 266; quoted, 279
Butler, Paul, cited, 256-7

Calvin, John, cited, xx

Canadian Broadcasting Company, xviii
Carroll, Wallace, cited, 235ff; quoted, 233
Cassirer, Ernst, quoted, 67
Catholic War Veterans, picketing, 150
Catledge, Turner, quoted, 218
Chafee, Zechariah, cited, 6; quoted, 108, 111, 127
Champaign (Ill.) *Courier*, quoted, 200-1
Chamber of Commerce, influence on publicity, 209
Chicago Daily News, 127, 141
Chicago Sun-Times, 110, 122, 226, 227
Chicago Tribune, 83, 110, 127, 128, 365
Christian Science Monitor, 216, 236
Church, Roman Catholic, as censor, 63, 67. *See also* Legion of Decency
Cincinnati Enquirer, 143
Collier's magazine, 327, 336
Columbia Broadcasting System (CBS), xviii, 23, 119, 127, 244, 256-7, 275
Commission on Freedom of the Press, cited, xiv, xvii, 3, 90, 94, 269; quoted, 91, 92, 96, 120, 147, 212, 235, 326, 328, 329, 330, 341, 348, 352, 353, 360-2
Committee (Sigma Delta Phi) on Freedom of Information, quoted, 194-6
Cone, Fairfax, quoted, 264
Confidential, 174-176
Congressional Record, vagaries, 223
Cooley, Charles, quoted, 274
Cowles, John, quoted, 124
Crosby, John, cited, 348; quoted, 174-5, 240-1, 328
Cross, Harold, cited, 192, 196

Dabney, Virginia, quoted, 126
Dale, Edgar, quoted, 270
Daniels, Josephus, 136
Davis, Elmer, cited, 203-239; quoted, 92, 236
DeForest, Lee, 15
Denver Post, 216

385

General Index

Accuracy (news), 218-32; obstacles: "firstness", 220-3; indirect quotation, 223-5; photographic difficulties, 225-7; short headlines, 227-9

Advertising, 24; influence on policy of media, 129-141, 151, 251-2; magazines and newspapers, xvii, 21, 22, 32, 130; obtrusive, xvii; radio and television, xvii, xviii, xix, 120-1, 131; response, 49, 53; responsibility of media, 261, 262-5; service, 34, 51-3; statistics, 24; support of media, 74, 130; use of boycott, 154; use of anonymity, 260

Advice columns, 261-2

Art, xv, xvi; assumptions, 295-308; debasement of, xvi, xvii; effects, 297; enlightenment vs. entertainment, 290, 291; limits on controversial subjects, 289; popular, 4, 5, 266-315; shallowness, 305; standards determined by media, 271-5

Authoritarianism, xiii, 3, 61, 62-66; censorship, 65, 66; licensing, 64; strands of, 63

Balance, 241-53; newspapers, criteria of, 246-251; special responsibility of radio and television, 244; violation of, 241-3

Books, 28, 29, 30, 47, 163; censorship, 64-6; comic, 293, 294, 336; responsibility, 46, 164

Boycotts, by pressure groups, 148-154, 278

Broadcasting, 115-123; investigation of, Congressional, 115, 119, 120-1; regulation of, by FCC, 115ff; service, local vs. network, 120-1; standards, 116-7. *See also* Monopoly, Television

caveat emptor principle, 104

Chain stores, 108

Change, dominance of, vii; effects upon human values, vii-viii; ethical implications, viii; persistence of ethics, viii; resistance to, 55-6

Christianity, as frame of reference, viii, xi, xii, xiii, xix, xx, xxi, xxii-xxiii

Church, *see* Christianity; television time allowed, 248

Class allegiances, 125-9

Codes, ethical, 292-3; books, 294; motion-picture, 287-8, 295, 337; newspaper, 286; radio, 288-90; television, 290

Communication, mass
beginnings, 14-5; growth, 24-5
centralization, 5, 28, 121-5
controls by government, 108-121; by monopoly, 121-5; by class allegiances, 125-9; by sources of support, 129-146; by pressure groups, 146-157; by manipulation, 157-162
diffusion, 28; duality, 5-7, 111, 139; effects on culture, xi, xii, xv, 49-57; ethical problems, 8, 131, 346; freedom, 6-7, 8-9, 107ff; functions, 32-34; objectivity, 8; pervasiveness, 26-7
philosophy, authoritarian, xiii, 3, 61; libertarian, xiv, xvii, 3, 5, 61, 62-66; social responsibility, xii, xiv, 1, 48, 61
rank as business, 28, 111; responsibility, 46-8, 76, 105-110, 131-162, 163-5; statistics of media, 30; structure, 26; support, 32; tabulation of concepts, 98-99; unprofessional, 344-5

Communism, 3, 61, 65, 66; theory, 77-86

Community, developed by mass communication, xix

Concentration of media, 124-5

Conformity, effected by mass communication, xix